The Golfer's Home Companion

Robin McMillan

SIMON & SCHUSTER
New York   London   Toronto
Sydney   Tokyo   Singapore

SIMON & SCHUSTER
Simon & Schuster Building
Rockefeller Center
1230 Avenue of the Americas
New York, New York 10020

DESIGNED BY BARBARA MARKS
Manufactured in the United States of America

1 3 5 7 9 10 8 6 4 2

Library of Congress Cataloging-in-Publication Data

McMillan, Robin.
The golfer's home companion / Robin McMillan.
p.   cm.
Includes index.
1. Golf—Handbooks, manuals, etc.   I. Title.
GV965.M35   1993
796.352—dc20   92-42554
CIP

ISBN: 0-671-70054-5

To my wife Gail,
who proved during the
compilation of this book
that her patience
is surpassed only by
her beauty, charm and wit;
and to our daughter
Madeleine,
who surpasses both of us
on every count
imaginable.

● ● ●

Contents

Money

157

Spectating

187

Books, Magazines, Videos

219

Games

249

Our Writers and Photographers *269*

Index *271*

The Golfer's Home Companion

Travel

The 17th green and 18th hole at the Old Course, St. Andrews, Scotland.

A Love Affair with Links Golf

by Jim Finegan

To put entirely too fine a point on it, this magnificent obsession began on September 11, 1952.

The aircraft carrier on which I was serving (as an assistant gunnery officer) had anchored the previous day at Gourock, on Scotland's Firth of Clyde, a few miles downstream from Glasgow. I was twenty-one, a lowly ensign, and abroad for the first time in my life—and within striking distance of St. Andrews.

I talked a fellow ensign into accompanying me on a pilgrimage clear across the country, from west to east. With our golf bags slung over our shoulders, off we went by train to "The Auld Grey Toon."

Arriving at the Royal & Ancient clubhouse, we informed the porter there that we had come to play the Old Course and could he be kind enough to show us where we could change our clothes.

He was polite but firm. Unless we were guests of a member, he said, we could not possibly go inside. He suggested we try the St. Andrews Golf Club, and pointed to a building just beyond the 18th green.

The secretary there directed us to a simple, locker-less room. We hung our navy uniforms on hooks, quickly donned our golf clothes, crossed Pilmour Links Road and the 18th fairway, and paid our green fee. I believe it was five shillings.

Now we stood on the first tee, looking down the vast expanse of fairway at what is surely the least demanding opening shot you will ever play (although the second shot over the Swilcan Burn does possess some character). We drove, hit to the green, got down in two putts and walked to the second tee, each of us silently wondering what all the fuss was about links golf and about this fabled course in particular.

But it was a pretty day—sunny mostly, with temperatures in the mid 60s and a brisk breeze driving white clouds out over St. Andrews Bay—and we were delighted to be away from the ship. Perhaps, we thought, the course would get better as we moved along.

And then, facing the long shot to the Old Course's second green, suddenly the game was on, and my sense of what a golf course should look like and feel like and play like and *daunt* like was changed forever.

The Old Course did not resemble any course I had seen before. Which is easily explained by the fact

St. Andrews.

that I had grown up caddying and playing in suburban Philadelphia on a diet of what Bernard Darwin once referred to as "windless golf in a park."

From my spot on the second fairway, the Old Course looked primitive and bleak. There seemed no definition to the holes around me. And who ever heard of a green so vast that it would play host to *two* different holes? And who ever saw such dips and rolls and swings—these on *putts* that could easily be 125 to 150 feet?

These links looked flat but didn't play flat. We found ourselves in a sea of heaving turf, all humpy and hillocky, with ridges and ripples, mounds and gullies,

hollows and plateaus and swales. Years later, I asked Jack Nicklaus whether St. Andrews posed the most difficult shots to the greens of any British Open course. "I wouldn't say the most difficult," Nicklaus replied. "I think *awkward* might be a better word."

Both "difficult" and "awkward" might apply to the bunkers on the Old Course. My shipmate and I were appalled at how penal these deep, sheer-faced pits were, to say nothing of their location in such odd places as the middle of a fairway, just where a good drive would land.

Then there was the heather and the gorse, the former likely to sprain a wrist, the latter prickly and

impenetrable, the very embodiment of the phrase "unplayable lie."

Yes, this was all very new and curious, this links golf—but enormously exhilarating. The close-cropped seaside turf had a resilience to it, a spring that somehow bred optimism as we approached our shots. You couldn't wait to hit your next shot from it. And the ball, whether because of the breezes or bounces, acted quite unpredictably, now skipping and squirting, now slipping and sliding, always introducing a large element of luck to the game.

Club selection seemed much more perplexing than on the courses we were used to, but when we did manage to choose the right club, and when the shot came off just as envisioned, after we'd considered the wind and the slopes and the bounce and the bunkers . . . ah, what sweet satisfaction.

But this business of hole after hole going straight out, and then the loop at eight, nine, ten and eleven so we could play as we turned, and then hole after hole heading straight back in—this fascinated us. Who had come up with this strange scheme? Why had we never run into it at home?

There was little in the way of pretty views as we strode along, but there still was the occasional moment, and none so striking as the scene from the Old Course's 12th tee. Straight ahead in the distance, the old town stood above the rocks and the sea on its modest bluff, its low, gray silhouette punctuated by four or five church spires. Immediately below and behind us was the River Eden Estuary. To our right lay holes on the adjoining Eden Course, with the rolling north hills of Fife beyond. To our left, the lightly capped waters of St. Andrews Bay rolled toward the town's West Sands. At every point of the compass our view was unimpeded. We could see as far as young men can see.

I remember that after our round we took high tea in the town. From our window table we watched the university students in their traditional red robes going home to their lodging and their books, and the townspeople, putters in hand, trooping down to the wildly undulating putting green, the Himalayas, beside the beach. There and then I promised myself that I would return to this links—to any links—as soon as I could.

The twin priorities of earning a living and raising a family meant I was unable to return to Scottish golf until late in the summer of 1971. This time a wife and three children (two teenage boys and a five-year-old girl) came with me. Our itinerary began at Gullane, ended at Turnberry, and in between saw us confronting the challenges of links golf at St. Andrews, Muirfield and Carnoustie in the east, at Nairn and Royal Dornoch in the north and at Prestwick and Royal Troon in the southwest.

At Muirfield the wind blew across the great links at 40 to 50 miles per hour, making a shambles of our swings. On any links there are those rare occasions when the flags hang lifeless, but ordinarily the wind ranges from a factor to a force. You are consistently called upon to hold shots up right or left into it, ride it for all it is worth, or tackle it unflinching, head-on. Links wind requires a combination of patience and skill: patience when the long two-shotters become unreachable, skill when the breeze from port or starboard is manageable—if you can swing within yourself.

All hazards, especially bunkers, are made more hazardous by links winds. Sometimes, as at Northern Ireland's magnificent Royal County Down, surely one of the four or five greatest links courses in the world, there are so many sand traps (125, I read somewhere) that there is simply no avoiding them when a fresh breeze is up. Other times, the wind seems to conspire with the bunkers to frustrate you. The slightly off-line shot which at first seems certain to evade the pits now inclines toward it. It is better not to watch, for the cruelty is too calculated. You see, the ground around these traps has been shaped and sheared to *lure* the errant shot, to suck it down hungrily as if into a vortex.

All of which demands that you play low, running shots which duck the wind and offer the most reliable way to get the ball somewhere near the hole on courses that are dry, firm and undulating. No dart games here. The shotmaking must be genuinely creative. One thinks immediately of Severiano Ballesteros and of Tom Watson, who could never have won eight British Opens between them without a mastery of the ground game, of the old-fashioned bump-and-run.

The locals in Scotland, in Ireland and in some coastal regions of England seem to take this for granted, and well they should. It's become second nature to them, probably because they have so much time to practice and play. That's because links golf, so splendidly open to the sky, enjoys more daylight than anything you'll find in a park or in woodlands. Royal Dornoch, the northernmost of the great links, is at the same latitude as Juneau, Alaska, and the long, lingering twilight never seems to end. In fact, it is possible on the summer solstice to tee off at Dornoch at midnight and get in the evening nine!

The need for a short game is just as critical at the opposite end of this 600-mile-long island, down on the English Channel in Sussex, where the Rye Golf Club lies. Rye must be the *fastest* links course in the world—fiery-fast in summer, when your ball races everywhere at alarming speeds. As at Dornoch, again and again you find yourself gingerly scuffling shots up and down greenside slopes. Rye also has one of the finest collections of short holes in the world, so demanding a group that it is frequently said—and not in jest—that the most important shot at Rye is the second shot on the par threes.

Inevitably at Rye we are reminded of Sir Guy Campbell, the late golf historian and course architect, for it was Sir Guy who so painstakingly analyzed the evolution of linksland into the earliest sites of the game.

Over tens of thousands of years, Sir Guy concluded, the sea gradually receded, leaving behind sandy wastes which the winds fashioned into dunes, knolls, hollows and gullies. Gradually grass began to grow in the hollows. It was a thick, close-growing mixture with stiff, erect blades—the key features of true links turf.

In due course other vegetation—heather, gorse, broom—took root, now resulting in terrain that would sustain animal life. First the rabbits appeared, then the foxes. When man came along, as either hunter or shepherd, the animal tracks were widened into paths. These began to serve as a rude kind of fairway and closely grazed ground, often lower areas where water also had gathered, acted as a putting surface. The earliest links, Sir Guy concluded, were actually a product of nature. He phrased it beautifully: "Nature was their architect, and beast and man her contractors."

As it happened, nature did not endow her links with trees. Oh, now and again a solitary, wind-whipped excuse for a tree will pop up, even a spinney on rare occasion (there's a small grove of pines near the fifth hole at Carnoustie), but generally the great links are treeless, beholding a severe, desolate kind of beauty. Encroaching limbs and claustrophobic foliage have no place on a pure links, so the player who opts to start his shot comfortably right or left and curve it back on line—if indeed he can—has plenty of room to do precisely that.

You will also rejoice on a links if you are the sort who has grown weary of masonry waterfalls and man-made lagoons (I am reminded of the high-handicapper in Florida who had to have his ball retriever regripped!). There is very little in the way of water hazards other than the occasional burn (the Barry Burn at Carnoustie, the Swilcan Burn at the Old Course, the Wee Burn at Turnberry and the Suez Canal at Royal St. George's come to mind, but I'm not sure I could name any more). Well, perhaps I should say there is little in the way of *small* water hazards. There are oceans (the Atlantic lies in wait on the sixth hole of Ireland's beautiful Enniscrone links). There are seas (the North Sea menaces the sliced shot on the inbound nine at Dunbar, a dozen miles southeast of

Muirfield). And there are firths (the Solway Firth penalizing slices at Powfoot, the Firth of Clyde dealing with hooks at Turnberry). But there is none of these piddling contrivances that constitute the "signature"—and the bane—of so much contemporary golf-course design.

Which is not to say that man has not at least on occasion played some role in forming the great links courses, but usually it's been in concert with nature. And when nature has been extravagantly generous, when the sea and the wind have fashioned imposing ranges of sandhills framing immense expanses of undulating ground, the result is usually a links course where both the shot values and the setting are nothing short of sublime.

An unheralded links, but without a doubt a personal favorite, is Cruden Bay, some 15 miles north of Aberdeen, on Scotland's east coast. This North Sea links, where Bram Stoker, author of *Dracula,* loved to roam and fantasize, is mighty stuff, routed through linksland probably unequalled for grandeur in all of Scotland. Here, amid the giant sandhills and the long bents and the stout gorse, you will encounter a four-hole sequence—numbers four through seven—that consists of a one-shotter, two par fours and a par five that together produces as much drama and excellence as you can wish for on any links course. Tom Simpson,

the man responsible for the Old course at Ballybunion, in Ireland, designed Cruden Bay. The kinship is plain to see.

Machrihanish, unlike Cruden Bay, is not near Aberdeen. Nor is it near Glasgow or Edinburgh or Dundee or Inverness. Nor, for that matter, is it near anywhere. You must make a concerted effort to reach this links that was laid out more than 125 years ago almost at the southernmost tip the remote southwestern peninsula of Kintyre. The drive from Glasgow takes nearly four hours!

The first shot at Machrihanish makes every hour on the road worthwhile. It is my favorite first shot in golf. It must be struck from a tee elevated some 10 feet above the beach and carry the diagonal across the Atlantic to a rolling fairway. This is the kind of start—how much should I bite off with the first swing of the day?—that can set you off in high spirits, ready to do battle with the course and all its quirks and, of course, the whims of the wind.

This rough-and-tumble course has everything you could wish for in a links. It has the scenery, its views from the more elevated tees stretching far out to sea; it has the characteristic hidden patches of fairways lying at every imaginable angle; and it has that challenging mix of targets—the unseen greens tucked into hollows and the windswept greens resting high atop plateaus.

It is much the same, if not as isolated, down in Kent, in the sleepy little hamlet of Sandwich, only a drive and a pitch up the English Channel from Dover. Here lies Royal St. George's, which has been host to a dozen British Open Championships beginning in 1894, when J. H. Taylor won the Claret Jug without managing to break 80.

Sandwich (the colloquial name for Royal St. George's) is a links that terrorizes with its merciless bunkering. Most notable are the pair carved into a mountain of a dune that menaces the drive at the fourth. The face of the shallower one is some 18 feet high.

Cruden Bay.

The real horror, right next door, is closer to 30 feet, bottom to top.

But my abiding affection for this extraordinary links stems rather more from the special sense of place: the mood, if you will. The holes at Sandwich run to every point of the compass, sometimes leaping from the pinnacle of the great dunes, more often routed through them, but all the while producing splendor and solitude that is utterly beguiling.

In a lifetime, you will not hear the shout "Fore!" at Sandwich. The only distractions, and that may be too harsh a word, are the lilt of the lark or the stunning seascape seen across Pegwell Bay to the white, chalk cliffs of Ramsgate beyond. Only Royal Birkdale, Northern Ireland's Royal Portrush or the back nine at Ireland's Waterville come close to the cloistered quality of Sandwich.

In a number of cases these irresistible links are integral parts of equally irresistible towns. Heaven knows it is nigh impossible not to be smitten by Sandwich or nearby Deal or by Elie, an old fishing village in the East Neuk (tr. "East Corner") of Fife (the course at Elie is where James Braid, five-time British Open winner, caddied and learned to play). Or by North Berwick, Gullane, Nairn and Dornoch (whose cathedral square may be even lovelier by night than by day), by Tain (like Dornoch, across the firth, a royal burgh) and by Rye (one of Joseph Wechsberg's "25 Dream Towns of Europe" and Henry James's home from 1898 until his death in 1916). In Wales, there is Conwy, with its castle still intact and its medieval walls even older than those at Rye; Aberdovey, a pretty, white village smack beside the broad, sailboat-dotted estuary of the Dovey River.

But do I have favorites? Of course I do. St. Andrews, Cruden Bay and Machrihanish are three of Scotland's best, but I would be ignoring my own Irish heritage were I to ignore the Emerald Isle. Let us head to County Kerry, to where the Shannon River enters the sea.

Standing on the first tee of the Old course at Ballybunion and scanning that vast sweep of shaggy, gray-green linksland, you are instantly struck—as you are not at St. Andrews or Prestwick or Portmarnock— by the formidable nature of the landscape. Ballybunion's huge, billowing, grass-covered sandhills reveal only an occasional patch of playing turf and promise high drama if you have the courage to foray into them. There is nothing here of that gentle, rumpled topography that greets the eye on the first tee at some links courses. Ballybunion's landscape is tumultuous and unyielding.

Among the many outstanding holes, there are two par fours, the seventh and the 11th, that will rank with the best you will ever play. On both of these 400-yarders, the tee is perilously high. To the right is a cliff that falls to the tawny, smooth sands of the Atlantic. Unnervingly close on our left are the awesome dunes, mantled in the long bent grasses that are never less than knee high. These two holes are both thrilling and terrifying, with the 11th possibly the harder. Its fairway is broken into three "pieces": the landing area for the tee shot; a scrap of closely mown grass perhaps a hundred yards farther, on a lower level; and finally, a path threading its way between low sandhills to the green just beyond them. And all of this with the ocean cliff tight on the right every foot of the way. I might add that you feel compelled to time your backswing on the drive so that the crash of the surf will not trigger a devastating lurch at the ball!

Ballybunion is unique. Not only are the sandhills substantially taller than those at other famous links, consistently attaining heights of 40 to 50 feet, but instead of paralleling the shoreline, they generally run at right angles to it. The effect is a mixture of dogleg holes of every description and of straightaway holes where the massive dunes stand sentinel at the entrance to the greens.

In sum, to play Ballybunion is to experience all that is challenging and complex and exhilarating in links golf—to savor the special joy of this earliest form of the game.

Golf Tours to Scotland, to Ireland—or Both

Scotland and Ireland are far and away the most popular foreign golfing destinations for North Americans. The lure of Scotland is undoubtedly its golfing heritage—a round at the Old Course in St. Andrews, for example—and the chance to play real seaside links golf. Ireland somewhat coattails that appeal; its best links are the match of anything in Scotland, but it cannot brag, at least not honestly, of having the golfing history of its neighbor to the northeast. (On the other hand, there are more Americans of Irish extraction than there are those of Scottish, which partly explains why there are as many tours to Ireland as there are to Scotland.)

Most tour operators visit the top layouts, such as Carnoustie, St. Andrews, Troon and Turnberry, in Scotland, or Ballybunion, Lahinch and Killarney, in Ireland. Still others might take a group off the beaten tracks, to the likes of Machrie, Cruden Bay or North Berwick in Scotland, or they may custom-fit a tour exactly to the courses requested. The last service obviously comes at a little extra freight.

Some of the operators listed below do offer golf in England, but Scotland always gets top billing. Rare is the travel company that takes golfers to Britain and neglects to cart them north. If in doubt, however, contact a travel agent or operator directly. Finally, be aware that all operators listed throw in nongolfing trips to Edinburgh or Dublin and occasionally to such golf tournaments as the Irish or British Opens.

The 8th hole, "Postage Stamp," at Royal Troon.

Tour Operator	Scotland	Ireland
Adventures in Golf 29 Valencia Drive Nashua, NH 03062 (603) 882-8367		X
Aer Lingus 122 East 42nd St. New York, NY 10168 (212) 557-1090 (800) 223-6537		X
Atlantic Golf 235 Post Road West Westport, CT 06880 (203) 454-0090 (800) 992-7700		X
Atlantic Group Tours 520 Oriole Drive S.E. Marietta, GA 30067 (404) 977-3072		X
Best Golf Tours Box 65 332 Forrest Ave. Laguna Beach, CA 92652 (714) 752-8881 (800) 227-0212 (800) 458-6888	X	X
Bestours Box 1596 Bonita Springs, FL 33959 (813) 495-1500 (800) 231-2431		X
Biblical Journeys 61 Main St. Southampton, NY 11968 (516) 283-8660 (800) 645-0298		X
Brian Moore International Tours 116 Main St. Medway, MA 02053 (508) 533-6683 (800) 982-2299	X	X
Byways of Britain 2543 NW 87th Drive Coral Springs, FL 33065 (800) 344-4485	X	
Celtic Golf Tours 1062 Pennsylvania Ave. Cape May, NJ 08204 (609) 884-8090 (800) 535-6148	X	X

Tour Operator	Scotland	Ireland
Championship Golf International 11665 Duenda Rd. San Diego, CA 92127 (619) 487-1523 (800) 222-0711		X
Chieftain Tours 235 Post Rd. West Westport, CT 06880 (203) 454-0090 (800) 992-7700		X
Culinary & Fine Arts Ltd. Box 153 Western Springs, IL 60558 (312) 246-6845	X	
Capricorn Tours 15 Penn Plaza 415 Seventh Ave. New York, NY 10001 (212) 967-2441 (800) 426-6544	X	
Close-Up Expeditions 1031 Ardmore Ave. Oakland, CA 94610 (415) 465-8955	X	
Destination Ireland 250 West 57th St. Suite 2511 New York, NY 10107 (212) 977-9629 (800) 832-1848		X
Evergreen Travel Service 19505 L 44th Ave. West Lynwood, WA 98036 (206) 776-1184 (800) 435-2288	X	
Exclusive Golf Holidays 5925 Kirby Dr. Houston, TX 77005 (713) 526-4040 (800) 433-9386	X	
Fourways Travel Ltd. 1324 Boston Post Rd. Milford, CT 06460 (203) 878-8854 (800) 223-7872	X	
Genesis Sports Tours 981 First Ave. Suite 135 New York, NY 10022 (212) 759-0480 (800) 888-8167		X

Tour Operator	Scotland	Ireland
Golf Adventures 1608 N. Milwaukee Ave. Suite 1103 Chicago, IL 60647 (312) 782-6226 (800) 878-0521		X
Golf Getaways Travel 30423 Canwood St. Suite 222 Agoura Hills, CA 91301 (818) 991-7015 (800) 423-3657		X
Golf Intercontinental 19 West 34th St. Suite 302 New York, NY 10001 (212) 239-3880 (800) 223-6114	X	X
Golf International 275 Madison Ave. Suite 1819 New York, NY 10016 (212) 986-9176 (800) 833-1389	X	X

Tour Operator	Scotland	Ireland
Golf Safaris 14429 Ventura Blvd. Suite 106 Sherman Oaks, CA 91423 (818) 788-5991		X
Golf Tours Unlimited Box 478 Bonita, CA 92002 (619) 475-6995	X	
Golfing Holidays (aka Holly Travel) 231 E. Millbrae Ave. Suite 109 Millbrae, CA 94030 (415) 697-0230		X
Golfpac Box 940490 901 North Lake Destiny Dr. Suite 192 Maitland, FL 32794 (407) 660-8277 (800) 327-0878		X

The 7th and 13th at Carnoustie.

Not all majestic golf links are in Scotland: the 15th green at Ireland's Ballybunion (Old).

Tour Operator	Scotland	Ireland
Grasshopper Golf Tours 403 Hill Ave. Glen Ellyn, IL 60137 (708) 858-1660 (800) 654-8712		X
Henry Hudson Tours Box 155 Maiden-on-Hudson, NY 12453 (914) 246-8453		X
The Hidden Ireland Box 40034 Mobile, AL 36640 (205) 433-5465 (800) 868-4750		X
Intergolf 1980 Sherbrooke St. West Suite 210 Montreal, Quebec H31 1E8 (514) 933-2771	X	X
Irish Fairways 455 Paces Ferry Rd. Suite 302 Atlanta, GA 30305 (404) 261-2326 (800) 447-2799		X
Ireland Golf Tours 251 East 85th St. New York, NY 10028 (212) 772-8220 (800) 346-5388		X
TC Golf Tours Box 5144 Long Beach, CA 90805 (213) 595-6905 (800) 257-4981	X	X
Journeys Thru Scotland 35 South Encino Rd. South Laguna, CA 92677 (714) 499-4410 (800) 521-1429	X	

Tour Operator	Scotland	Ireland
Leisure Destinations Marketing Box 220 Palm City, FL 34990 (407) 220-0410	X	
Lynott Tours 350 Fifth Ave. Suite 2619 New York, NY 10118 (212) 760-0101 (800) 221-2474	X	X
Marsans International (see Golf Intercontinental)	X	X
MJK Tours Box 14484 Portland, OR 97214 (503) 231-0905	X	
Northwest Worldvacations 5130 Highway 101 Minnetonka, MN 55345 (612) 470-1111 (800) 362-3520	X	
Owenoak International 88 Main St. New Canaan, CT 06840 (203) 972-3777 (800) 426-4498		X
Perry Golf 8302 Dunwoody Place Suite 305 Atlanta, GA 30350 (404) 641-9696 (800) 344-5257	X	X
Phelan Golf Box 1222 Darien, CT 06820 (203) 655-8084 (800) 274-7888		X
Rolfes Travel Inc. 1126 Charles St. Baltimore, MD 21201 (301) 244-0077	X	
Scottish Golf Holidays 9403 Kenwood Rd. Suite A205 Cincinnati, OH 45242 (513) 984-0414 (800) 284-8884	X	X

Tour Operator	Scotland	Ireland
SCGA Travel 3740 Cahuenga Blvd. North Hollywood, CA 92604 (818) 509-0662 (213) 877-0185	X	X
Showcase Ireland 586 Roma Court Naples, FL 33963 (813) 591-3447 (800) 654-6527		X
Travel Concepts 373 Commonwealth Ave. Suite 601 Boston, MA 02115 (617) 266-8450	X	
TraveLinks 1799 E. Gude Dr. Rockville, MD 20850 (301) 424-9330 (800) 322-0052	X	X
TravelTix International 400 Madison Ave. Suite 411 New York, NY 10017 (212) 688-3700	X	
Value Holidays 10224 N. Port Washington Rd. Mequon, WI 53092 (414) 241-6373 (800) 558-6850	X	
Vignette Holidays 270 N. Canon Dr. Suite 1053 Beverly Hills, CA 90210 (213) 479-3160 (800) 776-7660	X	
Wide World of Golf Box 5217 Carmel, CA 93921 (408) 624-6667	X	X

Culzean Castle, equally as interesting as nearby Troon or Turnberry.

Or Not to Golf—Nongolf Outings for Your Golf Tour

I've said it many times and I'll say it again: The single greatest fault with the golf tour is that golfers continually risk doing nothing but play golf.

There are some tours that scream out for addicts only. Marsans, for example, once limited an eight-night tour of Ireland—two rounds at Royal County Down, two at Royal Portrush and one round each at County Sligo, Ballybunion and Lahinch—to "20 Deadly Serious Golfers."

As a native Scot, I find it astonishing that someone from, say, California, would fly halfway round the world and *not* take the time to visit the ancient areas of Edinburgh, the Scottish capital, or spend quality time doing zero in the highlands. But it happens. It's like flying to play Royal Calcutta and ignoring the Taj Mahal. Like going to play the grand Australian designs, such as Royal Melbourne, and never thinking of popping north to see the Sydney Opera House.

Fortunately, most of the better tour operators arrange side trips. Unfortunately, they're labelled for "nongolfers." Personally, I think some of them should be mandatory for everyone. Here's what two of the more prominent operators, PerryGolf and TraveLinks, serve up in Scotland and Ireland, respectively.

PERRYGOLF

Where the golfers play: Royal Troon, Prestwick (Old) or Turnberry (Ailsa).

Nongolfers can: Visit Culzean Castle, which sits on cliffs above the sea and was designed by one Robert Adam, who, among other things, was responsible for that fine "southern" look of Charleston, South Carolina. Not bad for man from east-central Scotland (my hometown of Kirkcaldy, to be exact).

Where the golfers play: Western Gailes.

Nongolfers can: Visit the Burrell Collection of paintings, pottery, statues and tapestries, assembled by William Burrell, a Scottish industrialist. The collection is almost too eclectic to enjoy (your attention is constantly having to jump from one medium or period to another), but the parklands in which the collection is set is spectacular. Although there is a cafeteria in the Burrell, it is almost always crowded. A better bet is to stroll through the park to nearby Pollock House and enjoy a feasible lunch in a restored manse kitchen.

Where the golfers play: St. Andrews (Old).

Nongolfers can: Tour the town of St. Andrews or go north to Glamis Castle, where Queen Elizabeth spent much of her childhood. Another possibility is to drive south through the fishing villages of Crail, Elie, Anstruther and Pittenweem.

Where the golfers play: Nairn.

Nongolfers can: Visit Cawdor Castle or Culloden Moor, site of the Battle of Culloden in 1746, in which Bonnie Prince Charlie's army was defeated by the English. Also nearby is Loch Ness. Of course you'll see the monster.

Where the golfers play: Royal Dornoch.

Nongolfers can: Visit the Falls of Shin, famous for its salmon leap. A better bet: Drive anywhere to the northwest, into the highlands. This is as raw and spectacular as Scotland gets.

Where the golfers play: Cruden Bay or Royal Aberdeen.

Nongolfers can: Visit Balmoral Castle, the Scottish home to the Royal Family.

Where the golfers play: North Berwick or Gullane No. 1.

Nongolfers can: Visit Edinburgh, with its ancient castle and Holyrood House, the Royal Family's official residence in Scotland. In addition, Edinburgh has no shortage of Georgian architecture, museums, art galleries and watering holes. For the last, try the Half Way House, in Fleshmarket Close, above the main railway station. It spreads across a grand total of, oh, 120 square feet.

Where the golfers play: Gleneagles.

Nongolfers can: Enjoy the Gleneagles Hotel's other pursuits, such as horseback riding and clay-pigeon shooting. Or spend a day at the hotel's spa. Here's a tip: About 20 minutes drive east of Gleneagles, in a tiny hamlet called Glendevon, is a small hostelry called the Tarmauchin Hotel. The Tarmauchin serves the best bar food known to man. When I last visited, it was venison sausages and pigeon pot pie beside an open fire. Delicious.

TraveLinks

Where the golfers play: Killarney.

Nongolfers can: Take a horse-drawn jaunting cart around the Lakes of Killarney, a region not unlike the northerly parts of Scotland. Visit Muckross House, an Irish folk museum in which potters and weavers can be seen at work.

Where the golfers play: Waterville.

Nongolfers can: Go on a day tour of the Dingle Peninsula, where the movie *Ryan's Daughter* was set and staged. This is countryside at its bare essentials, glacial-scraped mountains and lakes, and rough, rocky outcroppings. Much Irish Gaelic is spoken in these parts.

Where the golfers play: Ballybunion.

Nongolfers can: Visit Glin Castle, built in the 13th century and which now houses a rich collection of 18th-century furniture and paintings.

Where the golfers play: Lahinch.

Nongolfers can: Visit Galway, from which most of the Irish immigrants to the U.S. left their homes during the potato famine of the 1840s. Close by are the Cliffs of Moher, rising 600 feet above the Atlantic.

Where the golfers play: Tralee.

Nongolfers can: Shop in the town of Killarney. Take a short boat ride (or drive, via a bridge) to Valentia Island, off the southwest coast of County Kerry. This is an interesting place, not necessarily because it was here, in 1858, that the first telegraph cable from the U.S. came ashore, and not because the views of the Irish coast from Valentia are some of the best in the country. Here's why: Valentia is said to have been the home of Mug Roth (translated as "Servant of the Wheel," whatever that means), a one-eyed magician who is the chap who decapitated John the Baptist. At least that's what the Irish say.

A Connoisseur's Collection

by Pat O'Bryan

Pat O'Bryan collects golf courses. As the gaffer at Golf Adventures, a golf travel company that will take you to some of the strangest places on earth, he is constantly on the road, talking to other golfers, other travelers, about new places to play.

The problem is, he just can't visit every place he hears of. So we asked Pat to list his top 10 "escapees"—those courses that have managed as yet to escape the pain and suffering that his golf game inflicts.

1. Puntas Arenas Golf Club, Chile

Only one water hazard here—the Strait of Magellan. At the southern tip of Chile, Puntas Arenas is the southernmost golf course in the world, with magnificent views of Tierra del Fuego. Puntas Arenas is about the only course in the world where it is easier to go over trees than around them. That's because the winds are so strong—gusting up to 100 miles per hour—that the trees grow vertically for about two feet and then detour at right angles. It's also because of the wind that the greens are set in hollows cut below the fairway level. The penguins that pepper the fairways don't seem to mind.

2. Stanley Golf Club, Falkland Islands

Play straight here. Out of bounds remains landmined from when Britain and Argentina squared off over ownership of these South Atlantic Islands in the mid 1980s. Word has it that the fairways have been cleared, but who really wants to find out? At any rate, Stanley ranks as the world's most dangerous golf course—especially now that the tank has been removed from the fifth hole of the Kabul Golf Club in Afghanistan and it's been all quiet at the Beirut Golf Club.

3. Livingstone Golf Club, Zambia

Since the great Elephant Hills Golf Club was bombed out of existence just across the Zambezi River in Zimbabwe, Livingstone has replaced it as the world's most "natural" course. Elephants, water buffalo and hippos stroll in the rough. Play can be uncomfortable here, with temperatures reaching well into the 100s in summer and the roar from nearby Victoria Falls deafening you as you play. Oh, while you're in Zambia, don't forget to play Ndola Golf Club, where there are 20-foot-high termite mounds all over the course.

4. Tuctu Golf Club

Some 14,000 feet up in the Andes, this quasi-mythical course is the highest in the world. Trouble is, people say it exists, but no one knows anyone who has ever played it! The story goes that a mining company created it for its workers. Maintenance costs are low, given that grass doesn't grow at that altitude—and golf explorers have been hunting it for years. I'm still looking.

5. GULMARG GOLF CLUB, KASHMIR, INDIA

We have this on one of our golf tours. I did visit once, but the course was under snow, which wasn't surprising considering it sits 8,500 feet up in the Hindu Kush. The original was built by British troops about a century ago, and was more or less covered over with a Thomson/Wolveridge design not that long ago. Imagine playing in an alpine meadow with millions of tiny flowers surrounding you. That's Gulmarg.

6. OUSTOEN COUNTRY CLUB, OSLO FJORD, NORWAY

You take a small motorboat from Oslo out into the fjord and to the island of Oustoen. The entire island is golf course. Deer wander on and off fairways that are carved through dense woodland. On the short ninth, you must carry the fjord to reach the green. Scandinavia's best-kept secret, no doubt about it.

7. SVEN TUMBA GOLF CLUB, MOSCOW, RUSSIA

This primitive nine-holer was created by the Swedish sportsman and entrepreneur of the same name. Just the idea of this most laissez-faire of all sports being played in the spiritual heartland of communism strokes a delightful chord of irony in my Irish soul.

8. ST. ENODOC, CORNWALL, ENGLAND

Nothing offbeat about this course. A classic links in southwest England with the largest dunes of any course in Britain. Depending on how the wind is blowing, the course can vary from a holiday treat to a hopeless challenge. In the middle of the layout sits an ancient church.

9. JOCKEY GOLF CLUB, BUENOS AIRES, ARGENTINA

This is the only course Alister Mackenzie built in South America. It is the haven now for Argentina's rich and famous and where Roberto de Vicenzo saw some of his greatest triumphs. Wouldn't mind 18 holes in his footsteps—followed by a dinner of wine and Argentinian steak, of course.

10. REAL GOLF CLUB DE CERDANA, PUIGCERDA, SPAIN

Okay, okay, I *have* played this one. And I want to play it again. Cerdana nestles in a Pyreneean valley close to the Spain-France border. Spanish architect Javier Arana laid out holes that are both natural and daring and in a wonderfully colorful mountain setting. There's an alpine Chalet de Golf attached to the club that offers magnificent food and comfort for the weary golf traveler. The whole place is restorative of the first order. If I hadn't been asked for courses I had *yet* to play, this would have been number one on my list.

Finns Det En Övningsbana?

A dozen useful phrases translated into the most common foreign languages

Although about every language on earth translates the word "golf" into "golf" (or sometimes gölf, "gølf" or even "gowf"—the last of those being Scottish), you could probably use a few translations of well-frequented idioms.

Not for when you're *on* the course, however. If someone doesn't automatically concede a "gimme," you can always just rake it and make your excuses later.

But actually getting to the first tee is where a smattering of foreign phrases may be useful. I can vouch for this. Several years ago I stood in a sweaty pro shop in Martinique hemming and hawing and pointing at numerous things, all the while wishing that my high-school French lessons had had the decency to cover greens fees and golf club rental.

So you don't run into the same quandary, we've taken 12 phrases that cover the basics of getting on to a foreign golf course or club. This brief linguistic Baedeker begins at your hotel and ends when you realize you've forgotten to bring golf balls.

It is taken from *Do You Speak Golf,* written by Gregg Cox and issued by Pandemic International Publishers. Although Cox is cosmopolitan enough to also include Portugese, Danish, Dutch, Swedish and Norwegian in his book, we're sticking to his French, German, Spanish and Italian translations. But we have taken the liberty of adding Scottish, which should on no account be confused with the Queen's English.

The chapter title above, by the way, is Swedish, and will come into heretofore unparalleled use on that bright, Scandinavian morning when you stroll in to the Falsterbo pro shop and inquire as to whether there's a practice green. Phonetically, it's "Feens deht en ohvneengsbahnah."

Let the Baedeker begin.

1. WHERE IS THE NEAREST GOLF COURSE?

French: Où se trouve le terrain du golf le plus proche?
German: Wo ist der nächste Golfplatz?
Spanish: Dónde está el campo de golf más próximo?
Italian: Dove'è il più vicino campo di golf?
Scottish: Whurza gowf course cloasbye?

2. DO I NEED TO BE A MEMBER?

French: Est-il nécessaire d'être membre?
German: Muss ich Mitglied sein?
Spanish: Se necesita ser socio?
Italian: Devo essere socio?
Scottish: Huvva goata be amemburanat?

3. DO I NEED TO MAKE A RESERVATION?

French: Dois-je réserver?
German: Muss ich vorbestellen?
Spanish: Se necesita reservar?
Italian: Devo fare una prenotazione?
Scottish: Huvva goata makka bookin'?

4. I WOULD LIKE TO MAKE A RESERVATION FOR TODAY/TOMORROW.

French: J'aimerais fair une réservation pour aujourd'hui/demain.
German: Ich möchte eine Vorbestellung für heute/morgen machen.
Spanish: Me gustaría tener una reservación para hoy/mañana.
Italian: Vorrei fare una prenotazione per oggi/domani.
Scottish: Geeza teetime furraday/furramorra.

5. WHERE CAN I PARK?

French: Ou puis-je me garer?
German: Wo kann ich parken?
Spanish: Dónde se puede aparcar?
Italian: Dove posso parcheggiare?
Scottish: Cunna park ower there, Jim?

6. IS THERE ANYONE HERE WHO SPEAKS ENGLISH?

French: Y-a-t-il quelqu'un qui parle anglais ici?
German: Spricht hier jemand Englisch?

Spanish: Hay alguien aquí que hable inglés?
Italian: C'è qualcono qui che parla inglese?
Scottish: We *ur* speakin' English, ya eejit!

7. IS THERE A PRO SHOP HERE?

French: Y-a-t-il une boutique spécialisée ici?
German: Gibt es hier ein Fachgeschäft?
Spanish: Hay alguna tienda de articuos de golf?
Italian: Il campo ha un negozio di articoli da golf?
Scottish: Whurragowfshoap?

8. HOW MUCH ARE THE GREEN FEES?

French: A combien s'élèvent les droits d'entrée?
German: Wie hoch sind die Grüngebühren?
Spanish: Cuánto es la tarifa del césped?
Italian: Qual'è la tassa d'ammissione?
Scottish: Humuch te play?

9. MAY I PAY BY CREDIT CARD?

French: Puis-je payer par carte de crédit?
German: Darf ich mit Kreditkarte bezahlen?
Spanish: Puedo pagar con tarjeta de credito?
Italian: Posso pagare con carta di credito?
Scottish: Tak plastic, Jim?

10. IS THERE A PRACTICE GREEN?

French: Y-a-t-il un green de putting?
German: Gibt es ein Übungsgrün?
Spanish: Hay algun cesped de practicas?
Italian: C'è una piazzola d'allenamento?
Scottish: Yu goata puttin' greenanat?

11. WHERE CAN I RENT CLUBS?

French: Où puis-je louer des clubs de golf?
German: Wo kann ich Golfschläger mieten?
Spanish: Done puedo alquilar de palos de golf?
Italian: Dove posso affittare mazze da golf?
Scottish: Yu goat oany rentals, Jim?

12. DO YOU SELL GOLF BALLS?

French: Vendez-vous des balles de golf?
German: Verkaufen sie Golfballe?
Spanish: Vende bolas de golf?
Italian: Vende palle da golf?
Scottish: Seeza fewo'they auld retreads.

On the Cheap
A guide to golf discount cards

Discount cards aren't a bad deal for anyone involved. You pay an annual fee, in return for which you get a few essentially useless knickknacks and discounts on green fees at "participating" golf resorts and occasionally other hotel and travel discounts. The resorts in return get a golfer set loose in a pro shop where no credit card is safe. Resorts that discount accommodations usually demand a minimum stay of several days.

Just about every state in the country has a card or two on the go, most of them tied in with a charity. For details, check with the local golf association. In the meantime, here are the major national programs. Always ask if there is an introductory membership discount.

▼ Hale Irwin's Golfer's Passport costs $59 per person per year or $85 for a two-ball. It offers two free greens fees at each of 1,500 participating courses, as long as you rent a golf car. Of the courses listed, 300 are resorts that offer 10 percent discount on accommodations. The Irwin card has one of the best international rosters. Call (800) 334-3140 or (800) 667-0173 in Canada.

▼ At $75 per person or $120 for two, *The Golf Card* is the priciest card, but it has the most extensive network of courses—1,750 in North America and the Caribbean. In addition to complimentary green fees for two at each course, you get a year's subscription to *The Golf Traveler* magazine and a golf atlas. The Golf Card has also spawned the "Grasshopper Club" for members who play in outings at Golf Card courses. Call (800) 453-4260 or (800) 321-8269 in Canada.

▼ Golf Access costs $49.95 per person per year. Each family member costs an additional $15. The card gives 50 percent discounts at more than 1,000 U.S. and Canadian courses (cart rental is required), 10 percent discounts on resort stays and discounts on more than 1,600 hotels and motels. Call (800) 359-4653.

▼ The *National Golfers' Association Discount Card* costs $50 and offers discounts on greens fees, golf lessons, range balls, cart rental, airline tickets, automobile rentals and accommodations. Almost 900 courses and resorts in the U.S., Canada and the Dominican Republic participate. A 244-page directory comes with membership. Call (303) 825-0944.

Oh, to Play 18 in Arikikapakapa

Few golf wholesalers make the big bucks off the beaten tracks. The real money comes from packing 'em off to Hawaii or Scotland and Ireland until they're crying out for more.

This is not to suggest that tour ops don't offer some of the weirder corners of the golfing world, where facilities may not be excellent in terms of course conditioning but which do offer more in terms of adventure. Golf Adventures in Chicago, for example, sends most of its clients to Scotland and Ireland but has a large selection of wayward areas, such as South America, North Africa and even India, Nepal and Kashmir.

Here are some of the more unconventional destinations. We've listed only one tour operator in each instance, but it should be pointed out that all of the numbers included below will likely be able to offer a similar tour.

AUSTRALIA

PerryGolf (800-344-5257) offers a 12-day tour that covers Melbourne, Sydney and Queensland, the portion closest to the Pacific known by the Aussies as the "Gold Coast."

Among other courses, the tour visits the New South Wales Club, an Alister Mackenzie layout designed in 1928, and Kingston Heath, another 1928 work by Mackenzie from original 1925 plans by Des Soutar.

FRANCE

Marsans International (800-223-6114) is one of several operators selling Air France's "Le Grand Golf" program. You tailor your own tour, fly Air France and then buzz around in a Hertz car or van. The program brochure devotes a page, sometimes two, to various regions, among them Brittany, Normandy, the Loire Valley, Bordeaux, Biarritz, Provence, Paris, Cognac country, the Rhone Alps and the Riviera. France doesn't have a group of classic courses in the way that the Costa del Sol does—but that could be due to public relations as much as anything else—so here are a few recommendations, all of which are part of the Le Grand Golf program: Omaha Beach, built on the cliffs of Normandy above the spot where the troops landed in World War II; Chiberta, a seaside course built in 1927 near Biarritz, which itself was a playground for the American wealthy at the turn of the century; Biarritz Golf Club; Les Bordes, a tough, 7,100-yard track by Robert Von Hagge, the American architect; and the Monte Carlo Golf Club, a course high above the principality with magnificent views.

INDIA AND NEPAL

Perhaps the most exotic of the Golf Adventures (800-878-0521) is this trek to four courses in India and Nepal: Royal Calcutta, Royal Nepal, Delhi Country Club and, in Kashmir, Gulmarg Country Club. *Kashmir?* You bet. When India was part of the British empire, army officers headed to this region to escape the heat and oppressiveness of Delhi and played golf in a mountain meadow some 8,500 feet above sea level. In more recent times, Peter Thomson and Michael Wolveridge designed a new course here.

NEW ZEALAND

As is the case with most operators, PerryGolf combines New Zealand with Australia. On its kiwi leg—as opposed to its wallaby leg—it offers golf at Muriwai, a links course near Auckland; Wairakei, a fine and very lush inland course; Arikikapakapa, a course that winds around thermal geysers.

NORTH AFRICA

The Royal Golf Rabat club, a Robert Trent Jones layout in Morocco, is tacked onto Golf Adventures' tour of Spain and Portugal.

SCANDINAVIA

Golf Getaways (800-423-3657) provides the only Scandinavian tour we could find. It plays six rounds of golf: Sollentuna and Skelleftea in Sweden; Sundsvall, Froso and Oslo in Norway, and the Copenhagen Golf Club in Denmark. Nope, we'd never heard of them either, which leads us to conclude that the tour itself is the key. In other words, can there be more sublime experiences than playing 18 holes in the morning then clambering 2,000 feet up a mountain by train in the afternoon—after a few Ringneses? GG is also kind enough to allot ample time to explore the Scandinavian cities at each stop.

SOUTH AMERICA

Golf Adventures' "Golf Carnival" tour first visits Brazil, where it plays the Gavea Golf Club south of Rio de Janeiro and the Itanhanga Golf Club, a Stanley Thompson design, then heads south to Argentina, De Vicenzo country, where it plays the San Isidro and Hindu courses.

Finding the Perfect Home
Away from Home

by Philip Gibson

As someone who grew up in the vicinity of St. Andrews, Scotland, but who never gave even a moment's thought to playing the Old Course—not with so many other golf courses closer to home—I have always been bewildered by the lengths that visitors are prepared to go to play my homeland's great courses.

Only a begging letter sent well ahead of time will give you a chance of playing Muirfield. So much as hint that you might be running a little late and the stuffy club secretary will dress you down sadistically.

Turnberry? Perhaps if you stay in the Turnberry Hotel, where room rates are Faroukian. Royal Troon? Another begging letter. Well, surely, the Old Course, a *public* course, is a simple conquest.

Simpler, maybe. For most of the summer you still have to put your name into a ballot one day in the hope of getting a tee time the next.

So if you want the British golfing experience, here's what to do: *Join one of the great old British clubs.*

This is superb idea, but not a new one. Stephen Goodwin, a contributing editor to *Golf Magazine* and the author of "A Hefty Drive Is a Slosh" (page 221), has been a member for years at Royal North Devon, aka Westward Ho!, in southwest England. So, too, has David Earl, the editor of the United States Golf Association's *Golf Journal*.

It costs them next to nothing. The overseas initiation fee is $250, or roughly a round and a half at Pebble Beach, while annual membership costs 17 of her majesty's pounds, which can be the equivalent of around $30 if the stock market goes through a dull patch.

For that paltry sum both Goodwin and Earl spend a week or so a year playing—nonstop—the oldest links course in England (1864), one that swoops above and down to the sea and which is inhabited by sheep and horses that graze what is common land. And when not on the course, they can be found in the clubhouse trying to learn the intricacies of snooker, or in the bar, glass in hand, talking golf with some very hospitable locals.

In fact, hospitality is much of what an overseas membership is all about. After all, which would you rather hear after a weatherbeaten day on the golf course: "Excuse me, but this is the *members'* lounge!" or "Looks like it was rough out there today. Will it be the usual—and perhaps a wee dram to warm you up?"

Below are listed a few of the better clubs you can join and enjoy, but you should by no means restrict your interest to this list. Human beings are creatures of habit, and if you find some nook or cranny in the British Isles that you know you will return to, you might want to look into joining the local golf club. All dollar figures, by the way, are approximate.

The 11th at Royal Dornoch: a home away from home at the latitude of Juneau, Alaska.

NAIRN

Location: Northeast coast of Scotland, east of Inverness.

Course notes: Archie Simpson designed this unheralded links course in 1887, and it was later remodelled and improved by Old Tom Morris and James Braid. It is not a Ballybunion-style links with towering sandhills and spectacular views. It is known more for being a solid design that is always challenging.

Cost to join: $280 covers the initiation. Annual membership costs $110.

How to join: Write to the club secretary David Patrick for an application form: Nairn Golf Club, Seabank Road, Nairn, Scotland.

Call for information: (0667) 53208

ROYAL DORNOCH

Location: Northeast coast of Scotland, north of Inverness.

Course notes: A fantastic, remote links course originally designed by Old Tom Morris in 1886, with major work carried out by John Sutherland and Donald Ross in 1922.

Cost to join: Royal Dornoch's "Rest-of-the-World" membership carries an initiation fee of $400 and an annual membership fee of $160.

How to join: Application must be accompanied by a proposer and a seconder from the club—which means you may want to visit and play a few times before joining up.

Call for information: (0862) 810219

ROYAL PORTRUSH

Location: North coast of Northern Ireland.

Course notes: The only course outside Great Britain to host a British Open, the 1951 tournament being won by Max Faulkner.

H.S. Colt, who built many fine courses in this country, and an associate, J.S.F. Morrison, designed Royal Portrush. While the course, sometimes known as Dunluce, spreads out over a broad expanse of links, it differs from many links courses in that the areas around the greens are not festooned with bunkers. They are instead festooned with pits and potholes, from which recovery can be just as difficult.

Cost to join: Annual membership is $40, but overseas members also pay a $1.85 green fee for each day. An overseas life membership costs $1,850, which also covers any green fees. The money goes toward repairing damage to the course caused by coastal erosion.

How to join: Only the lifers need not be proposed and seconded, so you may want to visit first. Write to the secretary, A.M. Woolcott, for an application form: Royal Portrush Golf Club, Bushmills Rd., Portrush, County Antrim, Northern Ireland.

Call for information: (0265) 822311

PORTMARNOCK

Location: East coast of Ireland, eight miles north of Dublin.

Course notes: The course sits on a peninsula of linksland between the Irish Sea and an inland bay. Like all the great links courses, it follows the natural rise and fall of the land, which in this case isn't very severe. The course has undergone several redesigns since George Ross and W.C. Pickeman first laid it out in 1894, but it has not lost any of its ancient flavor.

Cost to join: Initiation costs $280

while the annual membership is $250.

How to join: By being proposed and seconded by a club member.

Call for information: (0001) 323082

ROYAL NORTH DEVON, WESTWARD HO!

Location: North coast of Devon, a county that occupies part of the peninsula forming southwest England.

Course notes: The oldest links course in England, one laid out on common land—which explains the sheep and horses that graze as you play. It is a combination of sandhills, water carries and clumps of hard, thick "Great Sea Rushes." Honest.

Cost to join: $250 initiation and $32 per year. There is also an overseas life membership. Rates currently under review.

How to join: Write to club secretary, John Davies, for an application: Royal North Devon Golf Club, Westward Ho!, Bideford, Devonshire, England.

Call for information: (023 74) 73817

SKERRIES

Location: East coast of Ireland, 20 miles north of Dublin.

Course notes: A recently lengthened parkland course noted for panoramic views and a tough, uphill dogleg finishing hole. The course dates to 1906.

Cost to join: $125 annual subscription. There is no initiation fee.

How to join: You must be known to at least two members. Write to the club for an application form: Skerries Golf Club, Skerries, County Dublin, Ireland.

Call for information: (0001) 491567

CARNOUSTIE

The benefit of joining Carnoustie does not lie in easier access to the golf course. *Everyone* who plays Carnoustie has to go through a ballot. Instead, membership at Carnoustie opens doors at many otherwise private clubs around Britain.

Cost to join: Initiation is $85. Annual membership is $50.

How to join: Write to the club secretary David Curtis for an application: Carnoustie Golf Club, Links Parade, Carnoustie, Angus, Scotland.

Call for information: (0241) 52480

A State-by-State Guide to Golf in America

We wouldn't presume to dictate where you should play your golf. Have a raging fondness for the Boise area? Be our guest.

But we can help you decide where to play in certain areas by guiding you to the appropriate information sources.

With each state description below, we have included the number of golf courses—conservative figures derived from the National Golf Foundation's 1991 "Golf Profile"—some examples of the literature available from state and local agencies (we wrote and asked them for stuff) and from regional golf associations, the necessary address and telephone numbers and the best golf courses in each state as rated by *Golf Digest.* Two fairly comprehensive books that could be listed over and over are the eastern and western editions of *The Golf Resort Guide,* by Jim and Barbara Nicol, put out by Hunter Publishing, and *The Official United States Golf Course Directory and Guide,* from the Kayar Company (*psst*—there's nothing "official" about it).

The public, resort and semiprivate courses in the *Digest* ratings are asterisked. Some of the top courses, such as the TPC at Sawgrass's Stadium course in Ponte Vedra, Florida, are accessible if you stay in a hotel on the development (in Sawgrass's case, a Marriott, which controls almost all the tee times).

The others are private. But don't let that deter you. Except in the case of the superexclusive clubs—Augusta National in Augusta, Georgia, for example—most courses are accessible through business contacts or friends. And make enough telephone calls to the right people and even Augusta National is not a closed shop. Exhibit A: a friend, Jim Wysocki (sadly, now deceased), from New Orleans, who wanted to play Augusta National as part of an eventually fulfilled quest to play all of *Golf Magazine*'s "100 Greatest Courses in the World." Wysocki's wife's sister introduced him to a sixty-year-old couple in his hometown who had a daughter in Jackson, Mississippi. The lady in Jackson was important because she was married to a doctor from Meridian, Mississippi, who had a sister in Augusta, Georgia. The Georgia sister's husband ran a trucking business in Augusta, and the insurance agent for the business just happened to be an Augusta member and the starter at The Masters every year.

Wysocki shot an 88.

ALABAMA

Number of golf courses: 211
Municipal: 33
Daily fee: 53
Private: 125

The *Golf Digest* Top Five:
1. Shoal Creek, Birmingham
2. Country Club of Birmingham (West)
3. Turtle Point Yacht & Country Club, Killen
4. Montgomery Country Club
5. Mountain Brook Club, Birmingham

Literature:
Very little up-to-date literature is available. State gives out advertising supplement from *Golf Digest* from 1987.

Further information:
• Alabama Bureau of Tourism and Travel, 532 South Perry St., Montgomery, AL 36104; (800) 252-2262
• Alabama Golf Association, Box 20149, Birmingham, AL 35216; (205) 979-1234

ALASKA

Number of golf courses: 8
Municipal: 2
Daily fee: 4
Private: 2

The *Golf Digest* Top Four (the other four didn't make the ranking):
1. Eagleglen Golf Club, Anchorage*
2. Anchorage Golf Club, Anchorage*
3. Moose Run Golf Club, Anchorage*
4. Chena Bend Golf Club, Fairbanks

Literature:
None.

Further information:
• State of Alaska Division of Tourism,

Box E, Juneau, AK 99811-0800; (907) 465-2010
• Alaska Golf Association, Box 112210, Anchorage, AK 99511; (907) 349-4653

ARIZONA

Number of golf courses: 236
Municipal: 31
Daily fee: 131
Private: 74

The *Golf Digest* Top Five:
1. Forest Highlands Golf Club, Flagstaff
2. Troon Golf and Country Club, Scottsdale
3. Desert Highlands Golf Club, Scottsdale
4. Desert Forest Golf Club, Carefree
5. Golf Club at Desert Mountain (Renegade), Scottsdale

15th green at Desert Highlands.

Literature:
The Arizona Golf Course Directory can be obtained from the state golf association for $2.95.

The "Exclusive Golf Card" is a program that costs $125 and allows three rounds at each of 15 courses in the Scottsdale area for $15 per round, including golf cart.

A note on Arizona golf: This is the game at its most draconian. If your ball leaves the fairway, you should either abandon it and play the desert as a lateral hazard or risk cactus-attack and play it. If you plan to opt for the latter, carry an old club, preferably a wedge; that desert scrub can ruin a perfectly good golf club in seconds.

Further information:
• Arizona Office of Tourism, 1480 E. Bethany Home Rd., Phoenix, AZ 85014; (602) 255-3618
• Arizona Golf Association, 11801 North Tatum Blvd., Suite 247, Phoenix, AZ 85028; (602) 953-5990

ARKANSAS

Number of golf courses: 151
Municipal: 14
Daily fee: 50
Private: 87

The *Golf Digest* Top Five:
1. Pleasant Valley Country Club, Little Rock
2. Texarkana Country Club
3. Mountain Ranch Country Club, Fairfield Bay*
4. Maumelle Country Club
5. Hardscrabble Country Club, Fort Smith

Literature:
The state's Department of Parks and Tourism will send "Fairways and Greens," a supplement that appeared in the *Arkansas Times Magazine*. It is short on feature information but includes an excellent list of all public, private, semiprivate, resort and military courses in the state, with telephone numbers, green fees, pars and yardages, cart rental fees and rates for those belonging to clubs with reciprocal memberships. For some reason the list carried a rider that it contains "only 85% of the courses in Arkansas"—but that's enough to get you going.

Further information:
• Arkansas Vacations, Dept. 1643, One Capitol Mall, Little Rock, AR 72201; (800) 628-8725
• Arkansas Golf Association, Box 943, Little Rock, AR 72203; (501) 666-2834

CALIFORNIA

Number of golf courses: 853
Municipal: 168
Daily fee: 367
Private: 318

The 18th at Pebble Beach.

The *Golf Digest* Top Five:
1. Cypress Point Club, Pebble Beach
2. Pebble Beach Golf Links, Pebble Beach*
3. Olympic Club (Lakeside)
4. San Francisco Golf Club
5. Los Angeles Country Club (North)

Literature:
In book form, the best might be *California Golf: The Ultimate Guide,* by Mark Soltau, which includes details on more than 600 courses. Beyond that, all the chambers of commerce in California—and there are more than a hundred—have literature. But below are the contacts for some of the more popular areas:

Anaheim Area Visitor and Convention Bureau, 800 W. Katella Ave., Anaheim, CA 92802; (714) 999-8999

Eureka/Humboldt County Convention and Visitors Bureau, 1034 Second St., Eureka, CA 95501; (800) 346-3482

Lake Tahoe Visitors Authority, 1156 Ski Run Blvd., Box 16299, South Lake Tahoe, CA 95706; (800) 288-2463

Los Angeles Convention and Visitors Bureau, 515 S. Figueroa St., 11th Floor, Los Angeles, CA 90071; (213) 624-7300

Monterey Peninsula Chamber of Commerce and Visitors and Convention Bureau, 380 Alvarado St., Box 1770, Monterey, CA 93942; (408) 649-1770

Palm Springs Desert Resorts Convention and Visitors Bureau, 255 N. El Cielo Rd., Suite 315, Palm Springs, CA 92262; (619) 327-8411

Pasadena Convention and Visitors Bureau, 171 S. Los Robles Ave., Pasadena, CA 91101; (818) 795-9311

Sacramento Visitors Information Center, 1104 Front St., Sacramento, CA 95814; (916) 442-7644

San Diego Visitor Information Center, 2688 E. Mission Bay Dr., San Diego, CA 92109; (619) 276-8200

Santa Cruz County Conference and Visitors Council, 105 Cooper St., Suite 243, Box 8525, Santa Cruz, CA 95061; (408) 423-1111

Further information:
• Northern California Golf Association, Box NGCA, Pebble Beach, CA 93953; (408) 625-4653
• Southern California Golf Association, 3740 Cahuenga Blvd., #100, N. Hollywood, CA 91609; (818) 980-3630

COLORADO

Number of golf courses: 187
Municipal: 64
Daily fee: 64
Private: 59

The *Golf Digest* Top Five
1. Castle Pines Golf Club, Castle Rock
2. Cherry Hills Country Club, Englewood
3. Eisenhower Golf Club (Blue), USAF Academy
4. Bear Creek Golf Club, Denver
5. Country Club of Castle Pines, Castle Rock

Literature:
Colorado has become a major golf destination ever since the ski resorts realized that they had to turn a buck when the snow melted. Some of the finest golf courses are now being built by the top architects in such areas as Aspen, Vail, Breckenridge, Steamboat Springs and more. The state recently formed a nonprofit promotional organization to deal specifically with golf and updated and published its golf directory in April 1990. The various golf resorts and areas offer numerous discount programs, with details available through the state's tourism board. The Colorado Golf Association is just as helpful. For $1 it will send you its *SHAG* book,

which stands for "Schedule, Handicap and Association Guide." As well as information on the CGA, *SHAG* lists courses, pars, yardages and slopes from various tees, slope conversion tables and a schedule of tournaments. Great stuff.

Further information:
• Colorado Tourism Board, 1625 Broadway, Suite 1700, Denver, CO 80202
• Colorado Golf Association, 5655 South Yosemite, #101, Englewood, CO 80111; (303) 779-4653

CONNECTICUT

Number of golf courses: 168
Municipal: 35
Daily fee: 53
Private: 80

The *Golf Digest* Top Five:
1. Stanwich Club, Greenwich
2. Wee Burn Country Club, Darien
3. Yale Golf Course, New Haven
4. Woodway Country Club, Darien
5. Brooklawn Country Club, Bridgeport

Literature:
If you visit Connecticut, pray that it's on business and your client belongs to one of the choicer clubs. Nutmeggers tend to be privateers; daily fee and resort courses are scarce in comparison. The state golf association does not carry listings of its courses.

One good public tip would be Richter Park, in Danbury, one of the top munis in the land, at (203) 792-2552.

Or you could ask the MGA (below) to send a copy of its Yellow Pages that appeared in a 1991 edition of *The Met Golfer,* the MGA's official publication.

Further information:
• State of Connecticut Department of Economic Development, 210 Washington St., Hartford, CT 06106; (800) 243-1685
• Connecticut State Golf Association, Golf House, 35 Cold Spring Rd., Suite 212, Rocky Hill, CT 06067; (203) 257-4171
• Metropolitan (NY) Golf Association,

125 Spencer Place, Mamaroneck, NY 10543; (914) 698-0390

DELAWARE

Number of golf courses: 28
Municipal: 2
Daily fee: 5
Private: 21

The *Golf Digest* Top Five:
1. Wilmington Country Club (South), Greenville
2. Bidermann Golf Club, Wilmington
3. Wilmington Country Club (North), Greenville
4. Rehoboth Beach Country Club
5. DuPont Country Club (DuPont), Wilmington

Literature:
Not a lot at all. "Delaware: Small Wonder," from the state, lists a grand total of three courses.

Further information:
• Delaware Tourism Office, 99 Kings Highway, Box 1401, Dover, DE 19903; (800) 282-8667
• Delaware State Golf Association, Box 325, Wilmington, DE 19806; (302) 695-2175

DISTRICT OF COLUMBIA

Number of golf courses: 10
Municipal: 3
Daily fee: 3
Private: 4

The *Golf Digest* Top Five:
Golf Digest does not include the District of Columbia in its ratings.

Literature:
None. Better bets for golf are neighboring Maryland and Virginia.

Further information:
• Washington DC Convention and Visitors Association, 1575 Eye St., N.W., Suite 250, Washington, DC 20005
• Washington Metropolitan Golf Association, 8012 Colorado Springs Drive, Springfield, VA 22153

16th hole, TPC at Sawgrass (Stadium Course), in Ponte Vedra, Florida.

and the state's Department of Industry Trade and Tourism. The listing is by county and a map is provided. The listing includes public, semiprivate, resort and military courses, with pars, yardages, staff names, directions to the courses where necessary and the amenities at the courses, such as snack bars or swimming pools.

The American Lung Association benefits from the "Golf Privilege Card," which costs $35 ($30 for two or more) and gives discounts at about 40 courses. Call (800) 277-5864.

Further information:
• Georgia Department of Industry, Trade and Tourism, Box 1776, Atlanta, GA 30301; (404) 656-3590
• Georgia Golf Association, 4200 Northside Pkwy., Bldg. 9, Suite 100, Atlanta, GA 30327; (404) 233-4742

FLORIDA

Number of golf courses: 1,011
Municipal: 96
Daily fee: 442
Private: 473

The *Golf Digest* Top Five:
1. Seminole Golf Club, North Palm Beach
2. Black Diamond Ranch Golf and Country Club, Lecanto
3. TPC at Sawgrass (Stadium), Ponte Vedra Beach*
4. Jupiter Hills Golf Club, Jupiter Hills
5. Pine Tree Golf Club, Boynton Beach

Literature:
Both *Golf Magazine* and *Golf Digest* publish "Florida Golf Guides" in the fall. *GolfWeek*—named *Florida Golfweek* until it went regional—publishes a "Course Directory and Travel Guide" that breaks the state up into five regions and lists contacts, green fees, pars, yardages and off-course facilities. The North Florida PGA offers a "Passport" discount program. Bear in mind also that all the major hotel chains have resort properties in Florida, and airlines serving the states often work with resorts in producing packages; a good travel agent should be able to put you in the right direction.

John F. Kennedy once was denied a round at Seminole. Don't let that stop you.

Further information:
• Florida Division of Tourism, Visitor Inquiry, 126 Van Buren St., Tallahassee 32301; (no telephone)
• Florida Department of Commerce, Bureau of Visitor Services; (904) 487-1462 (phone only)
• Florida State Golf Association, 5710 Clark Rd., Box 21177, Sarasota, FL 34233; (813) 921-5695

GEORGIA

Number of golf courses: 324
Municipal: 42
Daily Fee: 109
Private: 173

The *Golf Digest* Top Five:
1. Augusta National Golf Club
2. Peachtree Golf Club, Atlanta
3. Port Armor Country Club, Greensboro*
4. Atlanta Country Club, Marietta
5. Atlanta Athletic Club (Highlands), Duluth

Literature
"Georgia on My Mind; Georgia's Official Golf Guide" is published by *GolfWeek*

HAWAII

Number of golf courses: 67
Municipal: 7
Daily Fee: 41
Private: 19

The *Golf Digest* Top Five:
1. The Prince Golf and Country Club, Kauai*
2. Kauai Lagoons Golf and Racquet Club (Kiele), Kauai*
3. Mauna Kea Beach Hotel Golf Course, Hawaii*
4. The King's Golf Club, Hawaii*
5. Princeville Makai Golf Course (Ocean/Lake), Kauai*

Literature:
Surprisingly, the Hawaii Visitors Bureau isn't too helpful with literature. Here's a better way to go about booking. Contact the major airlines that offer packages (American, United, America West) or the hotel companies that have properties (Sheraton, Westin, Hyatt, etc.) Two of the major packagers (there really isn't a better way to play in the state) are Real Hawaii at (800) 367-5108 and Golf Getaways at (800) 423-3657. An outfit called Hawaii Reservations at (800) 662-9906 specializes in twosomes and foursomes.

Further information:
- Hawaii Visitors Bureau, Suite 801, Waikiki Business Plaza, 2270 Kalakaua Ave., Honolulu, HI 96815; (808) 923-1811
- Hawaii Golf Association, 1859 Alaweo St., Honolulu, HI 96821; (808) 521-6622

IDAHO

Number of golf courses: 82
Municipal: 26
Daily fee: 42
Private: 14

The *Golf Digest* Top Five:
1. Sun Valley Golf Course*
2. Elkhorn Golf Course, Sun Valley*
3. Hillcrest Country Club, Boise
4. Quail Hollow Country Club, Boise
5. Crane Creek Country Club, Boise

Literature:
A listing of accommodations in Idaho, town-by-town, mentions golf courses and whether they're private or public but does not supply telephone numbers.

Further Information:
- Idaho Travel Council, 700 W. State St., Boise, ID 83720; (800) 635-7820
- Idaho Golf Association, Box 3025, Boise, ID 83703; (208) 342-4442

ILLINOIS

Number of golf courses: 606
Municipal: 151
Daily fee: 251
Private: 204

The *Golf Digest* Top Five:
1. Medinah Country Club (Number 3)
2. Butler National Golf Club, Oak Brook
3. Chicago Golf Club, Wheaton
4. Wynstone Golf Club, North Barrington
5. Cog Hill Golf and Country Club (Number 4), Lemont*

Literature:
It's not the sexiest looking booklet in the country, but it may be the most comprehensive. Illinois' *Golf List* comprises 46 Xeroxed pages of course listings. Each entry includes directions, telephone numbers, par and yardage as well as USGA course rating, related amenities, a budget range for greens fees and cart rental ($ to $$$), availability of special rates (for seniors, juniors, twilight times, etc.), and the name of the professional. It even tells you what credit cards the courses accept. Note: The Chicago area has one of the best public-course networks, which is the result of much hard work by a man named Joe Jemsek. The Cog Hill complex in Lemont, a suburb of Chicago, is one of the best in the land. It's Number 4 course was rated the fifth best layout in Illinois by *Golf Digest* and now hosts the PGA Tour's Western Open.

Further information:
- Illinois Department of Commerce and Community Affairs, Tourist Information Center, Suite 108, 310 South Michigan Ave., Chicago, IL 60604; (312) 793-2094
- Chicago Golf Association, 619 Enterprise Dr., #101, Oak Brook, IL 60521; (312) 954-2180
- Western Golf Association, 1 Briar Rd., Golf, IL 66029; (312) 724-4600

INDIANA

Number of golf courses: 387
Municipal: 63
Daily fee: 220
Private: 104

The *Golf Digest* Top Five:
1. Sycamore Hills Golf Club, Fort Wayne
2. Crooked Stick Golf Club, Carmel
3. Wolf Run Golf Club, Zionsville
4. Otter Creek Golf Club, Columbus*
5. South Bend Country Club, South Bend

Literature:
The state provides a partial list of courses, and the golf association provides only a copy of their mailing list; in other words, names and addresses but no telephone numbers, yardages or any information on the courses themselves. They also ask that you send a check for $35 and a written reason for the request. If the request is denied you get your $35 back.

Further information:
- Indiana Department of Commerce, Tourism Development Division, One N. Capitol St., Suite 700, Indianapolis, IN 46204; (800) 232-8860
- Indiana Golf Association, 111 East Main St., Carmel, IN 46032; (317) 844-7271

IOWA

Number of golf courses: 367
Municipal: 56
Daily fee: 141
Private: 170

The *Golf Digest* Top Five:
1. Wakonda Club, Des Moines
2. Des Moines Golf and Country Club (Red), Des Moines
3. Amana Colonies Golf Course*
4. Davenport Country Club, Pleasant Valley
5. Crow Valley Golf Club, Bettendorf

Literature:
"Bogey on down to Iowa" reads part of the Hawkeye State's "Visitors Guide & Calendar of Events." The guide allocates three pages to a listing of almost 150 public and daily-fee courses according to city, accompanying the names with addresses and telephone numbers. Although it doesn't actually list green fees, it does say that they are "noted for reasonable green fees."

Further information:
- Division of Tourism, Iowa Department of Economic Development, 200 East Grand Ave., Des Moines, IA 50309; (515) 281-3100
- Iowa Golf Association, 3800 Wilson Ave., S.W., Cedar Rapids, IA 52404; (319) 396-5968

KANSAS

Number of golf courses: 243
Municipal: 48
Daily fee: 71
Private: 124

The *Golf Digest* Top Five:
1. Prairie Dunes Country Club, Hutchinson
2. Hallbrook Country Club, Leawood
3. Shadow Glen Golf Club, Olathe
4. Kansas City Country Club, Shawnee Mission
5. Deer Creek Golf Club, Overland Park

Literature:
The golf association has a list of courses but is reluctant to release it as, in the past few years, snake-oil salesman have been beating down the doors of member clubs having secured said list. However, the association will discuss where to play with anyone who writes or calls directly.

Further information:
• Kansas Travel and Tourism Division, 400 West 8th St., 5th Floor, Topeka, KS 66603; (913) 296-2009
• Kansas Golf Association, 3301 Clinton Parkway Court, Suite 4, Lawrence, KS 66047; (913) 842-4833

KENTUCKY

Number of golf courses: 228
Municipal: 36
Daily fee: 99
Private: 93

The *Golf Digest* Top Five:
1. Valhalla Golf Club, Louisville
2. Persimmon Ridge Golf Club, Louisville*
3. The Champions Golf Club, Nicholasville
4. Kearney Hill Golf Links, Lexington
5. Country Club of Paducah

Literature:
The Kentucky Golf Association will send a golf calendar that lists member courses, addresses and telephone numbers, whether they're nine- or 18-hole layouts and whether they're public, private or daily-fee. You might also want to look out for a book called *Kentucky Golf,* by Laurie Paine-Stoneham.

Further information:
• Kentucky Department of Travel Development, 2200 Capital Plaza Tower, Frankfort, KY 40601; (800) 225-8747
• Kentucky Golf Association, Box

20146, Louisville, KY 40220; (502) 452-1584

LOUISIANA

Number of golf courses: 148
Municipal: 22
Daily fee: 28
Private: 98

The *Golf Digest* Top Five:
1. Southern Trace Country Club, Shreveport
2. The Bluffs on Thompson Creek, St. Francisville
3. Country Club of Louisiana, Baton Rouge
4. Oakbourne Country Club, Lafayette
5. English Turn Golf and Country Club, New Orleans

Literature:
Outdoor pursuits in Louisiana are more geared to the water—fishing, boating, swamp tours, etc.—but "Louisiana Outdoors" does list 40 courses, mostly municipal, with telephone numbers. It also tells you where to find the National Association of Louisiana Catahoulas for those interested in the Catahoula Leopard Dog, the official state *dog*.

Further information:
• Louisiana Office of Tourism, Box 94291, Baton Rouge, LA 70804; (504) 342-8119
• Louisiana Golf Association, 1305 Emerson, Monroe, LA 71201; (318) 342-4140

MAINE

Number of golf courses: 121
Municipal: 9
Daily fee: 89
Private: 23

The *Golf Digest* Top Five:
1. Sugarloaf Golf Club, Carrabassett Valley*
2. Sable Oaks Golf Club, South Portland
3. Waterville Country Club, Oakland
4. Falmouth Country Club
5. Portland Country Club, Falmouth

Literature:
The best information is to be found in the *New England Golf Guide,* a 300-

page handbook published by two youngish businessmen from the Boston area. It breaks the state into northern and southern chapters and, as with all its courses, lists the normal stuff, like par and yardage, along with detailed stuff, like whether there is a practice area and how much the local pro charges for lessons. Discount coupons are bound into the back of the book.

Further information:
• Maine Publicity Bureau, P.O. Box 2300, Hallowell, ME 04347; (207) 582-9300
• Maine State Golf Association, 40 Pierce St., Gardiner, ME 04345; (301) 467-8899

17th green at Baltimore Country Club at Five Farms.

MARYLAND

Number of golf courses: 146
Municipal: 27
Daily fee: 32
Private: 87

The *Golf Digest* Top Five
1. Congressional Country Club (Blue), Bethesda
2. Baltimore Country Club at Five Farms (East), Timonium
3. Columbia Country Club, Chevy Chase
4. TPC at Avenel, Potomac
5. Burning Tree Club, Bethesda

Literature:
Maryland's "Travel and Outdoor Guide" lists all public and semiprivate courses, according to the county in which they are located and the region in which the county is located. Each listing includes a map reference (the map is in the cen-

ter of the guide), address and telephone number.

Further information:
• Maryland Office of Tourism Development, 217 East Redwood St., Baltimore, MD 21202; (800) 543-1036
• Maryland Golf Association, Box 16289, Baltimore, MD 21210; (301) 467-8899

MASSACHUSETTS

Number of golf courses: 329
Municipal: 40
Daily fee: 166
Private: 123

The *Golf Digest* Top Five:
1. The Country Club (Open), Brookline
2. Kittansett Club, Marion
3. Salem Country Club, Peabody
4. Brae Burn Country Club, West Newton
5. Crumpin-Fox Club, Bernardston

Literature:
The sole golf-only literature issued by the Massachusetts Office of Travel and Tourism includes such details as addresses, distances from Boston, pars and yardages, hours of operation, green fees, services available and even the languages spoken by the staffs. But it covers only the areas immediately north and south of Beantown as well as

Cape Cod, which means no more than 32 courses. What are useful, however, are the general comments included with each course. We find out, for example, that "Donald Ross designed 14 of the holes" at the L.J. Martin Golf Club in Weston, Massachusetts.

A better source is the *New England Golf Guide*. See Maine.

Further information:
• Massachusetts Office of Travel and Tourism, 100 Cambridge St., 13th Floor, Boston, MA 02202; (617) 727-3201
• Massachusetts Golf Association, 190 Park Rd., Weston, MA 02193; (617) 891-4300

MICHIGAN

Number of golf courses: 749
Municipal: 87
Daily fee: 513
Private: 149

The *Golf Digest* Top Five:
1. Crystal Downs Country Club, Frankfort
2. Oakland Hills Country Club (South), Birmingham
3. Point O'Woods Golf and Country Club, Benton Harbor
4. Detroit Golf Club (North)
5. Grand Traverse Resort Village (The Bear), Acme

Literature:
Plenty of it, which comes as no surprise as Michigan is developing rapidly as a major golf destination. The Michigan Travel Bureau and the Michigan Association of Public Golf Courses issues *Celebrate Golf in Michigan,* a 100-page guide complete with addresses, pars and yardages, course amenities—and places to make notes. The various resort areas (note the abundance of daily-fee layouts) also package several courses; it's all in the booklet. The "Michigan Travel Planner" devotes a section to golf, but refers to the *Celebrate* booklet for listings. The *Michigan Golfers Map and Guide* is more complete and contains coupons giving discounts at more than 250 courses in the state. It's available for $14.95 from RSG Publishing (which also publishes the *Celebrate* booklet), Box 612, Plymouth, MI 48170; (800) 223-5877.

Further information:
• Michigan Travel Bureau, Department TPM, Box 30226, Lansing, MI 48909; (800) 543-2937
• Michigan Golf Association, 31800 Northwestern Highway, #130, Farmington Hills, MI 48018; (313) 855-4653

MINNESOTA

Number of golf courses: 394
Municipal: 81
Daily fee: 224
Private: 89

The *Golf Digest* Top Five:
1. Hazeltine National Golf Club, Chaska
2. Interlachen Country Club, Edina
3. Northland Country Club, Duluth
4. White Bear Yacht Club
5. Rochester Golf and Country Club

Literature:
While, like most golf associations, the Minnesota fraternity can send you a list, a better bet might be "Explore Minnesota Golfing," a rather ugly state brochure that nevertheless contains all the necessary information and sound advice on when and where to play. The

No. 7 at The Country Club (Open Course), Brookline.

regional golf association has a greens-fee discount program known as "The Minnesota Green Pages." Contact the golf association.

Further information:
• Minnesota Travel Information Center, 375 Jackson St., 250 Skyway Level, St. Paul, MN 55101; (800) 657-3700
• Minnesota Golf Association, 6550 York Avenue South, Suite 402, Edina, MN 55435; (612) 927-4643

MISSISSIPPI

Number of golf courses: 145
Municipal: 15
Daily-fee: 40
Private: 90

The *Golf Digest* Top Five:
1. Old Waverly Golf Club, West Point
2. Annandale Golf Club, Madison
3. Colonial Country Club (Deerfield), Madison
4. Laurel Country Club
5. Country Club of Jackson (Red/White)

Literature:
The state issues a "Mississippi Golf Guide" that lists about 40 courses, and a similar number of hotels that offer golf packages. But whether the two are connected or at which courses the packages are offered is anybody's guess. The Gulf Coast Hotel-Motel Association, (800) 237-9493, publishes a "Mississippi Gulf Coast Golf Planner" that lists the best courses between Pascagoula to the east and Pass Christian to the west, along with golf packages that actually do tell you where you might play depending on where you stay. This is a good little guide. It includes average temperatures as well as details on the Mississippi Coast Coliseum and Convention Center's Ram Indoor Golf Clinic, where for $10 (or the cost of a green fee at a participating hotel) a golfer can get instruction from a PGA pro, take a test on the rules, enter putting and chipping contests and partake in the occasional hand of gin rummy. They run afternoons and evenings in February and March. Call (601) 388-8010 for more details.

Further information:
• Division of Tourism Development, Mississippi Department of Economic and Community Development, Box 849, Jackson, MS 39205
• Mississippi Golf Association, 630 Cherry Lane, Laurel, MS 39440; (601) 649-0570

MISSOURI

Number of golf courses: 280
Municipal: 49
Daily fee: 115
Private: 116

The *Golf Digest* Top Five:
1. Bellerive Country Club, Creve Coeur
2. Old Warson Country Club, Ladue
3. Highland Springs Country Club, Springfield
4. St. Louis Country Club, Clayton
5. Lodge of the Four Seasons, Lake Ozark*

Literature:
Each of the golf associations can provide information on request.

Further information:
• Missouri Division of Tourism, 301 West High St., Box 1055, Jefferson City, MO 65102; (314) 751-4133
• Kansas City Golf Association, 9331 Ensley Lane, Leawood, KS 66206; (913) 432-5739
• St. Louis District Golf Association, 537 North Clay, Kirkwood, MO 65110; (314) 821-1511
• Missouri State Golf Association, Box 104164, Jefferson City, MO 65110; (314) 636-8994

MONTANA

Number of golf courses: 75
Municipal: 19
Daily fee: 32
Private: 24

The *Golf Digest* Top Five:
1. Eagle Bend Golf Club, Bigfork
2. Buffalo Hill Golf Course, Kalispell*
3. Briarwood Country Club, Billings
4. Whitefish Lake Golf Club (Woods/Lake)
5. Yellowstone Country Club, Billings

Literature:
As Montana's business isn't golfers, the "Montana Vacation Guide" pays but a passing reference to golf at the Grouse Mountain Lodge in Whitefish. But I hear it's quite an experience.

Further information:
• Travel Montana, Department of Commerce, Helena, MT 59620; (800) 541-1447
• Montana Golf Association, Box 3389, Butte, MT 59701

NEBRASKA

Number of golf courses: 173
Municipal: 36
Daily fee: 66
Private: 71

The *Golf Digest* Top Five:
1. Firethorn Golf Club, Lincoln
2. Highland Country Club, Omaha
3. Happy Hollow Golf Club, Omaha
4. Omaha Country Club
5. Country Club of Lincoln

Literature:
For *Nebraska?* Good luck.

Further information:
• Travel and Tourism Division, Nebraska Department of Economic Development, Box 94666, 301 Centennial Mall South, Lincoln, NE 68509; (402) 471-3111
• Nebraska Amateur Golf Association, 6001 South 72nd St., Lincoln, NE 68516; (402) 486-1440

NEVADA

Number of golf courses: 55
Municipal: 18
Daily fee: 30
Private: 7

The *Golf Digest* Top Five:
1. Shadow Creek Golf Club, North Las Vegas
2. Edgewood Tahoe Golf Club, Stateline*
3. Desert Inn Country Club, Las Vegas*
4. Canyon Gate Golf Club, Las Vegas
5. Incline Village Golf Club

Literature:
The *Las Vegas Golf Guide* lists twenty-

four courses in the Las Vegas area, with course maps, pars and yardages, accompanying facilities and details on lessons available. Send $5 to *Las Vegas Golf Guide,* 1555 East Flamingo Rd., Suite 301, Las Vegas, NV 89119.

Further information:
• Nevada Commission on Tourism, Capitol Complex, Carson City, NV 89710; (702) 885-4322
• Nevada State Golf Association, 3500 Sullivan Lane, Sparks, NV 89431; (702) 673-4653

NEW HAMPSHIRE

Number of golf courses: 99
Municipal: 4
Daily fee: 81
Private: 14

The *Golf Digest* Top Five:
1. Sky Meadow, Nashau*
2. Portsmouth Country Club, Greenland*
3. Country Club of New Hampshire, North Sutton
4. Bretwood Golf Course, Keene*
5. Manchester Country Club

Literature:
New Hampshire calls it a "Cruise Directory," but it includes a listing of 66 courses with telephone numbers. A better source, however, is the *New England Golf Guide.* See Maine.

Further information:
• New Hampshire Office of Vacation Travel, Box 856, Concord, NH 03301; (603) 271-2666
• New Hampshire Golf Association, 45 Kearney St., Manchester, NH 03104; (603) 623-0396

NEW JERSEY

Number of golf courses: 263
Municipal: 48
Daily fee: 80
Private: 135

The *Golf Digest* Top Five:
1. Pine Valley Golf Club
2. Baltusrol Golf Club (Lower), Springfield
3. Plainfield Country Club

4. Somerset Hills Country Club, Bernardsville
5. Ridgewood Country Club (East/West), Paramus

Literature:
Most of the top courses in the state fall under the wing of the Metropolitan (NY) Golf Association. The MGA has a veritable library of information, with details on all the area's courses, and publishes an off-beat but useful book of travel directions to each course.

Further information:
• New Jersey State Division of Travel and Tourism, CN-286, Trenton, NJ 08625; (609) 292-2470
• Metropolitan Golf Association, 125 Spencer Place, Box 219, Mamaroneck, NY 10543; (914) 698-0390
• New Jersey State Golf Association, 1000 Broad St., Bloomfield, NJ 07003; (201) 338-8334

NEW MEXICO

Number of golf courses: 82
Municipal: 29
Daily fee: 24
Private: 29

The *Golf Digest* Top Five:
1. Piñon Hills Golf Course, Farmington*
2. Inn of the Mountain Gods Golf Course, Mescalero*
3. Cochiti Lake Golf Course, Cochiti Lake*
4. University of New Mexico Golf Course (South), Albuquerque*
5. Rio Rancho Golf and Country Club (East/West), Albuquerque

Literature:
Contact the Sun Country Golf Association, whose "Tee It Up In Sun Country" brochure lists 83 golf courses in New Mexico and West Texas. It also describes the nongolfing possibilities, such as hiking or whitewater rafting, in each area.

Further information:
• New Mexico Economic Development and Tourism Department, Joseph M. Montoya Bldg., 1100 St. Francis Drive, Santa Fe, NM 87503; (800) 545-2040
• Sun Country Golf Association, 10035 Country Club Lane N.W.,

Albuquerque, NM 87114; (505) 897-0864

NEW YORK

Number of golf courses: 781
Municipal: 119
Daily fee: 401
Private: 261

The *Golf Digest* Top Five:
1. Shinnecock Hills Golf Club, Southampton
2. Winged Foot Golf Club (West), Mamaroneck
3. Quaker Ridge Golf Club, Scarsdale
4. Oak Hill Country Club (East), Rochester
5. Winged Foot (East), Mamaroneck

Literature:
The state's "I Love New York Travel Guide" breaks New York down into ten regions, plus New York City, and lists every accessible course in each region—except those in New York City. This isn't all bad. The New York City public courses tend to be overcrowded and in poor shape. The regional listings include telephone numbers, pars and yardages, related amenities and map locations. See also the MGA details listed under New Jersey.

Further information:
• Tourism, New York State of Economic Development, One Commerce Plaza, Albany, NY 12245; (800) 225-5697
• New York Golf Association, 530 W. Clinton St., Elmira, NY 14901; (607) 732-6446
• Buffalo Golf Association, Box 19, Cheektowaga, NY 14225; (716) 632-1936
• Metropolitan Golf Association, Box 219, Mamaroneck, NY 10543; (914) 698-0390
• Westchester Golf Association, 1 St. Anne's Rd., Poughkeepsie, NY 12601; (914) 471-5578

NORTH CAROLINA

Number of golf courses: 474
Municipal: 35
Daily fee: 242
Private: 197

The *Golf Digest* Top Five:
1. Pinehurst Country Club (Number 2)*
2. Wade Hampton Golf Club, Cashiers
3. Charlotte Country Club
4. Country Club of North Carolina (Dogwood), Pinehurst
5. Pinehurst National Golf Club

Literature:
The state issues a supplement prepared by *Golf Digest* that includes a listing, region-by-region, of about 200 courses. Although that represents only half of North Carolina's total, the supplement goes into good detail, especially about the Pinehurst area, in accompanying features.

Further information:
• North Carolina Division of Travel and Tourism, Department of Commerce, 430 North Salisbury St., Raleigh, NC 27611; (800) 847-4862
• North Carolina Golf Association, Box 844, Clemmons, NC 27012; (919) 766-5992

NORTH DAKOTA

Number of golf courses: 103
Municipal: 46
Daily fee: 26
Private: 31

The *Golf Digest* Top Five:
1. Fargo Country Club
2. Minot Country Club*
3. Oxbow Country Club
4. Edgewood Golf Course, Fargo
5. Riverwood Golf Course, Bismarck

Literature:
Call Rosemary at Associated General Contractors in Bismarck and ask for the membership directory of the North Dakota Golf Association. She is very helpful, and if she can't help you, she'll know who can. Her number is (701) 223-2770.

Further information:
• North Dakota Tourism Promotion, Capitol Grounds, Bismarck 58505; (800) 437-2077
• North Dakota Golf Association, see above.

OHIO

Number of golf courses: 704
Municipal: 92
Daily fee: 420
Private: 192

The *Golf Digest* Top Five:
1. Muirfield Village Golf Club, Dublin
2. The Golf Club, New Albany
3. Scioto Country Club, Columbus
4. Inverness Club, Toledo
5. Camargo Club, Cincinnati

Literature available:
The local golf associations are the best source. The Northern Ohio Golf Association, for example, has a tournament schedule book that also happens to list 125 nonmember clubs along with its 50 or so members. For each course, the guide gives course and slope rating from front, middle and back tees, but no contact numbers.

The same golf association offers a "Golf Privilege Card." It costs $25 and allows one free round at each of 31 courses, one free bucket of balls (with the purchase of the first) at seven participating driving ranges and discounts on golf clubs, shoes and resort accommodations. All proceeds go to the American Lung Association.

The Greater Cincinnati Golf Association lists all its member clubs, along with pars and yardages and the various course and slope ratings, but lists addresses and telephone numbers in a separate part of the book.

Further information:
• Northern Ohio Golf Association, Bainbridge Community Commons, 17800 Chillicothe Rd., Chagrin Falls, OH 44022; (216) 543-6320
• Greater Cincinnati Golf Association, Box 317825, Cincinnati, OH 45231; (513) 522-5780
• Ohio Golf Association, 7030 Huntley Rd., Worthington, OH 43085; (614) 885-4653
• Toledo District Golf Association, Box 6313, Toledo, OH 43614; (419) 866-4771

OKLAHOMA

Number of golf courses: 172
Municipal: 53
Daily fee: 55
Private: 64

The *Golf Digest* Top Five:
1. Southern Hills Country Club, Tulsa
2. Oak Tree Golf Club, Edmond
3. Golf Club of Oklahoma, Broken Arrow
4. Dornick Hills Golf and Country Club, Ardmore
5. Oak Tree Golf and Country Club (East), Edmond

Literature:
The "Pocket Guide to Oklahoma Golf Courses" lists both public and private courses, as well as noting the state-run courses where senior citizens aged 62 and over can play for half price. It also lists telephone numbers, locations, pars and yardages. The "Oklahoma Vacation Guide" does not list golf courses but does include several advertisements for golf resorts.

Note: The state's park system is undergoing a complete makeover, which includes renovation and improvement of its nine public golf courses.

Further information:
• Oklahoma Tourism and Recreation Department, Division of Marketing and Services, 215 NE 28th St., Oklahoma City, OK 73105; (405) 521-2409
• Oklahoma Golf Association, Box 449, Edmond, OK 73083; (405) 340-6333

OREGON

Number of golf courses: 159
Municipal: 15
Daily fee: 108
Private: 36

The *Golf Digest* Top Five:
1. Eugene Country Club
2. Tokatee Golf Club, Blue River*
3. Columbia-Edgewater Country Club, Portland
4. Portland Golf Club
5. Waverly Country Club, Portland

Literature:

A tip: Ask the state to send you the "Oregon Golf Courses" guide published by Fiddler's Green, a golf course, driving range and discount golf shop just north of Eugene. Or call Fiddler's Green direct at (800) 999-6565. The brochure pinpoints 136 courses with telephone numbers. The state's own publication "Golf Courses in Oregon" comprises nine xeroxed pages, with telephone numbers, pars and yardages (for men and women). It is broken into regions.

Further information:

• Tourism Division, Oregon Economic Development Department, 775 Summer St. N.E., Salem, OR 97310; (800) 547-7842

• Oregon Golf Association, 520 S.W. Sixth, 1003 Cascade Bldg., Portland, OR 97204; (503) 222-1139

PENNSYLVANIA

Number of golf courses: 643
Municipal: 44
Daily fee: 365
Private: 234

The *Golf Digest* Top Five:
1. Oakmont Country Club
2. Merion Golf Club (East), Ardmore
3. Laurel Valley Golf Club, Ligonier

4. Aronomink Golf Club, Newtown Square
5. Saucon Valley Country Club (Grace), Bethlehem

Literature:

Although Pennsylvania ranks seventh in the nation in terms of the number of golf courses, it cannot supply any general information on golf in the state. It does have a few brochures from resorts in the Poconos, in eastern Pennsylvania.

Further information:

• Laurel Highlands Tourist Office (Ligonier area), (800) 333-5661
• Poconos Travel Information, (800) 762-6667
• Eastern Pennsylvania Golf Association, Box 2, King of Prussia, PA 19406; (215) 687-2340
• Western Pennsylvania Golf Association, 1378 Freeport Rd., #1D, Pittsburgh, PA 15238; (412) 963-9806

RHODE ISLAND

Number of golf courses: 48
Municipal: 3
Daily fee: 25
Private: 20

The *Golf Digest* Top Five:
1. Wannamoisett Country Club, Rumford
2. Rhode Island Country Club, West Barrington

No. 3, Merion Golf Club (East).

3. Newport Country Club
4. Pawtucket Country Club
5. Metacomet Country Club, East Providence

Literature:

Simple, sound material from the Ocean State. "Rhode Island Golf" lists addresses and telephone numbers, nine- and 18-hole green fees, weekday and weekend green fees, reduced senior rates where applicable, cart availability, pars, yardages and a brief description of each course. Did you know, for example, that the 13th hole at the Exeter Country Club, a 324-yard par four over water, features Rhode Island's only covered bridge? Map included.

Also helpful is *New England Golf Guide*. See Maine.

Further information:

• Rhode Island Tourism Division, Department of Economic Development, 7 Jackson Walkway, Providence, RI 02903; (800) 556-2484
• Rhode Island Golf Association, 10 Orms St., Providence, RI 02904; (401) 272-1350

SOUTH CAROLINA

Number of golf courses: 316
Municipal: 7
Daily fee: 185
Private: 124

The *Golf Digest* Top Five:
1. Long Cove Club, Hilton Head Island
2. Harbour Town Golf Links, Hilton Head Island*
3. Haig Point Club (Calibogue), Daufuskie Island
4. Tidewater Golf Club, North Myrtle Beach
5. Greenville Country Club (Chanticleer)

Literature:

Now we know where the Amazon rain forest goes. South Carolina has reams of literature, some only about golf, others including golf. Myrtle Beach is the main area, with about 50 (and rising) first-class courses. The "Myrtle Beach Golf Holiday" brochure is as detailed a piece of literature as you'll find, with course descriptions, greens fees, accommodation rates, restaurants, and more. The area's "Tee Up" brochure describes all the courses, too. The Sumter area's "Swing Away" brochure lists seventeen courses, and so it goes, through the Charleston area, Kiawah Island, Hilton Head Island, the "Upcountry" area. . . .

Further information:
• South Carolina Division of Tourism, 1205 Pendleton St., Columbia, SC 29201; (803) 734-0135
• Myrtle Beach Golf Holiday, Box 1323, Myrtle Beach, SC 29578; (800) 845-4653
• Hilton Head Island Chamber of Commerce, Box 5647, Hilton Head Island, SC 29938; (803) 785-3673
• South Carolina Golf Association, 145 Birdsong Trail, Chapin, SC 29036; (803) 781-6992

SOUTH DAKOTA

Number of golf courses: 110
Municipal: 27
Daily fee: 38
Private: 45

The *Golf Digest* Top Five:
1. Meadowbrook Country Club, Rapid City*
2. Minnehaha Country Club, Sioux Falls
3. Westward Ho Country Club, Sioux Falls
4. Hillcrest Golf and Country Club, Yankton
5. Willow Run Golf Course, Sioux Falls*

Literature:
Both the state and the golf association work on a simple, one-page listing of courses, pars, yardages and where you can find them.

Further information:
• Travel Director, South Dakota Tourism, Pierre, SD 57501; (800) 843-1930
• South Dakota Golf Association, 509 Holt Ave., Sioux Falls, SD 57103; (605) 336-1100

TENNESSEE

Number of golf courses: 234
Municipal: 40

Daily fee: 86
Private: 108

The *Golf Digest* Top Five:
1. The Honors Course, Chattanooga
2. Belle Meade Country Club, Nashville
3. Holston Hills Country Club, Knoxville
4. Memphis Country Club
5. Colonial Country Club (South), Cordova

Literature:
The golf association has a list of member clubs, but is reluctant to release it to the public. Try the state.

Further information:
• Tennessee Department of Tourism Development, Box 23170, Nashville, TN 37202; (615) 741-2158
• Tennessee Golf Association, 4711 Trousdale Drive, Nashville, TN 37220; (615) 833-9689

TEXAS

Number of golf courses: 756
Municipal: 153
Daily fee: 231
Private: 372

The *Golf Digest* Top Five:
1. Colonial Country Club, Ft. Worth
2. Barton Creek Country Club (Fazio), Austin
3. Crown Colony Country Club, Lufkin
4. Preston Trail Golf Club, Dallas
5. Austin Country Club

Literature:
Not a lot from the state. It sends out a reprint from the Club Corporation of America's *Private Clubs* magazine, which, ironically, includes a listing of 71 public clubs that are also members of the United States Golf Association, but it doesn't tell you much about the courses. Golf is also covered in the *Texas Travel Book,* a general visitors' booklet.

Further information:
• Texas Department of Highways and Public Transportation, Travel and Information Division, Box 5064, Austin, TX 78763; (800) 888-8839
• Dallas Golf Association, 4321 Live Oak, Dallas, TX 75204; (214) 823-6004

• Houston Golf Association, 1830 S. Millbend Dr., The Woodlands, TX 77380; (713) 367-7999

UTAH

Number of courses: 94
Municipal: 49
Daily fee: 26
Private: 19

The *Golf Digest* Top Five:
1. Park Meadows Golf Club, Park City*
2. Green Spring Golf Course, Washington*
3. Jeremy Ranch Golf Club, Park City
4. The Country Club, Salt Lake City
5. Willow Creek Country Club, Sandy

Literature:
For a state with relatively few golf courses (only 10 have fewer), Utah impresses with its help. The local PGA section has put together *The Utah Book of Golf,* which includes courses, the pros' names and a calendar of events. The Utah Golf Association has a monthly magazine and a separate list of courses.

Further information:
• Utah Travel Council, Council Hall/Capitol Hill, Salt Lake City, UT 84114; (801) 538-1030
• Utah Golf Association, 1512 South 1100 East, Salt Lake City, UT 84105; (801) 466-1132

VERMONT

Number of golf courses: 60
Municipal: 0
Daily fee: 49
Private: 11

The *Golf Digest* Top Five:
1. Ekwanok Country Club, Manchester
2. Quechee Club (Highland)
3. Rutland Country Club*
4. Manchester Country Club
5. Burlington Country Club

Literature:
Not very colorful stuff, but plenty of it. *Vermont Golf Courses, a Player's Guide* is published by The New England Press.

The state office has a list of all the courses—split into north, south and central—with telephone numbers, pars, yardages and the availability of carts, rental clubs, etc. A general travel brochure from the state lists three golf courses in the state, at Stratton, Quechee and Mt. Snow. Also very useful is *New England Golf Guide*. See Maine.

Further information:
• Vermont Travel Division, State of Vermont, 134 State St., Montpelier, VT 05602
• Vermont Golf Association, 117 Crescent St., Rutland, VT 05701

Virginia

Number of golf courses: 256
Municipal: 26
Daily fee: 100
Private: 130

The *Golf Digest* Top Five:
1. Cascades Golf Club, Hot Springs*
2. Stoney Creek at Wintergreen
3. Water's Edge Country Club, Penhook
4. Country Club of Virginia (James River), Richmond
5. Golden Horseshoe Golf Club, Williamsburg*

Literature:
No luck at the state or the golf association. Best source is the *Southern Golfer* magazine, at (919) 759-9312.

Further information:
• Virginia Division of Tourism, Bell Tower on Capitol Square, 101 North 9th St., Richmond, VA 23219; (804) 786-4484
• Virginia State Golf Association, 6952 Forest Hill Ave., Richmond, VA 23225; (804) 378-2300

Washington

Number of golf courses: 240
Municipal: 50
Daily fee: 129
Private: 61

The *Golf Digest* Top Five:
1. Sahalee Country Club (North/South), Redmond
2. Semiahmoo Golf and Country Club, Blaine*
3. Canterwood Golf and Country Club, Gig Harbor
4. McCormick Woods Golf Course, Port Orchard*
5. Port Ludlow Country Club*

Literature:
The only list of golf courses I could get my hands on had tremendous detail but was from 1983. Best bet: Contact the local tourism agencies. The Olympic Peninsula, for example, publishes a travel guide that lists courses in the area.

Further information:
• Tourism Division, Destination Washington Project, 101 General Administration Bldg., AX-13, Olympia, WA 98504; (206) 586-2088/2102
• Pacific Northwest Golf Association, 10303 Meridan Avenue North, Suite 101, Seattle, WA 98133; (206) 526-1238

West Virginia

Number of golf courses: 109
Municipal: 17
Daily fee: 58
Private: 34

The *Golf Digest* Top Five:
1. The Greenbrier Hotel (Greenbrier), White Sulphur Springs*
2. The Greenbrier Hotel (Old White), White Sulphur Springs*
3. Lakeview Resort (Lakeview), Morgantown*
4. Williams Country Club, Weirton
5. Speidel Golf Course, Wheeling*

Literature:
The state's "Outdoor Recreation/Spectator Sports" brochure lists 24 public courses. The state parks department has a brochure listing packages at seven different resorts. "Golf West Virginia" is a straightforward listing of names and addresses of 59 clubs. But judging from the *Golf Digest* rankings, you probably want to look into The Greenbrier, a classic old American resort. Its telephone number is (800) 624-6070.

Further information:
• West Virginia Department of Commerce, Division of Parks and Recreation, State Capitol Complex, Charleston, WV 25305; (800) 225-5982
• West Virginia Golf Association, Box 7128, Cross Lanes, WV 25356

Wisconsin

Number of golf courses: 417
Municipal: 70
Daily fee: 265
Private: 82

The *Golf Digest* Top Five:
1. Blackwolf Run Golf Course, Kohler*
2. Milwaukee Country Club
3. Sentry World Golf Course, Stevens Point*
4. Maple Bluff Country Club, Madison
5. Oneida Golf and Riding Club, Green Bay

Literature:
Lots of material from the state tourism office and from the golf association. Wisconsin, like neighboring Michigan, is growing fast as a golf destination. The "Wisconsin Golf Directory" lists courses by city, by region and by nine or 18 holes. It also details addresses, green fees, pars, yardages, related amenities and the names of managers and pros. The golf association's directory ($5) lists even more, right down to the home telephone number of each course's golf course superintendent. Wisconsin Golf Course Association issues a "Wisconsin Golf Tour" coupon book that gives discounts on green fees and pro shop purchases. A tuned-in state, one might say.

Further information:
• Wisconsin Tourism Development, 123 West Washington Ave., Box 7970, Madison, WI 53707; (800) 432-8747
• Wisconsin Golf Course Association, Box 185, Pewaukee, WI 53073; (414) 547-2933

• Wisconsin State Golf Association, Box 35, Elm Grove, WI 53122; (414) 786-4301

WYOMING

Number of golf courses: 49
Municipal: 15
Daily fee: 22
Private: 12

The *Golf Digest* Top Five:
1. Teton Pines Golf Club, Jackson*
2. Jackson Hole Golf and Tennis Club*
3. Old Baldy Club, Saratoga
4. Olive Glenn Golf and Country Club, Cody
5. Cheyenne Country Club

Literature:
The state lists the names of all the courses—no further details—with the cities in which they're located. Still, if you're heading to Wyoming, you're probably after a dude ranch, not a golf course. You city slicker, you.

Further information:
• Wyoming Travel Commission, I-25 @ College Dr., Cheyenne, WY 82002; (307) 777-7777
• Wyoming Golf Association, Route 2, Box 287R, Sheridan, WY 82801

**Part of what the armed guard
won't let you see: the 10th green at Pine Valley.**

Five Golf Clubs *Mission Impossible* Can't Get You Into
(although a member can)

1. **Pine Valley Golf Club, Pine Valley, N.J.** Turn left at the amusement park, drive down a dirt road, cross the railroad tracks—and stare down the barrel of the armed guard's gun.
2. **Augusta National Golf Club, Augusta, GA.** More armed guards—but they will sell you a shirt at the guardhouse.
3. **The Honors Club, Ooltewah, TN.** Automatic gate; if you don't have the plastic, you don't get through.
4. **Seminole, Jupiter's Island, FL.** Club policy allows one pro—Ben Hogan, which meant Nicklaus's application was refused. JFK was turned away.
5. **Desert Highlands, outside Scottsdale, AZ.** Not as snobby as they used to be, but win a mention because they turned away Fuzzy Zoeller a few years ago.

—Tom Doak

A Province-by-Province Guide to Canadian Golf

Soon after *Golf Magazine* sponsored the Centennial of Golf in America in 1988, a letter arrived in the offices of the magazine from Canada's most prolific golf writer, Lorne Rubenstein. In a tone that was more educational than critical, Rubenstein pointed out that the only celebration that should have taken place was for 100 years of golf in the *United States.* The game had been played formally in Canada, Rubenstein noted, for 15 years before it arrived south of the border.

The man had a point, but one that masked a greater reality: When people think about golf in North America, they never even consider Canada.

But they should. In addition to having a 15-year head start on the United States, the Canadian Open is the world's fourth-oldest championship, and the only man to win a gold medal for golf in the Olympic Games is one George S. Lyon. He did it for Canada in St. Louis in 1912.

But it's not as if Canada doesn't have the stuff. The Highland Links is a tumbling and heaving Stanley Thompson design on the tip of Cape Breton Island. Herbert Strong, an Englishman who designed the first island green (at the Ponte Vedra Club in Florida in 1932, half a century before Pete Dye did likewise at the nearby TPC at Sawgrass), also designed a wonderful hillside course outside Quebec called Manoir Richelieu. The Banff course in the heart of the Canadian Rockies is revered as one of the most scenic courses on earth; Capilano, Robert Trent Jones's work in the coastal mountains outside Vancouver, gives it a good run for its money; and even Newfoundland is getting in on the act with a new course opening a few years back amid conifers and gurgling rapids at the Twin Rivers resort, two hours north of St. John's. And here's a *real* trivia question for you: Know who developed the Devil's Pulpit course, which opened for play outside Toronto in 1990? Answer: Chris Haney and Scott Abbott, the cocreators of the board game Trivial Pursuit. Some golfing cynics have suggested that the mustachioed pair have no business developing a course—even if it is one of the more acclaimed on the continent—because they know nothing about the golf business. To which Haney replies, "People said we didn't know anything about the board game business, either."

The best source for information on Canadian golf is *Score* magazine, otherwise known as "Canada's golf magazine," published five times a year; for information call (416) 928-1357. You might also check your local bookstore for a copy of *The Great Golf Courses of Canada,* written by John Gordon, executive director of the Royal Canadian Golf Association (and published by Prentice Hall). Beyond that, the national and regional associations should be able to help out. Here's where to find them, along with the top courses in each province, as published by *Score.*

ALBERTA

Total golf courses: 231
Private: 20
Semiprivate: 53
Public: 158

Score's top courses:
1. Banff Springs Golf Club, Banff
2. Wolf Creek Golf Club, Ponoka
3. Glencoe Golf & Country Club (Forest Course), Calgary
4. Kananaskis Country Golf Club (Mt. Lorette course), Kananaskis
5. Kananaskis Country Golf Club (Mt. Kidd course), Kananaskis

Who to contact:
Alberta Golf Association
#104 4116-64th Ave., S.E.
Calgary, Alberta T2C 2B3
(403) 236-4616

BRITISH COLUMBIA

Total golf courses: 231
Private: 10
Semiprivate: 52
Public: 169

Score's top courses:
1. Capilano Golf & Country Club, West Vancouver
2. Gallaghers Canyon Golf Club, Gallaghers Canyon
3. Royal Colwood Golf Club, Victoria
4. Rivershore, Kelowna
5. Victoria Golf & Country Club, Victoria

Who to contact:
British Columbia Golf Association
Suite 185
Sperling Plaza 2
6450 Roberts St.
Burnabym B.C. V5G 4EI
(403) 236-4616

The 10th at Devil's Pulpit, Caledon, Ontario.

MANITOBA

Total golf courses: 107
Private: 12
Semiprivate: 26
Public: 69

Score's top course (only one made its rankings):
St. Charles Country Club, Winnipeg

Who to contact:
Manitoba Golf Association
200 Main St.
Winnipeg
Manitoba R3C 4M2
(204) 985-4162

NEW BRUNSWICK

Total golf courses: 41
Private: 4
Semiprivate: 19
Public: 18

Score's top courses:
1. Mactaquac Provincial Park Golf Course, Mouth of Keswick
2. Riverside Golf & Country Club, Riverside

Who to contact:
New Brunswick Golf Association
565 Priestman St., Suite 103
Fredericton
New Brunswick E3B 5X8
(506) 459-5675

NEWFOUNDLAND

Total golf courses: 9
Private: 2
Semiprivate: 4
Public: 3

Score's top courses: None made the rankings, but you may want to check out the new Twin Rivers course at the St. Christopher's Resort, with the Atlantic in play on some holes and rapidly flowing salmon rivers on others.

Who to contact:
Newfoundland/Labrador Golf Association
17 St. Andrews Drive

Mount Pearl
Newfoundland A1N 1C8
(709) 368-0762

NOVA SCOTIA

Total golf courses: 49
Private: 3
Semiprivate: 36
Public: 10

Score's top courses:
1. Highland Links Golf Club, Cape Breton
2. New Ashburn Golf Club, Halifax
3. Digby Pines, Digby

Who to contact:
Nova Scotia Golf Association
14 Limardo Drive
Dartmouth
Nova Scotia B3A 3X4
(902) 368-1177

The 18th at The National Golf Course, Woodbridge, Ontario.

ONTARIO

Total golf courses: 646
Private: 112
Semiprivate: 290
Public: 244

Score's top courses:
1. The National Golf Club, Wododbridge
2. Glen Abbey Golf Club, Oakville
3. St. George's Golf & Country Club, Islington
4. Devil's Pulpit Golf Club, Caledon
5. Beacon Hall Golf Club, Aurora

Who to contact:
Ontario Golf Association
RR #3
Newmarket
Ontario L3Y 4WI
(416) 853-8511

PRINCE EDWARD ISLAND

Total golf courses: 11
Private: 0
Semiprivate: 5
Public: 6

Score's top course: Brudenell River,
   Montague

Who to contact:
P.E.I. Golf Association
Box 51
Charlottetown
P.E.I. C1A 7K2
(902) 368-1177

QUEBEC

Total golf courses: 332
Private: 38
Semiprivate: 132
Public: 162

Score's top courses:
1. Royal Montreal Golf Club (Blue Course),
   Ile Bizard
2. Royal Ottawa Golf Club, Hull
3. Kanawaki Golf & Country Club, Kanawaki
4. Carling Lake Country Club, Lachute
5. Beaconsfield Golf & Country Club,
   Beaconsfield

Who to contact:
Quebec Golf Association
3300 Cavendish Blvd.
Suite 250
Montreal
Quebec H4B 2M8
(514) 481-0471

SASKATCHEWAN

Total golf courses: 202
Private: 5
Semiprivate: 9
Public: 188

Score's top course: Riverside Golf & Country
   Club, Saskatoon

Who to contact:
Saskatchewan Golf Association
510 Cynthia St.
Saskatoon
Saskatchewan S7L 7K7
(306) 975-0834

Golf Museums and Collections

by Janet Seagle

Whether you are a casual fan of golf and its history or a golf collector or dealer conducting some form of research, there are enough golf exhibits around the country to satisfy your or anybody else's appetite.

They come in several forms: museums, which are open to the public and are therefore the easiest to visit; collections at private golf clubs, most of which will admit visitors; and the collections of individual collectors. Access to the last is probably the toughest—gained only with the permission of the collector (although some private clubs will put you through the gauntlet before allowing your mucky feet in their plush halls).

This portrait of Bobby Jones by Thomas Stephens hangs in Golf House.

The Great Triumvirate, by Clement Flower, also on display at Golf House.

MUSEUMS WITH LIBRARIES

These are wonderful research sources. However, all research must be done on the premises as these are not lending libraries. In fact, some of the books are very valuable collectors' items.

The American Golf Hall of Fame, Foxburg Country Club. Box 305, Harvey Rd., Foxburg, PA 16036; (412) 659-3196

The club and the collection was started in 1887 by Joseph Mickle Fox. In 1884 Fox traveled to Britain for a series of cricket matches—he was then a member of Merion Cricket Club, now Merion Golf Club—one of which happened to be in Edinburgh, Scotland. Fox took the opportunity to travel to St. Andrews to look into this pastime called "golf" and met with Old Tom Morris. Morris took a liking to Fox because, among other reasons, it was the Fox family who had founded the Quaker religion. The Scotsman taught Fox the fundamentals of golf. He started his club soon after his return. The collection comprises clubs, balls, books and artwork. Open seven days a week, April through October. Contact the club to check on access.

The United States Golf Association Museum and Library, Far Hills, NJ 07931; (908) 234-2300

This is the largest collection of books, clubs, equipment, artwork and memorabilia that is open to the public. It provides a historical display of the game as well as putting on special changing exhibits. For the best attractions, see the top choices of the museum's curator, Karen Bednarski (page 53). It is open daily and there is no admission fee.

The PGA World Golf Hall of Fame, PGA Blvd., Box 1908, Pinehurst, NC 28374; (919) 295-6651 or (800) 334-0178

Operated by the PGA of America, the Hall displays clubs, artwork, memorabilia, balls and a fine library. Its most interesting exhibits include a 90-foot long display depicting the complete history of golf, with original artwork, vintage clubs, featherie balls, etc; a "golf ball wall" covered with more than 13,000 logoed balls and a room devoted to the history of the Ryder Cup. It is open daily from March 1 to December 1.

Western Golf Association, 1 Briar Rd., Golf, IL 60029; (312) 724-4600

The collection is made up mostly of clubs and books, with some memorabilia, and is open only during association hours. Call for further information.

Ralph W. Miller Library, One Industry Hills Parkway, City of Industry, CA 91744; (818) 854-2354

This is a fine library that will provide more-than-able assistance for any researchers. The museum collection is small, and it is the library that is the best aspect of the Ralph W. Miller. Its 5,000

The Five Most Interesting Items at the USGA Museum

The United States Golf Association's museum and library in Far Hills, New Jersey, is the most complete collection of golf memorabilia in the world. There may be club collectors with more hickories, golf-ball collectors with more gutta perchas, but only the USGA has a collection that encompasses the entire game.

Rather than furnish a written tour of every dusty nook and cranny, we have instead asked Karen Bednarski, the museum's curator, to list what she considers the top five attractions, and we have accompanied her selections with some notes of our own.

1 Alan B. Shepard, Jr.'s Moon Club. This is the Wilson 6-iron that astronaut Shepard took with him to the moon on the Apollo 14 mission of February 1971. Actually, it was the head of a 6-iron attached to an implement otherwise used by moon walkers to pick up moon rocks and whatever else moonish they might find. Along with the "club," Shepard took two balls. He won't reveal the brand lest he open up all sorts of commercial cans of worms. Shepard shanked the first, but the second flew well. The balls are still up there, awaiting a truly enterprising retrieval company.

2 Bob Jones's "Calamity Jane II" Putter. This is a replica of Jones's original Calamity Jane, which is said to have originated in a shed at Nassau Country Club in Glen Cove, New York. But it *is* the putter with which Jones won most of his major championships, including those that made up the Grand Slam of 1930. It can be found in the Bob Jones Room, close to the museum entrance.

3 Ben Hogan's 1-iron. Hogan hit one of the most famous approaches in history when he reached the final green at Merion with a 1-iron in 1950. It was his first Open campaign after almost losing his life in an automobile accident a year earlier, and Hogan would eventually win the title in a playoff—one he would have to play *without* the aforementioned 1-iron: Someone took it from Hogan's bag soon after he hit the shot. In 1983, however, Jack Murdock, a golf-club collector from North

Carolina, swapped another collector several old clubs for the 1-iron. He then passed it on to an old friend from college, touring pro Lanny Wadkins. He in turn forwarded it to Hogan who, after verifying the club's authenticity, sent Murdock the following note: "I liken this to the return of a long-lost friend." Hogan donated the old MacGregor club to the USGA museum, where it can be seen in the first-floor hallway.

4 "Play Away, Please." This is an interactive video, a computer-driven laserdisc, on which you can:
   a. Design your own golf course;
   b. Study the swing styles of famous players at different speeds;
   c. Take a test on the rules of match-play;
   d. Watch film clips from golf history;
   e. Keep up to speed on USGA goings-on.
   The course design normally is the favored program. It works sort of like finger painting. Touch a tee, bunker, pond, green, etc., then touch where you want it to sit, and so on. Interactive video exhibits are becoming very popular at museums. The new British Golf Museum in St. Andrews, Scotland, has eight such machines, one of which is supposedly devoted to telling visitors where they can get a drink on a Sunday. Press the name of a bar, press a pint glass or a half-pint glass . . .

5 The USGA Library. With 8,000 volumes on golf, this is the largest collection of its sort in the world. Karen Bednarski speaks especially fondly of the periodical collection, which includes copies of Britain's *Golf Illustrated* from the 1880s and every copy of the now-defunct *American Golfer* from 1908–34. It is open to the public as a reference source.

When the museum is open: Monday through Friday from 9 A.M. to 5 P.M.; Saturday and Sunday, from 10 A.M. to 4 P.M.
Admission: Free
How to get there: From the New Jersey Turnpike, take Exit 14 to Route 78 West. Take Exit 33, Martinsville Road, Bernardsville. From 78 West, turn right off ramp. Proceed to third traffic light and turn left. From 78 East, turn left off ramp. Proceed to fourth traffic light and turn left. Follow signs to USGA. It is located on Liberty Corner Road in Far Hills. If you *still* can't find it, telephone (908) 234-2300.

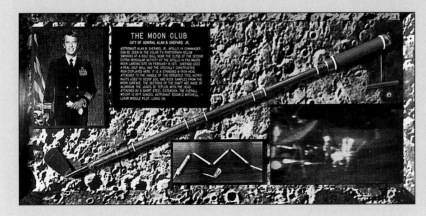

The Moon Club at Golf House.

The Luxurious
Bobby Jones Steamer Trunk

Don't you just yearn for the grand old days of Atlantic steamship crossings? Don't you miss the elegant clink of silverware in the dining room, the starched white jackets of the room-service staff, the black-tie dancing by the light of the moon?

Me neither. But I can't help but be impressed by the steamer trunk custom-designed and built in Italy for Hickey Freeman's Bobby Jones Golf Collection. It stands four feet high and is made from fine lacquered wood, with drawers and hangers and a classic interior fabric design bearing the Royal & Ancient clubhouse and the Swilcan Bridge in St. Andrews (and palm trees!). All that's missing is a couple of Marx Brothers.

Now the bad news. The retail price is $10,000-plus, but Hickey Freeman may give you a break if you order directly—and in bulk. Contact (800) 848-1289.

books are fully cataloged and include Scottish history, golf history, club histories, turf management, biographies, directories and annuals, humor, poetry and even old and new golf fiction. Among its treasures are a copy of W.W. Tulloch's *The Life of Tom Morris*—autographed by both Tullock and Old Tom; a 1597 edition of the *Scottish Lawes and Acts of Parliament,* which contains the first printed mention of golf (banning it, of course); and a fragile 1743 edition of *The Goff,* the first book published on the game.

A small research staff will help researchers, collectors, authors, historians, film production people or even the casual visitor who wants to settle a bar bet. They'll handle inquiries personally or by mail, telephone or fax. Although its titles are not circulated, the staff will photocopy—within reason. The library is currently indexing golf periodicals back to 1891. First up for its computer: *The American Golfer, Golf Illustrated* and the *Pacific Coast Golfer,* all long gone. "Our database is still young and small," says Saundra Sheffer, "but give us 10 years and it will be spectacular." It's certainly off to a grand start.

The museum and library, funded by the City of Industry as a public library and located in the Industry Hills Recreation and Conference Center, is open daily from 8:30 A.M. to 5 P.M. Admission is free.

The Ouimet Room, Massachusetts Golf Association, 190 Park Rd., Weston, MA 02193; (617) 891-4300/4301/4302

The collection contains many items related to the golfing activities of Francis Ouimet in particular but also devotes space to the equipment and memorabilia of other noted Massachusetts and New England golfers. Well worth a visit. Call for access.

Rev. Edmund P. Joyce Sports Research Collection, 102 Hesburgh Library, Notre Dame, IN 46556; (219) 239-6506

Contains fair selection of old and current golf books. Open Monday through Friday, 8 A.M. to 5 P.M. They prefer that you call ahead.

The British Golf Museum, St. Andrews, Fife, Scotland; (0334) 73423

This new museum opened behind the Royal & Ancient clubhouse in the summer of 1990. It contains clubs, balls, artwork and interactive videos that help tell the history of the game. The comprehensive Spalding Collection has moved to the new museum from its previous home in Dundee, just to the north.

Royal Canadian Golf Association, RR#2, Golf House, Oakville, Ontario, Canada; (416) 849-9700

Contains books, clubs, trophies and other memorabilia of golf in Canada, as well as the Canadian Golf Hall of Fame. Open weekdays only.

Jude E. Poynter Golf Museum, College of the Desert, 43-500 Monterey Ave., Palm Desert, CA 92260; (619) 341-2491

Opened in 1990, it contains memorabilia assembled by Jude Poynter, who endowed a golf department at the college. The collection includes a "kolven" club from the 19th century ("kolven" was the Dutch game that some heretics consider the forerunner to golf); a rare wicker golf bag made in Hong Kong and one of six 1926 reproductions of Bobby Jones's putter, "Calamity Jane."

Northern California Golf Association, Box 1157, Pebble Beach, CA 93953; (408) 625-4653

Books, clubs and balls housed in the association office may be studied during office hours.

Chicago District Golf Association, 619 Enterprise, Suite 101, Oak Brook, IL 60521; (708) 954-2180

The association has been looking to establish its own library for some time. For the moment, its collection of memorabilia and books can be studied during office hours, but it's wise to call ahead.

Canadian Golf Museum and Historical Institute, Kingsway Park Golf and Country Club, 1461 Mountain Rd., RR#2, Aylmer E., Quebec, Canada, J9H 5E1; (819) 827-4403

The exhibit is located in a historical building at the club and comprises the private collection of William Lyn Stewart, the founder and director of the club. It shows the evolution of balls and clubs and has a gallery of golf art as well as a small library. Among its most interesting exhibits are a leather-faced driver by Willie Park, winner of the first British Open, in 1860; an iron club by J. H. Oke, winner of the first Canadian Open, in 1904, and the earliest color golf illustration created in North America (in Montreal, in 1885). The museum is open daily, with no admission charge.

The BC Golf House Society, 2545 Blanca St., Vancouver, British Columbia, Canada; (604) 943-4998

Another new museum. Open Tuesday through Sunday, BC Golf House has a small but growing collection.

Japan Golf Association Golf Museum, Palace Building, 6th Floor, Tokyo, Japan

Most of this collection, which was established in 1987, hails from Britain.

MUSEUMS ONLY

American Golf Classics, 12842 Jefferson Ave., Newport News, VA 23602; (703) 874-7271

A collection of unusual clubs ranging from kolven clubs to famous classics, many once owned by famous PGA pros. Contact the owner, Bob Farino, to arrange a visit.

The Heritage of Golf, West Links Rd., Gullane, East Lothian, Scotland; (087 57) 277

This is a private museum that can be visited by appointment with its owner and curator, Archie Baird. It contains fine examples of early equipment, artwork and ceramics, all collected avidly by Baird and shown enthusiastically to visitors. Baird is particularly proud of his collection of early golf oil paintings and watercolors (some 30 to 40 in all), his collection of 50 featherie balls and his early golf books. Admission is free— "Contributions are welcome," says Archie—but visitors are asked to call

ahead for an appointment, which means you'll have to learn to use one of these strange British callboxes.

PRIVATE CLUB EXHIBITS

Atlanta Athletic Club, Robert T. Jones, Jr. Room, Athletic Club Drive, Duluth, GA 30136; (404) 448-2166

Honors great players of the past who were also members of the club. Concentrates on Jones, with his personal collection of 268 books as well as those books written about him. The Grand Slam Case includes replicas of the trophies won by Jones in 1930 in achieving what was named "The Impregnable Quadrilateral"—the U.S. and British Amateur Championships and the U.S. and British Open Championships. There also is a trophy case devoted to other great club members, including Alexa Stirling Fraser, Watts Gunn and Charlie Yates. Curator is Eugene Branch, former law partner of Jones and currently a member of the club. The collection is open from 9 A.M. to 9 P.M., Tuesday through Sunday. Call ahead for access.

Broadmoor Golf Club, Colorado Springs, CO 80901; (719) 577-5790

Although this is a private collection (of old clubs and artwork mainly), guests at the Broadmoor Resort have full access to it. Its display area recently was renovated.

Colonial Country Club, 3735 Country Club Circle, Ft. Worth, TX 76109; (817) 927-4200

On display are medals, trophies and other memorabilia of Ben Hogan.

Old Marsh Golf Club, 7500 Old Marsh Rd., Palm Beach Gardens, FL 33418; (407) 626-7400

Each site has a collection of golf clubs assembled by the late Laurie Auchterlonie, who was head professional at the Royal & Ancient in St. Andrews. Harbour Town is probably the easier to get access to, in that Old Marsh is private and you must be escorted by a member. But Old Marsh is the better-known collection. Of interest are a putter owned by Willie Park, who won the first British Open, in 1860; a brassie owned by six-time British Open winner Harry Vardon and a club made by James McEwan in 1770 in which a lead weight in the head has been hollowed out to suit the player (unknown) who used it. Funny how times change. Today they start out light and *add* lead tape.

James River Country Club Museum, 1500 Country Club Rd., Newport News, VA 23606; (808) 596-4772

The James River Museum claims to be the oldest golf museum in the world. It's certainly one of the best. It was founded in 1932 by Archer M. Huntington, a resident of New York City who didn't play golf but who, as the principal owner of the Newport News Shipbuilding and Drydock Company, did like starting up museums. Intrigued by the idea of a museum devoted totally to the display and research of golf, he both encouraged the James River club to open the museum and offered to finance it.

Among the most interesting items are a wooden putter made by Simon Cossar of Leith, Scotland, around 1790 (Cossar was a well-known clubmaker in his day); a brassie and two irons donated by Bob Jones; the clubs with which Harry Vardon won the 1900 U.S. Open Championship; a large collection of long-nose woods by Tom Morris, Hugh Philp and others; a putter made and used by Vardon, and a putter made by Horace Rawlins and used to great effect by him in winning the first U.S. Open championship, in 1895.

The curator, Weymouth B. Crumpster, welcomes visitors from 9 A.M. to 9 P.M. but prefers that you call in advance. Admission is free.

Los Angeles Country Club, 10101 Wilshire Blvd., Los Angeles, CA 90024; (213) 276-6104

This exclusive club contains a fine collection of clubs, balls, tees and other memorabilia carefully watched over by club manager Jim Brewer. Contact him for access.

National Golf Links of America, Southampton, NY 11968; (516) 283-0410

Has clubs, artwork and a fine collection of books. Access is limited only to members and their guests.

Oak Hill Country Club, Box 10397, Rochester, NY 14610; (716) 586-1660

Collection of clubs and memorabilia put together by Burt Kling, a longtime member at Oak Hill.

Pine Valley Golf Club, Pine Valley, NJ 08021; (609) 783-3000

This ultra-exclusive enclave owns a small but fine collection of clubs, balls and artwork, including a putter owned by Old Tom Morris, a Walter Hagen wedge and an assortment of rut irons. Access is limited to members and their guests. There also is a small library.

Royal North Devon Golf Club Museum at Westward Ho!, Westward Ho!, Devon, England; (02372) 3824

This is one of Britain's older clubs, but the golf collection didn't open until 1985. Visitors welcomed.

Architecture

Fifteen Steps to the Perfect Golf Course: The Art of the Golf Course Architect

by Rees Jones

Rees Jones is one of the famous Jones gang of golf-course architects. Robert Trent Jones, the father, and history's most prolific architect, began in the business in 1930 and now has a portfolio of some 500 courses around the world. Rees's brother, Robert Trent Jones, Jr., joined his father's firm in 1960; Rees followed four years later. Since setting out on their own, both have proven worthy heirs to their father's throne, perfect examples of the kind of men who look at land and see par threes, fours and fives and a finishing hole over water, when you and I see rocks and trees.

Some of the most recognized works of Rees Jones are Haig Point Golf Club, a coastal layout on Daufuskie Island, South Carolina; Pinehurst No. 7, a course built on rugged terrain within the Pinehurst Resort in Pinehurst, North Carolina; and the Blue Course at Congressional Country Club in Bethesda, Maryland, the site of the 1964 U.S. Open Championship and the 1976 PGA Championship, and which Jones completely remodelled in 1989 in preparation for the 1995 U.S. Senior Open. Rees also renovated and improved The Country Club in Brookline, Massachusetts, for the 1988 U.S. Open and the Hazeltine Country Club in Chaska, Minnesota, for the 1991 U.S. Open. The latter, interestingly, was originally designed and laid out by his father in 1962.

But no matter the architect or his bloodlines, certain steps have to be taken to take a golf course from an idea to completion and play. As you'll see, there is more to designing and building a golf course than a good eye, a good idea and a lot of heavy machinery.

STEP 1. WE HAVE CONTACT

The process normally begins with a telephone call from a potential client who will describe the project he envisages and propose the project to the architect. He will normally outline such elements as course location, the type of land and a preliminary schedule.

STEP 2. TIME TO COLLECT INFORMATION

Although some of this part of the procedure has been discussed in step one, the architect cannot rely solely on client information. Before accepting—or rejecting—a project he must also determine:

▼ The type of course proposed (private, public, resort, development or remodeling)
▼ Number of holes (usually 18, 27 or 36)
▼ The budget and how the project is being financed
▼ Scheduled starting dates for the design process and for construction
▼ The characteristics of the land, including acreage, topography, irrigation sources, vegetation, lakes, streams, wetlands, types of soil, presence of rocks and easements (such as gas and power lines or roads), access from surrounding areas, the nearest airport and any existing mapping
▼ Who will make up the design team (e.g., planners and engineers).

STEP 3. THE SITE VISIT

This is not necessarily a formality. A golf course architect can "read" a site better than anyone. In fact, it's not uncommon for an architect to go to a site and suggest to a developer that a golf course might not be the best method of developing the land.

STEP 4. SIGN THE DOTTED LINE

If the plan is feasible, the architect and the developer go to contract.

(STEPS 5–8 COMPRISE WHAT COULD BE CALLED "THE DESIGN PHASE.")

STEP 5. THE MAPPING

Mapping normally is conducted by an aerial photography company, which shoots the land and, as the name of this step suggests, draws up a map of the area. This map should indicate the property line of the proposed development, topography, vegetation, stream, lakes, flood plain, existing wetlands, existing structures, easements, any cemeteries and archeological sites and adjacent roads and properties. Some mapping companies will shoot ultraviolet film to reveal marshy and other wetland that might not be clearly visible on regular film.

STEP 6. BEFORE THE ROUTING CAN BEGIN . . .

Before the architect can come up with a rough outline of the route he wants the holes to follow, he must answer many more questions. To wit:

▼ What are the local, state and federal laws associated with wetlands on the property?

▼ Can I clear, dredge, reshape, fill or reconstruct any wetlands?

▼ Which agencies have jurisdiction over wetlands? Army Corps of Engineers? Coastal Commission? Environmental Protection Agency?

▼ Are there laws requiring that "buffers" be built into the design? (These are areas, normally about 50 feet wide, to be left untouched between natural areas and the proposed development.)

▼ Will I be able to construct around existing gas and power lines, roads or other easements?

▼ Will the course be associated with a housing development or a resort? (This question can be vitally important as a course winding its way around real estate probably will need a more extensive—and therefore more expensive—irrigation system.)

STEP 7. THE ROUTING BEGINS

First the architect determines the location of the clubhouse. This affects not only the design of the course, but also the location of access roads and parking, swimming pool, tennis courts and so on.

Integral to the location of the clubhouse is the number of holes planned for the development. In most instances the course will comprise 18 holes, with each nine returning to the club. That means the land around the clubhouse must accommodate four holes (first, ninth, 10th and 18th) and a practice area—not usually a problem.

But when the development calls for 36 holes, that means four holes running away from the clubhouse (two opening holes and two 10th holes) and four returning (two ninths and two 18ths). The area around the clubhouse could have to accommodate *eight* holes and a practice area.

All this time, the architect must keep in mind that there are five basic course configurations for a regulation, 18-hole golf course:

1. A single fairway, each side of which is lined by development, with returning nines;
2. A single fairway with nonreturning nines;
3. A double fairway—development on one side, another fairway on the other—with returning nines;
4. A double fairway with nonreturning nines;
5. A "core" layout—there is no development; the golf course is an entity unto itself.

The last type of course may sound like a boon to the architect from an aesthetic standpoint, but more often than not when there is real estate planned (or already existing), the routing is simply a matter of following the available land.

In deciding on the makeup of the layout, an architect takes into consideration several elements:

▼ He tries to include two par fives, two par threes and five par fours on each nine, while trying to avoid back-to-back par fives and par threes.

▼ He tries to vary the lengths of holes and position them in different directions so that players will encounter different slopes and rolls and, depending on the weather, different wind conditions.

▼ He tries to fit holes to existing land and use as many natural features, such as water and trees, as possible, while avoiding steep slopes. You will run into golf courses that you think may be too steep, but the rule of thumb for the architect is that the properly hit ball must *come to rest* in the desired landing area.

▼ He tries to make every landing area, including greens, visible from the tee. If he can't, he makes them visible from the landing area of the shot just played.

▼ He locates cart paths close to greens and tees—less walking—while keeping the paths sequestered wherever possible. He must also leave adequate access from the cart paths to the greens.

STEP 8. THE COST ESTIMATE

This is computed when the planners, engineers and client have all viewed the routing plan and everyone is satisfied enough to go ahead with the actual course construction.

STEP 9. STAKE-OUT TIME

"Staking" a golf course involves placing four-to-six-feet-high stakes in the center of where each hole's championship tee would be, in the crook of each dog-leg and in the center of each green. Now the architect can walk the course and make sure that the holes fit the land properly and make any necessary adjustments.

STEP 10. CLEARING THE LAND

Clearing opens and prepares the playing areas, as well as any lakes, detention basins and circulation routes for construction work and for turf development.

Clearing generally consists of three phases: Phase one involves clearing along the center of the holes to let the architect analyze the process visually and make any adjustments. The next phase involves clearing from 30 to 60 feet on either side of the center line. The third phase involves clearing areas assigned for feature construction (mounds, bunkers, etc.) and to allow adequate playing space.

STEP 11. EARTHMOVING

First we strip and stockpile topsoil. Basically we clean any debris from it, which an architect has to do if he hopes to end up with good turf.

Now the major earthmoving begins. We make the major cuts and fills and hollow out any borrow areas (where we take from one area to "make" another) or lakes.

The feature-shaping includes the contouring of tees, fairways, fairway and rough features, the green and any features on it. When the features have been shaped, the topsoil is respread, except on the greens.

While the clearing of a course can be conducted by any competent contractor, when it comes to shaping a course's features, a good architect uses only a contractor who is familiar with golf course work. In fact, some contractors specialize in shaping golf courses.

STEP 12. WATER, WATER . . . EVERYWHERE?

Most new courses install fully automatic, underground irrigation systems. How much the system covers is a function of budget and weather conditions. The two fundamental types of irrigation are hydraulic and electric.

STEP 13. GRASSING

To the untrained eye, a golf course looks like any old construction site and then—presto!—it turns green.

Clearing the center of the fairway at Fairview Country Club, Greenwich, CT.

Moving earth and stockpiling to shape features, here at Woodside Plantation, Aitken, SC.

Feature shaping of green, here at Charleston National Country Club, Mt. Pleasant, SC.

Fine grading of soil before sodding, Charleston National.

ety of Bentgrass or Bluegrass. In warmer climates, fairways generally are sodded or sprigged with strains of Bermudagrass or Zoysia. Roughs generally consist of Bluegrass or Fescues in cooler climates and Fescues and Bermuda in warmer climates. Bent is the most common grass to be found on putting greens, except in the south, where Bermuda is the norm.

STEP 14. THE GROWING PERIOD

Bermuda grows fast. A course planted in the south might be ready for play within three to four months. On the other hand, a northern course seeded with Bent might need an additional growing period, and might not be ready for a year. It's worth the wait.

Whatever the length of the growing period, the architect will visit the site intermittently to consult with the golf course superintendent, inspect the course and repair any erosion. And that's about it.

STEP 15. MULLIGAN ON THE FIRST TEE?

Life should be so easy. There are actually several different procedures.

First we must "regrade" the entire site. Since back around step 9, all kinds of heavy machinery have been driving over it and churning it up. Before we seed the soil, we must make it smooth. We'll first disc it to eliminate ruts and tracks, loosening the surface to between three and six inches. Then we'll rake the soil to remove any sticks, rocks and stones. This can be a back-breaking part of the process that very often requires hand labor.

We then treat the soil by applying lime—if necessary—to reach the desired pH factor. We next fertilize and seed according to the type of grass chosen.

This is a choice that local climate to a certain extent makes for you. But an architect must also take into consideration soil type, the amount of water on the land, salt, shade, traffic, disease and the possible intrusion of undesired grasses and weeds.

In cooler climates, fairways generally are seeded with a vari-

Sodding fairway, here at Peninsula Club, in Huntersville, N.C.

A Little Respect, Please, for the Short Par Four

by Tom Doak

In the family of golf holes, the short par four is often considered an outcast, unable to hold its own in the ongoing defense of par. Long-hitting Tour pros (as if there are any other kinds) dismiss short par fours as "birdie holes" and "lay up holes." Even the founding fathers of golf-course design cautioned against building holes which were "not of a good length." When golfers indulge in making up these eclectic and interminable lists of great holes, the short par four becomes the 98-pound weakling of golf, the last boy picked for the team.

For a time in the late 1950s and 1960s, the par four of less than 400 yards was almost in danger of extinction. Course developers always demanded a "7,200-yard championship course" from their architects to fend off the new generation of power hitters led by Jack Nicklaus. With four par threes as part of the picture, the new math didn't leave much room for anything around 330 yards. The Champions Club's Cypress Creek Course in Houston, venue of the 1969 U.S. Open and highly regarded in its time (it was built in 1959), was designed with only one par four shorter than 400 yards—its third hole, which weighed in at 397.

But the short par four seems to be making a strong comeback, thanks principally to designers placing a bit more emphasis on interest and a bit less on sheer length. The trend shouldn't be surprising. Pine Valley, Cypress Point, Merion (East), the Old Course in St. Andrews, Scotland, and Royal Melbourne, in Australia, each possess at least four short par fours, and all five courses are considered classics, among the top ten layouts in the entire world.

Probably the real reason for the unpopularity of short par fours was that the designers found it difficult to maintain the "proper" shot values for stroke play, which Robert Trent Jones once described thusly: "Every hole should be a difficult par, but an easy bogey."

Look at it this way. A 360-yard hole is just a drive, or maybe even a long iron, and a short pitch for an accomplished player (who we'll call "Tiger"). But it could well be a less-than-ideal drive and a middle- or long-iron second shot for an average, 15-handicap player (who we'll call "Rabbit"). In order to make the hole playable for Rabbit, a designer would have to build a large green, but our Tiger is highly unlikely to miss a large target with a 100-yard approach. So to make it a true par four for Tiger, the designer must build a small green—and Rabbit will be hard-pressed to hold, or even hit, such a small target. It's quite a dilemma.

Until you consider that this discussion of shot values is only relative to par, and that golfers do not play against par. They play match play against an opponent, stroke play against a field of opponents *or they play against their own expectations.* In effect, our Rabbit can play a 360-yard hole with a large green with reason to expect his four, but on the same hole Tiger believes he ought to be able to make three, or birdie. Indeed, the best players often *must* make a three to keep pace with an opponent or make up a stroke that has slipped away elsewhere on the course. Even the most modest par four therefore has real psychological value within a course—it can boost the ego of Rabbit and puts extra pressure on Tiger. And the fact that the green is large doesn't help Tiger much, because he figures he could hit even the smallest green: His real aim is to get close enough to the hole to leave a makeable birdie putt.

So bearing all this in mind, what exactly constitutes a good par four? It's tough to say exactly, but there are five distinct types of the genre from which the best will probably derive.

1. THE CLASSIC DRIVE AND PITCH

The usual formula is to make it very short and allow everyone to get close to the green with the tee shot—then demand perfection on the relatively short pitch. The classic hole of the type is the eighth at Pine Valley, with its tiny green surrounded by a frightening array of unraked bunkers. Something of an exception to the rule is the seventh hole at Augusta National, where specimen trees to either side of the fairway make a straight drive mandatory, after which the pitch to the shallow green must be carefully judged (but it is worth

The unraked bunkers guarding Pine Valley's tiny 8th green (alternate green at right) make this a classic drive-and-pitch hole.

3. THE DRIVEABLE PAR FOUR

On these, the designer has clearly intended that a strong player be able to knock his first shot onto the green. Any hole shorter than 350 yards could possibly be driven by the longest-hitting Tour players under favorable conditions; the key factor is that the green be large enough and oriented such that a full drive could bounce in front of the green and roll on, or hit the green and hold.

The most heroic of these holes designed in recent years is the 275-yard 10th at The Belfry in Sutton Coldfield, England, the site of the British PGA Championship and the Ryder Cup matches of 1985 and 1989. It offers just two options: A player can lay back off the tee or try to drive the green, the latter requiring a slightly left to right shot over a pond to a long narrow green flanked by the pond on the left and bunkers to the right. The green is clearly designed and oriented to allow a full shot from the tee to hit and hold. Those who play short and left are then presented with a shallow target. Several American designers, including Jay Morrish and Tom Fazio, have integrated this concept into their designs.

4. THE "ANYTHING GOES"

These offer a variety of strategies. A player could attempt to drive close to the green and leave a short pitch; lay well back of any fairway hazards and avoid any driving penalty, but leave a longer approach and little chance of birdie; or play into the heart of trouble with a controlled driver or iron shot to set up a reasonable pitch.

The classic example is the 312-yard 12th (or "Heathery") hole at St. Andrews. The fairway is peppered with pot bunkers that are not visible from the tee (and does *that* ever make the decision interesting). The green is two-tiered, the flagstick normally resting on the shallow top shelf, which favors the scrambling run-up approach, a shot that not every player is capable of (or ever sees, for that matter).

Thus, the golfers' choice is to try and clear the last

remembering that the same trees did not infringe so much on the tee shot when Augusta National was built 60 years ago).

Unfortunately, as courses receive more players every year because of the increased popularity of the game, a very small green is more likely to receive heavy damage from foot traffic; thus the classic drive-and-pitch hole may become a thing of the past. Pine Valley found a solution by building an alternate green, just as small, next to the eighth green to reduce the traffic on the original.

2. THE SHARP DOGLEG

On these, a long, narrow green is angled to receive an approach shot from one side of the fairway and to make an approach from the improper angle very difficult indeed. The classic hole of this type is the 311-yard 10th at the Riviera Country Club in Pacific Palisades, California. A dogleg right with its narrow green tilted sharply from right to left, it tempts the stronger player to try and drive all the way to the entrance of the green, but if the tee shot winds up even a little bit too far right, it is nearly impossible to stop the ensuing pitch shot on what has become a very narrow putting surface. A safe drive to the left makes the green relatively accessible. The 12th hole at Pine Valley, a dogleg left with the green falling away to its back left, is almost a mirror image of the Riviera hole.

of the bunkers, try to find safe haven between the bunkers and the edges of the fairway or lay up and leave a long approach to a tough pin.

A similar hole is the 291-yard ninth at Cypress Point, in California, which has a wide, short landing zone and a narrow neck of fairway leading up to a shallow green fronted by a deep bunker.

5. THE BLASÉ SHORT PAR FOUR

These can be used expressly for psychological value—not to scare players but to play with their minds.

The ninth hole of the Old Course at St. Andrews is one example. There is a small, deep bunker to be avoided with the tee-shot, but all things considered, this is an easy hole by present-day values: quite short at 356 yards with a green largely unguarded by bunkers.

But the very absence of trouble around the green can lull Tiger to sleep; perhaps it will cause doubt in his mind whether to run or pitch the ball up to the hole, and his decision will result in a poor approach to, say, 40 feet from the hole—from where he might take three putts while chastising himself for making a bad approach. Meanwhile, Rabbit, relieved of the subconscious fear of the greenside hazards that normally play havoc with his swing, is so encouraged by the probability of making par that he might, in fact, finish close enough to make a rare birdie. It has been known to happen.

Such turnabouts, it must be noted, may have ramifications for several holes thereafter, inspiring con- fidence in Rabbit for the tougher holes ahead and nagging at Tiger's mind when he should be concentrating on subsequent shots.

Thus, for the sake of subterfuge as well as increased variety, the best designers will seek to include short and interesting par fours on all their courses, whether destined for championship or public play.

As well they should.

The easy approach to St. Andrews's 9th green can create psychological hazards of its own.

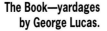

The Book—yardages
by George Lucas.

Where to Find . . .
The Yardage Books the Pros Use

They're compiled by George Lucas, not the Hollywood special effects wizard but a former Tour caddie who decided in the mid 1970s that carrying some young gun's bags for peanuts was a fairly dreadful lot. Lucas realized no single person was producing informative, reliable yardage books, so he stepped in. Now he travels the country with his faithful dog, Corky, surveying tournament courses for the men's and women's pro tours and for the major championships. Lucas's books are not what you'd call production numbers; they're black-and-white sheets, basically, with a few squiggles here and there for water and trees. Some holes will contain "auxiliary" yardages should a pro have to pitch out of trouble. Lucas labels these "J.I.C.Y.R.F.U."—as in "Just In Case You Really Fuck Up." What the books lack in production quality, they make up for in accuracy.

They're so accurate, in fact, that they've been held responsible for there being so many good players today. Lucas is a tough man to contact (so would you be if you spent your time driving from golf course to golf course), but you may want to try him at (406) 842-3121.

The Art of the Bunker

by Tom Doak

● ● ●

"I have used the word 'bunker' in what I have understood to be the traditional golfing sense, meaning a pit in which the soil has been exposed and the area covered with sand. I regard the term 'sand trap' as an unacceptable Americanization. Its use annoys me almost as much as hearing a golf club called a 'stick.' Earthworks, mounds, and the like, without sand, are not bunkers."

—BOBBY JONES

When golf first evolved in Scotland, bunkers existed naturally on the sandy, windblown, coastal terrain. Centuries later, they continue to be the preeminent hazard in golf, simply because time has shown them to have the ideal playing qualities for a hazard—they do allow a recovery but at the price of power and accuracy unless the shot is performed with *perfect* technique.

So golf-course designers continue to introduce bunkers as the principle hazards in their designs even though golf is more often than not played over terrain where sand does not exist naturally. Indeed, non-golfers often differentiate a golf course from open grassland because of the bunkers that break it up.

Legend has it that the early links bunkers were formed by sheep sheltering from the wind, but this is mostly fable. Sheep certainly did not dig out bunkers the size and depth of those we see today. But the animals that roamed the early links, sheep and rabbits mostly, scraped the native dune grasses bare in some areas, and over time the wind carved out more formidable bunkers in the shifting sands from these modest beginnings. On some remote British links courses—notably Westward Ho!, in Devon, where the course remains common ground and animals may graze freely—the evolutionary process remains evident today.

In the early days, these natural dune bunkers were the only real hazards that existed, and it was the holes that were designed around them to provide the sporting test. Once the game started to become popular, however, a new generation of bunkers arose. As areas of concentrated divots developed, it became difficult to maintain turf in certain areas of the fairway, and once the highly trafficked area began to erode, the players were forced to treat it as a new bunker. Thus many of the bunkers on British links courses are located in hollows precisely where a player might otherwise wish to drive the ball—not by accident or by the command of a sadistic golf-course designer, but because this spot was worn out before the practice of turf maintenance could rescue it. These bunkers are known as "pot" bunkers because of their concave shape and small size, and often a cluster of two or three—or many more—was built, as this would reduce the amount of wind erosion that would occur with one large bunker.

In the early days, players combatted the patterns of wear on a course by playing the holes in reverse order during certain months (it is a rite that is still sometimes performed in St. Andrews, but these days for novelty's sake). It gave worn-out areas a chance to recover. But few courses were as interesting backward as they were forward, and eventually fairways were widened around one side of the new bunkers, creating the first dogleg holes, or the bunker was allowed to remain actually in the middle of the fairway, such as on the 12th or 16th holes of the Old Course at St. Andrews today.

When the art of golf-course design became more sophisticated in the 20th century, and architects were free to design hazards around their holes instead of designing holes around existing hazards, new theories arose as to where bunkers should be positioned.

On most early courses, artificial hazards were placed primarily to punish an off-line shot, or a "cross-bunker" was laid across the line of play, short of a desired landing area, to punish a topped shot. But as the game became more popular, beginning players, who had trouble enough just hitting the ball from a good lie, saw this strategy as unfair.

Therefore this so-called "penal" school of bunkering has generally given way to a more "strategic" school, where fairway bunkers are placed selectively to guard the ideal spots in the fairways from which to approach the greens, leaving the player to choose between risking the bunker or driving away from it and leaving himself a more difficult approach. (A by-product of this strategic school is the modern belief that bunkers should be visible so that a player may readily identify his options, whereas frequently on the early links courses the bunkers are in hollows and are not easily discerned by a player unfamiliar with his surroundings.)

For a while it was even popularly held that bunkers should be added to a course only after it had received play for some time and the various lines of play had become apparent. Kingston Heath, outside Melbourne, Australia, is a notable example. It was laid out by Des Soutar in 1925 and bunkered by Dr. Alister Mackenzie three years later. Eventually, however, designers became secure enough to visualize the proper bunker placement during construction.

Today, bunkers can be found in all shapes and sizes, for all kinds of reasons. Some bunkers are built not only as a hazard but also to provide a target for a semiblind shot; to stop balls from running into deeper trouble in a natural hazard; to discourage players from playing close to an adjoining hole or even to cut off golf-cart traffic from going in a certain direction. The British-born designer, Desmond Muirhead, has even experimented with using bunkers as symbolic shapes for psychological effect or for some artistic purpose totally independent of golf. In fact, bunkers now offer the golf-course architect his greatest freedom of expression.

Nevertheless, nearly all bunkers can be categorized into two general types:

1. Those on an elevation, with sand flashed up against their forward face;

2. Those in hollows with grass faces and sand only at the bottom.

It is worth noting that the proponents of each are quick to trace the ancestry of each style back to the original dune and pot bunkers on the early links. Among the celebrated designers, Alister Mackenzie, Stanley Thompson, Robert Trent Jones, George Thomas and A.W. Tillinghast were all proponents of the dune-style bunker (sand flashed up the face). Charles Blair Macdonald, Seth Raynor and, today, Pete Dye, generally preferred to have grass faces on their bunkers as with the pot.

Visual quality of a particular site also has an effect on bunkering. Pot bunkers generally look out of place in a tree-lined setting, for example, while the best designers have always sought to harmonize the smoothness or jaggedness of the distinct edge between sand and grass with the background presented. Two successful examples of the latter include Mackenzie's lace-edged bunkers against the jagged outlines of the many Monterey cypress trees at Cypress Point in California, and Thompson's contrast between the bunker shapes and the shapes of the nearby snow-capped mountains in Banff and Jasper, in Canada.

Bunkers can also be divided for discussion into either "fairway" or "greenside," according to where they are found on a hole. Modern theory holds that fairway bunkers should be larger and shallower, in order to trap a full shot but to allow some chance of still reaching the green with a perfectly struck shot. This is clearly not the idea behind the small, deep pots of the early links courses, and while it has been argued that deep bunkers remove the strategy from the recovery shot, there is also a good argument that on a links course a player must choose carefully between trying to advance a ball 100 yards to present an easier approach or simply playing sideways and accepting the bunker as a one-shot penalty.

In the 1982 British Open at Troon, for example, Bobby Clampett held an eight-stroke lead on the sixth tee of the third round, but refused to concede one of those eight strokes after driving into a fairway pot. He

The 10 Best Bunker Names
(Self-explanatory unless noted)

1 "Pandemonium," sixth hole, Musselburgh Old Links, Musselburgh, Scotland.

2 "Hell's Half Acre," seventh hole, Pine Valley Golf Club, Pine Valley, New Jersey.

3 "Eleanor's Teeth," (as in Roosevelt!), fourth hole, The Apawamis Club, Rye, New York. Yup, a Republican club.

4 "The Devil's Asshole," 10th hole, Pine Valley.

5 "The Cardinal," third hole, Prestwick, Scotland. Once was shaped like a Cardinal's hat (and was much larger).

6 "The Principal's Nose," 16th hole, St. Andrews (Old), St. Andrews, Scotland. Just like the proboscis of one of the faculty at St. Andrews University.

7 "Soup Bowl," 18th hole, Rye Golf Club, Rye, England.

8 "Coffins," 13th hole, St. Andrews (Old).

9 "Spectacles," 14th hole, Carnoustie Golf Club, Carnoustie, Scotland. Two round bunkers set into a slope.

10 "Chalk Pit," third hole, Royal Eastbourne, England. Because it really is a chalk pit.

—Tom Doak

remained bunkered after his second shot, clipped the top of the bunker—but escaped—with his third, strained too hard to reach the green with his next shot and pulled it, and wound up with a devastating, momentum-shifting triple-bogey. He never figured in the Open again, eventually finishing tied for 10th.

While a bunker can be found almost anywhere "through the green"—which the rules define as the whole course except for tees and greens and hazards themselves—most designers place their fairway bunkers at relatively standard distances from the back tee markers. On old American courses, however, you are likely to find them about 200 yards from the original tees, as that was how far a good player could expect to carry the ball in the early part of this century. Today the best players can carry the ball between 240 and 260 yards with a driver, so fairway bunkers are placed farther downrange. In fact, on many older courses either the tees have been moved back or the bunkers have been moved toward the green by a subsequent designer so they once again come into play for the good player.

Greenside bunkers are generally deeper than fairway bunkers, since the ball does not have to be advanced a great distance out of them. Some designers believe the visual qualities of sand help to frame and define the target and may more than offset the effect of the bunker as a hazard per se, so they build large bunkers around a green with sand well flashed on their faces. But frequently a single, small, greenside bunker in just the right place can have great effect. Witness the Road Bunker on the 17th hole at St. Andrews—"Just big enough for an angry man and his mashie, but eating its way into the very vitals of the green," as Bernard Darwin described it long ago. Should a player try to hit the green with a long second shot and instead find the bunker, the narrowness of the plateau green on this hole makes it difficult to splash out of the sand and keep the ball on the green. But should the same player miss both green and bunker, he will find it even more difficult to stop the third shot, a short pitch, when the bunker intervenes. Thus, the difficulty of the recovery shot is in proportion to the degree of error on the approach.

Maintenance concerns also have affected the size and shape of bunkers over the years. Before 1950, when steep banks were mowed by hand and bunkers had to be raked by hand, bunkers tended to be fairly small and deep so they could be maintained in a short time but retain a menacing appearance. Most newer bunkers have been designed larger and shallower, with more regular edges and gentler banks, to accommodate "power" maintenance.

A related development is the "waste area" or "waste bunker," which began to appear on courses in the 1970s and has been identified with Dye, who popularized it at his TPC at Sawgrass course in Ponte Vedra, Florida. This is a long expanse of firmly packed sand, usually running parallel to the fairway, which by virtue of its length serves as an even-handed hazard for all players, regardless of the distance they hit the ball or which tee markers they choose to play from. The actual impetus of the design, however, was convenience-oriented: It's easier to find balls on bare sand than in long grass, and it's easier to drag the sand with a tractor than to mow grass. (While these waste areas have become popular, there has developed an argument as to their true identity: They are often con-

The famed Road Bunker.

sidered a through-the-green area where it is legal to ground the club, whereas a true "bunker" is a hazard where the club may never be grounded.)

Finally, it should be noted that although a bunker, by definition of the Rules of Golf, is a hazard and players are prohibited from taking relief from loose impediments, bunkers are nowhere near as hazardous as they once were. In early days it was not expected that a bunker would be smoothly raked, and cupped lies in footprints were common. In fact, for many years at Oakmont Country Club outside Pittsburgh, Pennsylvania, the scene of many major championships, a special saber-toothed rake was employed to furrow the sand and *guarantee* a poor lie.

But with the combination of tamer etiquette and the invention of the sand wedge by Gene Sarazen in 1932 (which in turn led to the proliferation of water hazards as stiffer punishment), professional players now expect to get up and down in two shots from a greenside bunker some 60 percent of the time—probably twice the average recovery percentage in Bobby Jones's day.

The Thirteen Commandments of Golf Course Architecture

In 1920, golf-course architect Alister Mackenzie, who was responsible for Cypress Point in California and, with Bobby Jones, Augusta National in Augusta, Georgia—plus a few dozen other great designs—drafted the following 13 "essential features of an ideal golf course" in his book *Architecture*.

Think about each one. You'll be pleasantly surprised how so many are applied to this day. You might also be shocked at how many are so blatantly ignored. Take number five, for example. In a nutshell, *that* was what critics have disliked most about Tournament Players Clubs.

1 The course, where possible, should be arranged in two loops of nine holes.

2 There should be a large proportion of good, two-shot holes, two or three drive-and-pitch holes, and at least four one-shot holes.

3 There should be little walking between the greens and tees, and the course should be arranged so that in the first instance there is always a slight walk forwards from the green to the next tee; then the holes are sufficiently elastic to be lengthened in the future if necessary.

4 The greens and the fairways should be sufficiently undulating, but there should be no hill climbing.

5 Every hole should have a different character.

6 There should be a minimum of blindness for the approach shots.

7 The course should have beautiful surroundings, and all the artificial features should have so natural an appearance that a stranger is unable to distinguish them from nature itself.

8 There should be a sufficient number of heroic carries from the tee, but the course should be arranged so that the weaker player with the loss of a stroke or portion of a stroke shall always have an alternative route open to him.

9 There should be infinite variety in the strokes required to play the various holes—viz. interesting brassy [fairway wood] shots, iron shots, pitch and run-up shots.

10 There should be a complete absence of the annoyance and irritation caused by the necessity of searching for lost balls.

11 The course should be so interesting that even the plus man [plus handicapper] is constantly stimulated to improve his game in attempting shots he has hitherto been unable to play.

12 The course should be so arranged that the long [high] handicap player, or even the complete beginner, should be able to enjoy his round in spite of the fact that he is piling up a big score.

13 The course should be equally good during winter and summer, the texture of the greens and fairways should be perfect, and the approaches should have the same consistency as the greens.

Greens

by Tom Doak

The green is the ultimate target in the play of every golf hole. Since so much of the game is spent either on the green—putting—or trying to hit an approach shot onto it, the green is naturally the focal point of every course architect's work.

While the construction of bunkers allows a designer more freedom of expression, and bunkers are therefore a more readily distinguished trademark of a designer's style, it is by his greens that his work will ultimately be judged.

Because the ground must be of a certain firmness to receive approach shots and because the surface must be so smooth for putting, greens naturally must meet more rigid standards of construction than any other part of the course. They must be designed to afford good drainage, both by surface flow and by tile drains built into the soil underneath. The soil with which they are built must be good enough that it will not compact from the concentrated foot traffic around the hole. And they must be large enough to accommodate the actual hole being moved frequently. (Most modern courses feature greens that are generally bigger than those you will find on older courses so they can cater to the increasing number of new golfers.)

Because of all this, as much as half of a new course's entire budget may be spent on green construction, and as much as half of the annual maintenance budget might go to their upkeep.

On a good golf course, each green is designed with a particular approach shot in mind. This shot determines a green's size, contouring, bunkering and opening. In general, the size is proportionate to the length of the expected approach; a par-three hole of 200 yards, for example, will usually have a larger green than, say, a par four of 320 yards, since on the latter most players will face an approach of between 50 and 120 yards. But these sizes may be adjusted based on the severity of the hazards around the green or on the whims of the architect who has in mind a desired difficulty for the hole in question.

When it comes to contouring, each designer has his own style. Some prefer relatively flat greens that give the advantage to the player who hits his ball closest to the hole: the premium, in effect, is on good iron play. Others prefer very undulating greens that place more emphasis on putting and chipping skills. Modern designers tend to think of their greens as several greens in one; they're made up of separate sections, or "pin-placements," where the hole may be cut; the challenges will differ from location to location.

While the best architects will provide variety by employing different types of greens on a single course, most of the more famous architects developed a preference over the years. Donald Ross, for example, generally preferred small, raised and slightly crowned greens such as those found at Pinehurst Number 2 at the Pinehurst resort in North Carolina. It is difficult to hold an approach shot on these greens unless it is played a certain way, and many subtly difficult chips are possible should a player miss a green.

Charles Blair Macdonald, on the other hand, built much larger greens with steep banks falling off at their sides toward more clearly defined trouble. The second hole at the Yale University course in New Haven, Connecticut, for example, has a bunker lying some twenty feet below the left side of the putting surface.

Alister Mackenzie is known for more severely sloped, multilevel greens, typified by those he built at Augusta National Golf Club in Augusta, Georgia. Their different pin placements on plateaus or in slightly concave areas place greater demands on putting skill.

A.W. Tillinghast's famous courses in the eastern United States—such as Winged Foot (West), in Mamaroneck, New York—all feature relatively small, well-guarded, sharply tilted greens which are slightly concave to the center but which also have rolls at their sides that make putts more difficult to read. Most of Tillinghast's greens are elevated because the heavy soils of the east did not permit him to build greens at ground level and still have good drainage.

Lastly, Robert Trent Jones is known throughout the world for his trademark large, elevated greens, often shaped with narrow tongues at their sides or corners to provide a difficult pin placement for tournament play.

But despite the preferences, interests and whims of different designers, there exist several distinct "types" of green, the most prevalent of which are the following ten.

1. THE GROUND-LEVEL GREEN

The seam between the putting surface and its surroundings has little or no change in elevation. This generally makes for easy recovery play, and is used only to keep down construction expense or in cases where the natural contours of the ground will keep play interesting. Example (of the latter): the ninth at the Old Course in St. Andrews.

2. THE TILTED GREEN

These normally pitch from rear to front, but sometimes tilt from one side to the other. This green rewards players who position their tee shots to play directly into the slope of the green. If the tilt is severe, the style also rewards those who can keep their approach shots below the hole and leave an uphill, easier putt. Example: the fifth at Merion.

3. THE FALL-AWAY GREEN

The tilt runs generally away from the line of approach. On short holes this may be employed to require the player to put extra bite on the approach shot; on longer holes, to require, or even encourage, the player to bounce in the approach and accurately gauge the bounce. Older courses frequently had one or two such greens, but they have since fallen out of favor as players have come to expect designers to make the targets more visible and receptive to approaches. Example: the 12th at Oakmont.

4. THE PLATEAU GREEN

A staple of most courses, the plateau green is elevated above its surroundings to reward a good shot and make the recovery for those who miss even more difficult. Elevated greens are especially common in the northeastern United States where, as noted, the native soils are heavy and only by elevating the green can a designer assure good drainage. Example: anything at Royal Dornoch, but the 14th is probably the best example.

5. THE TWO-TIERED (OR MULTITIERED) GREEN

This is used to reduce the area around the hole where a player would have a reasonable chance of holing a putt. The tiered green is also used on sloping sites to reduce the overall tilt between pin placement areas. Example: the 18th at Augusta National.

6. THE CROWNED GREEN

A version of the plateau green, this is sited on a bump or a knob in the ground which is high at the center and falls off to one or all sides. The difficulty of stopping an approach which lands on a part of the green that slopes away from the golfer effectively reduces the size of the target. In addition, recovery shots from the "wrong" side of the crown can be very difficult. Example: the 16th at Westward Ho!

7. THE PUNCHBOWL GREEN

The punchbowl green sits in a hollow or bowl in the terrain where the edges of the green and perhaps the surroundings slope in toward the center and to some degree gather approach shots (which are often hit blind). These greens pay homage to the early links of Great Britain. The best grass for greens often grew in such hollows, as that was where the most moisture collected. Today, however, irrigation techniques limit punchbowls to very sandy areas. Punchbowls have also fallen out of favor because they tend to provide poor visibility and few designers today favor blind approaches. Example: the 16th hole at the National Golf Links of America in Southampton, New York.

8. THE ISLAND GREEN

This heroic type is completely surrounded by sand or water and is often inspired not by architectural necessity but by the desire for public relations pizzazz. Such greens may look impressive, but generally a weaker player finds them too difficult to hit unless the green is fairly large and the carry is fairly short. Example: the 17th at the TPC at Sawgrass. Dye's design has since been knocked off all over the country, an iniquity for which Dye has yet to be forgiven by many in the world of golf.

9. THE DOUBLE GREEN

A vestige of the Old Course at St. Andrews, where the greens were widened and two separate holes were employed when the course became so busy that it was no longer feasible to use the same holes coming back to the clubhouse as had been used going out—as was the practice in the old days on the Old Course. But two greens within one creates problems with circulation and safety and, like the island green, the style is now more of a public relations ploy. (Jack Nicklaus had the audacity to put a double green on an island in one of his latest creations in Scottsdale, Arizona.) If

The World's 10 Best Nine-Hole Courses

1 **Royal Worlington & Newmarket Golf Club, Bury St. Edmunds, Suffolk, England.** It's affectionately known as "Mildenhall" after the tiny railway station at which students from Cambridge University would pile off with their clubs. It was designed by one Captain A.M. Ross, who ingeniously crammed nine holes into 65 acres and gave up course design thereafter. Pity. So compact is the course that the captain used most features several times. Example: A swale that sets off the green of the first also comes into play in front of the third green, behind the seventh green and in the landing area for the tee-shot on the fourth.

2 **Whitinsville Golf Club, Whitinsville, Massachusetts.** Another Ross nine—this one by Donald, the famous one. Because of the traffic a half-size course gets from a full-size club, it's tough to get on, but worth the hassle. The final two holes are almost perfect. The eighth is a short, dogleg par four on which a drive that cuts the corner finely is adequately rewarded. The ninth is a strong driving hole with some work left to do on the approach.

3 **Reigate Heath, Reigate, Surrey, England.** A heathland nine of unknown origin. It's strongest at the start and peters out toward the end, but the short, undemanding, uphill ninth allows you to at least finish on a good note.

4 **River Oaks Plantation, Richmond Hill, Georgia.** For all I know, this could be an 18-holer right now. The nine that were originally built were done so by Pete and P.B. Dye in beautiful woodland. The back nine was destined to be on an old paddy field engineered by Henry Ford when he lived in these parts, but I've yet to hear of it being completed.

5 **Millbrook Club, Greenwich, Connecticut.** A sound little nine tucked into wooded, rocky terrain. Don't play it if it rains—or don't *expect* to play the eighth. It lies on the lowest part of land in the entire county.

6 **Wawashkamo Golf Club, Makinac Island, Michigan.** A delightful experience: You can actually rent hickory clubs and gutty balls to play this turn-of-the-century restored layout that rests on farmland in the middle of the island. Warning: Get your short game in shape, for the greens are tiny.

7 **Urbana Country Club, Urbana, Ohio.** Stands out for two reasons: 1. The second and eighth holes are canted so steeply that they are the embodiment of "goat-hill" architecture; 2. Pete Dye's dad built it.

8 **The Sea Ranch Club, near Gualala, California.** The real estate development occupies the best of this coastal site, but at least the Pacific winds reach into the golf course. Two good finishing holes.

9 **Musselburgh Old Links, Musselburgh, Scotland.** If you know of an older, unchanged course, we want to hear from you. This was once the home of the Honourable Company of Edinburgh Golfers, who long ago moved on to Muirfield ("flitted" is the Scottish word). Now it fills the center of the town's horse racetrack and is given little attention by the town or any of the punters losing their shirts at the bookies' windows. Which is fine: You play the course the way it was more than 100 years ago.

10 **Carradale, Golf Club, Carradale, Scotland.** Sitting on a hilltop on the Mull of Kintyre, the Carradale course gives you wonderful views of the island of Arran, the Ailsa Craig rock, and the front- and rear-ends of the local sheep. Isn't that enough?

—Tom Doak

---

the routing requires that two holes make use of approximately the same green site, the greens could be laid out back-to-back just as easily. Example: the seven double greens at the Old Course.

10. THE POSTAGE-STAMP GREEN

Nicknamed because of its size. Tommy Armour gave the most famous example its name by offering that the eighth green at Royal Troon was so small it was harder to hit "than a postage stamp." While the contrast of a small green among larger ones on the course and the resulting shock value can be an interesting psychologi-

cal hazard, the requirements of maintaining good turf limit the use of postage stamps to courses that do not receive heavy traffic. Example (other than the original Postage Stamp): the eighth at Pine Valley.

In general, however, what makes a putting green good and interesting are its subtle contours which affect putting and chipping and which cannot be categorized easily. Simply to build a plateau or island green is not enough. For a course to be classified as "great" and hold lasting interest for players, each shot—including chips and putts—must present some challenge and some element of risk and reward.

How to Build Your Own Green

by David Earl

● ● ●

It started with putting. Atrocious putting. I'd been experimenting with all kinds of new putters since my old Ping Anser gave out, everything from an old Reachley hickory shaft to an Archie Compton flange. Nothing worked. Sympathetic, cynical friends (are there any other kind in this game?) suggested that the Ping had simply made all its allotted putts. I of course knew better. It was a matter of practice.

But frankly it was a pain driving all the way to the club for half an hour on the practice green. I was in a quandary. Should I just live with a game that made nothing? Thirty-six putts a round? Or should I take matters into my own hands and build my own practice green?

The dilemma was decided on the morning that a little box marked "Plant 'N' Putt: Professional Golf Course Green" arrived at the offices of *Golf Magazine*. Oh, I'd looked into practice greens before. The Jack Nicklaus catalog offered a green for $25,000—a bit rich for my blood. Figuring other builder/architects might be cheaper than The Bear, I'd hunted around and found I could have a whole dang golf course from Michael Hurdzan for a couple of million—again, well out of my range. I was thinking more along the lines of a couple of hundred.

The Plant 'N' Putt deal looked promising, however, so I read the literature. The building process, although it looked like some work, was clearly explained, so I figured it would do no harm to start pricing materials and tools. And since sand was one of the materials I'd be needing—and in quantity—I resolved to dig a little practice pot bunker as well.

For research material, I ordered the USGA booklet, "Specifications for a Method of Putting Green Construction" and photocopied the relevant pages from James Beard's excellent book, *Turfgrass*. I read them both carefully, then called a building supply company. Here's what I ordered:

½ cubic yard of large gravel (1½ inch average)
½ cubic yard of pea gravel (½ inch average)
2 cubic yards of sand
A green mower
40 feet of perforated 4-inch PVC drainage pipe

The whole deal came to around $320, which included the mower, a push-style seven-blade. No way was I blowing $600 for a gas mower for a twelve-foot by twenty-four-foot green! Mine was special-ordered through my local Ace Hardware store from American Lawn Mower. Works just fine, too.

Then came the sweat. As per the Plant 'N' Putt instructions, I staked out the green site and started excavating with a hand-held shovel. Ditto the bunker. At eight feet around, this proved to be the quicker task, so I decided to build the bunker before the green. In the corner of my garden I

For about $500. No kidding. This guy did it in his backyard.

Earl's green—after the gravel base, before the sanding and seeding.

Earl's practice bunker.

dug out a fifteen-inch-deep hole as well as trenches for the PVC drainpipe. The yard runs fairly severely downhill, so I knew the bunker and green would drain well.

I used the dirt I'd dug out to build a front lip to the bunker. Then, after filling the bottom of the trenches with large gravel to a depth of a couple of inches, I laid the drains in it. I glued the pipes together, then buried them in gravel. Then I spread another couple of inches of gravel, and filled it with sand. It looked divine. I hit a few shots—it worked! Next I got an old bunker rake from my club and seeded the ground around the bunker with good old Scottish-style Fescue grass. Two weeks later, it looked like Muirfield—at least to me. It still does.

Wish I could say the same about the green. One day, I was feeling peppy, so I decided to dig out the green. I had two options; dig it a foot deep, or build up the edges. After about half an hour, I decided on a compromise, six inches deep and six inches of buildup. Subtle Donald Ross style. So I dug and dug and dug. It took me almost eight hours to finish.

The drainage system—PVC pipe and gravel—went in just like in my bunker. It fit, it drained, and it covered well. Then I began covering with sand. At this point, I rented a 200-pound water-fillable roller. It would be needed at several stages.

The experts recommend about a foot of sand but no topsoil, surprisingly. As I filled the sand in I watered it to help compact it, then rolled it two or three times. It got so hard I could walk on it without leaving footprints. The process took almost two days, dawn to dusk. Finally it was shaped to my liking, and I applied seven pounds of 6-20-20 fertilizer and raked it into the surface. Then I regraded it, and it was time to seed.

The Clyde Robins Seed Company supplied the seed. It's Penncross Creeping Bentgrass, a common seed for greens in the Northeast. I asked Richie, the superintendent at my club, whether it would work. "Sure," he said. I then spread seed, cross-raked to work it into the soil, and watered it assiduously. The instructions said to keep it moist for the first two weeks.

Three days later came the first tragedy. We suffered a real gullywasher. In fact, over the next eleven days, six inches of rain fell. You can imagine what happened; all the grass became concentrated on the lower side of the green and down the drainage ditch (which I'd buried and covered in dirt and Fescue seed). I hoped the Creeping Bentgrass would creep enough to cover the bare areas. No such luck.

So I had to reseed. Fortunately, I'd followed the seed folks' recommendations and saved half of the seed. I reseeded, reraked and rewatered. It worked better. The grass grew in all but a few spots, and I mowed for the first time about two weeks after the second reseeding. It was fun—took about three minutes, as I recall. I refertilized, rolled during the grass's "establishment" and soon I had my putting surface.

A few warnings. First, building a green involves long hours of hard labor. Second, be prepared to be mightily frustrated. Greens are finicky beasts. They catch diseases. They need sunny, breezy areas to grow (which is why you'll find bare patches on greens that are surrounded by high trees). They need constant care. Count on mowing three times a week. You'll also have to water regularly and "syringe" (light applications of water) in hot periods. You'll have to aerate and topdress. It's no picnic.

But on the up side, when I look out my living-room window and see that little flagstick, I know the work was worthwhile. And maybe, just maybe, it'll help sell the house when the time comes to move. I can see the ad now: "Golfer's Special! Comes with green and pot bunker!"

Ten Schizophrenic Golf Courses

1 **Austin Country Club, Austin, Texas.** Five holes skirt a lake, the other 13 rest along ravines.

2 **Bodega Harbour Golf Club, Bodega Bay, California.** Splits its loops between mountains, links—and a housing development. Weirdest hole is the par five fifth, which doglegs twice, each time at 90 degrees, around huge bunkers.

3 **Carmel Valley Ranch, Carmel, California.** The 10th to the 14th take to the mountains; the rest is flat.

4 **The Creek Club, Locust Valley, New York.** Get through the first five holes fast. They're uninspiring parkland. The course begins at the sixth, when you head toward Long Island Sound and a stretch of marvelous seaside holes.

5 **Golspie Golf Club, Golspie, Scotland.** North of Dornoch—an area most golfers have yet to tread—lies this part-links, part-moorland layout.

6 **Hillside Golf Club, Southport, England.** The front nine is flat, the back takes off into sandhills.

7 **Inverness Golf Club, Toledo, Ohio.** Donald Ross built 14 holes in the early part of the century; George and Tom Fazio redid four in the 1970s. The difference in years pales next to the difference in style.

8 **Ojai Valley Country Club, Ojai, California.** The front nine is nothing; the back nine is an adventure through ravines. Or maybe it's the other way round; the club keeps reversing the nines.

9 **Pacific Grove Muni Golf Club, Pacific Grove, California.** The front nine is as close to Scottish as you get: rolling, duneland holes and not a lot spent on maintenance. The back nine, tightly laid out among trees and homes, you can miss.

10 **Spyglass Hill, Pebble Beach, California.** Similar deal. First five in sandy wastes, the rest running through trees.

—Tom Doak

Schizophrenic Spyglass: part waterside, part woodland.

Go Whole Hog—Build Your Own Golf Course

But you don't need a full-scale 18-holer. Here's an interesting story of a young man from Texas.

McAlister's 9th green. Also the 1st, 4th, and 7th. (See diagram.)

They come from miles around, from surrounding states, to this golf course hacked from forest and scrub in the countryside of eastern Texas. To a golf course that was named the most unique in the Lone Star State by a panel of experts convened by the *Dallas Morning News* which included Ben Crenshaw, Byron Nelson, Charlie Coody and Don January. To a golf course with only two greens—but nine holes, seven tee boxes, six bunkers, three fairways, two drop areas, two large lakes, three-quarters of a mile of concrete cart path and a dammed creek that is frequently referred to as "that *damned* creek."

The course's owner and builder is Mike McAlister, boss of the Sulphur Springs–based Lone Star Chemical Company and as good an example as any of an enthusiastic golfer who wanted to build his own golf course . . . and did. He accomplished the task simply by doing his homework, following instructions from experts and rolling up his sleeves and breaking a bucket or two of sweat himself.

Originally, McAlister wanted only to give guests at his weekend spread outside Sulphur Springs, Texas, what he thought was the best view of his property, from the far side of a lake behind his house. McAlister figured he could "lure" them across the water by building a golf green they would hit to.

Two years later, the McAlister Ranch Golf and Country Club was complete, and it's about as ingenious a piece of golf-course architecture as has been designed—and a blue print for anyone who has an inkling to build his own course.

By an intricate routing pattern, McAlister has managed to concoct a 3,270-yard layout with three par threes, three par fours and three par fives. With only two greens, you'll recall. The secret, McAlister says, is in having nine actual holes. "Five on the first green and four on the second," he explains. "Two groups play at any one time. We normally have six to a group and play a three-man team scramble. The lead group plays to the first green, then replaces the pin when they're done. Now, as they play to the second green, the second group plays to the first. When the second group has holed out, it moves the pin *clockwise* to the next pin placement, so that when the first group plays to that green for their third hole, they'll play from a different tee box to a different flag. And so it goes. You play to the first green five times, and you'll finish there, and to the second green four times. You never play to the same hole from the same tee box, so you never play the same hole twice."

Construction really began back in 1978, when the Lone Star Chemical head office overlooked the fifth green of the Bent Tree Country Club in Dallas. Each day McAlister would watch the maintenance crew at work. When the idea began to germinate, McAlister proceeded to pick the brains of everyone from greenskeepers and club pros to caddies and friends about green construction and maintenance. He contacted the United States Golf Association on how to build a proper subsurface, Texas A&M University about soil testing and the best grasses for the area. "Before we began, I thought a green would have sufficient drainage if it had a sloping surface," McAlister says. "I guess not. Our putting surfaces are built over French drains filled with pipe and gravel, covered by a six-inch layer of more gravel, covered by a 12-inch layer of mortar sand mixed with 20 per-cent peat moss. The peat moss aids in moisture retention to give the correct porosity so the surface moisture drains through the French drains properly."

To clear forest so dense that only the hungriest coyote would have ventured in, McAlister contracted a local firm to bulldoze and to dig and dam the water hazards. (The dirt from one the lakes helped shape much of the course's features, as well as the lighted putting green he still maintains in his yard.) McAlister then bought a track loader, backhoe, dump truck and a tractor with disc and ploughs, and completed most of the remaining work with the help of some friends.

"We root plowed, limed, deep disced and sprigged and dragged the fairways ourselves," he says. Before applying the final touches—the putting surfaces—McAlister contracted a Dallas company to install an irrigation system.

Finally, when the course was finished, McAlister traded in the heavy machinery for a fairway mower and a green mower and a

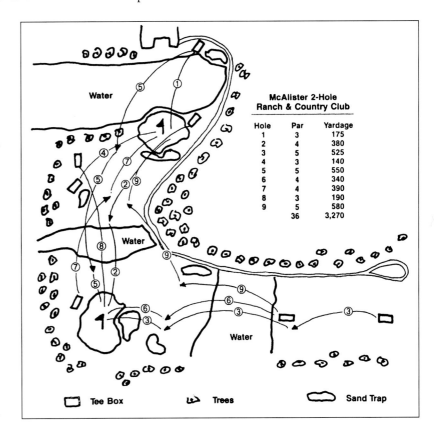

McAlister 2-Hole
Ranch & Country Club

Hole	Par	Yardage
1	3	175
2	4	380
3	5	525
4	3	140
5	5	550
6	4	340
7	4	390
8	3	190
9	5	580
	36	3,270

Tee Box   Trees   Sand Trap

gasoline-powered, three-wheel bunker rake. He still makes use of that stuff.

McAlister began playing on the course in 1981, held a small tournament for friends in 1983 and a year later launched what has become one of the hottest tickets on the Texan golfing calendar: the four-day "McAlister Two-Hole Ranch and Country Club Championship." The field is made up of McAlister's golfing friends, Lone Star Chemical customers, most of the pros from Dallas-area country clubs (and some who have since moved on to greener pastures farther afield) and various sporting personalities. Coming by an invitation is tough. It helps if you've coached at a local university, for instance. Darrell Royal, who won a few NCAA number-one ratings in football for the University of Texas, is a regular.

The championship is a four-day affair, but each team plays on only one day. During the rest of the weekend, those who have played or have yet to play join a mass of hecklers.

Local guests post scores on Thursday. Out-of-town guests roll in Friday; some play that day. That evening, McAlister's wife, Judy, stages a ladies' putting contest. The resident greenskeeper and estate manager, Junior Horton, runs continuous hayrides. Sam White, the legendary Texan bar-b-que king, keeps everyone's plate filled. A fishing contest is held over the entire weekend and is usually won by former Dallas Cowboys defensive end Randy White. "He *attacks* fish," McAlister says.

By Saturday afternoon, the gallery is up to 400. McAlister owns six golf carts and rents another 50 for the shindig, but many guests bring their own.

McAlister's own group is always the last to tee off, around 3 P.M. Sunday. "And let me tell you," he says, "it is *not* easy playing in front of my best friends after two nights of partying. To win a nine-hole golf tournament with a scramble format, *every* team member has to be on to win."

McAlister has been known to win because he practices the pin positions for weeks in advance and likes to team himself with the better players. But that's his prerogative. He built the course, he built the tournament and when the weekend is over, he has usually solicited enough donations to present a check, usually for more than $4,000, to a local charity that helps underprivileged children.

"It as one good friend has always maintained," McAlister says, " 'If you build a house of quality in the woods, the world will beat a path to your door.' "

As If Bunkers Weren't Enough . . .
Some of the more unusual hazards to be found on the world's golf courses:

Hazard	Where You Can Find It
Caves	The 18th at Barton Creek Club, Austin, Texas; the 6th at the Pete Dye Club, Clarksburg, West Virginia
Chalk Pit	third, Royal Eastbourne Golf Club, Eastbourne, England
Church	fourth, West Cornwall, St. Ives, England
Goats	All over Lahinch Golf Club, County Clare, Ireland
Gully (midfairway!)	15th, Boat of Garten, Boat of Garten, Scotland
Out of Bounds Across Hole (instead of lining it)	18th, Ganton, near Scarborough, England
Racetrack	Musselburgh Old Links, Musselburgh, Scotland; Northumberland Golf Club, High Gosforth Park, England
Road (current)	17th, St. Andrews (Old), St. Andrews, Scotland
Road (Roman)	12th, Royal Cinque Ports, Deal, England
Sinkhole	12th, Nefyn & District Golf Club, Morfa Nefyn, Wales
Thermal Vent	ninth, Rotorua Golf Club, Rotorua, New Zealand
Wild Horses	All over Pennard, near Swansea, Wales

—Tom Doak

Where to Find . . . the Information You Need to Build

Both the United States Golf Association and the National Golf Foundation distribute guides and pamphlets that will help you build your own practice green, bunker or golf course. All that is needed is:

a. space
b. the necessary tools
c. a patient spouse; or one who likes to build golf courses
d. slightly green fingers.

UNITED STATES GOLF ASSOCIATION

To order, call (908) 234-2300 or (800) 336-4446.

Specifications for a Method of Putting Green Construction
It's exactly what it says it is. Since it was first written years ago, a videotape has been produced to accompany it.
Cost: $2.50 for the pamphlet, $19.95 for the video (VHS or Beta)

Golf Course and Grounds Irrigation Drainage
You can't know enough about water on a golf course.
Cost: $43 (book)

A little light reading for the backyard greenskeeper.

Turfgrass Management (Revised Edition)
A.J. Turgeon's illustrated guide to turfgrass care.
Cost: $48

Green Section Record
Basically a magazine for those who operate golf courses, it comes out six times a year.
Cost: $9 per year

Turfgrass: Science and Culture
This is the classic reference guide to turfgrass, by James B. Beard.
Cost: $45

Turf Management for Golf Courses
A reference book by Beard on basic turfgrass cultivation and management.
Cost: $59.95

NATIONAL GOLF FOUNDATION

All of these publications are available from the NGF, 1150 South U.S. Highway One, Jupiter, FL 33477; (800) 733-6006.
A useful way to accumulate information is to purchase some of the NGF's "Executive Summaries." They range from two to four pages long, deal with numerous topics from ball flight laws to golf vacations, and cost $2, with a minimum order of $10. Let's say you want to spend the minimum and only on summaries that deal with building your own golf course or practice green. Here's a sample, along with the reference number you should note when ordering:

How to Build and Maintain a Practice Green (GC-8)
Sand Bunker Design, Construction and Maintenance (GC-28)
Building Concrete Cart Paths (GC-61)
Selecting Bunker Sand (GC-76)
Golf Course Irrigation—Design and Application (GC-4A)

A complete list is available from the NGF at the above address. Below are some other books sold via the NGF.

Planning and Building the Golf Course
Covers planning, different kinds of golf course design, guidelines on irrigation and information on construction.

Planning and Developing a Private Golf Facility
Comprises seven reports which, if bought separately, would cost more than $600. The reports include such NGF research reports as "The Golf Operations Handbook," "Golf Participation in the U.S.," and the "Golf Course Maintenance Report." It is designed to give a complete picture of where, when and what to develop as well as how.

The Evolution of the Modern Green
Explains how to get the best putting surfaces, and how to maintain them. Also analyzes what has gone into the creation of the modern green.

Turf Irrigation Manual
Uses more than 250 illustrations to take you through how to design and execute an irrigation system.

Rules

....

The Original Rules of Golf—and What They've Become Today

The Rules of Golf can be traced back to 1744, when the Honourable Company of Edinburgh Golfers (the first known golf club, which now roosts at Muirfield Golf Club, to the east of the Scottish capital) persuaded the city fathers to put up a trophy that members would compete for annually. To the Honourable Company, the "Silver Club" meant formal recognition. But in order to stage the tournament equitably, the club had to draw up a code of conduct.

The first "Code of Rules" amounted to 13 "articles," and remarkably (or perhaps not so remarkably, depending on your point of view) many of the original rules remain virtually unchanged today.

Of course, they have been added to. Golfing man has an astounding knack for debating and complicating, normally to get an edge. Today's rules, including appendices and indexes, stretch to 130 pages. The *Decisions on the Rules of Golf,* sort of a supreme-cum-appellate court for situations not immediately clarified in the rules themselves, are included in an inch-thick "booklet" that is almost 500 pages long.

Herewith the original articles with their closest living relatives, and comments:

1. YOU MUST TEE YOUR BALL WITHIN ONE CLUB'S LENGTH OF THE HOLE.

Rule 11 today is totally devoted to the "Teeing Ground," the progenitor of which was this area within a clublength of the hole. Of course, in the old days they didn't have double and triple mowers cutting putting surfaces to an eighth of an inch. The rules first referred to an actual teeing ground in 1875.

2. YOUR TEE MUST BE ON THE GROUND.

This one doesn't exist any more. Understand that the Honourable Company didn't use wooden tee pegs; those wouldn't be invented until 1922. They instead used little piles of sand or dirt. How this could be any place but on the ground is not clear. Maybe the original rulesmakers had been tippling too much claret during lunch.

3. YOU ARE NOT TO CHANGE THE BALL YOU STRIKE OFF THE TEE.

Today's Rule 15-1 is almost identical: "A player must hole out with the ball played from the teeing ground unless a Rule permits him to substitute another ball." Now if you whack your ball out of shape or blade it so badly it smiles at you, you can replace it; no such luck for the original players. Note also that the pro tours today invoke an indirectly related rule that dictates that players must play only one *type* of ball during a round—same manufacturer, same brand, same cover material, same compression.

4. YOU ARE NOT TO REMOVE STONES, BONES OR ANY BREAK CLUB, FOR THE SAKE OF PLAYING YOUR BALL, EXCEPT UPON THE FAIR GREEN AND THAT ONLY WITHIN A CLUB'S LENGTH OF YOUR BALL.

Today we refer to "Stones, Bones or any Break Club"—what was it these people had with their capital letters?—as "loose impediments." They're natural objects that aren't growing or fixed to something, and we can move them anywhere on the course except in hazards. But if our ball moves when we're moving any L.I.s within one clublength of the ball, we're penalized.

Note that we have it easier than our forefathers (don't we always?). Say a fallen branch lay between an Honourable Company golfer and the hole, about 10 feet in front of him. He was stymied. We can roll it out of the way and flail for home. It's all in Rule 23.

5. IF YOUR BALL COME AMONG WATTER OR ANY WATTERY FILTH, YOU ARE AT LIBERTY TO TAKE OUT YOUR BALL AND BRINGING IT BEHIND THE HAZARD AND TEEING IT, YOU MAY PLAY IT WITH ANY CLUB AND ALLOW YOUR ADVERSARY A STROKE, FOR SO GETTING OUT YOUR BALL.

If you've ever wondered why you have to drop your ball *behind* a hazard after hitting into it, look no further than original article 5. Personally, I prefer the original terminology. Can you imagine the CBS broadcasters whispering about the "wattery filth" around the 13th green at Augusta National?

Note also that the player hitting into the wattery filth did not add a stroke. Instead, his partner was awarded a free swipe. The reason is that the original rules were drawn up for match play; total strokes for the round mattered little.

6. IF YOUR BALLS BE FOUND ANYWHERE TOUCHING ONE ANOTHER YOU ARE TO LIFT THE FIRST BALL, TILL YOU PLAY THE LAST.

Rule 22 today is almost identical. If there's another ball in your way, get whoever hit it to mark it and lift it.

7. AT HOLING, YOU ARE TO PLAY YOUR BALL HONESTLY FOR THE HOLE, AND NOT PLAY UPON YOUR ADVERSARY'S BALL, NOT LYING IN YOUR WAY TO THE HOLE.

This one has all but disappeared. The idea was to stop you playing billiards with your opponent's ball. Nor were you to leave your ball between your opponent's ball and the hole, a practice known as a "stymie" that was outlawed in 1950. Nowadays players mark and lift on the green, so there is no need for the original rule.

8. IF YOU SHOULD LOSE YOUR BALL, BY ITS BEING TAKEN UP, OR ANY OTHER WAY YOU ARE TO GO BACK TO THE SPOT, WHERE YOU STRUCK LAST, AND DROP ANOTHER BALL, AND ALLOW YOUR ADVERSARY A STROKE FOR THE MISFORTUNE.

We call it "stroke and distance." If you lose your ball, you go back to where you played it from and hit again. We add a penalty stroke but, as noted before, the originals gave the opponent a free shot.

At this juncture, I'd like to applaud the Honourable Company for including the word "misfortune" in their rules. Lawmakers today are not nearly as understanding.

9. NO MAN AT HOLING HIS BALL IS TO BE ALLOWED TO MARK HIS WAY TO THE HOLE WITH HIS CLUB OR ANYTHING ELSE.

Today's Rule 8-2 prohibits you from "Indicating the Line of Play." It also prohibits you from touching the line of a putt, which is basically what original article 9 was all about.

10. IF A BALL BE STOPP'D BY ANY PERSON, HORSE, DOG, OR ANYTHING ELSE, THE BALL SO STOPP'D MUST BE PLAYED WHERE IT LIES.

We know this as a "Rub of the Green." In other words, tough luck if your ball hits something. However, if it happens on the putting green, we have to cancel the stroke and replay it, which is just as well given the proliferation of horses and dogs on putting greens today. We also refer to this as "Ball in Motion Deflected or Stopped by Outside Agency."

Don't you love the way the original article capitalized the words "Horse" and "Dog," but not the word "person"? These Honourable Company golfers had the darndest priorities, didn't they?

11. *If you draw your Club, in order to Strike and proceed so far in the Stroke, as to be bringing down your Club: If then your Club shall break, in any way, it is to be Accounted a Stroke.*

A stroke today is defined as "the forward movement of the club made with the intention of fairly striking at and moving the ball." Today's Rules don't cover a club breaking on the down-swing, but the decisions on the rules do. Decision 14/3 determines that a player whose club breaks on the downswing, and who misses the ball, must count the stroke because he *intended* to hit the ball. He probably intended to buy better equipment, too.

12. *He whose Ball lyes farthest from the Hole is obliged to play first.*

This sounds like the Rule of Golf that Moses brought down from Mount Sinai. And, like the other Ten Commandments, it's still around, but this one is disguised as "Rule 10: Order of Play." The Rule is a hell of a lot more complicated now, but the principle remains: Farthest from the hole plays first.

13. *Neither Trench, Ditch or Dyke, made for the Presentation of the Links, nor the Scholar's Holes or the Soldier's Lines, shall be accounted a Hazard. But the Ball is to be taken out and Tee'd and play'd with any Iron Club.*

Don't be put off by the terms. These are just features on the course over which the Honourable Company would compete for the Silver Club. That this particular geography would require certain exceptions to generally agreed rules proves that "Local Rules," which today occupy eight pages in the Rules of Golf and can be found on scorecards everywhere, were necessary from the get-go.

For the record, the first Silver Club was won by John Rattray, a surgeon who also happened to notarize the original articles and who later served as surgeon-general in the ill-fated army of Bonnie Prince Charlie during the Jacobite rebellion of 1745. For his efforts, he was appointed the inaugural captain of the Honourable Company.

Answers on a Postcard, Please

The Metropolitan Golf Association, which covers the New York-New Jersey-Connecticut area, issues a quiz each year comprised of 25 questions to the more than 200 rules and tournament officials on the MGA roster, as well as to member clubs and other local and regional golf organizations around the country.

What the other organizations do with it then is their business. The MGA officials, however, must send their answers in to the MGA. The MGA judges the answers, rates the questions in order of difficulty and sends the results back to the officials with a complete report on how each official fared.

Below are a dozen questions from a recent quiz. See how you fare. The answers are on page 88. Don't worry if you don't do well. Few answer all the questions correctly.

Rules of Golf Quiz

1 In a match, player A's tee shot may be lost or out of bounds. Player B, before he himself plays from the tee, goes forward to determine the status of player A's ball.
A. Player B incurs a penalty of loss of hole.
B. Player B is within his rights.

2 In stroke play, a competitor played out of turn from the teeing ground. When informed of his error, he puts another ball into play.
A. There is no penalty.
B. The second ball is in play under penalty of stroke and distance.

3 In a stroke play championship, the competition was conducted on only two nines of a 27-hole golf course. (The third unused nine was not classified as out of bounds.) After an errant tee shot on one of the holes, a player's ball came to rest on one of the unused putting greens. The player, deciding that it was not a "wrong putting green", played his next stroke from where the ball had come to rest.
A. The player has proceeded properly.
B. The player incurred a penalty of two strokes.

4 A player declared his ball unplayable and dropped his ball within two club-lengths of the spot where it lay. The ball rolled and came to rest in the original position at which the ball was called unplayable.
A. The player may re-drop without penalty.
B. The player must again invoke the unplayable ball Rule, incurring an additional penalty stroke.

5 In a match, a player searches for his ball for five minutes and cannot find it. He continues his search, finds the ball and plays it.
A. The player loses the hole.
B. The player incurs a two-stroke penalty.

6 In stroke play, player A's ball goes into a water hazard and is not found. Using her best judgement in determining the point where the ball last crossed the hazard margin, player A drops a ball under the water hazard Rule. Player A's marker and a fellow-competitor agrees with that judgement. Before player A plays her next stroke, player C, another competitor in the group, says that the ball last crossed the hazard margin some 20 yards away and the ball is then found there. Player A then picks up the ball she dropped in the wrong place and drops it in the correct spot and plays it.

A. The player incurs a penalty of two strokes.

B. There is no penalty.

7 In the same circumstances as described in Question 6, player A played from the wrong place before the original ball was found.

A. The player incurs a penalty of two-strokes.

B. There is no penalty.

8 In stroke play, two competitors, having completed play on the 11th hole, in error played from the 15th tee. They completed the hole and then played from the 16th tee. Before playing their second shots, they realized their mistake, returned to the 12th tee and completed the round. On reporting the incident, the competitors were each penalized two strokes, as the Committee interpreted the "next teeing ground" referred to in Rule 11-4b to be that of the 12th hole.

A. The players were disqualified.

B. The two-stroke penalty was the correct one.

9 In stroke play, both A and B are carrying 14 clubs. On one hole, player A, who had mistakenly left his putter at the previous green, borrows player B's putter and uses it. He then returns the putter to player B who uses it himself.

A. Only player A incurs a penalty of two strokes.

B. Players A and B each incur a penalty of two strokes.

10 In stroke play, a competitor, after announcing his intention to do so, lifted his ball to check for damage, showed it to his marker and claimed it was unfit for play. His marker disputed his claim, but the competitor insisted on substituting and playing another ball. Before completion of the hole, a Committee member was consulted and he ruled that the ball taken out of play was not unfit for play.

A. The player incurs a penalty of one stroke and must put the original ball back into play.

B. The player incurs a total penalty of two strokes and must hole out with the substituted ball.

11 In a match, a player wins the fifth hole with a wrong ball and the error is not discovered until the players had driven from the next tee. The opponent claims the fifth hole, the one on which the error had occurred.

A. Since the players had played from the next tee, the claim is invalid.

B. The opponent wins the fifth hole.

12 In stroke play, a competitor's ball came to rest on an artificially-surfaced road. The competitor, not sure whether the road was an obstruction or an integral part of the course, invoked the second ball Rule and announced that he wished his score with the second ball to count. He played the original ball as it lay and dropped the second ball almost two club-lengths from the nearest point of relief, instead of within one club-length, and played it.

A. The score with the original ball counts.

B. The second ball is in play with a two-stroke penalty for playing from the wrong place.

MGA Rules of Golf Quiz—Answers

Question	Answer	Applicable Rule/Decision	Why
1.	A	Rule 6-7 Dec. 9-2/16	Player B is in breach of Rule 6-7 (Undue Delay) by his action. A player may make such a determination only if it can be done without unduly delaying play.
2.	B	Rule 27-1 Dec. 10-2c/1	When the competitor put another ball into play, the original ball was lost.
3.	B	Rule 25-3	The definition of "wrong putting green" under Rule 25-3 states that if a ball lies on "*a*" putting green other than the hole being played, the player *shall* lift the ball and drop it off the green.
4.	B	Rule 20-4 Dec. 28/3	The ball was in play when it was dropped (Rule 20-4) and the additional penalty was correct.
5.	A	Rule 15-2 Dec. 27/8	After five minutes, the ball was lost and out of play. When the player played the ball which was out of play, he played a wrong ball.
6.	B	Rule 26-1b Dec. 26-1/16	Since the player had not played the ball from the wrong place, she could lift it and drop it in the right place, without penalty.
7.	B	Rule 26-1b Dec. 26-1/17	Player A must continue to play with the ball dropped in the wrong place. The player made a honest judgement when she dropped and played the ball from the wrong place and does not incur a penalty.
8.	A	Rule 11-4b Dec. 11-4b/4.5	When the competitors played from the 16th tee, they had played from the next teeing ground" and could not correct their error. Therefore, they were disqualified.
9.	B	Rule 4-4a and 4-4b Dec. 4-4b/2	Since player A started the round with 14 clubs, he incurs a penalty of two strokes for having an extra club. When player B played a stroke with his own putter, he too incurs a penalty of two strokes, for only the borrower may use such club for the remainder of the round.
10.	B	Rule 5-3 and 15-1 Dec. 5-3/3	Under Rules 5-3 and 15-1, the player is penalized a total penalty of two strokes and must hole out with the substituted ball.
11.	B	Rule 9-2 Dec. 9-2/8	Since the player failed to inform his opponent promptly that he had incurred a penalty for playing a wrong ball, he is deemed to have given wrong information even though he was not aware that he had incurred a penalty.
12.	A	Rule 3-3b Dec. 3-3/5	Rule 3-3b states in part: "If the Rulesallow the procedure selected in advance by the competitor, the score with the ball selected shall be his score for the hole." In this case, the procedure selected in advance (i.e., dropping the ball almost two club-lengths from the nearest point of relief) is not allowed under the Rules. Accordingly, the score with the original ball counts.

My Favorite Decisions

Every so often a golfer gets a break from a salamander.

An honest-to-god *salamander*. It says so right here in the *Decisions on the Rules of Golf*, a 500-page booklet that, as the name suggests, contains the United States Golf Association's verdicts on the weighty legal dilemmas that threaten to consume the game.

On page 332, under the heading "25/22 Salamander," the USGA's crack Rules Committee addresses the question, "Is a salamander mound a cast or runway made by a burrowing animal?" The answer is vital because a golfer is entitled to relief from casts or runways caused by burrowing animals. Of course, the *real* value of the decision is that those unsuspecting school kids who skipped their biology homework to bone up on the Rules of Golf will inadvertently discover that . . .

Yes! The USGA *does* consider the salamander a burrowing animal. "Relief is available under Rule 25-1b, unless the ball lies in a water hazard," reads the decision.

That is but one offbeat decision in what can be a fascinating, if initially forbidding, book. Granted, not all the decisions deal with arcane situations involving amphibians. Many deal with thoroughly technical matters, such as "Prohibiting Employment of Umbrella Carrier." Others deal with unbelievably simple situations, such as "Competitor's Ball Played by Fellow-Competitor; Competitor Substitutes Another Ball at Wrong Place, Plays It and Then Abandons It and Plays Out Original Ball from Right Place."

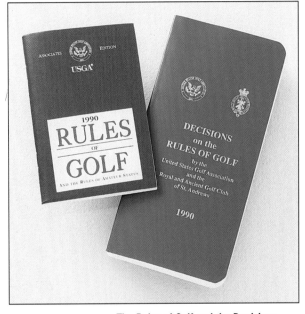

The Rules of Golf and the Decisions on the Rules of Golf: the game's holy books, except in your foursome and mine.

Shoot 'em both, I say.

In fairness to the USGA, it should be pointed out that all the decisions affect the game to some extent, and it's not their fault that they have to come up with the answers. It's usually the *questions* that are outrageous, the sort that should have the Rules Committee lobbying Congress to pass a law punishing any flagrant lack of common sense. Picture the salamander-man writing his letter. Now picture the USGA staffer reading it. ("Good god! Now we're being quizzed about *salamanders!*")

So as a favor to you connoisseurs of esoterica out there—and you know who you are—what follows are some of my favorite decisions from one of my honest-to-god favorite golf books:

14-1/7 USING MORE THAN ONE CLUB TO MAKE STROKE

Q. A player, whose ball was lodged in a bush, swung at the ball with three clubs to minimize the chance of missing it. Is this permissible?

A. No. Rule 14-1 requires that the ball be struck at with "the head of the club;" the word "club" is in the singular, the player was in breach of this Rule when he swung at the ball with three clubs.

I always marvel at how the USGA reaches its decisions. They penalized the player not because he tried to gain an unfair edge, but for his wanton disregard for *grammar*.

15/1 STROKE MISSES WRONG BALL

Q. A player swings at and misses a wrong ball. What is the ruling?

A. Since the player made a stroke with a wrong ball, he lost the hole in match play (Rule 15-2) or incurred a two-stroke penalty in stroke play (Rule 15-3).

It's not the question or the answer that's precious; it's the title of the decision. What ball was he *supposed* to miss?

23/6 DEAD LAND CRAB

Q. A ball lodges against a dead land crab in a bunker. May the crab be removed without penalty?

A. No. A dead land crab is a natural object and thus a loose impediment and not an obstruction. Removal of the crab would be a breach of Rule 13-4.

Just make sure the superintendent doesn't see you showering his greens with pieces of rotting land crab. (Just to avoid confusion with the decision below, loose impediments cannot be removed from hazards, and a bunker is a hazard.)

23/8 WORM PARTIALLY UNDERGROUND

Q. Is a worm, when half on top of the surface of the ground and half below, a loose impediment which may be removed? Or is it fixed or solidly embedded and therefore not a loose impediment?

A. A worm which is half underground is not "fixed or growing" or "solidly embedded" within the meanings of those terms in the Definition of "Loose Impediments." Accordingly, such a worm may be removed under Rule 16-1a(i) or Rule 23.

Okay, I'll buy the answer, but how exactly do you determine how much of the worm is *under* the ground?

18-1/7 BALL IN PLASTIC BAG MOVES WHEN BAG BLOWN TO NEW POSITION BY WIND

Q. A player's ball comes to rest in a plastic bag that is lying on the ground . . . a gust of wind blows the bag and the ball to a new position . . . should the player drop the ball directly under the place where it originally lay in the bag or where it now lies in the bag?

A. Wind is not an outside agency. However, if an object being moved by the wind moves a ball, the object is an outside agency in the circumstances. In this case, the bag, not the wind, caused the ball to move. Accordingly, the player must drop the ball directly under the place where it originally lay in the bag.

I don't get it. Surely the wind made the ball move by making the bag move, because a bag sure can't move a ball on its own. On the other hand, if the ball hadn't been in the bag, it probably wouldn't have been moved by the wind. So the bag must be to blame. This is exactly why we have committees.

23/3 HALF-EATEN PEAR

Q. A half-eaten pear lies directly in front of a ball in a bunker and there is no pear tree in the vicinity of the bunker. In the circumstances, is the pear an obstruction rather than a loose impediment, in which case the player could remove it without penalty?

A. No. A pear is a natural object. When detached from a tree it is a loose impediment. The fact that a pear has been half-eaten and there is no pear tree in the vicinity does not alter the status of the pear.

And you thought pears didn't have status.

·   ·   ·

Finally, some bad news. In my research into this salamander controversy, I happened to stumble on the fact that there are "salamanders" and there are "mole salamanders."

The former is basically the newt family. Its Latin name is *salamandridae*. The latter deals with tiger salamanders, Pacific giant salamanders, axolotls and the like. The Latin name is *ambystomatidae*.

What I'm driving at is this. Does Decision 25/22 (above) refer to *ambystomatidae*, which most definitely are burrowing animals, or *salamandridae*, which might not be and therefore would not leave any runways or casts?

Looks like the Rules Committee is going to have to come to another decision.

·   ·   ·

The book Decisions on the Rules of Golf *is available from the United States Golf Association at a cost of $12 to members of the USGA Members Program and regional and state amateur golf associations, and $15 to everyone else. Call (908) 234-2300 or (800) 336-4446.*

The Six Most Despised Rules

1. RULE 27-1: BALL LOST OR OUT OF BOUNDS.

Why the rule is despised: Because of the penalty for losing a ball or hitting out of bounds.

Take these two situations:

1. A golfer, Wild Wally, sends a ball screaming 50 yards out into a water hazard that lies to the right of the fairway, about 100 yards out from the tee. He can now drop his ball 100 yards from the tee and be hitting his third shot.

2. A golfer, Steady Stan, hits a fairly good drive that bobs and rolls for 260 yards but comes to rest nine inches out of bounds. According to the rules, he must play his third from where he played his first, which is to say 100 yards behind Wild Wally.

Why the rule exists: Because losing a ball or hitting out of bounds (beyond the jurisdiction of the course, as it were) is considered a more serious crime than hitting into an area designed to make play more difficult. There is also no way to determine proper procedure for a ball that is lost. You can't drop within two clublengths of where you lost it, for example, because if you knew where you'd lost it, it wouldn't be lost—it would merely be unplayable. In addition, a player hitting into a water hazard retains the option of playing from the hazard even if it is 20 or 30 feet deep; he's just not likely to, as death by drowning is rarely in his plans. A golfer who loses his ball, on the other hand, has no option at all but to start afresh—and that amounts to stroke and distance.

2. RULE 13-4B: THE PLAYER SHALL NOT TOUCH THE GROUND IN THE HAZARD OR WATER IN THE WATER HAZARD WITH A CLUB OR OTHERWISE.

Why the rule is despised: Because it deals with your touching the ground at any point in the hazard, even if you are nowhere near your ball or not in the process of hitting it.

Waiting to play from a hazard in the PGA Tour's Tucson Open one year, Mark McCumber leaned on his club, an understandable practice given the furnace-like conditions you can encounter in that part of the country. Taking a breather cost him two strokes.

In addition, Rule 13-4c says that you can't touch a loose impediment in a hazard. Fuzzy Zoeller once picked up a boulder to use as a bridge across a stream and was penalized two strokes for his initiative.

And if you're waiting to play, don't even consider chewing a strand of grass as you mull over your shot. Steve Elkington, the young Australian pro, did that once and found himself dining on a two-stroke penalty.

Why the rule exists: Because the rules cannot differentiate between someone deliberately improving his stance, lie or "area of intended swing" and someone who is innocent of any premeditated crime.

3. RULE 15: PLAYING A WRONG BALL.

Why the rule is despised: Basically it's not the golfer's fault that there are too many Top Flites and Titleists making the rounds. The penalty for playing a wrong ball—two strokes in stroke play or loss of hole in match play—is despised for much the same reason. The ultimate penalty—disqualification if you do not correct your mistake by the time you hit from the next tee or leave the final green—is despised because there is very little time to make amends.

Why the rule exists: Hitting someone else's ball could ruin someone else's performance.

4. RULE 14-4: STRIKING A BALL MORE THAN ONCE.

Why this rule is despised: Because the second hit means an automatic penalty stroke added to the original hit for a total of two strokes—yet the second hit almost always means a ball flying off in the wrong direction.

Why this rule exists: To stop you from hitting fungos.

5. RULE 16-1C: REPAIR OF HOLE PLUGS AND BALL MARKS.

Why this rule is despised: Because it keeps you from repairing ball marks on your line to the hole.

Why this rule exists: Because if it didn't, every Tom, Dick and Greg Norman would be gardening 'til dark.

6. RULE 4-3: NO FOREIGN MATERIAL SHALL BE APPLIED TO THE CLUBFACE FOR THE PURPOSE OF INFLUENCING THE BALL.

Why this rule is despised: Because there is evidence that if you apply a thin coat of clear nail varnish to the face of a driver, filling in the grooves, and then smooth the face with fine sandpaper, your ball will *zip!!*

Why this rule exists: Because there is evidence that if you apply a thin coat of clear nail varnish to the face of a driver, filling in the grooves, and then smooth the face with fine sandpaper, your ball will *zip!!*

Five Rules That Ought to Be Ignored

(except, of course, in formal competition)

1. RULE 10: ORDER OF PLAY

We're talking stroke play here. Although there is no penalty for accidentally playing out of turn in stroke play, golfers who *formally agree* that it's kosher to play out of turn are supposed to be disqualified.

What bunk.

Under most circumstances, which is to say anything that is not formal competition, order of play matters little. Most amateur golfers are more concerned with scoring as low as possible and playing the golf course as well as possible.

There may be some merit to giving someone who has made low score on the previous hole the consummate honor of getting to hit first from the next tee. You could even genuflect as he goes through his preshot routine.

Or perhaps there may be one of those rare occasions when a player has a putt to break his personal best or a putt to win a grudge match, and there is a longer putt on much the same line. He prefers to wait and go to school on the longer one. Fair enough.

But generally, here's what you should do: If you're first to the tee, tell your fellow golfers, "I'll just hit." If you're ready to play in the fairway, in a hazard or in the rough, do likewise. As long as you don't interfere with another player's swing, it won't make much of a difference.

Once on the green, keep putting until either you hole your ball or another player mutters, "That's good." There are several courses that have ordered players to practice "continuous putting" and swear that it speeds up play.

Then congratulate yourselves for getting done in under four hours.

2. RULE 4-4: MAXIMUM OF FOURTEEN CLUBS

Unless you're carrying your own or have a caddie with a bad back, take along as many as you want.

In most cases, there are only thirteen clubs that the average player can hit with any authority: The driver, a couple of fairway woods, the 3-iron (debatable), 4- through 9-iron and three wedges. If someone wants to fill out his set with four or five putters, let him. He (or she) probably can't putt anyway.

3. RULE 27-1: BALL LOST OR OUT OF BOUNDS

It's not the rule we object to: If you thwack your ball out of the golf course, you should be penalized.

We're more concerned with the practice of club committees placing out of bounds stakes *within* the boundaries of a golf course.

Normally this is done to protect players on an adjoining fairway, yet there is no evidence that shows these players need more protection from others than they do from those in their own four-ball.

Instead, when out of bounds is marked in a "maybe" situation, golfers neglect to hit provisional balls, then slow play down by eventually observing stroke and distance, then get into unnecessary arguments about how they should proceed and why the hell these white stakes were there in the first place.

Certain exceptions exist—almost. OB often segregates a hole and a practice range, the idea being to stop players from running in pursuit of a wayward shot as a hail of range balls descends. Wouldn't a high fence makes better sense? There are also occasions when residences are next to the hole. Why not mark these as lateral hazards? The color of a stake has yet to prevent a golfer from yanking a two-piece onto someone's deck.

4. RULE 19-2: BALL IN MOTION DEFLECTED OR STOPPED BY PLAYER, PARTNER, CADDIE OR EQUIPMENT

This carries a two-stroke penalty, or loss of hole in match play, but I just can't see where penalizing a player for endangering his or his caddie's life with a golf ball adds anything to the game.

Some may make the argument that abolishment of this rule would allow a caddie to go into the hole—so to speak—to field a ball that may be heading for a water hazard. I have no problem with that. My opponent will still get the penalty if it crosses the "margin" of the hazard but doesn't actually get wet—plus, he'll save three bucks on a new golf ball. Others may fear that a player may rake a putt that is about to trundle past the cup and down a 25-foot swale in a green. Sorry. Rule 1-2 already disqualifies a player for doing that.

But if I'm in a sandtrap and hammer the ball into the lip, whereupon it rebounds and hits me in the stomach:

A. I'm already so embarrassed that I'm not that eager to finish the hole anyway, and

B. I lose anyway, for if the ball hadn't hit me, it may have ended up sitting on the fairway in a perfect spot for me to chip in or make up-and-down a cinch (which was the original idea in the first place).

Now consider the poor caddie. He's two-bagging his third loop of the day. The first two loops stiffed him for the proper tip. It's the final hole, 97 degrees in the shade, and now some clown who made a fortune selling junk bonds to those who should have known better shanks an 8-iron and catches the poor chap on the back of the head. Not only is the player penalized, but if the caddie ever comes to, he will have to shoulder the blame for some rich jerk losing the hole and the entire day's wagers because of a shank.

And they say golf is a game of integrity.

5. RULE 23-1: LOOSE IMPEDIMENTS

According to this rule, a golfer is not allowed to remove or even touch natural objects—loose impediments—if his ball is in a hazard.

Fair enough. But let's say your ball is in a bunker, snug up against a stone. No, let's say a couple of stones. There is no way in Hades that you will be able to hit a decent recovery.

This situation has been a bone of contention between the game's lawmakers, the United States Golf Association and the Royal & Ancient Golf Club of St. Andrews, Scotland, for years. The Brits are in favor of removing large stones. They're aware that British courses tend to be in poorer shape than American courses for various reasons that include poor weather, smaller bankrolls and no real interest in spending thousands of quid on incessant small-stone removal. The USGA's position is that players will start removing every stone, little or large, because there's no way to determine where "large" begins.

My position is, "Why would you want to?" As someone who is worse in the sand with a $120 sand wedge than my four-year-old daughter is with a $5 plastic spade, I have long maintained that bunkers are supposed to be filled with sand only, that there is no place for stones in them, no matter the size. I believe that you should clean out any stone, whether little or large, because anything you can do to help out your overworked, underpaid golf course superintendent will be effort well spent.

No problem. You're welcome.

Three Rules That Are Ignored— but Shouldn't Be

1. RULE 27-2: PROVISIONAL BALL

You know the scene. Player hits out of bounds or into a thicket. Two things happen: Either the player says "I've got a bead on it," and off the group goes. Or else he'll say "Maybe I should hit another ball" and someone else in the group says "Nah, we'll find it."

In both cases, time and effort will be saved by a player hitting a provisional ball. It's the main reason one of the best rules in the book exists.

Let's take the first situation. If the player does have a bead on the ball, there still remains every chance he won't find it. Now he has to apologize to his group for holding up play and trot back to the tee with his tail between his legs.

In the second situation, the player knows he should have gone ahead with the provisional. Now he's mad at his *partners* when he has to head back.

And in each case, there is nothing more difficult or embarrassing than having to inform the group that's now on the tee that you've returned to hit another ball because the first one was hit so badly that you lost it. Now you have to hit with four less-than-sympathetic golfers wondering why you're out to spoil their day. And one of them is sure to say, "Why didn't you just hit a provisional?"

Good question.

2. RULE 13-1: BALL PLAYED AS IT LIES

Six words that strike contempt in the true golfer's heart:

"Are we rolling them over today?"

Few occasions exist when a golfer should not play the ball as it lies. There are those days when torrential rain makes play nigh impossible. If you go out in that weather, you deserve to make up the rules as you go along: Lift them, clean them and *throw* them into the hole if you want.

But the tendency is for greens committees to invoke "winter rules" when the temperature drops below 75 degrees. Now, for no apparent reason, golfers with perfectly decent lies start propping the ball up as though on a tee. They start to spit and polish balls

with no more than a smudgeon of dust on them. They have no right nor reason to do so.

Some golfers appease their guilt by rolling them only in the fairway of the hole being played, as though those who have played the proper shot should now need further help.

Lee Trevino once argued that rolling them over allows a player to hit a better shot and therefore enjoy the game more. But that denies the golfer the enjoyment of hitting the occasional wonder shot when he has no reason to do so—an infinitely better feeling, I'd say.

On a related note: Mulligans have about as much place in the game as winter rules.

3. RULE 18-5: BALL AT REST MOVED BY ANOTHER BALL

It is eminently fair that if a ball at rest is moved by an opponent's ball, it should be replaced in its original position.

Why? Because it's not fair that a player who has hit close to the hole should then have to hit from a position farther from the hole. Likewise, in the case of a ball being knocked closer, it is equally unfair that one player should gain an advantage out of a situation that was not his doing.

This rule is often ignored. Golfers' minds for some reason turn to bocce when one player's ball hits an opponent's. But the fact is that while the second player must play his ball as it lies, the first *must* replace his ball as close as possible to where it had earlier come to rest.

How to Join a Golf Club— Without Actually Joining a Golf Club

You form what is commonly known as a "golf club on wheels," or, officially, a "golf club without real estate."

This is an interesting new phenomenon that has arisen from there being too many golfers and not enough golf clubs to go around, and too many golf clubs asking too many dollars for the privilege of membership.

So groups of golfers—workmates, usually, but often just friends—are forming their own clubs. They don't have real estate (i.e., a clubhouse and locker-room), but they do meet all the provisions necessary for members to join the United States Golf Association's handicap system, which calculates and issues handicaps via regional organizations—which itself is a big reason for clubs on wheels existing in the first place.

All these clubs can then participate in competitions run by local golf organizations, run their own tournaments or leagues and, most important, can do so with the knowledge that everything is above board. No sandbagging. No "Put-me-down-for-a-seventeen" handicap estimates. And, come to think of it, no monthly restaurant minimums or random "assessments" that are so common when "real" golf clubs feel like hitting their members up for a chunk of change.

The only provisions laid down by the USGA are that a club have at least 10 members who play together regularly, and that they practice "peer review." The latter provision is designed to keep everyone honest and means basically that members must post scores that can be reviewed by other members and by an elected handicap chairman. In other words, if you are going to become part of the USGA's handicap system, you should at least have the decency to do things by the book.

Flamingo Gaze: no clubhouse, no greenskeeper, but a damned fine anagram.

The system works wonderfully. In the spring of 1989, for example, my colleagues at *Golf Magazine* formed the Flamingo Gaze (an anagram of the magazine title) Golf Club, partly to get yours truly an official handicap in the wake of my winning our annual editorial championship with a tremendously questionable 22—two years later I was an official 12—but also to accommodate those editors who either lived in New York City and did not have access to a "real" club or those who were not paid well enough to afford a club membership. Once we'd set aside a wall in one of our offices, thereafter known as the "Flamingo Gaze Room," and placed the handicap sheets on which each member would post his or her scores, we were off and running. Or playing, rather.

We began with a dozen members, but within a year enough salespeople and contributing editors had paid the $25 annual membership—which included a golf hat (loud pink)—to push the membership to 35. We also appointed two-time U.S. Open champion and playing editor Curtis Strange head professional, a position that Curtis accepted with customary grace and that his wife, Sarah, accepted with customary enthusiasm—within a month of his appointment, she'd sent a box of several hundred foam beer caddies, each emblazoned with our club logo (a flamingo) and the words "Curtis Strange—Head Pro."

The idea became infectious when we ran a column in June of that year, telling nonclubbers how to form their own. Within weeks, the USGA had received some 600 inquiries, about half of which cited Flamingo Gaze as inspiration. We also caught the attention of other clubs on wheels and soon were being challenged to matches. And we started a few traditions of our own. The Masters winners may have to don a fairly ugly green blazer, but that garment pales—literally—in comparison to the screaming pink jacket that goes to the unfortunate winner of our annual championship. With my new handicap I have yet to come within a lunar orbit of the thing.

For information on how to start your own club, contact the USGA and ask for their free booklet: "Bylaws for Clubs Without Real Estate." Phone: (908) 234-2300.

How to Figure Your Handicap

Nota bene, as they say in Italian circles: You can calculate your own handicap—or handicap index, as it is more accurately known—but you can't use it in competition. The folks at the United States Golf Association spent thousands of man-hours chained to computer terminals figuring out the best system and now guard it with the ferocity of a Minotaur. Or at least a phalanx of lawyers.

On the other hand, once you've joined their handicap system, they'll reveal the formula, and who's to stop you from sitting down with a calculator?

Before you calculate your handicap accurately, you must first understand how to return a score. To be more specific, you must understand "Equitable Stroke Control," or ESC.

ESC puts a lid on the amount of strokes that you can count on a hole (for handicapping purposes) and is designed to prevent an unearthly score on a hole or two from turning an otherwise accurate handicap into an aberration. Prior to January 1, 1993, a scratch golfer could not return anything higher than bogey. A one-handicapper was allowed one double bogey, a two-handicapper was allowed two, and so it went, up to the 18 handicappers who were restricted to 18 doubles, or one per hole if you're counting.

Things got interesting above 18. Those between 19 and 36 were allowed double on each hole and triple bogey on as many holes as their handicap exceeded 18 (a 24 was allowed 12 doubles and six triples, for example). Those over 36 were allowed four over on as many holes as their handicaps exceeded 36, and triple on the rest. Although they really should have considered taking up tennis.

I mention this only because that system made sense. Here's the new deal. Those with handicaps of zero to nine can return nothing higher than a six on a single hole; 10 to 19 returns seven or under; 20 to 29 returns eight; 30 to 39 returns nine; 40 to 49 returns 10; and 50 and above returns 11.

What this means is that a lousy player whose handicap is 35 is allowed six blows over par on a par three when the ball should have been burning a hole in his pocket after two. We'll see how the new system works out.

At any rate, having accurately recorded a score, the next step is to calculate a "differential." This is done by subtracting the Course Rating from your ESC-adjusted score (the Course Rating is the number a scratch golfer can be expected to shoot) and multiplying that by the ratio of 113 divided by the Slope Rating of the course played (the Slope Rating is a number that reflects the relative difficulty of a course for players of different ability; an average course is rated at 113).

Okay, let's do a test run. You shoot an 88 (adjusted) on a track with a Course Rating of 69.8 and a Slope Rating of 121. The calculation would be:

$$(88 - 69.8) \times \frac{113}{121} = 16.93$$

That's not your handicap, but we're getting there. Eventually you will post 20 scores and have 20 differentials. Take the 10 lowest and average them out. (On your way to 20 you'll use a proportionate amount of differentials.) When you've played more than 20 rounds, take the 10 lowest from the 20 *most recent* rounds.

Now, take that average and multiply it by .96. That, you arithmeticians out there, is what is known as your handicap index.

Why the .96 stuff? The USGA has many reasons, none of which I fully understand. One cynic has suggested that the hoi polloi at the USGA believes multiplying by a fraction expressed to two decimal points serves to bewilder the limited mental capabilities of the average PGA of America professional, but I won't go near that one.

At any rate, you should apply your handicap index to the Slope Rating at each course you play, and you'll find out what handicap to play off for a particular round.

There is, however, an easier way to reach a handicap index: Have someone do it for you, by joining a club that belongs to the USGA's handicap system or by forming your own club (page 95). It's worth it. Full details from the USGA at (908) 234-2300.

Speak Up! Or When It's a Crime to Stay Silent

Although an undeniable pleasure of playing golf is banter that floats between players, there is no denying that the golfer who chatters nonstop eventually runs the risk of having to ingest the forward areas of another golfer's FootJoys.

On the other hand, there may be occasions during a round of golf when, according to the Rules of Golf, a player *must* speak up. It's all a matter of keeping other players informed of what you're up to when a matter of procedure comes up.

▼ When you intend to hit a provisional ball—i.e., when you believe your existing, so to speak, ball is lost or out of bounds— you must tell your partners just that. "I'm gonna hit a provisional," is quite acceptable (just make sure you use the word "provisional"). If you don't speak up, the rest of your group has every right to consider the second ball the ball in play. In other words, you took the first ball to be lost and accepted the penalty.

▼ In match play, you must inform your opponent if you take a penalty stroke—unless he saw you following a procedure that obviously involved a penalty.

▼ If you believe that your ball is unfit for play—i.e., it is out of shape, cut or cracked—and you want to inspect it, you must tell the other players before you touch it. (You must also let the other players inspect it.)

▼ If you are inspecting another player's ball that may be unfit for play and you want to object to its removal, you must say so before he replaces it with another ball.

▼ If you have to lift your ball to identify it (which, by the way, you cannot do in a hazard), you must tell the other players. The rules also allow them to watch the whole procedure of lifting, identifying and replacing, so try and make it entertaining.

▼ If you're playing stroke play and you're not sure about proper procedure, you are allowed to play a second ball. But you must tell the other players—"fellow competitors" in this instance—before you play either ball. You must also tell the powers-that-be what happened when you finish your round and before you sign your card.

▼ In a similar vein, if you have any doubt about the correct score for a hole, you should discuss the situation with the powers-that-be before signing the card.

▼ Let's say you're carrying 22 clubs (some folks do!). The legal maximum is 14. You're on the third hole when the thought occurs to you, "Crikey! I forgot to take those eight extra clubs out of my bag!" You must now tell the other players which clubs you are optioning to the Triple-A locker and leave them untouched for the duration of the round. You'll also pick up a two-stroke penalty (or loss of hole in match play) for every hole played with the excess, with a maximum penalty of four strokes (or two holes). This can lead to the classic situation in match play in which a player ends up four holes down after only two have been played. While losing the first two holes, he was carrying too many clubs. So he lost two holes and was penalized two: four down with only 16 to play!

A Case for Slope

Since the early 1980s, the United States Golf Association has been cultivating and promulgating religiously its "Slope System."

It is a system that refutes the old, unchallenged credo that the discrepancy between a good golfer and a poor golfer, in terms of strokes, remains constant wherever they may play. The Slope System instead maintains that the discrepancy *grows* according to the difficulty of a course: A poor player will not only find trouble more easily, he will also take more shots to escape. Slope takes such factors into consideration and establishes handicaps *for a particular round.*

There's just one problem. While the system is in place throughout the country, it has still to be adopted by many golfers who shun it because:

1. They're unaware of it;
2. They refuse to use it because they're resistant to change; or
3. They are not completely sure *how* to use it and would rather leave it alone than learn it.

Most nonslopers probably fall into the third category, which is a shame since the Slope System is a simple system to use. Slope is simply the victim of a rotten moniker and a misperception on the part of the nation's golfers that in order to embrace the system they will have to replace the 3-iron in their bags with a slide rule.

Slope got its name from USGA officials with a better feel for numbers and charts than for public acceptance. When various performances by various handicaps on various courses were plotted during two years of research, beginning in 1978, the USGA's handicap experts noted that the graphs formed steady "slopes." The tougher the course, the greater the differential in scores and the steeper the slope on the graph. The easier the course, the gentler the slope.

The next strike was called against Slope when the USGA went to great lengths to describe how the system worked, something they were morally bound to do, though the game might have been better off if they had just played oligarchs and put the whole damn system in place, like it or not.

Ever have a computer buff explain to you how a hard drive works? This was the same. The USGA told people how each course was awarded a "Slope Rating," a number indicating difficulty according to hazards, length, topography, likely psychological effects, prevailing wind and so on. An average course would be assigned a rating of 113, an easy course a smaller number, down to about 90, a tough course a larger number, up to about 150. (Why 113 and not a round number like 100? Who knows? The USGA insists that 113 is the way to go.)

Meanwhile the existing system of "Course Ratings" would remain. They indicate what a *scratch* player should score on a course.

You got it. Things were getting confusing.

But not half as confusing as when the USGA informed golfers that instead of having a simple "handicap" they would now have a "Slope Handicap." And whenever they played—wherever they played—they were to look up their Slope Handicap (later changed to a "Handicap Index") on a "Course Handicap Table" posted in the locker room or pro shop and find out what their "Course Handicap" would be.

Now, they were told, if the Slope Rating is 113 (absolutely average) their Course Handicap would be identical to their Slope Handicap. Easy course? It would likely go down. Tougher? Up it would go. They would also be issued a "*Home Course* Handicap," which would be a permanent handicap to be used at their club. And guess what. The Slope Handicap would be expressed to a decimal point!

What the USGA *should* have pointed out was that golfers had only one number to remember, just as they had with their old handicaps.

So in the interest of fair play, here are five easy steps to help you use the Slope System.

1. Your handicap card issued to you by your local or regional golf association will include your Index and will be updated monthly and sometimes more frequently. Either memorize the Index or try not to lose the card. If in doubt, call the association.

2. When you go to a course, match your Index to the Handicap Table. If you take a 13.6 to a tough course (with a Slope of 135, for example), you might play to a 16 that day. You could probably use the extra strokes.

3. Enjoy your round.

4. When you finish, post your score and the appropriate Slope Rating and Course Rating.

5. If in doubt, ask for assistance at the pro shop or starter's box. If there is no help in sight, keep a record and contact your association.

My official handicap card—note the home club.

Instruction

The Case of *"The Lumpy Doughnut"* (or why perfect putts don't drop)

Leave it to a former NASA physicist to tell me that if I were to strike every 12-foot putt perfectly—perfect line, weight and swing—a good half of them wouldn't drop. This isn't good news.

But you have to listen to Dave Pelz because since leaving the space agency he's spent the best part of the past two decades studying the physics of golf; the short game in particular. He's now a top teaching editor with *Golf Magazine;* convenes a short-game school in Austin, Texas; works on the short games of many of the top PGA Tour professionals; and in 1989 put many of his thoughts about putting in a book called *Putt Like the Pros.*

So why do perfect putts stay out? Pelz has a three-word explanation. Given his background examining the upper atmospheres of every planet in the solar system, you'd expect the explanation to run something along the lines of "Interrelated Geophysical Deformation."

Nope. Pelz the physicist blames *"The Lumpy Doughnut."*

The gist of his theory is that a golf ball has to cross an obstacle course of bumps and hollows before it reaches the hole—even on greens that seem as smooth as the blade of a Gurkha's kukri.

Pelz confirmed this by running a series of putting tests at three different golf clubs, each with greens of different quality. The tests consisted of Pelz's "True Roller" putting device—an adjustable, eight-foot-long, metal ramp—rolling 100 identical putts, each 12 feet long, on each green at each club: 5,400 attempts in all.

The True Roller sank 48 percent of the putts at Greencastle Country Club, a private club in Silver Spring, Maryland, with greens a tad better than those at your average public course. It sank 54 percent at the Bethesda Country Club, a club in Bethesda, Maryland, with good greens and a considerable maintenance budget. At the Columbia Country Club in Chevy Chase, Maryland, the True Roller went to work on greens that had been cut in the morning but had not suffered a footprint, mower or roller the rest of the day. Score: 84 percent. Clearly the degree of damage inflicted on a green by the amount of play was a major culprit.

Pelz confirmed this by running yet another test at the practice green at the Westchester Country Club in Harrison, New York. He putted the *same* green, but at different times of day. Pelz had the True Roller putt at first light on pro-am day during the PGA Tour's Westchester Classic, when it scored 73 percent. In the evening the True Roller shot but 30 percent.

Pelz fingers several culprits:

▼ Diseased grass, which golfers can do little about, but which golf course superintendents can;
▼ Unrepaired ball marks, which can and should be repaired at any time;
▼ Spike marks, which cannot be repaired until you've finished the hole, but which should be nevertheless; and
▼ "Warts," the name Pelz gives to nubs of turf pushed up in front of a ballmark by the impact of the ball hitting the green. The etiquette-prone repair the holes they make, but few repair, or even know to repair, the warts. Hit any part of a wart—and they're tough to miss—and the putt will be knocked off line.

The biggest culprit, however, is Pelz's doughnut thing.

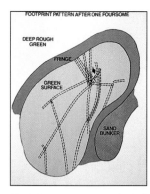

Footsteps were concentrated around the hole.

Pelz arrived at the theory by rising early one morning, traveling to a nearby course and watching the first group of the day traipse around the first green. He first noted where each ball was hit on the green; then, because he could see footprints in the dew, he tracked where each golfer walked and counted the footprints they left: 500!

Because it is commonplace for a golfer to line up his putt, hit it, miss it, then line it up again at a position nearer the hole, and because a golfer removes, replaces or tends the flagstick by walking or standing near to the hole, there appeared a mass concentration of footsteps within a six-foot radius of the hole.

In addition, because no one actually stands virtually on the hole, there were hardly any footprints within 12 inches of it. Pelz tracked all this information and the ensuing information looked like, well, a doughnut. It measured twelve feet across with its "hole" having a diameter of about one foot.

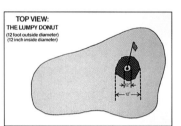

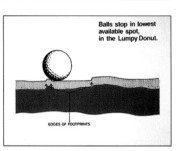

The official "doughnut" (top). Ballmarks and warts can leave an unseen mess (bottom).

That takes care of what the doughnut is. But how lumpy is it?

Pelz figures that footprints usually leave a depression of about one-eighth of an inch in a green at the heel and don't disappear for about two and a half hours. That may not seem very deep to you and me, but to a golf ball, which measures 1.68 inches in diameter, it's a trench.

Now consider that a busy course may see more than 100 groups a day. At 500 footprints per group per green, that translates to more than 5,000 footprints on a single green by the end of the day. Clearly this is one exceedingly lumpy doughnut.

Now the bad news really begins. Were your ball actually to stop *on* the doughnut, Pelz reasons, then the laws of gravity and the concentration of footprints suggest that it will settle into one of these depressions. As you won't be hitting the ensuing putt very hard, because you hit to within 12 feet of the hole, it will likely be knocked off line.

More bad news: The more play a green receives and the longer the hole is kept in the same position, the deeper (and lumpier) the doughnut becomes, with the result that the 12-inch, undamaged circle around the hole becomes a *ramp*. So if your ball does manage to negotiate the lumpy doughnut successfully, it then has to make like a ski jumper and hope for perfect form.

Now the worst news of all! When you putt from outside the doughnut your ball will cross this golfing minefield at exactly the same time that it slows down—exactly when it is most sensitive to lumps and bumps. The poor thing won't have a chance.

So there you have it. Your putting doesn't suck. Life does.

But some good news. There are ways you can improve:

▼ Play early in the day, when the doughnut has yet to reach its full, awesome lumpiness;

▼ Accept that half of your 12-footers would miss if you were one of the best golfers in the world, but that since you're not, almost all of them will miss;

▼ Buy a copy of *Putt Like the Pros*. It's published by HarperCollins, goes into even greater discussion about this most frustrating part of the game, and costs $18.95.

The flag goes in the hole in the center.

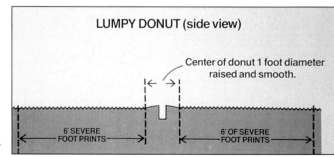

Learn from the Best

by Chris Yurko

The world is full of excellent golf instructors. But there is a level of golf instruction that is occupied by the superteachers, those teaching pros who more often than not work with touring pros, whose reputations have been amplified by the golfing media and whose stature, normally through their pupils' successes, is not inconsiderable.

The trouble with getting to these people, however, is that they're the instructors in the greatest demand. Books, videos, clinics, schools and touring pros take up the vast majority of their time, so arranging a private lesson with one of them can be tough. But not impossible. As their schedules permit, most of the superteachers will give private instruction. The waiting lists tend to be long, however, and the fees can be exorbitant, but if you have both the patience and the money, you're in business.

Here's a rundown of the top 10 instructors in the game, where you can find them and how much you'll have to pay.

DAVID LEADBETTER

Director of Golf, Lake Nona Golf Club, 1900 Chiltern Dr., Orlando, FL 32827; (407) 857-8276

Fee:
$300/hour for private lesson; $2,500 for two-day retreat (six hours a day, maximum of six students, three instructors, including Leadbetter).

Star pupils:
Nick Faldo, David Frost, Bob Tway, Tom Watson, Scott Simpson, Nick Price

Comments:
Leadbetter is the most sought-out teacher in the game today, due mostly to the success of Nick Faldo, whose swing Leadbetter rebuilt prior to Faldo's major triumphs. Leadbetter's time is consumed mostly by visits with touring professionals at tournaments throughout the United States and Europe. He has no set schedule for lessons but will accept reservations three or four months in advance.

PETER KOSTIS

Broken Sound Golf Club, Boca Raton, FL 33496 (407) 241-6860 (winter); Falmouth Country Club, One Congressional Dr., Falmouth, ME 04105; (207) 878-2864 (summer)

Fee:
$150/hour

Star pupils:
Mark Calcavecchia, Ken Green, Andy Bean, Tom Purtzer

Comments:
Kostis is reluctant to take on new students, mainly because his work as a television golf analyst has severely cut into his private-lesson time, which is spent mostly with his long-time students and touring pros. He will however take calls regarding new students and will make appointments on a time-available basis. "My concern is that a student is genuinely interested in getting better and not just using my name for cocktail party conversation," says Kostis. Kostis's lesson format is unique: Most of his students take an hour's instruction in the morning and then either practice or play a round later in the day. The next day, students undergo a fur-

ther hour's instruction to reinforce what they've learned or to move on to the next step. "I don't like to do much more than that in one session," says Kostis.

JIMMY BALLARD

Jimmy Ballard Golf Schools, Box 22686, Hilton Head, SC 29925; (803) 837-3000, or Jacaranda Golf Club, 9200 West Broward Blvd., Plantation, FL 33324; (305) 475-2250

Fee:
Minimum of $200/hour

Star pupils:
Curtis Strange, Peter Jacobsen, Hal Sutton, Sandy Lyle

Comments:
Ballard's "connection" and "loading the right side" swing theories, though considered unorthodox by many golf teachers, gained prominence with the ascension of Curtis Strange to the top of the golfing world. Ballard's primary responsibility is running his golf schools. He is available for private lessons, but only for those who have been through his school.

DAVE PELZ

Independent Golf Research, Hills of Lakeway Golf Club, 1200 Lakeway Dr., Suite 21, Austin, TX 78734; (512) 261-6493

Fee:
$2,500—but that's for a full-day, eight-hour lesson. Pelz demands a reservation of at least two lessons, each at least one month apart.

Star pupils:
Tom Kite, Chip Beck, Peter Jacobsen, Tom Sieckmann, Tom Purtzer, Beth Daniel

Comments:
Pelz is strictly a short-game instructor dealing with play from 60 yards in as well as putting. He uses scientific data extensively in his instruction programs to help students understand exactly what is happening during the golf swing. Pelz is another instructor who is on the road a lot—once or twice a month—working with touring pros. He

Peter Jacobsen has studied under Jimmy Ballard, Dave Pelz, *and* Jim McLean. This impression of Craig Stadler he presumably learned on his own.

recommends making private reservations at least six months in advance.

JIM MCLEAN

Head pro and director of golf, Sleepy Hollow Country Club, P.O. Box 345, Scarborough-on-Hudson, NY 10510; (914) 941-8070/3062. In winter: Doral Hotel and Country Club, 4400 NW 87th Ave., Miami, FL 33178; (305) 532-3600

Fee:
$200/hour

Star pupils:
Peter Jacobsen, Hal Sutton, Brad Faxon, Bill Britton, Tom Kite

Comments:
Since Sleepy Hollow is a private club, its members get first dibs on lessons. They also can "cancel" a lesson for an outsider if they feel like working on something with McLean. McLean runs the occasional class for four to six pupils at Sleepy Hollow and charges $400 a head for each four-hour session. In the winter, he runs his school at Doral Country Club in Miami.

ED OLDFIELD

Merit Club, Box 756, Libertyville, IL 60048; (708) 918-8800 (summer); Orange Tree Golf Club, Scottsdale, AZ 85254; (602) 948-3730 (winter)

Fee:
$100/hour

Star pupils:
Betsy King, Jan Stephenson, Tina Purtzer

Comments:
Oldfield was head pro at the Glenview Country Club in Glenview, Illinois, for 29 years before he left to become the president of the Merit Club, a course he designed. "I went from giving 20 lessons a day to about 20 every three months," says Oldfield. What this means is that if you want a lesson from Oldfield, you'll either have to join his new club—he teaches only members—or

take a winter trip to the Orange Tree Golf Club in Arizona, where Oldfield works as an independent contractor from October through March. "I don't give band-aid cures," says Oldfield. "Golfers who come to me generally are pretty desperate."

BILL STRASBAUGH

Columbia Country Club, 7900 Connecticut Ave., Chevy Chase, MD 20815; (301) 951-5050

Fee:
$75/45 minutes (lessons have been known to stretch to an hour)

Star pupils:
No one outstanding, but he does work with a lot of PGA club pros. A teaching pro's teaching pro, one might say.

Comments:
Strasbaugh has been head pro at Columbia for 23 years and has been teaching golf for 45. Time was when Strasbaugh gave lessons from dawn to dark. Now he's cut back to about five hours a day. He teaches students of all levels from beginners to professionals, but he'll only take new students on a referral basis, so you'll have to get a recommendation from a Columbia club member or another golf professional. Columbia has an indoor facility, complete with nets and video equipment, so Strasbaugh gives lessons year round.

JAY OVERTON

Innisbrook Resort and Country Club, Box 1088 Tarpon Springs, FL 34688; (813) 942-5312

Fee:
$100/hour

Star pupil:
John Huston

Comments:
Overton is head pro and director of golf at Innisbrook as well as vice president of golf operations for Golf Host Resorts, which owns Innisbrook as well as

Five Pieces of Instruction You Can Safely Forget

Surgeon General's warning: The following advice comes from a 12-handicapper and may cause irreparable damage to your game.

1 Keep your head still. Watch Curtis Strange. Watch Gary Player. Their heads sway to the right on the backswing and to the left on the downswing and follow-through. The idea is to keep your head *level*. Don't bob.

2 Keep your left arm straight. This is especially dangerous advice for a left-handed golfer, but on the basis that the advice is written for righties, it is worth pointing out that it is physically impossible—except, perhaps, for the severely double-jointed—to complete your backswing with a straight left arm. Just don't wrap it around your right ear.

3 Play the ball in the same position for every shot. Jack Nicklaus does it—opposite his left heel—so many amateurs figure they're good for 21 majors if they do likewise. The fact is that Nicklaus is on the record—in *Golf My Way*—as saying that "there can be no hard-and-fast rule on the matter."

4 Long irons and fairway woods should be hit with a "sweeping motion." Try to sweep a ball from the turf at exactly the bottom of your swing and you're likely to leave your ball with a smile that would make Carol Channing proud. As Bobby Jones pointed out years ago, the grooves in the face of a club and the dimples on a ball are designed to make the ball rise when the ball is hit with a *downward* blow. Which doesn't mean you should be scooping divots of Brobdingnagian dimensions, but you get the idea. Hit down and through.

5 The arc of your downswing should be a mirror image of the arc of your backswing. British writer Peter Dobereiner once asked Greg Norman what he was working on and Norman referred to the above advice. To which Dobereiner replied something along the lines of "You won't go far with that." Well, we all know how far Norman has gone, but I suspect that's because there is a subtle and very useful difference between *thinking* of the two actions being identical, and their actually being so.

Tamaron Resort and Country Club in Durango, Colorado. He spends about five weeks every summer at Tamaron and the rest in Florida playing in golf tournaments and running the Innisbrook Golf Institute. You generally can schedule a lesson with Overton with a lead time of seven to 10 days. He works with students of all levels but prefers to concentrate on the better players. "That's not because I won't or don't want to teach beginners," he says. "I just think that a one-on-one lesson can sometimes be intimidating for a first time player. Many times the first thing a teacher will say to a student in a private lesson is, 'Let me see you hit the ball.' That doesn't exactly put a poor player at ease."

JOHN REDMAN

Shadow Creek Golf Club, Las Vegas, NV, Mirage Hotel (702) 791-7111; Golden Nugget (702) 385-7111

Fee:
$150/hour

Star pupils:
Paul Azinger, Jim Hallet, Jim Benepe

Comments:
Shadow Creek is a very exclusive club. How exclusive? So exclusive, it has no members! You won't find the number listed in any directory either. The only folks with access are the friends of casino operator and boxing promoter Steve Wynn, who owns the course, and guests of the Mirage and Golden Nugget Hotels, which Wynn also owns. Redman is available for private lessons, but only if you're one of Wynn's hotel guests. So you won't likely see Redman working with Don King. When asked about his fee for private lessons, Redman said, "Are the other guys telling? I hear Leadbetter gets $300 an hour these days. Guess that means he's twice as good as me."

JOHN JACOBS

Stable Cottage, Chappel Lane, Lyndhurst, Hampshire, England SO4 7FG; 011-44-703-28-2743 (office)

Fee:
None

Star pupils:
Tony Jacklin a while back. None today.

Comments:
John Jacobs has probably worked with every great European professional at one time or another, his best-known student being Tony Jacklin. After a professional playing career and more than 40 years as a world reknowned instructor, Jacobs no longer lists "giving lessons" as part of his job description. But he does concede that he'll help out "good friends or desperate golf professionals," so if you fit either billing, give him a call. (For information on John Jacobs's Golf Schools, see page 112).

How to Find the Best Golf School

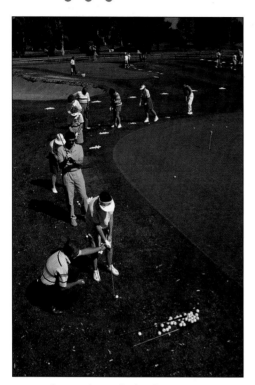

A group lesson in the short game.

There is no such thing as the perfect golf school in that perfection, to a certain extent, has to be convenient.

Finding the best golf school is therefore a function of time, money and geography: time, because you should count on at least a week of hard instruction to show any marked improvement in your game; money, because you will probably have to shoulder the cost of accommodation, as most golf schools are affiliated with resorts; and geography, because you may have to travel a considerable distance to school, as most of the better schools are to be found in the Sunbelt.

That's the good news. The bad news is that you cannot count on leaving a golf school with a great golf game any more than you can count on leaving a class in nuclear physics with the ability to split atoms like pistachio nuts. But you sure as hell can try.

Golf schools are full of triers, of all ages and handicaps. Most pupils have spent their golfing lives sclaffing balls right and left and figure that a vacation at a golf school would be better for them socially, aesthetically and educationally, than many long hours on a practice range with the local club pro. Besides, golf schools have cocktail hours. And these people are right, but that doesn't mean to say that the golf school is the domain of the golfer whose idea of a recovery shot is something you find in a bottle marked 90° proof.

Good golfers go to golf schools, too, mostly because turning a six handicap into a five takes as much, if not more, work than turning an 18 into a 12, and a formal education at school is far more *intensive* than piecemeal work on the range.

But what unites these two classes of golfer is exactly what makes a short semester at a golf school so feasible an idea for anyone: Golf schools, with very few exceptions, are staffed by some of the best teaching pros in the country who are all thoroughly versed in the game's *fundamentals.* Most use sound, clear instruction, state-of-the-art videotaping and expansive facilities, sometimes with a "private" course, to help you understand and improve.

The approach to the fundamentals will change from school to school, however, and this is something else you should bear in mind when choosing a school. Do you want a particular kind of instruction?

The "Swing's the Thing" schools, for example, place heavy emphasis on golfers' finding the optimum swing plane and swinging easily; the clubhead and the ball will take care of the rest. John Jacobs's schools teach something of an advanced approach; advanced in *thinking,* that is. The actual hitting of the ball is no less simple than at any other school. They teach you to deduce your faults from the flight of the ball, a practice that, once understood, can be applied at any time (and which can have tremendous longevity).

Some modern developments include the short-game-only schools run by Dave Pelz, discoverer of *"The Lumpy Doughnut"* (see page 103), who through his knack for numbers and analysis has ascertained that the *fastest* route to lower scoring is through better chipping, putting, sand and recovery play.

Up in California (and in several other areas), the Sybervision folks will have you repeatedly watch videos of the mechanics of well-known golfers, the idea being that you will watch and absorb this immense talent. Only in California . . .

Meanwhile, down in Arizona, an outfit called Sports Enhancement Associates teaches the power of positive thinking on the golf course through various kinds of imagery. Only in Arizona?

And while most top instructors will blurt out on command the credo that a teacher shouldn't change a pupil's swing, that he or she should find the swing that suits the pupil best, a couple of schools teach one—and only one—way to play this god-forsaken game properly.

Paul Bertholy, for example, teaches "The Bertholy Method" at his schools in North Carolina. His method involves learning seven key positions in the swing and keeping to them, an approach that, says Bertholy, "could very well be a generation or maybe two generations ahead of conventional golf-swing instruction." Who are we to argue?

Actually, this Bertholy chap is a genial, interesting and somewhat extroverted character in his mid-seventies who without a doubt has a hairdo that is "a generation or maybe two generations" ahead of conven-

Individual instruction also is available.

tional coiffure construction: a total comb-over that seems to start from the base of his neck and has the appearance of a large, hairy cycling helmet. (Author's note: There is no evidence that a teacher's hairstyle has anything to do with his ability to teach.)

Another character is Jimmy Ballard, who teaches his "Connection" theory, which holds that the body's "big" muscles control the swing and "connect" to the small muscles, which effectively are passive elements. Okay, try it this way: The idea is for the dog to wag the tail, not the other way round.

At any rate, you may have seen Ballard doing his thing on one of your local cable channels. He has tight curly hair, a staccato drawl—if such a

All right, class, keep the right elbow in . . .

John Jacobs School co-founder Shelby
Futch gives a lesson.

thing is possible—and he rushes through the instruction rather colloqui-
ally, regardless of who he is teaching.

A colleague of mine recalls traveling to a conference center outside
New York City a few years ago to listen in on Ballard addressing a group of
about a dozen well-dressed, well-coiffed, sunburnt old ladies from the
country clubs of tony Westchester County. At one point, Ballard was trying to explain how the buttocks (*gluteus maximus:* biggest muscle in the
body) should provide power during the swing—especially on the downswing, when they help the hips and legs move correctly. The buttocks do
this, Ballard says, by staying clenched tightly together.

"When Ben Hogan swung he used to imagine he was holding a dime
between the cheeks of his buttocks!" Ballard told an already blushing audi-
ence. "That dime *never* dropped out."

Then he motioned to one poor, blue-haired soul in the front row.

"Now I've seen *you* swing," he told her. "You sway over here to your
right and then you fall away over here to your left." He went through her
motion then looked at her again.

"Know what you just did?" he asked.

She didn't dare answer.

"Lady," said Ballard, "you just gave change of a quarter!"

A List of the Country's Top Golf Schools

School	Address/Telephone	School Locations	Accommo-dation?	Comments
Jimmy Ballard Golf Workshop	Jacaranda Golf Club, 9200 West Broward Blvd., Plantation, FL 33324; (305) 475-2250	At HQ, and Hilton Head, SC	Optional	Ballard's "Connection" theory is that the "big" muscles control the swing
Howie Barrow Golf School at Grenelefe	Grenelefe Resort & Conference Center, 3200 State Rd. 546, Grenelefe, FL 33844; (813) 422-7511 or (800) 282-7875	At HQ	Yes	Maximum four-to-one student/teacher ratio
Bertholy Golf School	Box 406, Foxfire Village NC 27281; (919) 281-3093	At HQ	Optional	75-year-old Bertholy claims to be light years ahead of the game in instruction
Bob Cooke's Golf School	2100 Emerald Dunes Drive, W. Palm Beach, FL 33411; (407) 684-GOLF	At HQ		One-on-one lessons by appointment
Craft-Zavichas Golf Schools	600 Dittmer Ave., Pueblo, CO 81005; (719) 564-4449	Pueblo, CO, Carlsbad, CA and Tucson, AZ	Yes	Only school run by women, and has a program solely for women
Exceller Golf Programs	3546 East Gold Dust Ave., Suite 1A, Phoenix, AZ 85028; (602) 996-7607 or (800) 424-7438	At HQ	Optional	Run by a rugby addict
Florida Golf School	2703 North A1A, Suite D Fort Pierce, FL 34949; (407) 464-3706 or (800) 365-6727	At HQ	Optional	Another new one
The Golf Clinic at Pebble Beach	Box 2594, Carmel, CA 93921; (800) 321-9401	Pebble Beach, CA and Houston, TX	Optional	High-end school in beautiful location. Don't expect free play on Pebble Beach.
Golf Digest Instruction Schools	Box 395, Trumbull, CN 06611; (800) 243-6121	Throughout the country	Optional	You can rely on the *Digest*
The Golf School	Plantation Inn & Golf Resort, Box 1116, Crystal River, FL 32629; (904) 795-4211 or (800) 632-6262 (802) 464-3333 or (800) 451-4211 From May 11 to Sept. 27, school is at Mount Snow Resort, Mt. Snow, VT 05356	At HQs	Yes	Novices grouped together
The Golf University at San Diego	2001 Old Highway, Fallbrook, CA 92028; (619) 723-9077 or (800) 426-0966	At HQ	No	Has comprehensive video library

A List of the Country's Top Golf Schools

School	Address/Telephone	School Locations	Accommo- dation?	Comments
The Grand Cypress Resort, Academy of Golf	One North Jacaranda, Orlando, FL 32819; (407) 239-1975 or (800) 835-7377	At HQ	Optional	Big on computerized instruction
The Illinois Golf Schools at Eagle Ridge Inn & Resort	444 Eagle Ridge Dr., Galena, IL 61036; (800) 892-2269 or (800) 323-8421	At HQ	Yes	Four-to-one student/teacher ratio
Innisbrook Golf Institute	P.O. Drawer 1088, Tarpon Springs, FL 34688; (813) 942-2000	At HQ	Yes	Good school at a great resort
International Golf	1018 East Indian School Rd., Phoenix, AZ 85014; (602) 248-0045 or (800) 752-9162	Phoenix, AZ and Reno, NV	Optional	Will do custom programs for groups
John Jacobs's Practical Golf Schools	7825 East Redfield Rd., Suite E, Scottsdale, AZ 85260; (800) 472-5007	Throughout the country	Optional	Great theory: Learn *why* a ball does things and adjust accordingly
Nice Shot Golf School	Sports Enhancement Associates, Box 2788, Sedona, AZ 86336; (602) 284-9000 or (800) 345-4245	Arizona, California, Georgia, Florida and Illinois	Optional	Think nice thoughts, hit great shots. They taught Tour pro Mike Reid to imagine he was putting along "a line of singing green worms." 'Nuff said.
Nicklaus-Flick Golf Schools	11760 U.S. Highway One N. Palm Beach, FL 33408; (800) 642-5528	Various resorts	Yes	Instructional manual given out is better than most books
Paradise Golf Schools	281 Hwy. 27 North, Sebring, FL 33870; (800) 624-3543	At HQ	Yes	Three-to-one teacher/student ratio
Dave Pelz Short- Game School	1200 Lakeway Drive, Suite 21, Austin, TX 78734; (512) 261-6493	At HQ	No	For those who want to *score* well. A great school
Pine Needles Golf School	Box 88, Southern Pines, NC 28387; (919) 692-7111	At HQ	Yes	Run by veteran LPGA teacher Peggy Kirk Bell
Phil Ritson Golf Studio at The Legends	Box 2580, Pawleys Island, SC 29585; (800) 544-8727	At HQ	Optional	Ritson released a multivolume instruc- tional series on video. Big promoter
San Diego Golf Academy	Box 3050, Rancho Santa Fe, CA 92067; (619) 756-2486	At HQ	Optional	Expensive school in another idyllic area
Golf Schools of Scottsdale	4949 East Linden Rd., Scottsdale, AZ 85253; (602) 953-2300 or (800) 752-9162	Arizona, Colorado	Optional	Does corporate group business

A List of the Country's Top Golf Schools

School	Address/Telephone	School Locations	Accommodation?	Comments
Mike Schroder's Strand Golf Academy	1204 Linda Drive, Conway, SC 29526; (803) 237-3447 or (800) 421-6296	Myrtle Beach, SC	Optional	Students receive one-hour tape from Schroder
Bill Skelley's Schools of Golf	Miami Lakes Inn & Golf Resort, Main St., Miami Lakes, FL 33014; (305) 821-1150, (800) 541-7707	At HQ	Optional	School has full-time clubfitter who'll check and advise on equipment
Roland Stafford Golf	Hannah Country Resort, Rte. 30, Margaretville, NY 12455; (914) 586-4841 or (800) 447-8894 Also: Peek 'n' Peak Resort, Ye Olde Rd., Clymer, NY 14724 Also: Pan American Ocean Resort, 17575 Collins Ave., Miami Beach, FL 33160	At HQs	Yes	Reduced rates in winter
Stratton Golf School	Stratton Mountain, VT 05155; (802) 297-2200	Vermont, Arizona and Biarritz, France	Yes	Yes, Biarritz. It's where the moneyed went before Hobe Sound. Provides clubfitting advice.
Ben Sutton Golf School	Box 9199, Canton, OH 44711; (800) 225-6923	Sun City Center (south of Tampa, FL)	Yes	Favored by the elderly set
Swing's the Thing Golf Schools	Box 200, Shawnee-on-Delaware, PA 18356; (717) 421-6666 or (800) 221-6661 Also: Orange Lake CC, 8505 W. Space Coast Parkway, Kissimmee, FL 32741; (305) 239-2050	Throughout the country	Optional	Instruction centers around the swing plane
Sybervision Golf Schools	111 Maiden Lane, Suite 400, San Francisco, CA 94108; (415) 391-1571 or (800) 432-2582	Throughout the country	Yes, except in Phoenix	More mental gurus. See a good swing enough and you'll inherit it is the idea, I believe.
Tamarron Golf Institute	Box 3131, Durango, CO 81302; (303) 259-2000 or (800) 678-1000	At HQ	Yes	Private instruction available
Paul Teseler's Golf Schools	3781 State Rt. 5, Newton Falls, OH 44444; (216) 872-7984 or (800) 553-7258	At HQ	Optional	Unsophisticated instruction in unsophisticated location—ya gotta love it
United States Golf Academy	5203 Plymouth LaPorte Trail, Plymouth, IN 46563; (219) 935-5680	At HQ	Yes	About a third of students are beginners
Vintage Golf Schools	Box 5045, Hilton Head Island, SC 29938 (803) 681-2406	At HQ	Optional	New school in great area for golf courses—play Harbour Town if you can!

For Juniors

Children need sound instruction from the start. A golf school is not necessarily the best source; they tend to be in the business of fixing damaged goods, not making new products. A kid could do what I did and work it out for himself, although he'd likely end up doing what I'm doing 25 years later—still trying to work it out for myself. He could learn and practice under the tutelage of his father or some other relative; a surprising number of the top PGA Tour pros' dads were teaching pros (Curtis Strange, Raymond Floyd and Davis Love, to name three). Or, better still, he could get formal instruction at a golf camp from a trained professional in a class inhabited by his peers.

Below is a list of more than 55 junior camps listed alphabetically by state. You'll notice that most camps are held either at a major college campus (got to keep these coaches busy through the summer) or by a local PGA section at a resort. In other words, these are established bodies you'll be packing the rug-rats off to.

But before deciding on a camp, you may want to consider these points:

Prices change, sometimes radically.

Space is tight at most camps, especially those that offer but a few sessions. As the camps normally take place in June, plan to book by mid-March at the latest.

Equipment, except for balls, is not usually supplied.

The best known of the college coaches include Mike Holder at the Oklahoma State camp (Holder has churned out a passel of good touring pros); Jesse Haddock at Wake Forest, North Carolina (coached Arnold Palmer and Curtis Strange, among others); Buddy Alexander at Gator Golf Camp, Florida (1986 Amateur champion).

The Golf Digest School on St. Simons Island, Georgia, offers parent-child sessions. The Bertholy School (North Carolina) *requires* that an adult attend.

The Falcon Camp (Colorado) offers a special "competition camp" while the PGA Schools (Florida) offer "tournament players" schools. Try these if you want to get them hungry young.

The Penn State camps take them earliest, age limits being seven to twelve.

Some of these camps have been around for decades, the veterans being Penn State at 24 years, Pinehurst (North Carolina) at 27 years, Chase (Massachusetts) at 34 years and Bertholy (North Carolina) at 46 years.

ALABAMA

Crimson Tide Golf Academy
Box 40405
Tuscaloosa, AL 35404
(205) 752-0675
Age limits: 10–17; coed
Accommodations: motel

ARIZONA

ASU Golf Academy
Arizona State University
306 ICA Bldg.
Tempe, AZ 85287
(602) 965-3262
(602) 821-1232
Age limits: 10–17; coed
Accommodations: dormitories

CALIFORNIA

Billy Casper's Hall of Fame Golf Camp
32 Washington Ave.
Point Richmond, CA 94801
(415) 215-1000
Age limits: 8–18; coed
Accommodations: dormitories

Northern California PGA Resident School
3645 Fulton Ave.
Sacramento, CA 95821
(916) 481-4506
Age limits: 13–17; coed
Accommodations: dormitories

COLORADO

Falcon Junior Golf Academy
U.S. Air Force Academy
Colorado Springs, CO 80840
(719) 472-2280
(719) 472-1895
Age limits: 10–17; coed
Accommodations: dormitories

CONNECTICUT

Golf Digest Junior Instruction Schools
Box 395

Trumbull, CT 06611
(800) 243-6121
Age limits: 12–18; coed
Schools are actually held in Florida, Georgia and Ohio

FLORIDA

Fellowship of Christian Athletes Golf Camp
Box 664
Ponte Vedra Beach, FL 32004
(904) 273-9541
Age limits: 13–18; coed
Accommodations: resort and hotel
Schools actually are held in Florida, Indiana, North Carolina, Texas and Wisconsin

Gator Golf Camp
Box 2313
Gainesville, FL 32602
(904) 375-4683
Age limits: 11–17; coed
Accommodations: dormitories

Innisbrook Junior Golf Institute
Box 1088
Tarpon Springs, FL 34688
(800) 942-2000
Age limits: 10–17; coed
Accommodations: resort

PGA Junior Golf Schools
Box 109601
Palm Beach Gdns., FL 33410
(407) 624-8456
Age limits: 12–17; coed
Accommodations: resort
Schools are held at various destinations; call for details

GEORGIA

Georgia Junior Golf Foundation Academy
4200 Northside Parkway
Bldg. 9, Suite 100
Atlanta, GA 30327
(404) 233-4742
Age limits: 10–17; coed and boys only
Accommodations: dormitories

Georgia Southern Golf Camp
L.B. 8082
Statesboro, GA 30460
(912) 681-9100

Age limits: 9–17; boys only
Accommodations: dormitories

Golf Digest Junior Instruction Schools
Box 395
Trumbull, CT 06611
(800) 243-6121
Age limits: 12–18; coed
Accommodations: resort
School is at Sea Island Golf Club, St. Simon's Island, GA

INDIANA

Sam Carmichael's Junior Golf School
Indiana University
Assembly Hall
Bloomington, IN 47405
(812) 855-7950
Age limits: 10–16; coed
Accommodations: dormitories

FCA Golf Camp
Box 664
Ponte Vedra Beach, FL 32004
(904) 273-9541
Age limits: 13–18; coed
Accommodations: resort and hotel
School is held in Winona Lake

IOWA

Cyclone Country Golf Camp
Box 1995
Ames, IA 50010
(515) 232-3999
Age limits: 11–18; coed
Accommodations: dormitories

KANSAS

Girls' Jayhawk Golf Camp
904 Prescott Dr.
Lawrence, KN 66044
(913) 842-6724
Age limits: 10–18; girls only
Accommodations: dormitories

Jayhawk Golf Camp
2104 Inverness Dr.
Lawrence, KS 66047
(913) 842-1907/1714

Age limits: 10–18; boys only
Accommodations: dormitories

Shocker Golf Camp
Wichita State University
Campus 18
Wichita, KS 67208
(316) 689-3257
Age limits: 12–17; coed
Accommodations: dormitories

KENTUCKY

Murray State University Golf School
305 Sparks Hall
Murray State University
Murray, KY 42071
(502) 762-2187
Age limits: 10–17; coed and boys only
Accommodations: dormitories

LOUISIANA

Tiger Golf Camp
4008 Irvine St.
Baton Rouge, LA 70808
(504) 383-8714
Age limits: 11–17; boys only
Accommodations: dormitories

MARYLAND

Ronnie Scales Golf Camp
University of Maryland Golf Course
College Park, MD 20740
(301) 403-4299
Age limits: 10–17; coed
Accommodations: n.a.

MICHIGAN

Katke Golf Camp
Ferris State University
Big Rapids, MI 49307
(616) 592-3765
Age limits: 12–17; coed
Accommodations: dormitories

Michigan State University Summer Sports School
222 Jenison Fieldhouse

E. Lansing, MI 48824
(517) 355-5264
Age limits: 13–17; coed
Accommodations: dormitories

University of Michigan Summer Camps
1000 S. State St.
Ann Arbor, MI 48109
(313) 998-7239
Age limits: 12–17; coed
Accommodations: dormitories

MINNESOTA

Rob Hary Junior Golf School
6300 Auto Club Blvd.
Bloomington, MN 55438
(612) 884-2409
Age limits: 8–18; coed
Accommodations: n.a.

Minnesota PGA Junior Golf Academy
Bunker Hills Golf Club
Hwy. 242
Foley Blvd.
Coon Rapids, MN 55433
(612) 754-0820
Age limits: 12–17; coed
Accommodations: houses

MISSISSIPPI

Ole Miss Golf Camp
Center for Continuing Studies
Box 879
University of Mississippi
University, MS 38677
(601) 232-7282
Age limits: 10–H.S. seniors; coed
Accommodations: dormitories

NEW MEXICO

Sun Country Section PGA Junior Academy
111 Cardenas N.E.
Albuquerque, NM 87108
(505) 260-0167
Age limits: 10–17; coed
Accommodations: dormitories

NEW YORK

Pepsi Met PGA Golf School
Box 268
Wykagyl Station
New Rochelle, NY 10804
(914) 235-0312
Age limits: 9–17; coed
Accommodations: n.a.

NORTH CAROLINA

Bertholy Method Golf Schools
Foxfire Village, NC 27281
(919) 281-3093
Age limits: 14–21; boys only
Accommodations: dormitories

Campbell University Golf School
Box 10
Buies Creek, NC 27506
(919) 893-4111
Age limits: 10–17; coed
Accommodations: dormitories

Duke University Golf School
Route 751 at Science Dr.
Durham, NC 27706
(919) 684-2817
Age limits: 11–17; coed
Accommodations: dormitories

Elon College Golf School
Elon College Athletic Dept.
Elon College, NC 27244
(919) 584-2420
Age limits: 8–18; coed
Accommodations: dormitories

Jesse Haddock Golf Camp
Wake Forest University
Box 7567
Winston-Salem, NC 27109
(919) 759-6000
Age limits: 9–18; coed
Accommodations: dormitories

North Carolina State University Golf School
3000 Ballybunion Way
Raleigh, NC 27613
(919) 846-5382
Age limits: 9–17; coed
Accommodations: dormitories

Pine Needles Youth Camp
Box 88
Southern Pines, NC 28374

(800) 634-9297
Age limits: 11–17; coed
Accommodations: resort

Pinehurst Junior Golf Advantage Schools
Box 4000
Pinehurst Hotel & Country Club
Pinehurst, NC 28374
(800) 634-9297
Age limits: 11–17; coed
Accommodations: resort

FCA Golf Camp
Box 253
Winter Park, FL 32790
(407) 629-1073
Age limits: 10–13; coed
Accommodations: resort and hotel
School is at Pine Needles Lodge in
Southern Pines

University of North Carolina Golf School
Box 4402
Chapel Hill, NC 27515
(919) 962-2041
Age limits: 10–18; coed
Accommodations: dormitories

OHIO

Golf Digest Junior Instruction Schools
Box 395
Trumbull, CT 06611
(800) 243-6121
Age limits: 12–18; coed
Accommodations: dormitories
School is at Hueston Woods Golf Club in
Oxford

Fighting Scot Golf Camp
College of Wooster
Wooster, OH 44691
(216) 263-2170
Age limits: 11–17; coed and boys only
Accommodations: dormitories

OKLAHOMA

Mike Holder's Cowboy Golf Camp
Gallagher-Iba Arena
Stillwater, OK 74078
(405) 377-4289
Age limits: 11–17; coed and boys only
Accommodations: dormitories

PENNSYLVANIA

Kiski Golf School
1888 Brett Lane
Saltsburg, PA 15681
(412) 639-3586
Age limits: 10–18; boys only
Accommodations: dormitories

Penn State Golf Camps
Penn State University
409 Keller Building
University Park, PA 16802
(814) 865-5141
Age limits: 7–12; coed
Accommodations: dormitories

Philadelphia PGA Junior Golf Academy
Penn State University
410 Keller Conference Center
University Park, PA 16802
(814) 865-6231
Age limits: 11–17; coed
Accommodations: dormitories

SOUTH CAROLINA

Furman University Golf School
Furman Golf Club
Greenville, SC 29613
(803) 294-9091
Age limits: 9–18; coed
Accommodations: dormitories

TENNESSEE

Tennessee Golf Academy
4711 Trousdale Dr.
Nashville, TN 37220
(615) 833-9689
Age limits: 11–17 for boys, 12–17 for
girls
Accommodations: resort

TEXAS

FCA Golf Camp
Box 253
Winter Park, FL 32790
(407) 629-1073
School is at Tapatio Springs, in Boerne,
TX

Age limits: 10–13; coed
Accommodations: resort and hotel

Texas A&M Golf School
c/o Athletic Dept.
Texas A&M
College Station, TX 77843
(409) 845-4533
Age limits: 13–16; boys only
Accommodations: dormitories

Texas Tech Junior Golf Academy
Box 4070
Lubbock, TX 79409
(806) 742-3335
Age limits: 12–17; coed
Accommodations: cabins

WISCONSIN

FCA Golf Camp
Box 253
Winter Park, FL 32790
(407) 629-1073
Age limits: 13–18; coed
Accommodations: resort and hotel
School is held at Greenlake, WI

Silver Sands Golf Academy
South Shore Dr.
Delavan, WI 53115
(414) 728-6120
Age limits: 10–17; coed and boys only
Accommodations: resort

Put in the Time—Two Practice Schedules

In the absence of a way to turn the pounding of balls into real entertainment, most golfers are going to view practice the way most of us view televised golf tournaments—from the comfort of an armchair.

It's sad really, for the same golfers who will shun an hour on the range if it's labelled "practice" will easily spend twice as long on the same range if the exercise is labelled "warming up before you play with your boss." Which is to say that most golfers *do* spend more time than they probably think on the practice tee.

With that in mind, here are two practice schedules. Each is reprinted from the *PGA Teaching Manual: The Art and Science of Golf Instruction,* a 600-page book published in 1990 by the PGA of America that covers everything from the fundamentals of instruction to equipment analysis and information on *how* to instruct. As golf books go, this may be the most thorough ever, which is not too surprising when one considers that its author, Gary Wiren, took five long years to put it together.

The *Teaching Manual* also is available as a shorter, consumer edition published by MacMillan. For further information, contact the PGA of America at 100 Avenue of the Champions, Palm Beach Gardens, FL 33418; (407) 624-8400.

A PRACTICE PLAN FOR THE SERIOUS PLAYER

Practice sessions should have a purpose. The serious student should have a written schedule of *what* he is going to practice. In planning practice time, the player should concentrate on what he and his professional have agreed needs the most work. The schedule may include both the short and long game, specific shots, remedial work, physical and psychological training, playing and information gathering. Below is the type of one-week schedule that someone contemplating a career in golf or who is training for national-level competition might follow. For other serious golfers with more modest objectives or more serious time restrictions, this sample schedule can be used as a guide.

PRACTICE FOR THE WEEKEND AMATEUR

The majority of golfers practice only occasionally, and even avid amateurs will find that time constraints limit their opportunities. The *what* to practice for them has to be more limited in scope than for the aspiring tournament player. Here are some suggestions:

1. Make practice swings whenever possible. Place old clubs around the house in various locations so that it will be convenient to pick one up and swing it.

2. Without a club, make imaginary swings with the arms and hands in front of a mirror or window. Picture and feel the correct positions.

3. Grip a club while watching television. Swing during commercials.

4. Create a practice area in the house or office which makes practice more convenient. Include short game practice.

Below is a schedule for the weekend player who wants to improve but has full-time work, family or other obligations.

A Practice Schedule for the Serious Player

	Mon.	Tues.	Wed.	Thurs.	Fri.	Sat.	Sun.
Short Game (Chip & Pitch)	1 hr.	2 hrs.	30 min.	2 hrs.	1 hr.	1 hr.	15 min.
Putting	30 min.	1 hr.	15 min.	1 hr.	X	2 hrs. (Pre-shot routine)	15 min.
Irons	30 min. (Short & Mid.)	1 hr. (Pre-shot routine)	15 min. (Short only)	1 hr.	30 min.	1 hr.	10 min.
Woods	15 min.	45 min. (Pre-shot routine)	15 min.	1 hr. Fairway	15 min.	30 min. (Pre-shot routine)	10 min.
Bunker Play	30 min.	15 min.	X	30 min.	15 min.	30 min.	X
Play & Course Management	9 holes	X	18 holes	9 holes	18 holes	9 holes	18 holes
Mental	Read golf & watch videos 1 hr.	Relax, meditate, & visualize 15 min.	Relax, meditate, & visualize 15 min.	Read golf & watch videos 1 hr.	X	Relax, meditate, & visualize 15 min.	Read Rules 30 min.
Physical	Aerobics & stretching 1 hr.	Strength 30 min.	Aerobics & stretching 1 hr.	Strength 30 min.	Aerobics & stretching 1 hr.	Strength 30 min.	Rest
Miscellaneous	Trouble shots, (select) trajectory, curving the ball, uneven lies, left-handed, recordkeeping, rough 15 min.	Trouble shots & left-handed	X	Uneven lies 20 min.	Take equipment for lie-angle check	Curving the ball	Recordkeeping & schedule

A Practice Schedule for the Weekend Amateur

	Mon.	Tues.	Wed.	Thurs.	Fri.	Sat.	Sun.
	Health Club Workout 12:30–1:30, include golf drills	Evening Swing club at home in front of mirror	Health Club Workout 12:30–1:30, include golf drills	Evening Swing club or chip	Health Club Workout 12:30-1:30 include golf drills	Practice 1 hr. and play 18 holes	Watch Golf Tournament T.V.
	Putt on rug 15 min.	X	Read golf magazine, watch a video 9:00–10:30 p.m.	X	Practice range 5:00–6:30 p.m.	X	Practice 30 min. Play 9 holes evening
Notes	Work on keeping left left wrist from breaking down in putting stroke	X	Watch for preshot routtine in video	X	Practice keeping the driver in play	X	

How to Make Practice Fun

This is an idea passed on to me by my editor at *Golf Magazine,* George Peper.

Peper is a low-handicapper known for a precise short game and the occasional ability to play different lengths and shapes of shots with the same club. The latter is certainly not a unique ability; most low handicappers and all scratch players can do that. I can do it with the middle irons, probably because the course I grew up on in Scotland had neither yardage books nor distances marked on sprinkler heads. We would hit to the green by sight and feel rather than by programming our clubs and swings to a certain yardage (which still doesn't explain my handicap).

There are several ways to go about learning such a valuable talent. I advise Peper's practice method: *Take only a 4-iron to the driving range and aim every shot at the guy in the caged tractor who sucks up the used balls.*

Imagine how easy it will be to hit a stationary object—a green—when you've mastered the art of pranging a moving tractor. As the tractor drives toward you, practice progressively short shots until the poor bombarded golf course employee makes a U-turn and heads for the far end of the range. Now your shots get progressively longer. As he drives right and left, you can practice draws and fades—again, of different lengths.

You think this sounds extreme? Try this story. At The Players Championship in 1986, I had to hunt down Bob Tway for an interview. Told he was hitting balls at the opposite end of the range (practicing the opposite wind), I asked how I could get to him.

"Jump in a golf car," said the girl from the tournament. "We'll drive up the side of the range."

The drive took about three minutes. Two and a half of those were spent dodging the golf balls that began to strafe our car immediately after the pros noticed us. I guess we were fair game.

The pros like to practice by hitting a moving target. So should you.

Five Tips That Should Never Be Forgotten

1 Don't look up.
Once you have swung back and through and the ball has taken off in the direction you probably didn't intend, no amount of peeking can help. All that happens is that the head lifts, the shoulders lift, the hands change directions, and there is every chance that you'll take a divot out of your ball.

2 Stay behind the ball.
A popular piece of instruction tells you to drive your legs toward the target as you swing through. This is sound advice—it is all a part of good weight-shift—but an awful lot of players find themselves lurching from right to left and smothering their ball into the ground in front of them. The key is to keep your head behind the ball as you swing through. If your head is behind, there's a fair chance that your upper body will also be behind the ball, allowing you to drive your legs through without collapsing your left side. Try it.

3 Miss breaking putts on the high side.
Or "the pro side," as it is sometimes known. The logic is simple: If a putt breaks sidehill it makes more sense to roll the ball toward the cup from the high side. If it approaches from the low side, it would have to defy gravity and turn uphill to have even a chance of falling in. This tip is playing percentages.

4 Don't hit from the top of your swing.
A lot of players are so eager to crack their ball record distances that they begin their downswing before they finish their backswing. This in effect pulls the club down on a too-narrow arc and makes clean ball-striking impossible.

There are several ways to cure this.

1. Swing back more slowly. Although it is true that no man ever hit a ball with his backswing, hitting from the top often is a result of a rushed backswing.

2. Count "one-two-three": "One" as you take the club away, "two" as you reach the top—the counting makes you consciously finish your swing—and "three" as you swing down and through the ball. Some instructors recommend that you go through the numbers in French—"un-deux-trois"—so that you concentrate even harder.

3. Stop at the top of the swing. Just take the club back and stop cold. Gordon Brand, an English pro on the European tour, does it routinely.

4. Valium.

5 Make sure you follow through on bunker shots.
Many players concentrate so hard on settling into sand, aligning their feet left of the target while opening the clubface, then hitting an inch or so behind the ball—that they forget to follow through and thus leave the club dug into the bunker and the ball a yard or so farther on.

The best way to remember to follow through is to slap the *back* of your sand wedge against the ground immediately underneath the ball and let it "bounce" through.

Build Your Own Practice Area

Everyone can and should have their own practice area somewhere at home. It can benefit the skilled golfer who wants to keep in tune as well as the novice golfer who is too embarrassed to take his game out to a golf course infested with so-called experts. There are many items available from numerous sources, and be aware that many companies don't picture in their catalogs everything that they stock. (For catalog information, see page 143.) Prices may change.

FULL SHOTS

The toniest of all practice nets has to be the **Personal Indoor Driving Range,** an eight-by-ten foot bright red fiberglass frame that resembles the outline of a huge igloo, with a flamboyant yellow target in front.
From: Hammacher Schlemmer, $199.50

The **Par-Fect Golf Net** attaches to the top of a garage door area like a window shade: Pull it down and you're ready to hit. It comes in three versions, eight, nine or 10 feet high and always 12 feet wide. A separate target can be hung at any height.
From: The GolfWorks, $229.95 to $274.95

The **Indoor/Outdoor Practice Range** actually includes two nets: The main one, for driving into, and a secondary net set low behind the first to catch topped shots. It measures nine by seven feet.
From: Golfsmith, $65.50; Golf Day, $59.95; Las Vegas Discount, $59.95; National Golf Distributors, $59.95

The **Hot Shot All Sport Net** comprises a red igloo-shaped frame and a target area inside a net.
From: Golf Day: $129.95

The **Stroke Saver Driving Net** leaves little room to miss. For outdoor use, it measures 15 by 8½ feet.
From: Golf Day, $119.95

J. White Industries sells three different nets, **a square net to be hung, a net on a frame and a cage net.** It will also make nets according to a customer's specification.
From: J. White, $41.95–$177.45

CHIPPING

The **Chipper** practice net is the most popular. It's two feet wide, about the same height off the ground and can also be used indoors.
From: Competitive Edge, $19.95; Golf Day, $14.95; Golfsmith, $13.65; Las Vegas Discount, $19.95; National Golf Distributors, $16.50; J. White, $16.90

The **Chip-N-Pitch Net** measures three feet by four feet and works much like a window that opens horizontally in that it can be set at different angles to receive different short shots.
From: Austad's, $39.95

The **Plastic Bucket** can be used for everything from practicing your short shots to holding a few gallons of dirty water as you scrub your kitchen floor. Comes in many colors.
From: Your local hardware store, about $10

PUTTING

A word of warning: Putting, more than any other part of the game (except perhaps trouble play) requires experience on real grass on a real green.

The **Longest Putting Green** measures 12 feet by 18 inches and has two holes at each end. In addition, each hole has a different break around it.
From: Golf Day, $29.95

The **Electric Auto-Return Putting Mat** is nine feet long, the last 18 inches or so of which slope up to the cup. Anything that misses is channeled toward a trigger that kicks the ball back to you.
From: Austad's, $48; Golf Day, $49.95

The **E-Z-Way Super Electric Putting Cups** should not be taken into the bathtub. When plugged in, it fires back putts according to the distance you set it for. The "Birdie" version divides sections of the entrance area into numerical values so you can have competitions.
From: Golfsmith, $13.85 or $18.25 (Birdie)

The nine-foot-long **Double Break Putting Green** slopes up at opposite corners, allowing you to practice putts that break uphill and to the right, uphill and to the left, downhill then uphill and to the right, downhill then uphill and to the left, downhill then to the left and uphill and to the right, uphill and downhill and left and right and all over the goddamn . . . anyway, it says it rolls up for quick storage, which is the best news I've had all day.
From: Golf Day, $49.95

Calling All Southpaws

When the left-handed golfer makes the decision to stick with his style, instead of learning to play right-handed as is so often done, he is making a courageous decision. He'll have to spend more time looking for good left-handed equipment, choose from a smaller selection of clubs, find it tough even to *find* a golf glove, and be viewed wherever he plays as some abnormality or eccentric.

So thank your lucky stars, all you lefties out there, for the National Association of Left-Handed Golfers.

NALG was launched in Chicago in 1935 and today has more than 150 members, hailing from as far afield as Australia, New Zealand, Japan, Hong Kong and Ireland. There is also a women's division.

The association distributes a newsletter titled *Southpaw Activities* to its membership nine times a year. It includes a golf equipment exchange as well as contact numbers for lefty-only tournaments. And there are many of those—more than 30 on the 1991 calendar, for example, ranging from the Seventh International NALG Championship in Taiwan to smaller, regional events, such as the sixty-team event in Cape Coral, Florida, that starts the year. The idea is for a lefty to check the calendar when he's about to travel, and if there's a tournament in the area, he can enter. The only requirement is that he or she play all shots, including putts but not necessarily trouble shots, left-handed.

Membership in NALG costs $20 per year and includes the newsletter, a bagtag, an iron-on logo and a pocket planner and calendar.

NALG is at Box 810223, Houston, TX 77280-1223; (713) 464-8683.

A regular advertiser in *Southpaw Activities* is "Lefties Only" a Burlington, Vermont, store that stocks only . . . well, the name says it all.

This is not some outlet selling freak golf clubs. A recent issue of the Lefties Only catalog had a set of MacGregor Muirfield 20th persimmon woods and forged blades for $675, a broad selection of metal woods and putters and a number of close-out sets and individual irons and woods. It also listed a pair of left-handed shoes from Etonic, which feature rubber turf "grippers" along the right side of each sole, instead of the left side as with the right-handed model, and a left-handed umbrella. Mmmmm.

As Senior Tour pro Bob Charles has created the only instruction material by a southpaw, Lefties Only keeps a good stock of Charles's *Golf from the Other Side* videotapes as well as the book version. (Most other video outlets also carry it.)

Lefties Only is at 1972 Williston Rd., South Burlington, VT 05403; (800) 533-8437 (that's 800-LEF-TIES). It takes MC, Visa and Discover.

Equipment

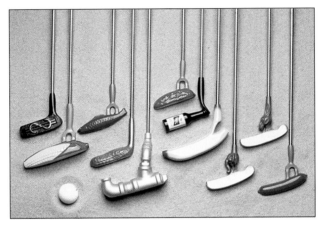

Getting a Handle on Your Golf Game

by Mike Royko

It is said that there is an R&D crisis in this country. That means research and development: inventing new products, creating, devising, improving. And our leaders say we are lagging behind other eager-beaver countries.

To them, I say bull!

At least that is what I am saying since becoming aware of an American company called International Biologics, Inc.

This small firm, showing the kind of original thinking that has made this country the world's leading manufacturer of almost any kind of thingumajig imaginable, has now found a way to successfully make commercial use of an, uh, of, uh, an, uh . . .

I'm not sure how to say it. So why don't I just go ahead and repeat the advertisement, exactly as it appeared recently in a magazine called *Potentials in Marketing.*

The ad, accompanied by a picture of a pretty model holding a golf putter, said:

A GOLF PUTTER MADE FROM WHAT?

You may not believe it, but the golf putter this young lady is holding is made from the pizzle of a bull.

That's right. The entire intact male reproductive organ of a grown bull . . . and this beautifully finished, full-sized, functional putter would make a unique gift for your colleagues, employees or some of your best customers.

Also available are walking sticks, billiard cues, gavels, ashtrays, back scratchers, pointers, etc., all made from the same raw material.

Send for your brochure and prices today!

I've always been intrigued by the workings of the inventive mind, by the ability to see the same things others see but in a creative way.

For some great minds, the ideas come in an instant revelation, as was said to be the case with Newton and his apple. For others, such as Edison, it could be a long hit-and-miss process.

So, after seeing the ad, I became curious. Under what circumstances does a person look at, as the ad put it, "the pizzle of a bull" and envision it as a golf putter, walking stick, billiard cue, back scratcher, etc.?

A few phone calls led me to Walt Mackey, a rural veterinarian in New Brighton, Minnesota, who heads International Biologics, which is located there.

Dr. Mackey, a cheerful, outgoing man of 55, was eager to talk about his creations, of which he is quite proud.

"I'll tell you how the idea came to me. It was many years ago, when I was a youth. I saw a farmer had hung this deceased bull's appendage on a fence to dry. I asked him why he did that, and he said they used them as the handles for bullwhips.

Four Golf Clubs You Should Remove from Your Bag . . .

1 Your driver. Honest. And especially if it's made of wood. Most companies make a 2-wood, which doesn't have the machismo of the big dog, the big gun, the big lumber or the ticket to the high-rent district, but which does have the extra degrees of loft that will give you a little more control and not a lot less distance.

2 Your 1-iron. Admit it. You hit the damn thing well once in your life and are convinced you can knife any tight tee shot with the soaring distance and accuracy of Jack Nicklaus. The 1-iron's good for retrieving balls from bushes or ponds, but that's about it.

3 Your 2-iron. Do you honestly think that a shaft that's half an inch shorter and an extra three degrees of loft is going to make a difference? Closet.

4 Your substitute putters. None of them work, so you might as well stick to one.

. . . And Four You Might Want to Add

1 A 2-wood. See above.

2 A 5-wood. A ball that doesn't get airborne doesn't get very far. A 5-wood has loft and punch, especially out of rough.

3 A third wedge. Heck, you might want to add a fourth wedge, too. Most of the average golfer's shots are hit—and missed—within wedging distance of the green, so the greater the number and variety of weapons you can carry, the closer you're likely to land to the pin, no? A third wedge, with extra loft (58° or 60°), allows you to hit the ball high in a hurry from a tight lie that won't accommodate the heavy bulge of a conventional sand wedge.

4 A new putter. You never know . . .

"So, I've always remembered that. And a few years ago, I was thinking about it and it occurred to me that they can be used in other ways, too. I began experimenting. I found I could make all kinds of products with the pizzle, so that's how the business got started."

How does one go about obtaining that portion of a bull's anatomy?

"Well, when a bull gets old and he's not able to do what bulls are well known for doing, then he is retired from his earthly domain. He ends up in a packing plant. We buy our pizzles from the packing plants."

Is it possible for you to explain, I would hope in delicate terms, how one goes about converting a bull's pizzle to a golf-club grip or a cane or a billiard cue?

"I'll try. When the pizzles arrive from a packing plant, naturally, they are kind of uh, uh, limp."

Naturally.

"Fortunately, Mother Nature has provided us with a solution to the problem. We insert an aluminum rod in order to make them firm and functional. Then we dry it until it is dry as a potato chip. Then there is sanding and cleaning and finishing and the result is a very beautiful, shiny, lustrous, sturdy, functional item."

When you speak of using them as a walking stick or billiard cue, I assume you are referring only to the handle.

"Not at all. For some items, such as the putter, it is only the handle, which would come from a modestly endowed bull. But for walking sticks, canes and pool cues, the entire item is the pizzle."

There are pizzles that long?

"Definitely. Believe me, there are some impressive bulls in this land of ours. Obviously, a pool cue would take a well-endowed beast."

I'll say. Now the word "pizzle" itself. Did you make that word up?

"No, when we first began advertising, we had a problem. Most publications would not accept ours ads using the more clinical word. Then somebody told me that the word 'pizzle' meant the same thing. It wasn't in my dictionary, so I called the St. Paul public library and asked the lady there if she could look in some of the real old dictionaries for the word pizzle.

"She asked me what it meant. I said I'd rather not say what it meant. So she went and looked it up and when she came back, she said: 'Well, it means what you probably think it means! And I'm glad you did not tell me what you thought it meant!' I guess she was kind of shocked."

How is business?

"Great. It started slow but now that we have the word 'pizzle' and can advertise, it's really going. One man in Texas ordered 70 putters to give to his friends. And the putters sell for $80. That's our most expensive item."

Do you expect that the mortality rate of old bulls will be high enough to keep you in pizzles?

"I think so. And I'll tell you a joke that's going around. Folks are saying that we've got every bull in Minnesota nervous. Ha!"

That's a real thigh slapper.

"I'll send you our brochure. You might want to think about something we've got for your Christmas list."

Do that. One never knows when he will meet a cow.

(Reprinted by permission: Tribune Media Services.)

50 Questions on Golf Equipment—and 50 Answers

by Rob Sauerhaft

BALLS

1. How Big Is a Golf Ball?
According to the Rules of Golf, a ball may not be smaller than 1.68 inches in diameter nor heavier than 1.62 ounces.

2. Is the So-called "British Ball" Still Legal Anywhere?
No. The smaller "British Ball," 1.62 inches in diameter, has been illegal for more than a decade.

3. What's in the Core of a Three-piece Ball?
Within the windings of a three-piece ball is a hollow, rubber core. Some cores are filled with a mix of sugar water and corn starch. Others have sulphates with the texture of toothpaste. Filling the core gets the ball to the proper weight and concentrates more weight in the center for more spin.

4. Do Golf Balls Lose Compression as They Age?
In a balata-covered wound ball, the windings will lose some tension and as much as 10 to 15 points of compression over three to four years. A Surlyn-covered wound ball also can lose compression, although more slowly than balata. The core of a solid, two-piece ball hardens as it ages, so the compression actually increases. A ball's original compression does not affect the rate at which that compression changes.

5. Do Balls Go Out of Round?
Regardless of cover material, balls will go out of round during 18 holes, but only by one one-thousandth of an inch—not enough to affect performance. Pros change balls every three or four holes, on average, but unless the ball is physically damaged there's no reason to.

6. What's Wrong with an "XXX-Out" Ball?
XXX-outs have some sort of small cosmetic blemish, such as a speck of dirt on the cover. Their specifications (compression, roundness, etc.) and playing characteristics are basically the same as other balls.

7. What Effects Do Dimples Have on Golf Balls?
In general, dimples make balls spin and, most important, rise. They also control the flight of the ball, so a ball can be maneuvered. A ball's trajectory is primarily influenced by the size and placement of its dimples; different balls do have different trajectories. A ball with no dimples will fly approximately 60–80 yards. The ball takes off like an ordinary dimpled ball but will drop quickly back to earth instead of making the gradual ascent and rapid descent we are accustomed to.

8. Does the Height That a Ball Bounces Off Pavement Indicate Anything About How It Will Play?
If you bounce two balls off pavement, a two-piece ball will bounce noticeably higher than a wound ball. This is relevant on putts when the two-piece ball jumps off the clubface faster and rolls farther than wound.

9. Should Weather Conditions Dictate Your Choice of Ball?
Yes, because temperature affects the way a ball feels. In cold weather, high-compression (100) wound balls will feel hard and can hurt the hands on mishits. Balata-covered wound balls fly significantly shorter and feel harder in cool weather. Climate should have less effect on a two-piece ball's performance.

10. Can Leaving the Golf Bag in the Trunk of a Car Harm Balls or Clubs?
Temperatures can rise to more than 100 degrees Fahrenheit in the trunk of a car parked in the summer sun. Such high heat can cause wound balls (both balata- and Surlyn-covered) to lose compression as the threads loosen and the dimples smooth out. The heat also can cause wooden woods to expand and contract, leading eventually to cracking.

11. What Effect Does a Cut or "Smile" Have on a Ball's Performance?
Damaged balls can be aerodynamically affected by the cut. Cut balls usually won't fly as far as they should, and sidespin will be exaggerated, resulting in more hooks and slices. The bigger the cut, the greater the harmful effect on ball flight. Still, there is no substantial evidence suggesting that the cut can be aligned on the tee in such a way as to correct a hook or slice.

CLUBS

12. When Were Clubs First Called by Number?
Calling clubs by numbers first became popular in the 1930s when manufacturers began building matched sets of clubs. Until that time, clubs were sold individually. The major impetus behind the matched set was the advent of the steel shaft; steel shafts were uniform in specifications (or at least more uniform than hickory), which allowed for the creation of matched sets.

13. Are There Limits on a Club's Length?
The only limit in the Rules of Golf states that the shaft must be at least 18 inches in length.

14. Are There Limits on the Size of a Clubhead?
The only limit is that the clubhead be wider—measured across the face from heel to toe—than it is deep, from front to back.

IRONS

15. What Are Forged Irons?
Clubs made by stamping red-hot metal bars between a pair of dies.

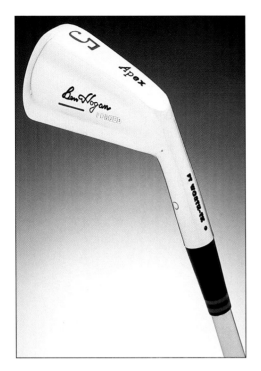

Forged irons from the Ben Hogan Company,
blades and cavity-back.

Clubmakers then imprint scoring lines
on the face and shave the metal to
weight. These clubs most often are
made of carbon steel.

16. What Are Investment-Cast Irons?
Irons made by pouring molten steel
(usually stainless steel) into ceramic
molds.

17. What Is Offset?
Building the club so the leading edge of
the face is set slightly behind the shaft.
This allows a split-second longer to
square the clubface before impact,
combating the average player's tendency to leave the face slightly open at
impact and hit a slice.

18. What Is Loft Angle?
The amount that a clubface deviates
from perpendicular to the ground, measured in degrees. Loft angle is crucial in
determining the ball's trajectory and
spin. If all other factors such as shaft
flex and flex point remain equal, then the
higher the loft angle (in degrees), the
higher the ball flies and the faster it
spins.

19. Do Similarly Numbered Clubs—Say, All 5-Irons—Have the Same Loft?
No. Although the industry standard
says, for example, that 5-irons should
have a loft angle of 31 degrees, manufacturers vary their specifications to
accommodate different modes of construction (such as forged vs. cast or
steel vs. graphite), different shaft characteristics and other variables.
Five-irons can vary as much as eight
degrees from company to company.

20. What's the Highest-Lofted Wedge Available from Stock?
Cobra, Slotline and Ram each make a
64-degree club.

21. What Is the Best Way to Clean Grooves?
Use a toothbrush and soapy water.
Never use a knife or wire brush, which
can scratch the finish and lead to rusting.

WOODS

22. What Is the Purpose of Grooves on the Clubface of Woods?
Grooves serve no purpose on either
wooden woods or metal woods. They
are purely cosmetic.

23. Do the Face Screws in a Wooden Wood Serve Any Purpose?
Not anymore. Face screws were neces-
sary before good epoxies came into
use more than 25 years ago. Before
that, the screws helped hold the insert
in place. Today, with the use of strong,
reliable glues, face screws are purely
cosmetic.

24. Why Do Wood Heads Become Smaller as Loft Increases?
A smaller head is easier to hit from the
fairway because there is less drag and
resistance. The smaller head also low-
ers the center of gravity, making it
easier to get the ball up in the air.

25. What Is the Effect of Runners on the Bottom of Woods?
Some fairway and trouble woods have
runners on their soles. The runners act
like the keel of a ship, guiding the club
through high grass, preventing it from
snagging.

26. How Long Have Metal Woods Been Available?
An aluminum-headed club with a leather
insert was introduced in 1891.

27. What's Inside the Head of a Metal Wood?
A foamy epoxy is injected into the head,
where it expands and hardens, adher-
ing to the inside walls of the shell. The
foam filling affects the sound made on
impact—the more foam, the duller the
sound. The amount of foam also can
affect the club's weight: Graphite-
shafted clubs require more foam,
adding weight to the head, to balance
the lighter weight of the graphite.

28. What Is the Most-Lofted Wood Available?
The Stan Thompson Company stocks a
15-wood with 46 degrees of loft—mid-
way between a standard 8- and 9-iron.

SHAFTS

29. Are Hickory Shafts Still Legal?
Yes, although they are not commonly
used because steel and the exotics
(graphite, boron, etc.) can be more precisely matched to flex, weight and feel.

30. When Was the First Major Won with Steel?
The 1931 U.S. Open, when Billy Burke
beat George von Elm in a two-day playoff at The Inverness Club in Toledo,
Ohio.

31. What Is Shaft Flex?

The measurement of the shaft's willingness to bend under a given stress or weight. Shafts are regularly available in ladies (L), flexible (A), regular (R), stiff (S), extra stiff (X) and double extra stiff (XX) flexes. As a rule, the stiffer the flex, the more strength and clubhead speed are needed to make the shaft straighten out at impact. Therefore, shaft flex influences ball flight and direction.

32. Is Shaft Flex as Important on a Sand Wedge as on the Other Clubs?

Yes. The flex can determine the flight of the ball on full shots and can influence feel on half and three-quarter shots.

33. What Is the Flex Point and How Does It Influence Ball Flight?

Flex point is that spot on the shaft that bows the most during the swing. Shafts generally have one of three flex points: low, medium or high. If all other variables remain the same, the lower the flex point, the higher the ball flight. Women and seniors benefit from low flex points because it helps them get the ball into the air. Better players benefit from the mid or high flex-point shafts, which hit the ball lower and offer more control.

34. Why Do Steel Shafts Have "Steps"?

Stepping is the easiest method of "sizing" a steel shaft so its diameter shrinks from the butt to the tip. Steps also give the manufacturer more control over the location of the flex point and the staff stiffness.

35. Is There Such a Thing as Shaft Fatigue?

No. Under normal circumstances, neither graphite nor steel shafts should weaken with age or use.

36. Graphite Shafts Are Often Referred to as High Modulus. What Does This Mean?

Modulus is the ability of a material to resist elasticity. The higher the modulus of a shaft, the lower its tendency to twist.

37. Why Are Some Graphite Shafts Gold?

In the early 1980s, gold paint was applied to higher-quality graphite shafts. Today, gold paint is purely cosmetic and not necessarily an indication of shaft quality.

38. Does the Flex in the Shafts Have Any Effect on Putters?

Stiff shafts are better in putters because they reduce the twisting caused by off-center hits.

GRIPS

39. Is There a Limitation on Grip Length?

There is no stipulation in the rules of golf regarding the length of a grip.

40. How Do You Maintain Grips?

To keep grips clean and a little "tacky," scrub them after every three or four rounds in warm water with a mild detergent and an abrasive pad, then rinse thoroughly and dry.

41. How Do I Tell If I Need New Grips?

Grips that are slick, hard, worn or shiny should be replaced. The final determinant is how secure the club feels in your hands. If you're still not sure, have one grip changed and see how it feels compared to the others.

42. What Happens If My Grips Are the Wrong Size for My Hands?

Grips that are too big inhibit proper hand rotation, leading to a tendency to fade or slice. Grips that are too small cause draws and hooks because the hands rotate too quickly.

43. Why Is There a Hole in the End of a Grip?

The hole relieves the air pressure that builds up when the grip is applied to the shaft.

RULES

44. Why Do Golfers Carry Only 14 Clubs?

The *USA Yearbook* of 1936 indicated that the Implements and Ball Committee was considering a limit on the number of clubs in a bag. "For some time the Committee has noted with concern the increasing number of golf clubs carried by players. It is the opinion of the Committee that the carrying of so many clubs tends to minimize the skill of the game and make it too mechanical as well as increase the cost." A 14-club limit went into effect on Jan. 1, 1938. Fourteen simply because the USGA felt that enough for a standard set of two woods, 1- through 9-iron, pitching and sand wedges, and a putter.

45. Is There Any Limit on How Many Woods or Irons You Are Allowed to Carry?

No. If you wanted to carry all woods or all irons—or all putters!—it's legal—as long as the total does not exceed 14.

46. If I Play Right-handed, May I Carry a Left-Handed Club?

Yes. Some right-handed players carry a left-handed club to help in trouble situations. But as Ray Davies of The Kinks once wrote, "Paranoia will destroy-ya."

47. When I Take Relief, Do I Have to Use the Same Club with Which I Intend to Hit My Next Shot?

No. The general practice is to take relief with the longest club in your bag, usually the driver. (However, to establish that you are *entitled* to relief, you must use a club "reasonable" for the shot you would play.)

48. Is It Legal to Play with Clubs That Can Be Broken Down for Travel?

A change in this rule is pending. As it now stands, a telescoping shaft (which collapses on itself) is legal only in its standard, or fully extended, position; the club becomes illegal if you play with its shaft shortened. Clubs that can be separated into two or more pieces are always illegal.

49. Are Adjustable-Loft Irons Legal?

No. Under Rule 4.1a, technically you'd be carrying more than 14 clubs.

50. What Happens If You Have a Nonconforming Ball or Club in Your Bag?

If you're carrying a nonconforming club and haven't declared it out of play before the round begins, you face automatic disqualification in both match and stroke play. There is no penalty for carrying a nonconforming ball; the rules are violated only if you put the ball into play, at which point disqualification is automatic in match and stroke play.

(Reprinted with permission from Golf Magazine.*)*

An Easy Four-Step Guide to Buying Golf Equipment (Really)

In a typical annual buyer's guide, the major golf publications will list about 250 different models of woods on the market and 200 models of irons. They probably will *not* list new and existing wedges or new putters and utility woods. They will not include the work of custom-club manufacturers or club lines built specifically for golf discount houses and mail-order firms. Nor, for that matter, will they include club lines no longer manufactured but still kicking around the shelves of pro shops and discount stores.

This is just as well, for the normal golfer's mind can accommodate only so much information when the aim is to purchase but a single set of golf clubs or a box of a dozen golf balls.

Yes, it's a jungle out there. The major equipment manufacturers are constantly announcing new golf clubs with revolutionary shafts or head designs, thrilling developments in manufacturing techniques, unheard-of innovations in golf ball construction. And for what?

For the manufacturers, it's for as large a handful as possible of the more than $3 billion that golfers spend every year on all forms of equipment. For you and me, it's for perhaps a few extra yards on a shot hit perfectly.

That's it?

'Fraid so.

So why is the job of buying golf equipment so difficult?

The fact is, it doesn't have to be. Our aim here is to untangle the golf equipment jungle and simplify your decision.

We have devised a four-step process. It's designed to give you as *little* information as is necessary to allow you to make the best purchase possible.

Step One. Understand that there are only so many ways to make a golf club or golf ball, and therefore only so many different *styles* of clubs and balls on the market. Once you understand the relatively few principles involved, you can narrow your choice of clubs down drastically. Look at it this way: If you intend to buy a car and you have decided that you want a two-seat sports car, why would you pore through all the catalogs detailing four-door sedans?

Step Two. There is a style of clubs that will suit you best, based on your age and sex (and therefore, generally speaking, your strength) and your skill level. There are no hard-and-fast rules in this area, but certain styles of clubs and balls have been designed specifically for certain groups of golfers. It's something the equipment companies actually do rather well.

Step Three. You will want to know what golf clubs cost, assuming that you have assigned yourself a budget.

Step Four. Familiarize yourself with who makes what. Which manufacturers stock ladies' clubs, for example? Which make long-shafted putters? Returning to the sports-car analogy, if Oldsmobile doesn't make a sports car, there's no point in going to an Oldsmobile dealer and asking for one. Our listings cover woods, irons, putters; junior, ladies' and lefties' clubs. Cross this hurdle and you're 90 percent of the way to a perfect set.

STEP ONE—THE DIFFERENT TYPES OF EQUIPMENT

Woods

Most are made from metal or solid persimmon wood.

Metal woods are hollow or filled with foam, which lets the manufacturer distribute more weight around the perimeter of the clubface, which makes for a much more forgiving club. Wooden-headed woods are shaped from solid blocks of persimmon (or sometimes ash) and normally are wielded by classic-minded players who prefer the click of wood to the plink of metal. They are less forgiving than metal woods.

Some companies manufacture woods whose heads are shaped from strips of maple laminated together.

Such exotic materials as graphite, Kevlar and boron have found their way into the golf-club market. These normally have the advantage of being light but durable, but they tend to be relatively expensive.

Oversized woods have made the greatest impact of late. The theory is that more weight distributed around the outside of a metal head makes already forgiving metal woods positively priestly. But they tend to come with longer than average shafts (to increase club-head speed) and these babies can be tough to control.

Irons

The three main types of irons are

▼ forged
▼ investment-cast
▼ forged *and* cavity-backed

Forged clubs are stamped from steel, with most of the weight in the sole of the club to help get the ball airborne. Forged clubs put a tremendous premium on contacting the ball on the sweet spot of the clubface.

Like metal woods, investment-cast irons have most of their weight distributed around the perimeter of the club to forgive off-center hits.

The third form of iron is the forged version with extra weight distributed around the back perimeter of the club.

Yes, such exotic materials as graphite and beryllium copper irons do exist, but I'm not convinced that they are appreciably better than steel-headed clubs.

Shafts

Do not overlook this area. Shaft flex is very important. Generally, *the faster you swing, the stiffer the shaft you should use.*

Most shafts are made from steel, but graphite, boron/graphite and titanium shafts have come back into vogue. As with exotic irons, I'm not convinced that they reward the extra time—in ordering—and money that may have to be spent securing them.

Colored shafts? A fad, like the colored ball.

Wedges

Most players should carry three wedges and stay within the legal 14-club limit by leaving a long iron at home.

Why? Because while the longest irons are usually the toughest clubs to hit, the wedges are often the easiest, and average golfers spend an inordinate amount of time attacking the pin from the area immediately surrounding the green. A third wedge with more loft than either your pitching or sand wedge will help you play high soft shots from tight situations. Recommended for *all* players.

Putters

Choosing a putter depends so much on the idiosyncrasies of the golfer that I'd rather not recommend a particular kind. The average golfer accumulates a small collection of them anyway. However, if you suffer from back problems, you may want to try one of the long-shafted models.

Balls

Golf balls come in

▼ Two-piece
▼ Three-piece with a Surlyn-blend (or similar) cover
▼ Three-piece with a balata cover

Two-piece balls have a solid center and normally have a tough, synthetic, Surlyn-blend cover. Normally they fly less far than three-piece balls, but roll more on landing.

Three-piece balls have a soft center covered by rubber winding, which is then covered by either a Surlyn-blend or a synthetic balata (which is a natural rubber). These balls spin well and are very responsive to draws or fades. Recent technological advances notwithstanding, they have a softer feel than two-piecers.

Recreational golfers should not use three-piece balata balls unless they can hit a golf ball so precisely that the ball never breaks a "smile"—balata cuts *very* easily.

The white cubes are balata. Or maybe tofu.

Still Confused About Balls?

Golf-ball manufacturers take certain liberties in their quest to have every golfer hit a golf ball farther than his wildest dreams. They all claim to be the longest, the most durable, the ones that spin most, fly highest and cook up a seven-course gourmet meal in less than five seconds.

Some would call this "lying." I have a friend who calls it "seeking a higher truth." The correct term is "advertising."

Because the ads are so bent on impressing you, they seldom *educate* you on golf balls. So if it's a crash course on golf balls you're after, send a card to Titleist.

Titleist publishes a solid little booklet (and a video, but that's a bit of a stretch) called "The Golf Ball." It begins with United States Golf Association's specifications; goes into the history of the ball; the aerodynamics of lift, drag and spin; explains cover materials, interior construction, dimple design and compression; toots its own trumpet for a page or two and then recommends six Titleist and Pinnacle balls (both made by Acushnet) that will—and this is advertising again—meet your need for such things as control, feel, low or high trajectory, a lot of roll or durability. Sad to say, there isn't a golf ball out there that gives you the lot.

The booklet is free from: Titleist Golf Division, Box B-965, New Bedford, MA 02741.

Inside Titleist.

Balls normally come in two compressions, 90 or 100. I could spend a few thousand words explaining compression (it's got something to do with how much the ball squashes against the clubface at impact), but this would only complicate matters. Take my word for it, if you hit the ball hard and solidly, try the 100s. Most of us will go no wrong with 90s.

Colored balls serve no real purpose unless the ground is covered by snow or leaves.

Gloves

Buying a glove is pretty much a function of knowing your size and picking your color. The only recommendation I'd make is that you keep your old gloves and use them when that storm front blows in.

Shoes

I'd recommend two types of shoes: A sturdy, leather, waterproof model and a lightweight "sneaker" with spikes. Many country clubbers frown on the sneaker models, but these shoes feel magnificent on hot days when you're carrying your own clubs.

Bags

Most manufacturers now stock a line of excellent lightweight bags, some of which weigh as little as three pounds (before you put the equipment in). I would not recommend one of these for storage in a golf club, however, as they are not designed to be hauled on and off shelves and golf carts.

Ideally, you should have a lightweight *and* a larger bag, the latter with several pockets. It's sometimes known as a "cart bag." The largest bags are known as "staff bags"—they make you *feel* important, but they'll also kill your caddie.

No matter the bag you choose, make sure it comes with a rain cover.

Rainsuits

A good rainsuit—one built to keep out rain and wind—may be the best purchase you will ever make. Beware of shoddy nylon jobs sold through mail-order houses and at discount shops. Rule of thumb: Do not skimp on a rainsuit.

Umbrellas

I prefer a good rain suit and a good hat, because toting an umbrella involves so much lifting and putting down—and it's illegal to hit the ball while being sheltered by an umbrella. Because they tend to be twice the width of other umbrellas, golf umbrellas are much more useful *off* the golf course.

STEP TWO—UNDERSTANDING WHAT STYLES OF CLUBS AND BALLS WILL SUIT YOU BEST

Those who play the PGA Tour tend to use persimmon or metal woods, forged irons and three-piece balls with balata covers. They hit forged irons and three-piece balls because the former allow them to work the ball better when hit on the sweet spot (and Tour pros almost *always* strike with the sweet spot) and the latter are softer and therefore allow more feel, or feedback. Many touring professionals have switched to metal drivers because they increase the margin for error on what is often felt is the most important shot in the bag.

In other words, the pros choose the equipment that best suits their games.

So should you. If you are a high-handicap player who does not hit the ball very hard, you will perform best with forgiving clubs, i.e., investment-cast irons and metal woods. You will also not likely need a ball with spin (three-piece). You will want one with *roll* (two-piece). Likewise, if you are a medium-handicap player, you probably hit the ball hard enough to warrant a ball that spins, but you could still probably use irons and woods that are forgiving.

Bear in mind that you may toss these recommendations out the window whenever you wish. If you are an average player who wants to sacrifice consistency for the occasional *zip!* on an iron shot, by all means hit three-piece balls with forged clubs. I do. Pretty badly, too.

One final note: You will notice in the chart that follows that we have recommended that junior players use persimmon woods and forged irons and have not advocated *any* golf ball. The first two recommendations come from the mind of someone who believes that youngsters should be taught to add, subtract and multiply in their heads before they be allowed access to an electronic calculator—and that if a junior player starts with low-handicap equipment, he will be a better player as an adult. As for the ball recommendation or lack thereof: Kids, play anything you can lay your hands on.

A USER'S GUIDE TO THE EQUIPMENT GOLFERS SHOULD PLAY*

	Metal Woods	Persimmon Woods	Investment Cast Irons	Forged Irons (or Forged Cavity-Backs)	Two-Piece Ball	Three-Piece, Surlyn Blend	Three-Piece, Balata
Low-Handicap (0–9) Male		✓		✓			✓
Low-Handicap (0–15) Female	✓		✓			✓	
Med-Handicap (10–18) Male	✓		✓			✓	
High Handicap (19 and above) Male	✓		✓		✓		
High Handicap (16 and above) Female	✓		✓		✓		
Senior Golfer	✓		✓		✓		
Junior Golfer		✓		✓			

*These are simply *recommendations* for what each "category" of golfer should play. There are no hard-and-fast rules.

STEP THREE—FIT YOUR CLUBS TO YOUR BUDGET

Once you have decided what style—not what brand—of golf clubs will suit you best, the logical thing to do is to buy them. Shop around, for prices will vary according to where you buy. Off-course golf stores will probably give you the best price, as many belong to chains and can translate their savings from bulk purchases into consumer discounts. Mail-order houses also offer discounts, but you had better know exactly what you want. Pro shops at golf courses won't give you as deep a discount and may try to foist clubs from a limited stock upon you, but the chances are that a certified PGA professional will find the best fit for you in terms of shaft-length, size of grip, etc. They will also be able to offer more thorough advice.

If you must buy in a sporting goods store, bear in mind that the person trying to flog you golf clubs may have been flogging basketballs or running shoes the day before. Department stores make a poor source, unless they have a section, in terms of space and personnel, devoted solely to golf.

The chart below contains some of the makes of golf clubs that have become almost "standards" in the business, arranged according to budget. The budgets are based on the manufacturers' 1992 recommended retail prices. Although the names of the clubs may change, the prices tend to be more stable. Expect to pay anything up to 35 percent lower than listed. Or rather, *try* to pay 35 percent lower than listed.

Low	Medium	High
Wooden Woods		
n/a	Bridgestone Precept Pro Model ($300)	Wilson Staff ($400)
	Spalding Tour Edition ($358)	Palmer Peerless ($540)
	Ping Eye 2 ($345)	Titleist Tour Model ($375)
	MacGregor Nicklaus Muirfield 20th ($350)	Slazenger Crown Ltd. ($492)
		Hogan Apex ($426)
Metal Woods		
Northwestern Ultimate ($110)	Lynx Parallax ($285)	Callaway S2H2 ($405)
Spalding Executive ($175)	Dunlop Maxfli Tour Ltd. ($342)	Mizuno MPC ($465)
Mizuno MIZ ($195)	Tommy Armour EQL ($339)	Taylor Made Tour ($375)
Wilson 1200 TN Gear Effect ($190)	Wilson Ultra System 45 ($300)	
Forged Irons		
Mizuno Silver Cup ($200)	Founders Series 200 ($512)	Titleist Tour Model ($675)
	Daiwa Adviser 273 ($560)	Ben Hogan Edge ($600)
	Bridgestone Precept Pro Model ($520)	Dunlop Maxfli Australian Blade ($688)
	Mizuno MS9 ($360)	Ram Laser FX ($656)
	Spalding Tour Edition ($550)	
Investment-Cast Irons		
MacGregor DX ($208)	Spalding Executive Ltd. ($339)	Ram Laser ZX ($656)
	MacGregor CG1800 ($400)	Tommy Armour EQL ($584)
	Browning Mirage ($384)	Titleist DCI ($600)
	Wilson 1200 TN Gear Effect ($400)	Taylor Made ICW ($616)

Step Four—Who Makes What?

Manufacturer	Persimmon Woods	Laminated Woods	Metal Woods	Jumbo Woods
WOODS				
ACCUFORM		X		
TOMMY ARMOUR	X		X	X
BRIDGESTONE			X	X
BULLET			X	X
CALLAWAY			X	X
CLEVELAND	X		X	X
COBRA			X	X
DAIWA			X	X
DUNLOP (MAXFLI)			X	X
FOUNDERS			X	X
H&B	X		X	X
HEAD			X	X
BEN HOGAN	X		X	
KARSTEN		X	X	
LANGERT			X	X
LYNX			X	X
MACGREGOR			X	X
MARUMAN	X		X	X
MERIT	X		X	X

Manufacturer	Persimmon Woods	Laminated Woods	Metal Woods	Jumbo Woods
WOODS				
MIZUNO			X	X
NICKLAUS GOLF			X	
PINSEEKER			X	
PRGR				X
PRO SELECT (NORTHWESTERN)			X	X
RAM	X		X	X
SLOTLINE			X	X
SPALDING	X		X	X
SQUARE TWO			X	
TAYLOR MADE			X	X
STAN THOMPSON		X	X	
TIGER SHARK			X	
TITLEIST			X	
RYOBI-TOSKI			X	X
WILSON	X	X	X	X
YAMAHA	X		X	X
YONEX				X
ZETT			X	X

Manufacturer	Forged Irons	Forged, Cavity-Backed Irons	Investment-Cast Irons	Other Irons
ACCUFORM			X	
TOMMY ARMOUR	X		X	
BRIDGESTONE	X	X	X	
BULLET	X		X	
CALLAWAY	X		X	
CLEVELAND	X		X	
COBRA	X	X	X	
DAIWA		X	X	GRAPHITE
DUNLOP (MAXFLI)	X		X	
FOUNDERS	X		X	
H&B	X		X	
HEAD			X	
BEN HOGAN	X	X	X	
KARSTEN			X	
LANGERT			X	

Manufacturer	Forged Irons	Forged, Cavity-Backed Irons	Investment-Cast Irons	Other Irons
IRONS				
LYNX			X	
MACGREGOR	X	X	X	
MARUMAN	X		X	CARBON-KEVLAR
MERIT	X	X	X	CARBON
MIZUNO	X	X	X	
NICKLAUS GOLF			X	
PINSEEKER			X	
PRGR			X	GRAPHITE
PRO SELECT (NORTHWESTERN)			X	
RAM	X	X	X	
SLOTLINE		X	X	DIE-CAST COPPER-COBALT
SPALDING	X	X	X	
SQUARE TWO			X	
TAYLOR MADE			X	

	IRONS			
Manufacturer	Forged Irons	Forged, Cavity-Backed Irons	Investment-Cast Irons	Other Irons
STAN THOMPSON			X	
TIGER SHARK			X	
TITLEIST	X		X	
RYOBI-TOSKI			X	
WILSON	X	X	X	
YAMAHA	X		X	CARBON-GRAPHITE
YONEX		X	X	GRAPHITE
ZETT	X	X	X	VECTRAN

PUTTERS/JUNIORS/WOMEN/LEFTIES

Manufacturer	Putters	X-Long Putters	Junior Clubs	Women's Clubs	Left-Handed Clubs
ACCUFORM	X		X	X	X
TOMMY ARMOUR	X		X	X	X
BRIDGESTONE	X			X	X
BULLET	X	X	X	X	X
CALLAWAY	X			X	X
CLEVELAND	X			X	X
COBRA	X		X	X	X
DAIWA				X	X
DUNLOP (MAXFLI)	X		X		X
FOUNDERS	X			X	X
H&B	X		X	X	X
HEAD				X	X
BEN HOGAN	X		X	X	X
KARSTEN	X	X	X	X	X

Manufacturer	Putters	X-Long Putters	Junior Clubs	Women's Clubs	Left-Handed Clubs
LANGERT		X		* see below	X
LYNX	X			X	X
MACGREGOR	X	X	X	X	X
MARUMAN				X	X
MERIT				X	X
MIZUNO	X			X	X
NICKLAUS GOLF				X	X
PINSEEKER	X		X	X	X
PRGR	X			X	X
PRO SELECT (NORTHWESTERN)	X			X	X
RAM	X	X	X	X	X
SLOTLINE	X	X		X	
SPALDING	X		X	X	X
SQUARE TWO	X			X	X

* Langert prefers not to differentiate by sex, instead issuing all its lines in five shaft flexes and three lengths—enough to cover most of the human race.

PUTTERS/JUNIORS/WOMEN/LEFTIES

Manufacturer	Putters	X-Long Putters	Junior Clubs	Women's Clubs	Left-Handed Clubs
TAYLOR MADE	X			X	X
STAN THOMPSON	X		X	X	X
TIGER SHARK	X			X	X
TITLEIST	X			X	X
RYOBI-TOSKI	X	X		X	X
WILSON	X	X	X	X	X
YAMAHA	X			X	X
YONEX				X	X
ZETT	X			X	

What Is Standard?

You'll read and hear a lot about three standards—standard lengths, lofts and lies—when you set out to purchase golf clubs. You'll also hear phrases like "longer-than-standard" and "shorter-than-standard" or "two degrees upright" and "three degrees closed," all of which are *related* to a standard. (The first two phrases refer to shaft-length, the third to the lie of a club, the last to the face angle of a clubhead.)

But if there are industry standards, what exactly are they?

Good question, for the golf-equipment industry seems unable to agree on a single set of standards. So in place of something that doesn't exist, here's as accurate a guide as you'll find, based on an informal survey of different manufacturers, repairmen, etc.

But first, an explanation of length, loft and lie.

Length. Refers to shaft-length, from the butt of the grip to where the shaft meets the club head. The ideal length of a club is determined not by a golfer's height, but by how far his hands are from the ground when he stands up straight. As a shorter person may have disproportionately short arms, it is not uncommon for a short player to need longer-than-standard shafts.

Loft. This is the angle of the clubface to the ground and determines to a great extent how far you will hit the ball. Although manufacturers graduate their lofts regularly throughout a set (you will never find a 6-iron with more loft than a 7-iron, for example), lofts of the same-number club can vary from manufacturer to manufacturer. A club designed to get the ball into the air more easily—offset irons, for example—might need stronger, or lower, lofts to compensate for a loss in distance. Bear in mind, also, that companies make several wedges with different lofts to accommodate the various short-game shots that a player will encounter during a round (sand shot, pitch, high lob, recovery from deep rough, etc.).

Lie. This is the angle, when viewed from either side of the golfer, between flat ground and the club when a player soles his club. The greater the angle, the more upright the club (which usually benefits tall players). You can tell if a club's lie is too upright or too flat if the heel or toe, respectively, is raised off the ground when the club is soled.

The industry standards:

CLUB	LENGTH	LOFT	LIE
Woods			
Driver	43"	11°	55°
2-wood	42½"	13°	55½°
3-wood	42"	16°	56°
4-wood	41½"	19°	56½°
5-wood	41"	22°	57°
6-wood	40½"	25°	57½°
7-wood	40"	28½°	58°
Irons			
1-iron	39"	17°	55°
2-iron	38½"	20°	56°
3-iron	38"	24°	57°
4-iron	37½"	28°	58°
5-iron	37"	32°	59°
6-iron	36½"	36°	60°
7-iron	36"	40°	61°
8-iron	35½"	44°	62°
9-iron	35"	48°	63°
Pitching wedge	35"	52°	63°
Sand wedge	35"	56°	63°

Sorting Out the Catalogs— the Lowdown on Mail-Order Golf

Victoria's Secret they ain't. Most of golf's mail-order catalogs are flimsy, four-color pamphlets, all looking pretty similar and all selling trinkets and less-than-perfect golf equipment at more-than-attractive prices.

So what's so wrong with that?

They're also convenient. Even though we call them mail-order, they should really be termed "credit-card-order" catalogs. One telephone call to a toll-free number and you can have a set of Spaldings or Yamahas or a major manufacturer knock-off on your doorstep the next day. Just make sure you know exactly what you want—and what you're likely to get—before you call.

This is not to say that catalogs sell only equipment. Want a golf jigsaw puzzle? A set of coasters? A Jack Nicklaus video? An elegant print of some auld St. Andrews gowfers? Call a mail-order house.

Austad's
4500 East 10th St., Box 1428, Sioux Falls, SD 57196
Call: (800) 759-4653
Fax: (605) 339-0362
Pay with: Visa, MC, Amex, Discover, GoldChex
Much the same as Las Vegas Discount (see that entry, below). You name it, they have it.

Golf Day
395 Beacham St. Chelsea, MA 02150
Call: (800) 669-8600
Pay with: Visa, MC, Discover, Amex
Golf Day doesn't carry as many different lines of equipment as Austad's or Las Vegas Discount, but you will find some top-of-the-line equipment. A full set of Wilson Staff irons for $329, for example.

Competitive Edge Golf
536 Broadway, 7th Floor, New York, NY 10012
Call: (800) 892-0200
Fax: (212) 941-8554
Pay with: Visa, MC, Amex
A good selection of metal woods and investment-cast irons; not too much junk.

GolfSmart
Box 639, Chicago Park, CA 95712
Call: (800) 637-3557 or (916) 272-1422
Pay with: Visa, MC
GolfSmart is the consumer branch of The Booklegger, which is the principal supplier of books and videos for some 4,500 pro shops, golf discount stores and catalogs around the country. See also "Where To Find Golf Videos," further in this section.

Golf Fantastic
6637 North Sidney Place, Glendale, WI 53209
Call: (800) 558-3058 or (414) 351-7070
Fax: (414) 351-6907
Pay with: Visa, MC, Discover
Most of this stuff is about as tasteful as golf junk gets: Tiny golf shoes for babies, golf-ball paperweights, silver moneyclips, elegant black-and-gold golf watches. Also included, however, are two gift ideas that must rate as the most inane around: A toilet-seat cover that says "Drop in Any Time" and a toilet-paper holder with a brass plaque on which is engraved the words "Closest to the Hole Award." This is humor?

My Favorite Catalog of All

WITTEK, 3650 Avondale Ave., Chicago, IL 60618
Call: (800) 869-1800 or (312) 463-2626
Fax: (312) 463-2150
Wittek is a wholesaler that supplies mainly pro shops and driving ranges. So what makes this such a great catalog? Wittek also happens to be the place to order miniature golf supplies! Need a six-foot-high "Fatso the Pig" statue with a little hole between his feet to prang a golf ball? It'll cost you $1,046. How about a 10-foot-high, 12-foot-long elephant? Beats the hell out of garden gnomes, but it will cost you $4,270. So let's find something in our budget. How about a trash can with a hippo head? Won't your garbage collectors love it? It's only $395. The point is, although you'd never order any of this stuff, it's wonderful to know that a giraffe and clowns and windmills and mice (*five-feet-high* mice) are only a phone call away.

Edwin Watts Golf Shop
Box 1806, Fort Walton Beach, FL 32459
Call: (800) 342-7103 in Florida; (800) 874-0146 nationwide
Fax: (904) 244-5217
Pay with: Visa, MC
Watts is one of the few catalogs that will sell you a *vacation* over the phone. Choose from Mobile, Alabama; Pensacola, Florida; or Fort Walton Beach/Destin, Florida.

National Golf Distributors
400 Galleria #400, Southfield, MI 48034
Call: (800) 999-0050
Fax: (313) 351-9013
Pay with: Visa, MC, Amex, Discover, Diner's Club, TeleCheck
Same as Austad's and Las Vegas Discount: plenty of golf clubs, plenty of junk.

Las Vegas Discount Golf and Tennis
5325 S. Valley View Blvd., Las Vegas, NV 89118
Call: (800) 933-7777 or (702) 798-7777
Fax: (702) 798-6847
Pay with: Visa, MC, Amex, Discover, JCB (Japanese Credit Bureau)
LVD is one of several discount houses that carries everything from top-of-the-line models—Taylor Made Metalwoods, for example—to trinkets you wouldn't think anybody would want.

INSTRUCTION ONLY

J. White Industries
405 Bradford Drive, Canfield, OH 44406
Call: (216) 533-5986
Pay with: Visa, MC
Perhaps the ugliest catalog in the history of the medium, the J. White booklet looks like a handicraft class project from a local elementary school. But we do like the fortune-cookie advice sprinkled throughout. Example: "Poor selection of clubs can severely hamper your enjoyment of the game." Got that right! All kinds of trainers and gadgets herein.

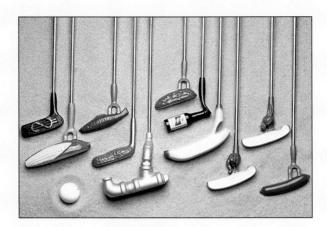

Where to Find . . .
a Left-Handed Putter Shaped Like a Pickle

From Matzie Golf, whose serious side brings you the Slim Jim, the original extra-long putter, but whose whimsical division makes putters in the shapes of bananas, beer bottles, telephones, peanuts, teeth, coffins, cobs of corn, dollar bills, pickles, pipes and hot dogs. The last three come in left-handed models. Each putter costs $36. Call (800) 722-7125.

JEF World of Golf
110 Laura Drive, Addison, IL 60101
Call: (312) 628-3540
Fax: (312) 628-3536
Pay with: Check
JEF wholesales putting trainers, practice nets, etc.

GIFTS AND PRIZES
These are wholesale outlets mostly, so call to check if you can actually buy. Unless you're already in the retail business, that is.

Maryco Products—The Golf People
7215 Pebblecreek Rd., W. Bloomfield, MI 48322
Call: (800) 334-7757 or (313) 851-4597
Pay with: Check (must accompany orders of $25 or less)
Small catalog, heavy on trinkets.

Marketcraft
Heritage Drive, Portsmouth, NH 03801
Call: (603) 436-7983
Fax: (603) 436-3417
Pay with: Visa, MC, Amex, Diner's Club
This is actually two companies: Marketcraft, which specializes in American-made gifts, and Hurley Style, which stocks British-made gifts and small leather goods. The companies also deal in hunting, riding, polo and sailing. First order has to total more than $250!

The Duck Press
Box 1147, San Marcos, CA 92069
Call: (800) 233-2730 or (619) 471-1115
Fax: (619) 591-0990
Pay with: Check
Wholesales goofy greeting cards, key chains, calendars, golf prints, plaques with unoriginal quotes ("Old golfers never die, they just lose their balls").

Field & Associates
269 Southeast 5th Ave., Delray Beach, FL 33483
Call: (407) 278-0545
Fax: (407) 278-8463
Pay with: Check
Produces a line of quality products geared toward tournament prizes, gift packages, etc. Which is why you'll find the likes of Rolex watches and Orrefors crystal in the catalog.

CLASSICS

Not a lot cheesy here. These outlets sell quality products at . . . well, you be the judge.

The United States Golf Association

Golf House, Box 708, Far Hills, NJ 07931
Call: (800) 336-4446 or (908) 234-9687
Fax: (908) 234-9687
Pay with: Visa, MC, Amex
If you missed out on your U.S. Open souvenir during the tournament, you can probably still get it from the USGA through their seasonal "Collections." The stuff in here is classic; no golfer's toilet paper or 14k gold putters. One weird inclusion is *Golf in America: The First 100 Years.* It was put together by the editors of *Golf Magazine* to celebrate the game's centennial in America, a birthday celebration the USGA adamantly refused to recognize.

Golf Arts & Imports

Dolores near 6th, Box 5217, Carmel, CA 93921
Call: (408) 625-4488
Pay with: Visa, MC, Amex
Old clubs, balls, prints, etc., available from Michael Roseto, who also runs the Wide World of Golf travel company. Which means you can book a vacation in the Far East as you order a set of Francis Ouimet stamps.

The Jack Nicklaus Golf Collection

20 Golden Bear Drive, Box 182220, Chattanooga, TN 37422
Call: (800) 544-2327
Fax: (615) 867-5318
Pay with: Visa, MC, Amex, Discover
A blatant—and no doubt very successful—attempt to cash in on Nicklaus's name and reputation. Some of the stuff is worthwhile and interesting: a portfolio of newspaper reports of Nicklaus's 20 major championship victories, for example. But most of it is overpriced—a leather address book with the Golden Bear insignia for $195?

FOR THE SERIOUS GOLFER

There are three main outlets for anyone interested in becoming a cottage industry.

The GolfWorks

4820 Jacksontown Rd., Box 3008, Newark, OH 43055
Call: (800) 848-8358 or (614) 323-4193
Fax: (614) 323-0311
Pay with: Visa, MC
This is the best source for the serious golfer—one who is interested in not only owning clubs but building them or repairing them himself. GolfWorks also is one of the few catalogs that also makes its own, top-of-the-line clubs. It's run by Ralph Maltby, author of the PGA of America's *Complete Golf Club Fitting Plan.*

Golfsmith

10206 North IH-35, Austin, TX 78753
Call: (512) 837-4810 or (800) 456-3344
Fax: (512) 837-1245
Pay with: Visa, MC
Golfsmith actually has two catalogs, one devoted to equipment and clothes for the player and a "Components and Repair Catalog" for the growing population of do-it-yourselfers. It's kind of a southern version of The GolfWorks. Weird in the catalogs are the philosophical golf quotes, some in English, others in Japanese. I'm not sure what to make of 26 Japanese characters followed by the credit "Plato."

Florida Golf Warehouse

4085 L.B. McLeod, Suite D, Orlando, FL 32811
Call: (800) 346-6574
Fax: (407) 423-5345
Pay with: Visa, MC, Discover
A complete supply store. Stocks everything from arthritic grips to "Belch," a polyurethane preservative.

Where to Find . . . a New Putter for Ten Bucks

Most average golfers could get down in two from 25 feet with an umbrella, yet they insist on spending lawyers' fees on a state-of-the-art putter.

You don't have to. If Lee Trevino can win the 1984 PGA Championship with a second-hand job he found in a bargain bin at a golf shop in Holland, you can collect with a $10 replica of the Titleist Bullseye that you can find in Chicago.

Wittek Golf Supply makes four models of putter for minigolf courses and putting tracks: three center-shafted jobs—in brass, chrome or "silver satin" finish—and an end-shafted chrome model. The brass putter is the Bullseye lookalike.

It comes in 33- and 35-inch adult versions, and 27-, 29- and 31-inch junior versions, and costs $10.20. Should you feel the urge to buy more than 24 of them, they'll cost $9.85 each. An order of 50–99 comes in at $9.45 each, while 100 or more cost $9.15. So maybe you've got a large family.

Call (312) 463-2636.

Where to Find . . . Boxes to Pack and Ship Clubs

The post office is probably the last place you'll find boxes long enough to pack clubs when you're ready to send them off for refinishing or repair. So The GolfWorks will send the boxes to you. They charge $5 per box, including shipping. Then, when the clubs are sent to The GolfWorks, a $2.50 credit is applied to your repair bill. Call (800) 848-8358 or (800) 877-4775.

10 Golf Gadgets the World Could Do Without . . . and a few that really work

by Bill Hogan

Bill Hogan is the world's leading expert on golf gadgets, principally because he wrote a book called Golf Gadgets *that Collier Books published a couple of years ago. Hogan reviewed every gadget known to golfing man in his book, but didn't really rate them. He had at least one kind word for almost everything.*

Welcome to the real world. Here Bill nominates the gadgets he finds of little use to even the most hopeless gadget addict. And just because he's kind of a nice guy, we've allowed him also to nominate a few gadgets he confesses to finding "terrific." Contact numbers are on pages 143–145 if not listed here.

Take it away, Bill.

1. MAGGIE'S STROKE-SAVER GOLF BOOTS

These are for those rare occasions when your ball isn't in water but your stance is. You're going to get your feet wet . . . unless you happen to be packing a pair of Maggie's Stroke-Saver Golf Boots. These heavy-bottomed, rubber-spiked, watertight knee-highs let you take a whack at all those shots that, for love of dry socks or dignity, you might otherwise have declared unplayable at a penalty of one stroke. Of course, you're carrying *a few* extra pounds around for that one shot in twenty rounds when they *might* help. Wanna be a hero? Boot up and swing away. Wanna be smart? Take the penalty. Wanna waste $19.95?

If you must: Las Vegas Discount

2. THE ONCOURSE INSTRUCTOR

You're in deep rough. You don't know what to do. You reach into your hip pocket and extract your Oncourse Instructor, punch in your predicament and get a quickie lesson from Bill MacWilliams, a real pro. Thanks to the marvels of microchip technology, his pointers are permanently etched in the 4K memory of the Oncourse Instructor, a hand-held computer that addresses more than 130 shotmaking situations.

MacWilliams tells you exactly how to approach and execute the shot: "Use three-quarter upright swing. Ball in center of stance. Hit down and through ball. High finish—face target. Hands lead during impact. Strike behind the ball."

Now, keeping those six swing thoughts in mind, put the thing back in your pocket and prepare to hit.

Wait. Did he say, down, through and behind, or down, behind and through? Reach into your hip pocket again. . . .

If You Must: Las Vegas Discount, Hammacher Schlemmer

3. STANCE GUIDE

"It's so simple that even I can't believe how well it works," says Bob Delgado, the Stance Guide's inventor.

"It" is a pair of bright-colored adhesive arrows that, when properly applied to the toes of your golf shoes, point in the same direction as your intended target line. One package (three sets of waterproof, soil-resistant stickers) should last a season; a golf ball designed to aid alignment on the putting green is included, too. But remember this: When your golfing companions joke about the funny-looking arrows on your shoes, you have no one but yourself to blame.

If You Must: Golf Rite, (516) 231-9530

4. THE REEL PUTTER

This fishing-reel-on-a-putter gizmo lets you retrieve any putt, made or missed, with a few twists of the wrist—its monofilament line is attached on a swivel to a gold-colored golf ball. The brass-plated putter telescopes from 36 inches down to 17 and can be mounted along with the ball on a wooden base that doubles as a practice putting cup. If you admire Rube Goldberg more than Gary Hallberg this might be perfect for you.

If You Must: Exec-U-Putt, (609) 786-1588

5. THE SUPER STICK ADJUSTABLE CLUB

No club can be all things to one golfer, but maybe this one can be all things to you. In the tradition of indoor-outdoor carpeting and reversible raincoats comes Super Stick—a collapsible, 17-in-one golf club. A twist of a coin turns its investment-cast, stainless steel clubhead into an entire arsenal: A driving iron with 12 degrees of loft, nine conventionally lofted irons, three wedges, a chipping iron and three putters. Even the swingweight is adjustable (D-2, D-4 or D-6). It's fitted with a telescoping True Temper shaft that locks for play and shrinks to 24 inches for travel. One thing: Ever actually see anyone playing with one of these things?

If You Must: Golfsmith—and just about every other catalog

6. THE SOLAR-POWERED, VENTILATED GOLF CAP

Getting a little hot-headed on the golf course? This headgear may look kind of funny, but its visor has a built-in fan that keeps a steady breeze directed at your forehead. The fan's motor normally is powered by six half-volt solar cells, but when mother nature clouds over, simply flip a toggle switch and two batteries pick up the slack. The cap also comes with a sponge that can be wetted and fitted (via Velcro) in its headband. If you dare to wear this contraption, however, the truth is you're not cool.

If You Must: Hammacher Schlemmer

7. CHECK GO

This battery-powered gizmo purportedly identifies a golf ball's optimal spin axis—its sweet spot. Place a ball in Check Go, push a button and a motor spins the ball at 10,000 rpm. After 20 seconds, the ball stops oscillating and spins on its OSA. Mark the sweet spot with a special pen, place the ball on the ground (or on a tee) with the mark facing you, and you're ready to hit. Sound kind of silly? It is.

If You Must: Sharper Image and others

8. THE RENEGADE 410 GOLF BALL

Troy Puckett, a 25-year-old veteran of the golf-ball manufacturing business, says his recipe for the Renegade 410 included "all the ingredients I knew to maximize distance." (Ironically, it was Puckett who also developed MacGregor's Mactec half-distance ball.) The three-piece Renegade has 410 dimples of three different sizes on a blended Surlyn cover. It's slightly smaller and heavier than USGA specifications allow, which helps it exceed the USGA distance standard. But why break the rules just for a few extra yards off the tee? Why not just lie about your score? Any golfer with an ounce of honor shouldn't touch this ball, or any of its clones, with a 10-foot ball retriever.

If You Must: Competitive Edge, Austad's, Herrington, (800) 622-5221 or (603) 437-4939

9. THE TASCO GOLF SCOPE

This is a precision-made, roof-prism monocular with a yards-to-the-pin scale etched on its lens. Sight the flagstick through the scope, making sure that the lowest crossbar on the yardage scale is aligned with the cup. Look where the top of the flag intersects the yardage scale and read the distance to the pin. This one is also against the rules. It's also kind of useless unless you can hit a golf ball that accurately.

If You Must: Haverhills, (800) 621-1203

10. THE POWER POD

Oh, go ahead. When push comes to slice, pull this bizarre-looking baby out of your bag, ignore the snickers and start singing "Yes, We Have No Banana Balls." If this maroon, plastic "wood" actually lives up to its billing as the ultimate slicebuster you'll have nothing to worry about. On the other hand, what if the Power Pod doesn't let you kiss all those skied and other skewed shots good-bye? What if it magnifies your *hook?* What if you run out of the six-inch high tees you're supposed to prop your ball up on? No problem. Just tell your friends that the strange thing gathering dust in the corner of your garage is a rattlesnake tenderizer.

If You Must: Austad's, Las Vegas, J. White

. . . and a few that really work

1. THE GOLF SWINGER

Wally Davis built his first prototype of his Golf Swinger in the early 1970s. It was a plastic bottle filled with water and attached to a sawed-off golf shaft. Davis played around with the idea for a few more months then came up with a metal "clicking" mechanism, which the company has basically sold ever since: a practice club and exerciser that, when swung correctly, clicks at the bottom of the downswing and automatically resets on the follow-through. If the Swinger clicks prematurely, you're hitting from the top and losing both distance and accuracy. If it resets too early after the click, you're not executing a full-follow-through with the arms extended.

The Swinger comes in two weights (26½ ounces and 21½ ounces) and, at only 25 inches long, is downright perfect for indoor practice. So if you want some reliable and affordable feedback on your golf swing, here's the perfect tool.

Worth the Effort: Kerdad, (415) 352-8662

2. HIT & TELL DECALS, IMPACT DECALS, LABELON TAPE

Any of these products can do your game a world of good by helping you determine how and where the ball is coming off the clubface. Apply any of them to the clubface and hit. An elliptical imprint left behind means the ball hasn't been hit squarely. A mark toward the heel usually means a shot that starts left, loses distance, then fades slightly. And so it goes. Simple help always was the best help.

Worth the Effort: Any catalog

3. THE MIYA COMPUTER PUTTER CHECKER

This portable practice unit checks in at only three pounds and features a series of light-beam sensors that track both the angle of your putter face and the position of its sweet spot as you stroke the ball. A computerized screen instantly displays the exact path your putter traveled over the sensors. If your putting stroke leaves something to be desired, the machine emits a short beep. Achieve perfection, however, and you'll hear a long beep of congratulations. The device works indoors or out, with any putter, with or without a ball.

Worth the Effort: Miya Epoch, (213) 320-1172

Who Makes a 1-Iron?

Lots of people. Next question: Why would you want to hit such an "advanced" club? Next answer: Because maybe you're one of those weirdos who hit long irons better than they hit woods. Or maybe you've just qualified for the U.S. Open and want to be one of the boys.

Bear in mind, also, that a cavity-backed 1-iron with a little offset is a kinder, gentler club than many 2- and 3-iron blades. Here's a partial list.

MAKER	LOFT (IN DEGREES)	LENGTH (INCHES)	MAKER	LOFT (IN DEGREES)	LENGTH (INCHES)
Tommy Armour			**Ben Hogan**		
Silver Scot 845	16	39½	Apex	17½	39¾
Silver Scot 986 Tour	17	39½	Edge	15½	39¾
Butterfly	16	39½	**Lynx**		
Browning			Parallax	14	39½
440 Gold	17	39½	Predator G	14	39½
Premier	18	39½	**MacGregor**		
Bullet			Jack Nicklaus Personal	16	39¾
.444	16	39½	**Northwestern**		
Cleveland			NR60	17	39½
TA 588	17	39½	**Slotline**		
Cobra			Inertial II	18	39⅞
Baffler Blade	15	39½	**Spalding**		
Lady Cobra	15	38½	Tour Edition	17	39½
Super Senior	15	40½	Executive Ltd.	17	39½
Dunlop			**TaylorMade**		
DP-30 Aussie	15	39½	Tour Preferred	17	39½
Maxfli Tour Ltd.	15	39¾	**Titleist**		
Max 357 MP	14	39¾	DTR	16	39⅝
The GolfWorks			Tour Model	17	39½
Bio Mech	17	to fit			
H&B Powerbilt					
TPS	16	39½			

4. THE ORIGINAL BAG SHAG

This is the old reliable. Since it first took the dirty work out of shagging golf balls, there have been plenty of imitations but few real improvements. Its zippered canvas bag holds up to 90 golf balls, and its aluminum pick-up tube is the next best thing to a well-trained Golden Retriever. What's more, the folks who manufacture the Original Bag Shag guarantee it to be man's best friend for five years.

Worth the Effort: Golf Day, Golfsmith, J. White

5. WIFFLE GOLF BALLS

The one, the only, the original. If your backyard doubles as your practice range, you'll be pleased to know that the folks at Wiffle, who still make the best plastic balls money can buy, haven't forgotten golfers. These hollow, regulation-size balls are made of white plastic and have holes instead of dimples. You can whack these babies around anyplace without the slightest regard for the premiums on your homeowner's insurance policy.

Worth the Effort: Sportime, (800) 444-5700

Headcovers, Headcovers, Headcovers

In a sense, headcovers are the last great bastion of humor in the golf bag. Ever see a funny raincover? Below are the best, from Team Effort, Inc., and the rest . . .

ALMA MATERS

Team Effort Inc., (800) 758-5857, offers these collegiate mascot headcovers: Florida Gator, Georgia Bulldog, Iowa Hawkeye, Michigan Wolverine, Ohio State Buckeye, Wisconsin Badger, Colorado Buffalo, Kansas Jayhawk, Nebraska Cornhusker, Arizona State Sun-Devil, UCLA Bruin, Texas Longhorn, Arizona Wildcat, Georgetown Hoya, Syracuse Orangeman, Iowa State Cyclone, Alabama Crimson Tide, Miami Hurricane (it's a bird!), Duke Blue Devil, Arkansas Razorback, Missouri Tiger, Louisville Cardinal, Auburn Tiger, Clemson Tiger, Florida State Seminole, Michigan State Spartan, USC Trojan, LSU Tiger, Kentucky Wildcat, Pitt Panther, Washington Husky, Purdue Boilermaker, Minnesota Gopher, Oklahoma State Cowboy, North Carolina Tar Heel, Houston Cougar, Penn State Nittany Lion, North Carolina State Wolfpack, BYU Cougar, Wake Forest Demon Deacon, Maryland Terrapin, Virginia Cavalier and Georgia Tech Yellow Jacket.

I know what you're thinking: "What does a Boilermaker look like?" As Team Effort says, "It's a guy with a big chin."

Given our druthers, however, we would have liked to have seen a Raging Cajun from Southwest Louisiana or perhaps an Anteater from Cal-Irvine. We would *kill* to find a set of headcovers in the shape of a Scottsdale (Arizona) Community College Battling Artichoke! *Golf Magazine* editor Jim Frank once challenged them to make a Kenyon (Ohio) "Lord." God arrived in the mail a few weeks later. Looked like Charlton Heston . . .

. . . AND THE REST

Sheepskin: Golfsmith has a set of four gray covers for $37.95 and a tan-colored putter cover for $9.50.

Animals: The Bronx Zoo has a smaller collection than the golf world. Las Vegas Discount has a panda, an elephant (pink), a frog, a lion and an alligator for $12.95 each. Austad's has a "Caddyshack Gopher"— just like the movie star—for $16.95, a rabbit coming out of a magician's top hat for $12.95, and a goofy looking gorilla for $9.95. National Golf Distributors has the gopher for $19.95. Edwin Watts has a gorilla, an elephant (brown), a dog wearing a deerstalker (they call it "Sherlock Dog"), a shark and a panda for $7.99 each. Golf Day has a skunk and a mallard for $19.95 each.

Cartoon characters: Golf Day sells the "Looney Tune" collection of Daffy Duck, Bugs Bunny, Tweety Bird, Sylvester and the Tasmanian Devil for $9.95 each or $8.25 each when you buy three or more. Golf Day also lists Snoopy—of Charlie Brown fame— wearing a tartan bonnet, for $10.95.

Beer cans: Golf Day and Austad's offer Bud, Bud Lite and Michelob. Golf Day's come in at $19.95 per set, Austad's at $24.95. Beer not included.

Plaid: Golf Day offers Gordon tartan (a dark green) bearing the town crest of St. Andrews at $34.95 for three.

Window covers: The idea is that you look through a vinyl window to see what club you're selecting, which I suppose is an advantage if you have a habit of putting the covers on the wrong clubs. $4.25 each from Las Vegas Discount Golf & Tennis.

Getting Started in Golf Club Repair

by Mark Wilson

It was in the early part of this century that John Dunn, a famous Scottish clubmaker and repairman of the time, commented that, "I should not advise anyone who has no knowledge of handling tools to attempt the art of clubmaking, since he is pretty sure to make a bungle of it."

That was then. This is now: Thousands of golfers are taking up club repair and assembly every year. Nary a bungler among them.

Apart from the obvious satisfaction these tinkerers get from returning a decades-old golf club to pristine condition, there are numerous reasons for the growth in interest. Some golfers pursue club repair simply as a hobby; they have the interest, are pretty good with their hands and already have a workshop in their basements. Others do it to supplement their income during retirement. Still others might see club repair as a form of therapy. Seriously. As Arnold Palmer or Greg Norman, two noted dabblers, will attest, you can lose yourself for hours tinkering with golf clubs. Some repairmen are also club collectors who get a thrill out of restoring old clubs as well as discovering them. And there are those who like the prestige; a club repairman's partners may be more patient with him in his hours of need on the golf course because he has the power to bestow free repair service upon them.

Much has changed since Dunn's day. Gone are the days of apprentices doing hard labor for such names as Forgan, Morris and McEwan, in return for only room and board. The work today is as easy as purchasing a manual and practicing the techniques contained in it. Or better still, going to a club repair school.

The GolfWorks, in Newark, Ohio (where I serve as Technical Services Manager), began running repair schools in 1982 and now convenes 16 "Total Golf Club Repair Classes" per year (see sidebar), with a student body made up of diverse backgrounds. How often do you find a retired IBM executive refinishing an old club alongside a teacher, a bricklayer and a fired air traffic controller?

A class of budding tinkerers at a repair school run by The GolfWorks.

Topics covered include the principles of golf-club and shaft design, antique club restoration and basic club-fitting. There is also an extensive session on reshafting and refinishing. We always try to get across the idea that golf-club repair does not refer only to the fixing of broken clubs. Golf-club *improvement* might be an equally valid description, for repair includes installing different grips, changing loft angles and, as noted, reshafting and refinishing.

Such was the popularity of the "Total" schools that The GolfWorks launched two new schools:

▼ "The Golfers School," which custom-fits golfers for new clubs (the cost of which is included in the $895 tuition fee) and then teaches them how to swing them; it convenes three times per year;

▼ "The "Advanced Golf Club Assembly School," which is really for commercial club assemblers. It convenes twice a year.

A third school concerns itself with advanced clubfitting.

Start-up costs are minimal. You may even possess some of the necessary tools already. If not, The GolfWorks offers a "Beginning Repair Shop Kit." Throw in a workbench and some pegboard and you'll be ready to get started. We recommend that your workshop be at least 60 square feet, including a bench measuring eight feet by two feet.

Club Repair Schools

The GolfWorks's Club Repair & Fitting Schools are held 16 times a year at the company's headquarters in Newark, Ohio, 30 miles east of Columbus. Each school lasts five days, Monday through Friday, and costs around $495. While students are responsible for their own travel and lodging, The GolfWorks is able to get lower rates at several hotels and motels close to HQ. The GolfWorks will supply a list on application.

Because space is limited, the company waits until they can reserve space for applicants before asking for a $100 deposit (refundable in the event of cancellation). Approximately one month before school convenes, each applicant receives a list of the materials he or she must bring. They include:

The basic repair kit.

▼ A wood with a loose insert or soleplate;
▼ A wood in need of a totally new insert;
▼ At least one iron (not necessarily a 1-iron) to be reshafted;
▼ A couple of irons whose loft and lie can be adjusted;
▼ At least two woods that need refinishing but do not need replacement inserts or soleplates;
▼ If possible, a hickory club for restoration;
▼ A tape recorder and notebook;

The GolfWorks provides the tools and supplies—and the workspace. For further information, contact The GolfWorks at 4820 Jacksontown Rd. (Rt. 13 South), Box 3008, Newark, OH 43055; (614) 323-4193 or (800) 848-8358. From Canada, call (800) 877-4775.

In the south, Golfsmith (best-known for its mail-order catalogs) runs repair schools every week at its facility in Austin, Texas. The schools costs $395, with an initial deposit of $50. Contact Golfsmith at 10206 North IH-35, Austin, TX 78753; (512) 837-4810 or (800) 456-3344.

How Much It Costs to Get Your Clubs Repaired

The cost of club repair varies according to where you live and where you "shop." A pro at a hoity-toity country club is going to charge you more than his counterpart at the local muni, for example. To get a handle on the range of charges, we contacted Mike Bowers, president of the Professional Golf Club Repairmen's Association, an organization founded in 1977 by his father-in-law, the late Irv Schloss, a longtime PGA master professional. Bowers provided the following menu. Anyone charging lower prices is giving a bargain, and anyone asking more is ripping you off.

REGRIPPING (PER CLUB)*

Men's Grips	Low	High
Lamkin Black	$2.50	$3.50
Lamkin Conquest (men's, ladies')	$3.00	$5.00
G.P. Victory (black, aqua)	$3.00	$5.00
Lamkin Ultra Tac Tour	$3.00	$5.00
Lamkin Silhouette (men's, ladies')	$3.00	$5.00
HiTack Black	$2.50	$3.50
Victory Jumbo	$3.00	$6.00
Air Cushion (brown)	$3.00	$6.00
G.P. Crown	$3.00	$6.00
G.P. Velvet Victory Cord	$4.00	$7.50
G.P. Victory Half Cord	$4.00	$7.50
G.P. Crown Cord	$4.50	$8.00
Classic Cord	$4.50	$8.00
Lamkin Half Cord Ultra Tac Tour	$4.00	$7.00
Lamkin Full Cord Ultra Tac Tour	$4.00	$7.00

Ladies' Grips	Low	High
Hitack (blue)	$2.50	$3.50
G.P. Victory (black, aqua)	$3.00	$5.00
G.P. Victory (blue, white)	$3.00	$5.00
G.P. Crown	$3.00	$6.00

Putter Grips	Low	High
Pro Only	$3.00	$5.00
Golf Pride	$3.00	$5.00
Hitack Pistol	$2.50	$4.00
Hitack Paddle	$2.50	$4.00
Classic Putter	$3.00	$5.00
Tiger Shark	$10.00	—

*For regripping old leather grips with paper underlisting, add 50 cents per club.

CLUB REPAIR

	Low	High
Replace epoxy, aluminum, phenolic insert, with minor touch-up	$7.00	$12.00
. . . with complete refinish	$14.00	$20.00
Rewrap whipping on wood	$2.00	—
Tighten wood head	$7.00	$10.00
Change swing weight (wood heads only)	$4.00	$8.00
Reshafting irons (with steel shaft and new grip)	$14.00	$20.00
Reshafting woods (with no refinish)	$16.00	$22.00
Reshafting aluminum woods	$16.00	$20.00
Lengthen shaft, old grip	$4.00	$8.00
Refinishing wood (if no major insert or soleplate work necessary)	$16.00	$22.00
. . . if 3 or more clubs	$14.00	$20.00
Refinishing metal woods (if no dents)	$8.00	$18.00
Change grip size (per club, full set)	$2.00	$4.00
Change grip size (one club)	$3.00	$5.00
Adjust loft and lie (per set)	$20.00	—
Adjust loft and lie (per club)	$2.00	$5.00
Assemble club from supplied components	$8.00	$12.00
Check loft and lie of woods	$2.00	—
Change swing weight (per iron)	$4.00	$8.00

Auction Fever

● ● ● **by Joe Murdoch**

How Golf Auctions Became Big Business (and where to find them)

It was a few years after the Golf Collector's Society was formed in 1970 that the rest of the world first became aware that there were men, and a few women, who collected golf artifacts. Occasional feature articles would appear in various newspapers and magazines telling how this fellow or that was collecting old, wooden-shafted clubs or golf books or scorecards, and how the growing interest in memorabilia was inflating the cost of such items.

We can only suppose that the major auction houses grew aware of this increasing interest, for in the late 1970s they widened the scope of their "sporting memorabilia" auctions to include valuables from the world of golf. Previously they had been restricted mainly to angling and cricket items. (As a matter of fact, the earliest account of a golf sale was a book sold in the 1890s, but that was in a general sale of books and not, specifically, golf books.)

This gradual attention to the golf market can also be attributed to Earle Nicklas, a book dealer in Cooperstown, New York. In 1977, his firm, Nicklas & Parker, auctioned off by mail a collection of golf books, soliciting bids via a catalog Nicklas distributed. The auction's gross receipts of $7,500 shook the private world of golf collecting, particularly as $3,000 was realized by a single copy of Thomas Mathison's *The Goff; A Heroi-Comical Poem in Three Cantos,* which was first published in 1743.

Also responsible was a small sale conducted by MacGregor's, an auction house in St. Andrews, Scotland, in 1979. Among 266 items of furniture, paintings and objets d'art was a featherie ball that went for about $220. The next morning, the ball was front-page news.

In August of that year, Sotheby's, which with Christie's and Phillips forms the big three in auction sales, conducted a sale of angling and golf memorabilia at the Gleneagles Hotel in Scotland. Again the press took note of the prices acquired. Four months later, Phillips held a sale restricted to golf, and by the following year Christie's had jumped aboard what had become a very loud and musical bandwagon, the music of course being the tinkling of cash.

Since 1980, these firms have conducted golf auctions annually and sometimes twice a year. Since 1985, the sales have been timed to coincide with the playing of the British Open and have been held within driving distance of the tournament site: in Glasgow when the Open was at Troon in 1989, for example, or in Edinburgh when the Open was at St. Andrews in 1990, or Muirfield in 1992.

These sales were to be found only in Britain until January 1988, when Phillips decided to test the temperature of the American golf addict and held a sale in New York. The mercury rose to sufficiently giddy heights— Phillips realized some $200,000—to inspire R.W. Oliver, a Kennebunk, Maine, auction house that had established itself auctioning off decoys and angling equipment, to hold its first golf sale the same year. Next up was

Mort Olman, the longtime proprietor of The Old Golf Shop in Cincinnati. Olman employed Robert Gowlan, a Phillips auctioneer and an ardent collector himself, to preside.

These houses were joined recently by Kevin McGrath, who had masterminded the first Oliver sales and who held his own sale in Andover, Massachusetts, in April of 1990. McGrath's sale realized some $380,000.

These sales, along with the big three sales in Britain, attract buyers from all over the world and gross, annually, more than $1 million. If attending one of the sales cannot be equated to playing a round at Pine Valley or Pebble Beach, the experience can be fun and, should you emerge victorious, very satisfying. But like playing a great golf course for the first time, the newcomer should treat the experience with care and respect.

The novice to the golf auction must be careful. The excitement that is built up at the hands of a skilled auctioneer is contagious; the beginner should beware and not get caught up in it. It is usually advisable to entrust the bidding to the experienced hands of a dealer who can be a bit less passionate about the occasion. Dealers charge for their services, normally about 10 percent of the price, but their skills and knowledge are well worth the premium.

A preview of the sale is normally held the preceding day or on the morning of the auction, during which time the potential buyer can view the items and, taking into consideration age, condition and rarity, decide in his own mind how much he is willing to spend.

This writer has attended a number of these auctions and has yet to pluck up enough courage to tender a bid, but I will not deny that the experience is exciting and somewhat enervating. I would encourage anyone to at least attend, if only to meet other collectors or dealers or just plain habitués like myself who show up really to observe.

The following auction houses can be contacted for information on their sales:

The Old Golf Shop
325 West Fifth St.
Cincinnati, OH 45202
(513) 241-7797

Richard Ulrich Sr.
2806 Pierce St.
Wall, NJ 07719
(201) 681-0928

Oliver's
Box 337
Kennebunk, ME 04043
(207) 985-3600

Sporting Antiquities
(Kevin McGrath)
47 Leonard Rd.
Box 1386
Melrose, MA 02176
(617) 662-6588

Christie's
502 Park Ave.
New York, NY 10022
(212) 546-1000

Phillips
406 East 79th St.
New York, NY 10021
(212) 570-4830

Sotheby's
1334 York Ave.
New York, NY 10021
(212) 606-7000

Money

How to Become a Golf Pro

● ● ● **by Roger Graves**

To anyone with even a reasonable addiction to golf, the club pro has the perfect job.

How bad can it be? His office is a golf course. His days are spent selling golf equipment, running golf tournaments, dispensing golf wisdom and occasionally playing a few holes—basically what a lot of us do anyway, only we don't do it for a living.

Which says something significant about the club pro: Because he (and to a greater extent these days, she) *does* do it all for a living, he has to do it well. Very well. Gone are the days when anyone could hang the shingle and go into business. Today, a golf pro must be accredited as a Class A member of the PGA of America, a process that involves countless hours of studying, on-the-job training, and testing. He must become an expert on a shag bag of subjects ranging from turfgrass and instruction to golf-shop operations and marketing. In fact, it's been said that today's PGA pros are as much businessmen and teachers as they are competent players.

There are several ways to earn certification, but all roads pass through the PGA Apprentice Program that was set up in 1970 and now has around 7,000 aspiring pros in its "classrooms." Apprentices must be 18 years old, must first work at least 40 hours a week, for six months, under a Class A head professional (or Class A LPGA professional) and must pass an orientation interview at their local PGA section. The final interview is basically a weeding-out process in which local PGA officers can ascertain which prospects intend to make the eventual position a lifetime pursuit.

Apprentices then begin a three- to six-year process that is not unlike progressing around a Monopoly board. To pass Go—to collect full accreditation, not $200—the PGA apprentice must:

▼ *Complete Business School I.* Six-day business schools are held at various sites around the country, throughout the year. Registration costs $250. Attendance, Sunday through Friday normally, is mandatory. Classroom time is spent reviewing the contents of the PGA Apprentice Business School Handbooks, which include such subjects as personal growth; the psychology of selling; the PGA Constitution ("We, the PGA. . . ."); turfgrass maintenance; an introduction to teaching golf; junior golf program operations; the rules; product knowledge; golf shop operations; applying for a position as an assistant pro; equipment design and repair, and golf-cart maintenance. God rested after six days, but apprentice pros have to take a 150-ques-

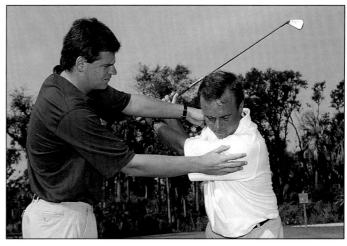

The part of the pro's job you relish: giving lessons.

tion test that is administered by the American College Testing Program, the same body that tests tens of thousands of American high school kids every year to determine their college eligibility. (Sample test questions appear on the following page.)

▼ *Pass a playing ability test.* These are administered by local PGA sections and can take any of several forms. Many sections will designate a state open championship or other PGA-sanctioned events as "Test Tournaments," meaning players satisfying predetermined scoring guidelines for a 36-, 54- or 72-hole tournament would pass the test. Normally a 36-hole score of 12 over the course rating is enough. Most PGA sections also organize tests in which apprentices play alongside two or three Class A pros at a specified course. Again, the passing grade is 12 over the course rating for 36 holes. As might be expected, some applicants breeze through the 150-question test and struggle to make the 12 over; others do exactly the opposite.

The part of the pro's job you could do without: pushing polyester.

▼ *Complete Business School II.* This one focuses on PGA membership application procedures, goal setting, motivation and communication, advanced teaching of golf, job arrangements and setting up a golf shop, the rules, clubfitting, tournament management, golf-cart management and how to hire another professional. Again, the 150-question test wraps things up.

▼ *Accumulate 36 working credits.* Apprentices can muster these at the rate they please; they're tied to the number of hours worked. The most an apprentice can make in one year is 18. A two-year college degree earns four credits automatically; a four-year degree earns eight.

▼ *Complete the PGA Apprentice Workbook.* This is no more than proof that the apprentice has studied the material provided during his apprenticeship.

▼ *Apply for PGA Membership.* An applicant must be 21 years old, a U.S. citizen or a resident alien for at least the last five years, have proof of high school or college education and have all employment substantiated. The application is processed at PGA headquarters in Palm Beach Gardens, Florida, and forwarded to the local section to which he applied.

▼ *Pass a membership interview.* Local PGA officials will interrogate the applicant. Pass it and he's home free, knighted as a Class A professional in the Professional Golfers' Association of America.

Do You Have What It Takes to Be a PGA Pro?

These are sample questions posed to PGA apprentices *before* they sit for the 150-question tests that conclude Business School I and II. The answers are on page 162.

BUSINESS SCHOOL I SAMPLE QUESTIONS

1. The distance from the center line of a shaft hole to the farthest portion of the face [of a golf club] is the:
   (A) hosel offset
   (B) loft
   (C) lie
   (D) face progression
   (E) length

2. A fully charged battery (100%) will have a specific gravity value of:
   (A) 1.190
   (B) 1.225
   (C) 1.175
   (D) 1.260
   (E) 1.245

3. If a ball is in a lateral water hazard, the player may, under penalty of one stroke, take any of the following actions *EXCEPT:*
   (A) Drop a ball outside margin of hazard within two clublengths of where the ball crossed the margin and no nearer the hole;
   (B) Drop a ball as close as possible to the spot where the original ball was played;
   (C) Drop a ball outside margin of hazard at a point on the opposite side of hazard equidistant from where the ball last crossed the margin and within two clublengths of that point;
   (D) Drop a ball anywhere along the line of flight of the ball, between original point of play and point where margin of hazard was crossed;
   (E) Drop a ball behind hazard, keeping spot crossing between himself and hole, with no limit to how far behind hazard he may drop the ball.

4. The responsibilities of the PGA President include which of the following?

   I. Authorizing Executive Director to sign contracts;
   II. Appointing committees he deems necessary;
   III. Presiding at all meetings of the Board of Directors.
   (A) I only
   (B) I and II only
   (C) I and III only
   (D) II and III only
   (E) I, II and III.

5 and 6. Match the turf term with the two definitions below (Example: A-5).
   (A) Scald
   (B) Scalp
   (C) Foliar burn
   (D) Brown spot
   (E) Fertigation

5. A fungus disease that occurs in warm, wet weather.

6. An injury that is caused by chemical application.

BUSINESS SCHOOL II SAMPLE QUESTIONS

1. Which of the following statements is a legal procedure that may be used if a ball having been hit from outside the hazard buries under the "lip" of a bunker and is deemed unplayable by the player?
   (A) With a one-stroke penalty, a ball may be dropped anywhere within two clublengths of where the ball lay but no nearer the hole;
   (B) With a two-stroke penalty, ball may be dropped anywhere within two clublengths of where the ball lay but no nearer the hole;
   (C) With a one-stroke penalty, ball may be dropped behind the hazard on the line formed by the point where the ball lay and the hole;
   (D) With a stroke and distance penalty, ball may be played from outside the bunker as near as possible to the spot from which the ball was played;
   (E) None of the above are legal.

2. If a golf cart accident occurs on your course, you should first take care of the injured parties and then do which of the following?
   I. Get statements from those who viewed the accident.
   II. Check the brakes, steering and mechanical parts in the presence of witnesses.
   III. Refrain from renting or operating vehicle until it is inspected by the insurance adjuster.
   (A) I only
   (B) I and II only
   (C) I and III only
   (D) II and III only
   (E) I, II and III.

3. Which of the following procedures must be followed in order to properly amend the [PGA] Constitution?
   I. The Sections or Board of Directors may propose and submit amendments to the Resolutions Committee at least 100 days prior to the National Meeting;
   II. The Board of Directors shall submit amendments to the Sections at least 15 days prior to the National Meeting;
   III. Proposed amendments may be adopted by a three-fourths majority of those voting at the National Meeting.
   (A) I only
   (B) I and II only
   (C) I and III only
   (D) II and III only
   (E) I, II and III.

ANSWERS TO PGA OF AMERICA BUSINESS SCHOOL SAMPLE QUESTIONS

Business School I
1. D.
2. D.
3. D.
4. E.
5. D.
6. C.

Business School II
1. D.
2. E.
3. A.

Tour Pros Are PGA Pros, Too

A touring professional does not *have* to join the PGA of America, but most do. Apart from the safety net that Class A accreditation provides should a Tour pro contract the yips and end up needing a club job, membership is required to play in the Ryder Cup, the top international team competition. Several Tour pros have blown a place on the U.S. Ryder Cup team for the biennial matches against Europe because they either neglected to attend a business school—Paul Azinger, Steve Jones—or, in the case of Jeff Sluman, simply didn't take the time to mail the application for full membership after having gone through all the other rigmarole. To a man, they regret their actions (or inactions).

The PGA of America refers to its members on the PGA Tour as "approved tournament players." Graduates of the PGA Tour's 108-hole qualifying school are automatically enrolled in the PGA's Apprentice Program, must pay the $250 initiation and must earn their 36 credits, in their case by competing in sanctioned golf tournaments here and overseas.

The Tour pros do not have to put their playing ability to the test, but they go through the business schools, where they encounter a curriculum, says Jan Gilpin, the PGA's director of education, that is geared toward the aspects of golf they will most likely encounter: ruling situations, club-fitting specifications and golf-course architecture. There is some crossover with the club pros' more business-oriented curriculum in that, says Gilpin, "the tournament player has to know about finance and investment."

Another free ride for the Tour pro: No need to take the 150-question test. "At one time," adds Gilpin, "we had an essay question examination for the Tour players that was administered at the end of the business school. We eventually eliminated that, even though most did very well on it. They were quite conscientious. But I don't know that an essay served much purpose."

However, if the Tour pro wants to turn club pro, he *will* have to sit through the 150 questions, and that means going through the study and homework once again. One such example is Peter Oosterhuis, a transplanted Englishman who was a Class A-3 professional on the PGA Tour until deciding, a few years ago, to get himself recertified. After poring through the Apprentice Program handbooks and passing the Business School I and II tests, Oosterhuis was reclassified as a Class A-4 golf director, a position he holds today at Forsgate Country Club in Jamesburg, New Jersey.

—**Roger Graves**

Where to Prepare for the Big Show

You know how all those old golfers talk about how the game isn't the same as it used to be? How today's pros aren't hungry because they're not one big mallard of a duck hook away from losing the house, the car and the chance of a lifetime? How now you can finish 20th and pocket $15,000, but in the old days it was win, baby, win, or you'd better arm yourself with a grade-A game of pool?

Well, those days are still around, only you won't find them on the PGA Tour. You'll find them on the mini-tours, a collection of traveling circuses that plays all over the continent, throughout the year, for their own entry fees and anything extra an equipment sponsor can toss in.

On any given weekend, more than 1,000 mini-tour players will leave the luxury of their beds in the back seats of their cars, or a cheap motel room if they've been flushing the ball lately, and tee it up—not because the idea of playing in front of a handful of puzzled onlookers is appealing, but because these young men and women are addicted to hitting golf balls and to the idea that someday they'll play the big tent.

Of course, maybe only one in ten, maybe less, will get a chance to even try the PGA Tour—Mark Calcavecchia and Paul Azinger are two of the few star players today who spent any real time in the minors (although the lower echelons of the PGA Tour overall is stocked full of 'em). But why let the facts get in the way of the perfect dream? Just as the PGA Tour is stocked with pros who might never win but who at the same time will never concede defeat, so the mini-tours are rife with players possessed with relatively mediocre games but who are absolutely convinced that soon the putts will fall and each week will be, "Where do I pick up my courtesy car?"

And they might just be right.

So if you can consistently break 70 from the tips and can get it up and down from a gator's jaw in a 60-mile-an-hour wind, here's where to find the main mini-tours, how to sign up and what you can expect to win. Or lose. Or both.

NIKE TOUR

Sawgrass
Ponte Vedra, FL 32082
(904) 285-3700

The Nike Tour is to golf what AAA is to baseball and for that reason may not even fit the life-is-hell profile of the average mini-tour. It was created in 1990 after the Ben Hogan Company agreed to put up $100,000 a week, 30 weeks of the year, for three years, to provide a somewhat lucrative training ground for young pros and a holding pattern for the 40-something crowd who wanted to remain competitive until they turned 50 and could play the Senior Tour. At the end of 1992, however, Hogan bowed out and Nike was brought in. Hence the name change.

The biggest difference between the Hogan Tour and the other minis, however, was best put by one young pro after the first few events. "The checks don't bounce," he said.

The Nike Tour has 17 different criteria under which you can qualify. If you have to read this to find out, you probably haven't already qualified. You probably want information on local qualifying. Here goes.

Each tournament site holds a Monday qualifying event at which the eight low scores win a place in the tournament. It's open to any professional, or to amateurs with a handicap of two or less. Entry is $100, but if you qualify you'll have to fork up a further $150 to bring you in line with the regular entry fee.

Each event is 54 holes, preceded by a Thursday pro-am. There is a 36-hole cut, with the top 50 and ties playing Sunday. Top prize usually is $20,000; 50th place pays $500.

EUROPEAN TOUR

The Wentworth Club
Wentworth Drive
Virginia Water,
Surrey, England, GU25 4LS
(0101) 9904 2881

The Eurotour probably won't like being tagged a mini-tour, what with such megastars as Seve Ballesteros, Nick Faldo and Ian Woosnam playing there regularly. But the fact remains that Europe is the hunting ground for many Americans who can't make the PGA Tour and don't want to labor on the Florida minis. Mike Smith, Jerry Haas, Peter Terevainen and Bryan Norton are just a sampling of the golfers flying the stars and stripes across the water. Tommy Armour III and Corey Pavin are two American pros who played in Europe before returning to moderate success here.

The European Tour's qualifying school is held in Spain in December. The top 50 qualify.

Certainly this is the most lucrative mini-tour, with a total of around 40 events and an average purse of around $500,000.

CANADIAN TOUR

254 Royal Salisbury Way
Brampton
Ontario, Canada, L6V 3H4
(416) 452-8232

Again, a national tour, but one that draws a lot of American golfers unable to make the PGA Tour. In fact, the Canadian Tour holds a qualifying school specifically for American golfers in the spring, just before the annual schedule kicks off in late May. When the roster of about a dozen events is completed in late September, the tour holds a Q-School for Canadian pros, who may win their cards then hibernate until the events start up again the following year.

Canadian purses range from $85,000 to $175,000 (Canadian dollars), with most hanging around the $100,000 territory. The Nissan Canadian Tournament Players

Championship offers $150,000, but also carries a $100,000 cash bonus for the winner. The extra dough is put up by Chris Haney and Scott Abbott, the owners of Devil's Pulpit, the tournament site, and the creators of the Trivial Pursuit board game. Did someone say, "Canadian golf trivia for cheese?"

GOLDEN STATE TOUR

2252 Via Del Robles
Fallbrook, CA 92028
(619) 728-7687

Now the hard-core minis. This is probably the most extensive of those, with more than 150 tournaments held around southern California (and occasionally in Nevada) during the year. It even has seven divisions:
• The Spalding Golden State Players Tour is the big event, a series of 14 tournaments, each 54 holes, each with an 18-hole pro-am and each with a purse around $50,000 (thanks to a subsidy from Spalding). The average field numbers around 120, with each entry costing $425. While the series began in southern California, it now visits Las Vegas, and the Napa Valley wine country. Anyone can play, provided you're not in the top 125 on the PGA Tour money list.
• The Professional One-Day Series runs up to 52 events, year-round, with the purse determined by the size of the entry. Fields vary from 50 to 80, with 65 the average. First-place usually pays between $1,000 and $1,300. Entry fees are $160, and there is an annual membership fee of $110, or $75 after June 1.
• The Spalding Pro Series comprises a dozen 36-hole tournaments. It began in 1989 and is now played every winter. Through Spalding's subsidy, each tournament can guarantee a $20,000 purse, with first place normally around $2,500. Fields are limited to 100, with each entry costing $275. The annual membership fee is $100.

This division has an interesting twist. It's fair to say that anyone blowing up on the first day has little chance of clam-

bering back into the money on the final 18 holes, so those in the bottom half of the field after the first day can toss in another $20 to a "Second-Day Purse." It pays the top two or three participants. The moral? It's better to lie 51st than 50th at the halfway mark.
• The Scratch Amateur division runs about 50 18- and 36-hole tournaments year-round. Fields sometimes reach 80–90 players, normally with handicaps of six or less but who all play even. Most events have an entry fee of $50–$90, and there is also an annual membership fee of $80, or $50 after June 1.

The top finishers, normally the top 10, win scrip.
• The Senior Professional division is open to golfers aged 49 and up (although that may have changed; it started in 1988 at 50, went to 45 the following year and then back up, to 49). The size of the fields varies drastically, from as little as a dozen players to as many as 60 and more, which usually means that the purses vary drastically, too. A good first-place check would be $600. Entry fees run $130–$140 with the annual fee set at $75. Each tournament also offers an over-60 flight, but if not enough sextegenarians enter, the limit is lowered to 57 or 58.
• The Senior Pro/Mid-Life Tour. Twice a month the age limit for the Senior Pro division (above) drops to 40 to allow "mid-lifers" a chance to play. This division actually evolved from what was known a few years ago as the "Mid-Life Crisis Tour." It wasn't a bad idea. Amateurs and pros aged 36 and up teamed up to play better-ball twosomes on good public courses. Trouble was, no one showed up. So the tour merged the mid-lifers with the senior pros. Just proves yet again that those who play tournament golf are interested only in their own balls. So to speak.
• Golden State's Senior Amateur division has been around for seven years even though first-place scrip seldom rises above $60. Entry fees range from $55 to $80 and there is a $45 annual membership. There is one low gross prize and several low net prizes for different flights.

SPALDING SPACE COAST GOLF TOUR

Box 2125
Plant City, FL 33564
(813) 996-2361
(407) 351-0275

August 14, 1988, must have been a big day for J.C. Goosie. That was the day the sometime Senior Tour pro and former regular Tour pro was able to watch Jeff Sluman and Paul Azinger finish one-two, respectively, in the PGA Championship. Why the big deal? Because both Sluman and Azinger are graduates of "The Goose"—the Goosie-owned Spalding Space Coast Golf Tour.

The Space Coast is, with the Florida Tour, the main mini-event in the east. It runs from September to March in the Orlando-Kissimmee area and normally comprises seven groups of three or four 36-hole tournaments each. Players sign up—and pay—to play one or more series. A four-tournament series entry runs $1,200–$1,400; a three-event series runs at $900. Single-tournament entry costs $350–$400.

With Spalding a major sponsor, purses normally run about $40,000–$50,000, with prize money paid to around 50th place. First place can pocket around $5,000. Fields are limited to 168, with any professional eligible unless he has fared too well on the PGA Tour and has landed himself in the top 125 on the money list. Second-day tournaments are available.

THE FLORIDA TOUR

Box 876
Tarpon Springs, FL 34688
(813) 937-9259
(800) 352-7767

Mark Calcavecchia is the most prominent Florida Tour alumnus now collecting major championships (1989 British Open). You'll also see the occasional big name playing—that is, a relative of a big player. Jack Nicklaus II, Wayne Player (son of Gary), Anthony Ballesteros (brother of Seve) and Jesse Trevino (cousin of Lee) have all shown up.

This is a year-round tour: 50 events, all in the Orlando-Kissimmee-Haines City area. Most are played at 36 holes. Any professional can play provided he didn't finish in the top 125 on the PGA Tour's money list in the previous year. If he has already qualified for the Tour, he may participate only until he plays his first Tour event. Amateurs with a handicap of four or less can play for scrip.

Entry fee is $250 per 36-hole event. Amateurs pay $135 per event. Eighteen-hole tournament fees are $125 and $60. There is also an annual registration fee of $100, amateur or pro.

A typical 36-hole purse runs between $20,000 and $30,000 in the winter and between $8,000 and $12,000 in the summer, when fields are smaller. The top third of the field is paid, which usually amounts to about $3,600 for first. An 18-hole victory might fetch $2,000.

One other note about the Florida Tour: It slaps a $100 fine on anyone neglecting to rake a bunker.

PLAYERS TOUR OF FLORIDA

105 Camille Court
Oldsmar, FL 34677
(813) 787-7687

The PTOF was launched in 1991 by Bill Keller, for six years the tournament director on the Florida Tour. The Players Tour has 45 tournaments a year, with contestants playing either 36 holes over two days or 18 holes the first day for a smaller prize.

Fields were small at the outset, but Keller was figuring on fields of 100 and purses of around $20,000 within a year of start-up.

Entry fees are $250 for 36 holes and $125 for 18. Registration fee is $100.

The PTOF is open to any professional not in possession of a PGA Tour card and any amateur with a handicap index of four or less. Amateur fees are $100 for 36 and $60 for 18.

T.C. JORDAN PRO GOLF TOUR

3261 Atlantic Ave.
Suite 216
Raleigh, NC 27604
(800) 992-8748

This was known as the U.S. Golf Tour until June 1991, when T.C. Jordan, a North Carolina businessman who now lives in Hawaii, decided to name the mini-tour after himself. Hey, he owns the thing. The Jordan tour, which traipses around the Carolinas, Georgia, Tennessee, Kentucky and up into Illinois, is about the closest that you'll get to the big show. Each of the 20 or so tournaments has fields of around 150, plays 72 holes and has a 36-hole cut; 60 or so play the weekend. It also has an end-of-year championship in which the top 60 "Jordan Point" earners have their entry fee of $475 waived. As entry fees go, that's a chunk of change, and it comes on top of a hefty $650 annual membership. But the T.C. does offer $75,000 purses and first-place money of around $12,000. Among those who play for such stakes are Kyle Coody (son of Charles), Gibby Gilbert (son of Gibby), Dave Stockton (son of Dave) and Randy Maris (son of Roger).

FUTURES GOLF TOUR (WOMEN ONLY)

2003 U.S. 27 South
Sebring, FL 33870
(813) 385-3320

This is *the* minitour for young ladies with aspirations to play the LPGA Tour. In fact, around 85 percent of all golfers who qualify for the LPGA spend some time on the Futures. It began in 1981 as a small circuit based around Tampa Bay, Florida, but soon moved north and west. The Futures runs between 15 and 22 events, mostly in the southeast (Florida, Georgia, the Carolinas, Virginia, etc.) and also in the midwest and northeast (Ohio, Illinois, New York, Pennsylvania, etc.).

The big difference between the Futures and the equivalent tours for men (Space Coast, Golden State) is that the Futures does not set its purses based on the size of fields. It has a local organization at each tournament site which raises the purse from local corporations. One of the biggest supporters is McDonald's, which puts up $65,000 for a tournament in York, Pennsylvania, and $50,000 the following week in Columbus, Ohio (the burger chain's partners in fast food, such as Coca-Cola, contribute to the purses, too—at the "suggestion" of McDonald's, of course).

Entry fees instead go to the administration of the tour. It employs around 10 staffers, seven of which are constantly on the road.

Fields range from 80–140 contestants and purses can range from $25,000–$65,000. The low end pays $3,300 for first place, down to $200 for 36th, while the high end pays $8,500 for first, down to $200 for 59th.

Entry fees are $225 per tournament and there is an application fee of $100. Amateurs (six handicap or less) must pay the same as the pros unless they are guests of the host club.

LPGA pros to have gone through the Futures ranks include 1989 duMaurier champion Tammie Green, 1986 U.S. Women's Open champion Jane Geddes and 1988 Women's Open champion Laura Davies.

Interestingly, the Futures is now run by Vicki Wainwright, like Davies an English girl and, like Davies, a product of the West Byfleet Golf Club where, Wainwright is quick to point out, *her* name appears before Davies's on the roster of women's club champions.

PLAYERS WEST GOLF TOUR
(WOMEN ONLY)

1901 Old Middlefield Way, #7
Mountain View, CA 94043
(415) 962-1267

Players West could be said to be the distaff equivalent to the Space Coast Tour in that it comprises five different series of between four and seven tour-naments, with most players signing up for a series at a time.

The 27-tournament schedule moves around California, Arizona and Nevada from March to August and in October and November. It is open to any women golfers who are at least 18 years old—amateurs with handicaps of six or less or LPGA pros who have yet to reach $15,000 in LPGA tournament earnings.

Entry fees for pros are $200 per event or from $720 to $1,260 per series, and $100 per event for amateurs. There is also an annual membership fee of $170, amateur or pro.

Purses range from $8,000 to $15,000, with first place paying $1,200 to $2,250. Tournaments pay between 18 and 25 places, depending on the size of the purse, which in turn depends on the size of the field and whether there is any sponsorship or funds raised at the tournament site.

NORTH ATLANTIC TOUR

Box 5724
Portsmouth, NH 5724
(603) 332-0002

It offers only 15 events, but what the North Atlantic Tour has in its favor is that it fills a large void in the golfing drifter's summer. Aware that the geography of New England means that several state open championships are within driving distance of each other but are usually scheduled weeks apart, the mini-tour decided to schedule its events during the "off" weeks between opens. That means a player who in the past hoboed his way around the south during the winter then headed north to play a few state opens and anything else he could hustle up, can now look forward to a pretty full schedule in a pretty area of the country.

Another big plus about the North Atlantic Tour: You can pay your entry fee by credit card—if the bank has not already withdrawn it.

The tournaments are played mainly in New Hampshire, where the tour is headquartered, but also in Massachusetts and Maine. Each event features a nine-hole evening shoot-out, in which groups of nine golfers are whittled by one at each hole (high score sits out) until one golfer remains. The idea is that the format creates camaraderie, hardens the constitution for future sudden-death playoffs and sure beats the hell out of a lonely evening in a motel room watching "Three's Company" reruns.

Entry fee is $225 per tournament or $600 for three. Annual membership costs an additional $100. Amateurs pay $75 per event and no annual membership.

A typical field numbers between 40 and 60 with a typical purse ranging from $5,500–$9,000. First-place usually pays between $1,350 and $1,750.

THE DAKOTAS PROFESSIONAL
GOLF TOUR

300 Apple St.
Box 424
Tea, SD 57064
(605) 368-2347

The Dakotas Tour resembles the big show in that it exempts previously successful players from qualifying for many of its 14–15 events, and it runs an open qualifying tournament for ten spots in the field.

Those fields can number up to 140—pros and amateurs—with purses ranging from $2,500 for some of the smaller "satellite" events (pros only, one-day events with small fields) to $60,000 and up for the larger, 54-hole pro-ams. Entry fees range from $40 (for satellites) to $300.

The tour begins in August and by the time its winds up in mid-September it has visited such places as Yankton, Pierre, Sioux Falls, Huron, Watertown, Milbank and Rapid City, in South Dakota, and Bismarck, Minot, Jamestown and Fargo, in the North.

Norman Dollars

Greg Norman, the founder of a new economy—but if anyone can be worth this money, he is.

Need a name at your corporate outing? Don't figure on booking the top golfers for peanuts. Plan on at least $75,000 per day plus expenses for Greg Norman. Arnold Palmer? His agent at International Management Group says Palmer also commands "Norman dollars," although that's a general category; Palmer can be had for $50,000 these days.

If you can get him, that is. Palmer and a few other top pros have so many outings already written into their sponsor contracts or have such outside interests as golf-course architecture that they seldom have the time or the inclination to pencil in what might be termed "transient" business. For exactly the same reasons, you will not be able to book Jack Nicklaus.

What do you get for your money? Normally the pro will show up in the morning, meet your clients over breakfast, make a couple of introductory remarks and then hold a clinic on the practice tee. During the golf after lunch, he'll either play a few holes with each group, passing on an instruction tip or two, or station himself at a par three and hit to the green with each group that comes through. If he does the latter, wager closest to the hole and demand *at least* three to one. In the evening, the pro will host an awards dinner and will likely be history by 7 P.M. It can be a full and busy day.

It's unlikely you'll be disappointed in your investment. Golfers tend not to show up reluctantly, and if they do they won't show it. Unless they want to cut off a lucrative supply of cash.

Some, of course, are just accommodating by nature. On the morning after the 1986 U.S. Open, for example, Norman showed up at the Inwood Country Club outside New York City for a corporate outing, only hours after blowing his third-round lead and the entire U.S. national championship with a final-round 75. It was a miserable, rainy morning, but Norman greeted everyone cheerfully. And when a member of one of the first groups that Norman played with sclaffed his ball into a large, thick bush, Norman wasted no time in getting down on all fours and accompanying the poor chap into the shrubbery.

Such an approach is not lost on those with the money to spend.

What follows is a rate card for the top players, based on information from the top agents. Bear in mind that prices can go up if the professional suddenly meets with major success, while the pro may ask but a fraction of the rate should a worthwhile charity or similar be involved. And even pros offer discounts on bulk orders.

$75,000
Greg Norman

$60,000
Nick Faldo

$50,000
Arnold Palmer
Isao Aoki

$40,000
Fred Couples

$35,000
Curtis Strange
Tom Watson
Tom Kite

$30,000
Gary Player

$25,000
Raymond Floyd
Ben Crenshaw
Bernhard Langer
Gary Player
Chi Chi Rodriguez
Fuzzy Zoeller
Hale Irwin
Nancy Lopez

$20,000
Peter Jacobsen
Lanny Wadkins
Ian Baker-Finch
Payne Stewart
Davis Love III

$17,500
Ken Venturi

$15,000
Paul Azinger
Mark Calcavecchia
Mark O'Meara
Nick Price

$12,500
Jan Stephenson

$12,000
Larry Mize
Bob Tway

$10,000
David Frost
Hubert Green
Scott Hoch
Betsy King
Johnny Miller
Mark McCumber
Doug Sanders
Scott Simpson

$7,500
Andy Bean
Chip Beck
Laura Baugh
John Brodie
Bob Charles
Beth Daniel
Bruce Devlin
Dale Douglass
Blaine McCallister
Gary McCord
Steve Pate
Joey Sindelar
Craig Stadler (the bargain in the list)

$6,000
Don Pooley
Mark Wiebe

$5,000
Danny Edwards
David Edwards
Bob Gilder
Mike Hulbert
Gary Koch
Don Massengale

Tournament Tickets—How Much You Want, How Much You're Prepared to Spend

Most tournaments have a range of prices for pro-am play. Or, rather, a range of packages that includes one or more places in the pro-am as well as a bundle of add-ons, such as access to hospitality tents, VIP seating, and so on.

What's on offer at the Honda Classic, played in Florida in March, is fairly typical of what's available at a PGA Tour event. Here are the packages and prices:

$150
Two weekly badges with access to the clubhouse
One VIP parking pass
Four tournament tickets, each good for any single day (any-day tickets, grounds only)

$250
Six clubhouse weekly badges
15 any-day tickets
Two VIP parking passes
Your name posted at the tournament and in the program

$350
One spot in a pro-am. The good news: The pro-am *will* be at the tournament site, the Weston Hills Country Club in Coral Springs, Florida. The bad news:
It won't be directly connected with the tournament, i.e., during tournament week, and you'll be paired with a PGA Section professional.
Six clubhouse weekly badges
15 any-day tickets
Two VIP parking passes
A gift package
Your name posted at the tournament site and in the program

$750
16 clubhouse weekly badges
50 any-day tickets
Eight VIP parking passes

Four stadium seats (Saturday and Sunday)
Your name posted at the tournament site and in the program

$850
One spot in the Monday pro-am
A gift package
Free parking
Six clubhouse weekly badges
15 any-day grounds tickets
Brunch
An invitation to an awards reception
Two invitations to a bar-b-q on the Tuesday of tournament week
Your name posted at the tournament site and in the program

$2,000
Note: This is the fee for a four-man team to enter the Honda's "Corporate Cup," which is played at Weston Hills a few weeks before the tournament.
Each team gets:
Green fees, carts and on-course refreshments during the cup
Four gift packages
Cocktails and snacks after play
16 clubhouse weekly badges
Eight VIP parking passes
25 any-day tickets
Your names listed in the program
Invitation to tournament awards banquet (two winning teams only)

$2,500
One spot in the Wednesday pro-am, the one the better players play in
One gift package
Five VIP parking passes and one regular parking pass
Player's guest credential
Six clubhouse weekly badges
25 any-day tickets
Four stadium seats for Saturday and Sunday
Two invitations to tournament pairings party on the Sunday before the tournament
Two invitations to bar-b-q on Tuesday of tournament
Two invitations to a gala ball during tournament week
Food and drink at designated part of the tournament site throughout the tournament
A round at Weston Hills on the Sunday before the tournament
Your name listed at the tournament site and in the program

$5,000
Eight sky box tickets per day ("Sky box" is the name given to glorified bleachers around the finishing holes where waiters will keep you eating and drinking while the golf goes on below you.)
Beverage service in the sky box (hey, we weren't kidding . . .)
Lunch in the sky box

For just $5,000 minimum, access to these skyboxes affords you a magnificent view at the Honda Classic.

Four clubhouse weekly badges
10 any-day tickets
10 VIP parking passes
One premier parking pass (closest to tournament)
A hospitality gift
Your name listed at the tournament site and in the program

$5,500
Note: This buys you into corporate row, where all the tents full of booze and shrimp are erected.
The fee gets you:
One tent, 20 feet × 20 feet
14 clubhouse weekly badges
Five VIP parking passes
One premier parking pass
25 any-day tickets
    One half-page, black-and-white ad in the tournament program
    15 grounds weekly badges for your staff
    A listing in the tournament preview, normally published in local newspapers and at the tournament site

$7,500
12 sky box tickets
Beverages and lunch in the sky box
Six clubhouse weekly badges

Tents on corporate row—for a few dollars more. (Providing cheerful hostesses is your own responsibility.)

25 any-day tickets
12 tickets to the Tuesday "shoot-out," in which ten pros begin a nine-hole tournament, one dropping out at each hole until the match comes down to the last two players on the ninth hole. The fans love it.
20 VIP parking passes
One premier parking pass
One half-page, black-and-white ad in the tournament program
A hospitality gift
Your name posted at the tournament site and in the program

$14,000
24 sky box tickets
Beverages and lunch in the skybox
25 any-day tickets
10 clubhouse weekly badges
24 shoot-out tickets
40 VIP parking passes
One premier parking pass
Full-page, black-and-white ad in the tournament program
One-eighth page, black-and-white ad in tournament preview
A hospitality gift
And, of course . . . your name listed at the tournament site and in the program.

Turn a Trick for $1,500— or Where to Find the Country's Golf Trick-Shot Artists

It's convention time. Eighty of the finest actuarial minds in America have spent six hours discussing pension schedules. Tomorrow they will play golf, after discussing pension schedules. Yesterday they played golf, after discussing pension schedules. Today is the day to break the rhythm after a two-hour lunch discussing—what else—pension schedules.

Answer?

A golf clinic. Or better still, a trick-shot exhibition.

Most professionals will put on a golf clinic. The trick-shot artists, on the other hand, go one better. For the simple reason that since you have to know how to hit a regular shot—have complete command and understanding of the golf swing—before you can start dealing with trick shots, the trick shot artists can give you a clinic *and* a circus act.

The best-known trick-shotter is Dennis Walters, not necessarily because his tricks are better, but because he also happens to be a paraplegic. Walters was a competent player—he once finished 11th in the U.S. Amateur Championship—in his home state of New Jersey until a spinal injury he suffered in 1974 when his golf car tipped over and left him paralyzed from the waist down.

After several months of rehab, Walters tried hitting golf balls from his wheelchair and did well enough to consider going out to the golf course. But in a wheelchair? Walters solved his problem by cutting the legs off a stool and mounting the top on a golf car. The car he now uses has a seat that swivels in and out.

A few of Mike Calbot's tricks.

The Walters show includes shots hit with crutches (this man has a black sense of humor), fishing rods, baseball bats and radiator hoses. He'll hit two balls with a 12-iron—a 5-iron welded to 7-iron. One flies 5-iron trajectory, the other 7-iron trajectory. Like many trick-shot artists, he hits shots from two-foot high tees, shots with a club whose shaft is hinged at several points and shots with extra-long clubs.

The first trick-shot artist was Joe Kirkwood, although who knows what some of the early Scots got up to with their cleeks and rakes after a couple of jars at the Jigger Inn. Kirkwood, a native of Australia, rose to fame on a series of tours with Walter Hagen in the 1920s (Hagen, incidentally, was an ice-skating trick artist; he could jump over seven barrels at once). Kirkwood was followed by Count Yogi, an oddball trick-shot artist who would dress up as Transylvanian nobility and who kept on tricking until his death in February 1990, and Paul Hahn, a former Tour pro who died in 1976 and who made famous the art of driving a ball from someone's mouth. Few trick-shotters, not even his son Paul Hahn, Jr., who continues the family business, will try that nowadays. It has something to do with lawyers.

Other well-known trick-shot artists include Wedgy Winchester, who won the National Long Drive Contest in 1984 using a driver that was five feet long, Bob Grobe, the oldest living trick-shot artist (he's 84) and Mike Calbot, who hits a shot with a clubhead attached to a samurai sword.

Whoever you contract, figure on spending in the low four figures for a clinic plus floor show. The average day rate is between $1,500 and $2,000. That's for a club outing. Charity events usually get a break—$1,000 normally—while corporate outings pay the most.

The following is a list of some of the top trick-shot artists in the country.

Dennis Walters
8991 S.W. Eighth St.
Plantation, FL 33324
(305) 474-3350

Paul Hahn Jr.
Box X
Boynton Beach, FL 33425
(407) 433-9393

Wedgy Winchester
c/o Karsten Manufacturing
Box 9990
Phoenix, AZ 85068
(602) 277-1300

Bob Brue
4316 N. Sheffield Ave.
Shorewood, WI 53211
(414) 962-6449

Buddy Demling
3512 Stony Brook Dr.
Jeffersontown, KY 40299
(502) 491-1891

Swing's the Thing
Dick Farley & Rick McCord
Shawnee Inn
Box 200
Shawnee on Delaware, PA 18356
(800) 221-6661
(800) 877-6522

Mike Smith
Swing-Time Golf
PGA West
54-489 Southern Hills
La Quinta, CA 92253
(619) 564-7429

Tom Mullinax
Links O'Tryon Golf Club
11250 New Cut Rd.
Campobello, SC 29322
(803) 468-4995

Mike Calbot
Pelican's Nest Golf Club
4450 Bay Creek Dr. SW
Bonita Springs, FL 33923
(813) 481-8734

Bob Grobe
61 Dayton Ave.
Somerset, NJ 08873
(908) 249-7550

Pete Longo
c/o White Pines Golf Club
500 W. Jefferson
Bensenville, IL 60106
(708) 766-0304

Joey O
Box 1196
124B Ave. NE
Cedar Rapids, IA 52406
(319) 365-7546

Paul Bumann
223 Hamilton Station
Columbus, GA 31909
(404) 324-3504

Buddy Shelton
8718 Rancho Court
Orlando, FL 32836
(407) 876-3745

Where to Get a Caddie Scholarship

It was in the early 1920s that Chick Evans, the 1916 and 1920 U.S. Amateur champion, made a series of instructional phonograph records in his native Chicago and received $5,000 in royalties. To accept the money would have been tantamount to turning professional, so Evans put it and numerous other payments he received for similar assignments into an escrow account.

Evans really didn't know what to do with the money until finally his mother, who had always been a big influence on his golfing life, suggested that, as the money had come from golf, it should go back to golf. "She believed," Evans recalled a short time before he died in 1979, "that it could be used to help caddies, by sending some outstanding boys to college."

Evans wasn't new to such philanthropy. During the first world war he'd conducted several exhibitions to raise money for the Red Cross. That was how golf got into the charity business in the first place. This time around, Evans spoke to friends at the Western Golf Association in Chicago and suggested that a caddie scholarship be set up at nearby Northwestern University. And in 1930, two young bag-toters by the name of Harold Fink and Jim McGinnis became the first "Evans Scholars."

The program changed little until after World War II. In the 1950s, chapter houses were established at the Universities of Illinois (1951), Michigan ('52), Wisconsin ('53), Michigan State ('55), Marquette ('55) and Minnesota ('58). Since then the universities at Ohio State, Purdue, Colorado, Missouri, Indiana, Miami (Ohio) and Northern Illinois have come on board, and 20 golf associations, mostly in the midwest, are now affiliated with the Evans Scholars Foundation (see below for complete list).

Indeed, there is hardly a local or state golf association that does not administer a scholarship program, and the total monies raised for scholarship funds runs easily into the millions of dollars—which is usually enough to cover the cost of tuition and board for the recipients.

In most cases, money comes from fund-raiser tournaments or individual donations. In the case of the Evans program—which many associations have duplicated—golfers can join the "Par Club" by donating more than $100, while donations of $200 and $300 get special "Birdie" or "Eagle" memberships, respectively. In return, Par Club members get bag tags, visors and money clips. A bag tag program involving contributions of $10 to $25—you get the bag tag—also helps raise cash.

In general, any caddie is eligible provided he or she meets the criteria of "scholarship, fellowship and leadership" established by J. Leslie Rollins, the dean at Northwestern when Evans first suggested the program. To be more specific, the potential scholar must,

▼ Have completed his/her junior year in high school and rank in the top 25 percent of the class or have a high enough grade point average. The Sun Country Amateur Golf Association's program in Albuquerque, New Mexico, for example, asks for 3.0 or higher. The Francis Ouimet fund in Massachusetts, on the other hand, asks only for 2.0.;

▼ Have caddied for at least two years, and have caddied well enough—and have behaved well enough—to be recommended for a scholarship by the club members. Some associations, however, require only that the candidate have worked in some golfing at the club; in the bag room or on the maintenance crew, perhaps;

▼ Be in true need of financial assistance.

In return, most caddie-scholars are expected to participate in some form of charity fund raiser while attending school. The Evans Scholars at Michigan State stage a blood drive for the Red Cross, for example, as well as a benefit run on behalf of the blind.

Details of the caddie programs can be obtained from any state golf association. Hereunder is a sample.

Western Golf Association
1 Briar Rd.
Golf, IL 60029
(708) 724-4600

This is the Evans Scholar Foundation. The foundation pays tuition and board directly to the chosen university. About 200 awards are presented each year, the average value being more than $5,000. The affiliated golf associations are:
Arizona
Colorado
Greater Cincinnati
Illinois Women's
Minnesota
Buffalo
Michigan
Indiana
Kansas City
Kentucky State
Northeastern Wisconsin
Ohio
Pacific Northwest
St. Louis
Toledo
Northern California
Oregon
South Dakota
Syracuse
Wisconsin

Some other contacts:

Francis Ouimet Caddie Scholarship Fund
Mr. Robert Elmer
Executive Director
190 Park Rd.
Weston, MA 02193
(617) 891-6400

Francis Ouimet was barely out of the caddie ranks himself when, as a sapling 20-year-old, he took on and beat veteran British professionals Harry Vardon and Ted Ray in a playoff for the 1913 U.S. Open. His victory did more for the growth of golf in this country than any other.

A Ouimet scholar can use his or her grant to attend any accredited college *anywhere,* which has seen Ouimet scholars studying anything from art history to languages at schools as far away as Italy, France, England and the U.S.S.R.

The Ouimet Fund asks for a 2.0 grade point average and admits those who have worked three years—most programs require two—in some golf-related capacity at a club. The fund raises up to $350,000 per year, splitting that among 200–250 recipients.

William Widdy Neale Scholarship Fund
Russell Palmer
Executive Director
Connecticut State Golf Association
35 Cold Spring Rd. #212
Rocky Hill, CT 06067
(203) 257-4171

Established in 1954 in memory of a former CSGA executive director, the Neale Fund helps about 50 caddies per year to the tune of about $65,000.

Northern Ohio Caddie Foundation
Northern Ohio Golf Association
17800 Chillicothe Rd., Suite 210
Chagrin Falls, OH 44022
(216) 543-6320

The NOGA split a total of $89,175 among 46 scholars in 1989, for example.

Sun Country AGA Scholarship Program
James Sweeney
Executive Director
10035 Country Club Lane, N.W.
Suite 5
Albuquerque, NM 87114
(505) 897-0864

This is a small association with a small fund. It gives two scholarships each year, each worth $1,200. The idea is to support eight scholars in any one year (two in each of four years at college) for a total annual award of $9,600.

Westchester Golf Association, Caddie Scholarship Fund
1875 Palmer Ave., Room 204
Larchmont, NY 10538
(914) 834-5869

Awards around 35 scholarships per year, with an average value of $1,500.

Yates Scholarship,
c/o Georgia State Golf Foundation,
4200 Northside Parkway
Building 9, Suite 100
Atlanta, GA 30327
(404) 233-4742 or (800) 992-4742

Begun in 1986 by the state golf association, the Yates gives out 10–12 scholarships a year, ranging from $200 to $2,000. The foundation runs a similar program with its Georgia Turfgrass Scholarship, in which recipients must follow turf-related studies at either the Abraham Baldwin Agricultural College in Tiston, Georgia, or at the University of Georgia in Athens.

Six Steps to Getting a Golf Scholarship

1. GET A GOLF GAME

This always helps. You'll have to win or finish high in a handful of junior tournaments before a college golf coach will come to check out your stuff. The coaches spend a lot of time in summer visiting the major junior events. They'll track the results of most of the local and regional junior tournaments, looking for the same names to crop up, then scout those names for themselves.

2. SKIP YOUR CLUB CHAMPIONSHIP

College coaches tend not to place much emphasis on how you fare on your home course against players you know. Of what good is that if you are, say, a Chicago golfer, and Jesse Haddock, coach at Wake Forest, is in the hunt for someone who can kick Furman's *glutei maximi* all over the Southern Conference?

3. GET REAL

Let's see . . . according to *Golf Digest,* there are almost 700 college golf programs around the country. That means that once you subtract such powerhouses as Florida, Georgia, UCLA, Oklahoma State, and so on, you're still looking at more than 500 colleges looking for anyone who can hit a 5-iron and chew gum at the same time. So lower your sights. Consider an NCAA Division II or III school or something from the NAIA.

4. SELL YOURSELF SENSIBLY

Basically this means you should do what prospects do in any other line of business: They prepare a resume that has a professional look to it. There are designers and typesetters all over the country. A few hundred dollars will buy you advice and something that college coaches and sports admissions departments will read.

5. LEARN HOW TO MAIL MERGE

Really. The time you'll save can be spent on the range or playing tournaments. Excuse me? What *is* a mail merge? It's a word-processing program that allows you to write a form letter that doesn't look like a form letter. You'll be able to write "Dear Mr. Williams, Your 17 NCAA championships leave me speechless . . ." where other kids are sending off, "Dear *coach,* I've heard a lot about your golf program." Coaches love this stuff.

6. DO YOUR HOMEWORK

If you play to scratch, you might make a top-10 school and won't see homework for the rest of your life. So do it now. Below are the books you should consult.

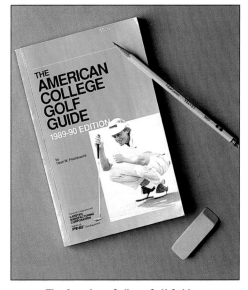

The American College Golf Guide—
see Step Six.

How to Find a Scholarship When You Can't Break Par

The College Golf Service is kind of a dating service for colleges who can't compete with such golf powerhouses as Texas, Florida or Oklahoma State, and for college-bound kids who don't play well enough to make the top squads.

It was begun by Nancy and Neil Saviano in Danvers, Massachusetts, in 1985. Originally the couple placed only tennis players, but in 1989 they started working with golf. According to Neil Saviano, numerous scholarships go unclaimed every year simply because schools do not have the funds to scout and recruit at junior tournaments around the country, and many high school golfers who play between a three and a 10 handicap never realize that money is available. Or, he says, there may be a pupil bright enough to go to an Ivy League school but who may miss out simply because very few applicants are actually accepted. The kid's chances would increase dramatically if a Harvard or Yale happened to need someone for their golf squad.

CGS charges a family $250 up front. That's a nonrefundable fee that covers the cost of putting together a resume package of high school and junior tournament results and academic performance. Then, having graded each client on a scale of one to six—golfing and academic performance—CGS forwards the resume to 15–20 schools that match. The would-be students then visit the schools to talk with the coaches and admission officials. If a school actually takes on a client—and CGS claims a success rate of 95 percent—the family ups a further $200.

Saviano cites Villanova, in Pennsylvania, and Seton Hall, in northern New Jersey, as the types of schools with which he works. He also claims close ties to the American and Canadian Junior Golf Associations and junior golf organizations in Europe, South Africa and the Far East.

CGS can be contacted at Box 2061, Danvers, MA 01923-5061; (508) 777-9828.

▼ *The American College Golf Guide.* Karsten Manufacturing, makers of Ping equipment, subsidizes it; maybe "Get 'Em Young" should be the company motto. At any rate, it lists every school with a golf program, goes into eligibility requirements and financial aid and is available for $11.45 from Dean Frishknecht Publishing, Box 1179, Hillsboro, OR 97123; (503) 648-1333.

▼ *The NCAA Guide for the College-Bound Student-Athlete.* This one runs down the do's and don'ts as spelled out by the NCAA. It costs $12 and is available from the NCAA, Box 1906, Mission, KN 66201; (913) 384-3220. Should you choose a NAIA school, you can get their rules and regulations from NAIA, 1221 Baltimore, Kansas City, MO 64105; (816) 842-5050.

▼ *The National Directory of College Athletics.* This is similar to the *American College Golf Guide.* It contains names, addresses and telephone numbers of every NCAA and NAIA college. The men's edition costs $16 while the women's edition costs $12, and that's because there are 550 college golf programs for men and only 130 for women. Geez, cent-for-cent the women get short shrift again. Both directories are available from Ray Franks Publishing, Box 7068, Amarillo, TX 79114; (806) 355-6443.

▼ *The Student Athlete's Recruiting Handbook.* This is like one of those life-enhancing deals you can catch on Sunday morning television. As well as the book you get a cassette tape, each of which deals with getting financial aid, dealing with recruiters, choosing the right college, etc. I'm not exactly sure why this has to be put on an audiotape, but I would guess that someone suspects that some prospective college athletes have trouble understanding anything more complicated than a play book—or, in golf's case, a yardage book. Just a hunch . . .

It's available from Human Kinetic Publishers, Box 5076, Champaign, IL 61825; (800) 747-4457.

How to Plan Tournaments as a Business, or at Your Club

AS A BUSINESS

"Companies will gladly pay you lots and lots of cold, hard cash to plan and manage their golf outings and golf-related meetings. When they turn the details over to an outside 'consultant' (you), they can then devote all of their attention to playing golf and having fun. They are left hassle-free to concentrate on entertaining important people."

That, in a nutshell, is the basis for a 70-page manual, *Corporate Golf Outing Management,* produced by Smyrna, Georgia-based Marshall & Associates. The company president, John Marshall, has been a tournament consultant to the PGA, LPGA and Senior Tours for several years.

Marshall's manual won't impress you in terms of production, but it does cover all the bases, pointing out from the very start the ten basic responsibilities of the outing manager:

1. Inspecting sites
2. Picking a golf course
3. Booking tee times
4. Selecting and ordering gifts and prizes
5. Booking meeting and sleeping rooms for an out-of-town event
6. Designing the playing format
7. Arranging for a still and/or video photographer
8. Coordinating the printing of invitations, cart signs, course signage, etc.
9. Mailing invitations, confirmation letters and thank-you notes
10. Meticulous attention to every detail

It then goes into such topics as which type of course to schedule (private, public or resort), suggested tournament formats, suggested gifts and prizes and how to go about getting the best prices, booking a touring professional and even setting up and publicizing the services of the firm you will have to incorporate to go into business.

For further information, contact Marshall & Associates, 3434 Vinings North Trail, Smyrna, GA 30080; (404) 436-2643.

AT YOUR GOLF CLUB

The National Golf Foundation's 84-page guide *Planning and Conducting Competitive Golf Events* was compiled specifically for use by club tournament chairmen, recreation directors, golf instructors and coaches.

It covers team and league play, various club tournament procedures and tournament golf for business outings.

For further information, contact the NGF at 1150 South U.S. Highway One, Jupiter, FL 33477; (407) 744-6006.

The United States Golf Association has updated its brochure "How to

---

How to Become a Tournament Volunteer

Although the members of the club that hosts a particular tournament tend to get first dibs on volunteer jobs—as do those who have volunteered in previous years—you should be able to sign up as some species of volunteer at the tournament of your choice. The only deterrent is that you may have to put up with golf fans who have been exposed to too much sun and light beer, and you'll probably be hit for around $30–$50 for the privilege of wearing a fairly ugly outfit. But, depending on your job, you could have one of the best seats in the house.

General categories are greens reporting (scores), scoring tent, leaderboards, walking scorers, standard bearers, concessions, marshals, parking, admission gate, transportation, hospitality, and construction. Expect to serve an apprenticeship collecting tickets before you begin driving the star players to the airport.

You also can expect zero compensation, but you do get a tournament admission badge that can be used when you're not at work. Depending on the tournament and the number of shifts you work, you may also get a ticket or two for a friend or relative.

To apply, contact the host club. A complete list of pro tournaments is available from the PGA Tour at (904) 285-3700 or the LPGA Tour, at (904) 254-8800.

Conduct a Competition." In this, the emphasis is on efficiency as opposed to fun, but such aspects as preparing a golf course and guidelines for rules officials are just as vital components of a good tournament as anything else.

The USGA also publishes "Tournaments for Your Club," a small pamphlet whose title says it all. Contact the USGA at Golf House, Far Hills, NJ 07931; (908) 234-2300.

How a Golf Tournament Makes Money

Ever wondered how a tournament can offer its players $1 million in prize money yet still make a buck for itself?

Here's the breakdown for a typical Greater Hartford Open, which is run by the Greater Hartford Jaycees, who take the proceeds and distribute them to various causes (such as books for schools, housing for the poor, hospital equipment). The GHO is a fairly typical Tour event: It's attached to a moderate-sized city, has a network television contract and offers the obligatory $1 million. What sets the GHO apart from other tournaments, however, is that it draws the largest galleries on the schedule. You'll notice that the *smallest* expense ($1,011) covers legal fees. This is astounding. Must have been one telephone call.

INCOME	
Corporate sponsor contributions	$1,000,000
Sponsor, pro-am sales	859,280
Ticket sales and pairing sheets	505,423
PGA Tour and television rights	491,107
Food and beer concessions	402,714
Corporate tent rental	265,081
Interest income	129,691
Clothing and novelties	115,692
Miscellaneous	57,571
Advertising	56,940
Parking	54,673
TOTAL	$3,938,262

EXPENDITURES	
Prize money	$1,000,000
Sponsors	210,832
Grounds	205,328
Food and beer concessions	197,414
Office expenses	188,917
Security and communications	158,272
Marketing	99,221
Clothing and novelties	91,857
Depreciation	80,077
Printing	64,038
Player relations	41,356
Miscellaneous	40,301
Dues and meetings	36,459
State sales tax	33,060
Pro-am purses	31,900
Corporate tents	29,260
Personnel	19,479
Celebrities	11,607
Interest expense	3,245
Legal expense	1,011
TOTAL	$2,543,814

PROFIT	$1,394,448

Own Your Own Golf Shop: How to Get into the Franchise Business

by Chris Yurko

Franchise golf shops are springing up all over, and anyone with a decent financial background and a healthy liking for the game can get in on the act. Even you.

A golf-store franchise is an independently owned off-course specialty store affiliated with a parent company. You probably know the names: Nevada Bob's, Las Vegas Discount and Pro Golf are some of the better known. Although the franchise conditions vary from company to company, the most common arrangement calls for each owner to pay a one-time franchise fee to get started (some parents have a flat fee or vary the rate according to the size of the store and the potential of the market) and thereafter pay a royalty fee of two to three percent of gross monthly sales.

The franchise contract gives the franchisee exclusive rights to a particular geographic area. He can then open further stores within that area, paying a reduced start-up fee and royalties. Of course, "exclusive" refers only to the parent company to which the franchise owner belongs. There's nothing—except good sense, perhaps—to stop Pro Golf opening for business right next door to Nevada Bob's.

Still, a franchise is probably a better commercial risk than an unaffiliated golf store. Franchise owners are helped by the parent through every step of the operation, from site selection and inventory to sales training and advertising. They also benefit from the parent's practice of volume buying, which makes merchandise available at reduced rates, which in turn means the franchises can sell their stock at reduced and *very* competitive prices.

Other benefits include having a recognizable name on their shingles and their locations listed in the parent's national advertising.

So where do you start?

The first step is as easy as picking up the telephone, which happens to be exactly what you do (contacts numbers are listed below). A parent representative will explain the business in brief and then mail you a packet of information.

Included in the packet are an introduction letter from a corporate officer espousing company philosophies and the benefits of owning a franchise, general information on franchises and the golf industry, an outline of financial requirements and a rundown of the services provided by corporate headquarters. The parent rep will probably contact you after you've had time to study the information, to address any questions or concerns you may have.

Where to Find . . . Help in Starting Your Own Driving Range

This is not a bad business to get into, assuming you can find reasonably priced land near a large enough market. According to the National Golf Foundation, a floodlit range of around 35 tee stations, with a small administrative building, minimal landscaping and range balls of decent quality, can cost between $100,000 and $300,000 to start up (excluding the cost of the land), but could be paying for itself within three years. A top-of-the-line range with additional tee stations, concessions, advanced landscaping and high-quality equipment can cost twice as much to launch but, again, could be raking in profits by the third year. The key, according to the NGF, are the lights, for the more people you can get onto your tee stations in the course of *24 hours*, the greater your revenue.

All this is explained in full in two NGF manuals. *Planning and Developing a Golf Range Complex*, costs $50, while *Golf Range Manual* costs $37.50. Discounts available for NGF members. Call (800) 733-6006 or (407) 744-6006.

In another section of this book, you will find guidelines on how to set up your own miniature (or micro) golf course. But say you want to take over an existing miniature golf course operation. Where would you look?

In State College, Pennsylvania. The home to Joe Paterno and his Nittany Lions is also home to the Miniature Golf Association of America, an organization set up a few years ago both to keep existing minigolf operators on the same page and to help newcomers get into the business.

Membership, which costs $40 per year, includes a newsletter—six times per year—that includes classified advertising, and *that's* where the courses go on sale. It also includes a listing of minigolf suppliers. Here are a few examples from a recent issue (without the contact numbers), that should give a rough idea of price ranges.

For Sale: Miniature golf course located in central PA. Prime location near regional mall. Good lease. Three batting cages included. Sales $110K+. Price neg.

For Sale: 18-hole, highly landscaped miniature golf course in Ft. Myers, FL. 2⅓ acres, 270′ frontage, office, parking, $715,000 neg.

The next step is to fill out an application form, which asks for information on your education, business background and financial situation. You'll have to supply professional and personal references, answer questions on the demographics of the area in which you propose to open up and sign a "credit investigation waiver," which allows the parent to run a check of their own.

A corporate committee will then review and evaluate your application. According to Larry Jordan, president of Las Vegas Discount, "The two most important areas are financial background and geography [the potential market]."

But that's not all. Says Lee Vlisides, director of corporate development at Pro Golf, "We want people with business sense who can communicate and are willing to learn the golf industry. You don't have to be a scratch golfer, but generally, franchisees are people who love golf and just enjoy being around the game."

If your application is approved, you may (depending on the company you intend to sign with) be invited to corporate headquarters, where the parent staff will explain the fundamentals of their operation and give you a tour of a model store.

You will then receive a Uniform Franchise Offering Circular (UFOC), which contains information about the parent (financial disclosure forms, a sample contract, corporate references, an outside evaluation of the company) and is required by both state and federal law.

Federal regulations also require a "cooling-off" period of 10 days before any contracts can be signed or money changes hands. If, after that time, you are still interested, you will sign the contract that defines and delineates your "territory" and put down a nonrefundable deposit to reserve your territory, usually for 90 days. The deposit, the amount of which varies from company to company but usually ranges from $2,000 to $4,000, will be deducted from your franchise fee if you go into business.

Next the franchisee and the parent look for commercial space, taking into account accessibility and visibility and parking and traffic flow in the neighborhood. When a promising location is found, the parent will help you negotiate a lease. The balance of the franchise fee is paid on the signing of the lease.

The time between signing a contract to opening for business can be up to three months. This will be your training period, when you attend a training program at company headquarters. You may bring along as many prospective staffers as you wish, and all of you will be briefed on accounting, personnel management, purchasing, product knowledge, selling techniques and clubfitting. You'll also spend some time working in a model store.

The parent's space planners will design the most effective layout for your own store and recommend vendors from which you can purchase such fixtures as cash registers, golf-club and clothes racks, carpets, displays, signage and so on. The parent will also recommend an inventory list and help set up accounts with suppliers. Most parents have their own product lines and require that you stock at least some of these products. Others impose no such conditions and leave any decisions on stock to the franchise owner.

Shortly before you open, the parent staff will set up a computer system to handle inventory, cash register and your general ledger, and train you and your staff how to use it. In the few days immediately before you open, an operations manager will be on hand for any last-minute assistance.

This assistance from the parent normally continues after you open—assuming you need it, of course. Most franchisers have a toll-free hotline to handle inquiries. "One owner used to call ten times a day," Vlisides recalls. "One time he asked where to put the shirts. Now he's got three shops and is one of our most successful owners."

A parent rep will always stop by at an owner's request, but it's not uncommon for them to stop by unannounced, just to help out with the daily operation. "If the owner is scrubbing floors on the day we show up," says Vlisides, "then we'll help scrub floors."

Franchise owners also keep in touch with each other via annual meetings, where they share planning and purchasing techniques and discuss new merchandise, and monthly newsletters, which contain general information on the golf business and list new franchisees. Stores also have been known to help each other out by shipping product when one store runs low.

That takes care of the start-up. But what are your chances of getting that far? Very good, assuming you are financially sound and have a good market. Pro Golf receives about 500 callers every week, but most are dreamers with but a few thousand dollars in their accounts. Most parents warn, also, that unless you plan to open in an area with a population of at least 200,000, the deal won't fly. They tell prospective franchisees that up front. Those who do proceed beyond application, however, will likely go the whole hog. Most parents claim a "closing" (on the contract, not the store) rate of at least 75 percent.

And if the business doesn't work out? The franchisee is expected to take care of his outstanding bills, but it's a rare occurrence as the parents spend so much time and effort insuring against a failure. "We want to keep our stores open at all costs," says Bub Hurley, franchise director of Nevada Bob's. "We won't let it get to the point of bankruptcy, if we can help it. If we have to, we will help an owner sell the store."

At right is a list of the major franchise parents. Included is the size of their networks, the franchise fee and the royalty payment (monthly unless stated otherwise).

. . . or take the word of a consultant

If you neither want to go it alone nor operate in the shadow of a parent company, there is another option.

You can do a bit of both.

Integrity Golf provides many of the same services as a franchise parent, but does not charge high start-up fees or royalties. Instead of a franchise fee, you pay a consultancy fee of $10,000–$25,000.

You will start by filling out a questionnaire and submitting a financial statement. A deposit of $1,500, which is eventually deducted from the consultancy fee, will pay for an Integrity staff member to visit your

Clubhouse Golf
7321 N. Broadway Extension
Oklahoma City, OK 73116
(405) 840-2882
Franchises: 29
Fee: $28,500
Royalty: 4%

Golf USA
1801 South Broadway
Edmond, OK 73013
(405) 341-0009
Franchises: 68
Fee: $25,000–$40,000
Royalty: 2%

International Golf Discount
9101 N. Thornydale
Tucson, AZ 85741
(602) 744-1840
Franchises: 21
Fee: $32,000
Royalty: 2%

Las Vegas Discount Golf & Tennis
5325 S. Valley View Rd.
Suite 10
Las Vegas, NV 89118
(702) 798-7777
Franchises: 72
Fee: $40,000 (up front)
Royalty: 3% (weekly)

Nevada Bob's Discount Golf & Tennis
3333 E. Flamingo Rd.
Las Vegas, NV 89121
(702) 451-3333
Franchises: 300
Fee: $47,500–$77,500 (up front)
Royalty: 3%

Pro Golf of America
31884 Northwestern Hwy.
Farmington Hills, MI 48018
(800) 521-6388
Franchises: 175
Fee: $45,000
Royalty: 2%

Integrity Golf
Professional Golf Consultants
1409 N. Kelly
Edmond, OK 73034
Clients: 60
Fee: $10,000–$25,000
Royalty: none

prospective market area, study the market potential, discuss financing and assist in selecting a location and signing a lease.

The company consults on inventory selection, store layout, and personnel training and will make arrangements with merchandisers for volume discount buys.

Of course, you won't benefit from national advertising and awareness, and a consulting firm can't supply the ongoing support services of a franchise parent.

But you will be an independent operator and you can name the store whatever you like. In other words, at last you'll see your name up in lights.

Wheeling and Dealing
A few glimpses of how the discount stores do business

▼ Many discount stores sell golf balls for *less* than they've already paid wholesale. Why? It's a combination of balls bearing the lowest profit margin of anything a discount golf store stocks, and the fact that golfers always need more balls. So rock-bottom prices are used to lure customers into the store, the assumption being that they'll also buy a new shirt, or putter or driver—all high-margin goods.

▼ Discount stores sell clubs at lower prices than other sources of equipment because they buy high volume wholesale at good prices. Although the profit per set may be smaller, the stores come out ahead in the long run; they'd rather sell 100 sets of Taylor Made metal woods for $290 per set than 25 sets at $310.

▼ Manufacturers encourage volume buying by offering "specials" to discounters. These might comprise a sixth set of clubs at 50 percent off when they buy five sets, or 10 dozen golf balls free for every 1,000 dozen a discount store buys during the year. The more the discounter buys, the easier it is to lower the net cost per unit.

▼ Manufacturers might also offer "closeouts" if they find themselves laden down with a particular product at the end of the year. A sand wedge free with every set of irons for every order of 50 sets is a good way to unload 50 surplus sand wedges while moving 50 sets of clubs.

▼ Some manufacturers produce private lines of equipment and apparel for franchisers and discount-store buying groups. For example, Roger Dunn Golf Shops, Supreme Golf and several other retail stores, are members of the B.A.G. group, which carries "Cougar" equipment and apparel. The B.A.G. groups buys tens of thousands of shirts, millions of golf balls and thousands of sets of clubs per year—so many that Cougar gives huge discounts, which translates into huge retail profits.

▼ A franchiser will often request that a manufacturer produce a low-end copy of a top-selling line, with a few minor modifications. Sometimes, however, a manufacturer will prevent a discount house from stocking a copy if an agreement has not been reached. The Ben Hogan Company, for example, stopped one discount house from selling a line of "Ege" clubs: forged, cavity-back clubs a bit too similar to Hogan's "Edge" line.

▼ Some franchisers require that franchisees sell a certain amount of a private line—100 sets a year, perhaps—or risk having to pay higher wholesale costs for other equipment.

▼ If a discount store tries to push a customer toward a private brand in lieu of a national advertised line, such as Hogan, Taylor Made or Wilson—even though the quality is poorer—it's usually because the mark-up, and therefore the profit, is greater on the private brand.

▼ Whatever the discount store buys, most manufacturers give retailers a good chance to sell the merchandise before making them pay for it. Most offer a two- to four-percent discount if the invoice is paid within 30 days, a one- to two-percent discount if it's paid within 30–60 days and no discount at all if it's paid within 60–90 days. Immediate payment brings discounts of more than four percent. The system is known as "anticipation" or a "Net 90" policy. Some manufacturers have "Net 60" policies, but that's usually the shortest amount of anticipation a retailer gets.

—Roger Graves

Before You Pay Up . . .

by Roger Graves

● ● ●

A few warnings about the discount-store business from a man who very nearly lost his life-savings— and then some.

"Join the multi-million-dollar retail golf business," the advertisement said. *"Own your own retail golf shop with minimum investment. If you love golf, this business is for you. Store features pro-line equipment, loyal clientele and desirable Salt Lake City location. Perfect business for the golf enthusiast."*

To me and two friends who had been chipping and putting around ideas for the ideal business venture for years, and who had been constantly observing and envying a particularly successful discount golf store in our own neighborhood, this sounded too good to be true. Between the three of us, we figured, we knew enough about golf, about the difference between Surlyn and balata, between forged and investment-cast golf clubs, to last us a lifetime. How could we fail?

Pretty easily, it almost turned out.

Within two months of spotting the newspaper ad, in the fall of 1985, we were the proud owners of a 3,400-square-foot, off-course retail discount store called Caddyshack Golf. Unfortunately, we also owned a hidden location in a virtually deserted strip mall in West Valley City, a middle-class suburb of Salt Lake City, and approximately $65,000 worth of outdated, shelf-worn inventory that was actually worth about $25,000. Within the next year we would find out that we also owned the previous proprietors' bad debts, a horrendous credit rating and a questionable reputation.

Caveat emptor, indeed.

"Pro-line equipment," the ad said? Well, there was one set of new Hogan Radial irons, a set of year-old Wilson Staffs, and an intriguing array of forged irons gathering dust and cobwebs in their display cases. The several dozen Titleist and Spalding golf balls we inherited had yet to be paid for, and the few LaMode sweaters and shirts that we could see had languished on the shelves so long that the plastic bags in which they lay had virtually disintegrated.

"Loyal clientele?" I suppose you could call both of our regulars loyal. They'd come in each morning for a cup of coffee and conversation, after which they'd saunter back to our indoor driving range and test-drive whatever demos were available or sit and discuss Ben Crenshaw's putting and the emergence of Paul Azinger, Mark Calcavecchia and Steve Jones. But buy anything? Not a chance.

I could also harp about the cash register we inherited, the one that wouldn't print parts of customers' receipts but which would add sales tax automatically—anything between five and 10 percent, depending on its mood. I could speak volumes about our "spacious storage area," which comprised approximately six square feet with no shelving, or what we'd been told was a "complete work bench for golf repairs," but was actually two square feet of work space and a vise. I could also mention the $7,000 neon sign out front that would flicker to life at midday, but go to sleep as soon as darkness fell.

But why dwell on the negatives? Each of our threesome had plunked down $20,000 and had ourselves a golf shop—such as it was. It would take two or three years to transform this shambles into the five-star megastore of our dreams. But we'd do it.

The first thing we discovered was that while each of us knew golf, none of us knew the golf business. Reality promptly replaced fantasy. In addition to monthly rent, insurance premiums, utilities, endless invoices and a few salaries, there were fixtures and inventory to buy. And the three of us had just handed our entire life savings of $60,000 to a man who'd skipped town and had left us with "all rights and duties of debt pertaining to Caddyshack Golf of Salt Lake City." If we'd bought into a franchise chain, we would have been able to estimate reasonably what kind of funds we'd have needed. Having bought from a previous owner, however, all our money had gone into his pockets instead of into the shop. With nothing to draw on, we had no choice but to go cap-in-hand to the banks and take out a $50,000 loan.

That done, we learned, to our great chagrin, that Caddyshack Golf's credit was so abysmal that those manufacturers who would deal with the store would do so cash-on-delivery only. No credit. No 30-, 60- or 90-day terms to help us establish a credit rating.

It was paramount that we improve our rating, so we filled out about 50 credit applications to all the big names—Spalding, Wilson, Dunlop, Titleist, Taylor Made, Ram, Hogan, Foot-Joy, Etonic, Nike, Mizuno, Pro Group, Yonex, Yamaha, LaMode, Browning, Bag Boy and an alphabet soup of others. Then we waited.

And waited.

And waited.

And found out, six months later, that some manufacturers don't like doing business with off-course shops at all. Even if the owners were three college graduates, one of whom (me) was a former member of the PGA of America Apprentice program. We also found out that some manufacturers prefer to evaluate new retailers for a year before even thinking of doing business.

Some companies were downright harsh with us. Karsten Manufacturing, whose designs were originally scorned and rejected by on-course professionals when Karsten Solheim, the company president, was trying to establish his business in the late 1960s and early 1970s, and so could be expected to show some loyalty to the off-course stores, rejected our credit application immediately. We cursed Solheim loudly, because his rejecting us meant we couldn't stock his hot-selling Ping Eye2s. But we endured this indignity.

Other manufacturers agreed to open an account when outstanding bills had been settled. Ultimately, we worked out compromises. Still others, most notably Dunlop, Taylor Made and Titleist, accepted our integrity and opened new accounts, and we developed an understandable allegiance to these companies immediately.

Then we had to decide which of our troika would quit his day-job and work the store full-time (we'd been working shifts around our existing jobs, but knew that good business meant on-site management and decision-making). It so happened that Chuck Schell, one of our three, had recently left his job as assistant general manager of the Salt Lake Golden Eagles, a pro hockey team, and although Chuck had played golf for only five to six years, he had a business and marketing background. He decided to give it a go.

Chuck then spent quality time on the telephone trying to persuade manufacturers to "open" Caddyshack Golf. If rebuffed, he'd call back a week later with renewed enthusiasm. Finally, two years after we bought in, we were "open" with every manufacturer—except Karsten, of course—and the cash registers were ringing consistently.

En route, however, we stumbled onto one of the great myths of the business—that you might actually *play* some golf yourself. Hah!

You want bankers' hours? Off-course shops keep supermarket hours. You have to open at dawn to catch the early-bird nine-holers, and you have to stay open late to capitalize on the high traffic of businessmen passing your store on the way home from work (or, in summer, on the way to and from the golf course).

We also found out how competitive the business is. You compete with department stores, drug stores, other retail golf stores, PGA pros at country clubs, resorts and munis, and with mail-order outlets.

As we were not part of a franchise chain, we had to take it upon ourselves to register the

A Franchise's Typical Start-Up Costs*

These numbers are based on a store of 2,800–3,000 square feet. They will vary according to geographic location, the parent company's fees, and the length of the golf season in the chosen area.

Franchise Fee	$40,000
Furniture, fixtures, equipment	$15,000–$30,000
Opening inventory and supplies	$100,000–$150,000
Rent	$2,500–$5,000
Preopening costs	$5,000–$8,000
Management training	$1,000–$3,000
TOTAL INVESTMENT	$163,500–$236,000
OPERATING CAPITAL	$20,000–$40,000

*Source: Las Vegas Discount Golf & Tennis

name of the shop with local and state authorities, design signage, lease building space, purchase cash registers, arrange our advertising, hire and train employees, and so on and so on. It never stopped.

But gradually we learned the business. We learned that starter sets and inexpensive full sets made by such "name" clubmakers as Spalding, Wilson and Dunlop, are huge sellers during traditional holidays. Golf-related gifts, such as gift-wrapped balls, socks, towels and tee packages go like hotcakes at Christmas. A sale on women's shoes and tops before Mother's Day, or men's shoes and accessories before Father's Day, can be immensely successful.

We also realized that the on-course professional was not so much a competitor as a source for us to promote our own shop. We'd buy advertising space on scorecards at local courses or buy signage on benches. We'd sponsor prizes at charity tournaments, all the while aware that each expenditure on promotion and advertising meant that we had to generate more retail sales to cover the cost.

But the most important thing we learned was that you can't go into this business without two key virtues: preparation and patience.

We really didn't expect to be handed a booming business on a silver platter when we bought the shop. But we didn't expect the seller to misrepresent the value of his stock so drastically. Given the chance again, we would have taken our own inventory of his stuff, right down to the last rusting sand wedge. Of course, we went after him to retrieve some of our money when we realized what we'd bought into, but almost immediately after selling he declared bankruptcy and all bets were off.

Our patience did pay off. After a few years of what amounted to trial and error, we got ourselves to a position where we could consult our *own* records to determine buying trends and what we should order. Copious record-keeping eventually told us, for example, that ball sales slumped in winter, but we still had to have the shelves stocked for Christmas.

It took us five years of hard work to get into the black. Today, the shop is turning a profit. Chuck is still managing it and employs a staff of three. I and our third partner, Glenn Davidson, are little more than silent partners. In fact, I think I've visited Caddyshack Golf about twice in the past year.

Then again, I saw enough of it when we started out.

Spectating

Why You're Better Off Watching the Pros Than Being One

by Thomas Boswell

Be glad that you don't play golf for a living. Be glad that you can watch it instead. You're better off snickering at the pros than being one. Here are 10 reasons why.

1. FIRST AND FOREMOST, THE PROS NEVER WIN.

Bobby Wadkins, brother of Lanny, has teed it up more than 30 times a year on the PGA Tour, for almost two decades of seasons.

HE'S NEVER WON A TOURNAMENT.

How would you like to spend the rest of your life pretending you're an athlete and a competitor when you know in your heart that in 600 tournaments your "best-ever finish," as they say in the press guides, was a second at the IVB-Philadelphia Classic, whatever that was, back in 1979?

Wadkins isn't alone. The PGA Tour has inferiority complexes industrial-strength Brillo couldn't scour away. Meet some of the guys in the 10-year club: John Adams, Brad Bryant, Buddy Gardner, Pat McGowan, Larry Rinker, Loren Roberts, Clarence Rose, Bill Sander, Lance "Q-School" Ten Broeck, Frank Connor, Mike McCullough.

Yes, at least 10 full seasons each on the PGA Tour and not one of them has ever won a tournament. Some of them have never even finished second! What does it take to get these guys off the Tour—detox?

The amazing thing is, most of these guys can play. They're good enough, year-after-year, to qualify to stay on Tour. But the dynamics of the sport dictate that if Jack Nicklaus is going to win 70 times, and Tom Watson insists on winning 32, there's just not enough to go around for the rest.

2. YOU'D NEVER BE AT HOME.

By the way, where *is* home? When the pros go on Tour, they're ON TOUR. When one event ends Sunday, they travel to the next town Monday to practice on Tuesday and play the pro-am on Wednesday. The tournament begins Thursday. For 25 to 30 weeks a year they play golf six days a week—not for fun, but to pay the bills—and on the seventh day, they travel.

Nice life.

Take the case of Mike Donald, who lost the U.S. Open in a playoff in 1989. On average, he'll enter 35 tournaments a year. Then there are exhibitions, outings and foreign events. The man is almost forty and until recently kept his stuff *at his mother's house.*

When the pros are at home—if they have one—they practice more days than not. Out of guilt. Or that inferiority complex. "I bet Greg is practicing today," they think. "And if he isn't, Curtis sure is. Oh God, I'd better go hit 400 balls and practice for two hours."

So the next time you get back from Divots-by-the-Parkway Public Golf Course and Video Arcade, which happens to be my home track, feel good about yourself. At least you're home sweet home. Hey, mow the lawn. You promised.

3. YOU'D NEVER HAVE FUN.

Ever seen a pro golfer have fun? No, Hale Irwin after making a 50-foot birdie putt at the 72nd hole of the U.S. Open doesn't count. We're talking about the other eighty million guys out there grinding for par in the spinach.

Golf is not like baseball where you can joke with the other team at second base or hotdog a little in front of 40,000 fans in your home park. If we don't count Lee Trevino and 7.3 other human beings this century, it is safe to say that it is impossible for a pro to play his best golf and enjoy himself at the same time.

If he smiles, he'll bogey the next hole. Laugh, and it'll be a double. If he actually tells a joke to the crowd, he'll probably sign an incorrect card and be DQed.

To the pro, golf is funny only after he's finished playing it. And even then, most of the jokes are at his own expense. Nice game.

Admit it, you may be a lousy golfer, but at least you have a ball. No matter how mad you may have gotten, no matter how badly you may have played, have you ever put in a round when you did not have a better time than you could possible have had doing anything else—with the possible exception of going to Madonna's house and pretending you're the new masseur?

4. You'd have no job security.

Nobody has ever mastered golf. It can't be done. Johnny Miller went from number two on the money list to 14th the next year to 48th to 111th. Generally speaking, he just woke up one morning, at the height of his career, as the greatest player in the world, or pretty close to it, and forgot how to play golf. There was no happy ending. He played diligently for another 10 seasons and never cracked the top 10. He just lost it.

At various times, much the same thing has happened to Lanny Wadkins, John Mahaffey and dozens of other stars. In 1979, when Jack Nicklaus dropped to 71st on the money list at a healthy 39, he wasn't the least bit sure he'd ever win again.

Even lawyers, who don't deserve to have *anything* good ever happen to them, know that by the age of 30 they will never have to learn anything else for the rest of their lives. They'll just bill higher and higher rates until they're 90. A pro golfer has to keep making five-foot putts to make a cent.

5. You'd have to sell your soul to Deane Beman.

When *you* step onto a course, you can wear a beard and Bermuda shorts, play in smelly old sneakers, carry 15 clubs and forget to rake the stupid sand traps.

The touring pros, on the other hand, all have to report to a central discount outlet store in Hattiesburg, Mississippi, where they get fitted for a gawdawful gruesome wardrobe of doubleknit pants, polyester shirts and Aureus visors that would throw Dan Quayle into a fashion crisis.

Don't these guys laugh when they pass each other in the locker-room? They all look like Ozzie Nelson in 1959. The only guy who tries to be different and modish is Tom Watson, and he looks worse than anybody! The man's a fashion mute. Companies should pay him *not* to wear their logos.

And as if the official Tour clothes, with the official Tour logo, sold at 700 equally boring Tournament Players Clubs throughout the Sunbelt, aren't bad enough, just think how much pure pleasure these guys are having in Memphis when it's 105 degrees—*in long pants.*

6. You'd have to play by the rules.

We get to make up our own.

This is very important. The devil invented golf, so the least we can do is return the favor and cheat like hell when we play.

Pro golfers are denied this prerogative. Mike Reid walked over to Curtis Strange at the U.S. Open in 1990, when both were in contention, and said he was calling a penalty stroke on himself. His club had accidentally brushed the ball, moving it about a quarter of an inch. Nobody but Reid saw it.

This is noble. This is the very spirit and core of golf, not to mention America. But is it possible that Mike Reid has given one too many banquet speeches?

Sorry, sorry, I didn't really say that. But in my group, we roll 'em over in the fairway. Of course, we never—*never*—touch the ball in the rough to improve the lie. Unless it's kinda hot. Or if you're in a bad mood. Or if you really, *really* have to.

7. The press.

I think this has something to do with being in a position where sportswriters—professionals with no known minimum standards—are paid to stand in judgment over a professional golfer, making fun of his mistakes and impuning his character, just before they go out on Monday and play the same course in 112 blows. For free.

8. You wouldn't be able to get mad.

So what's the point of golf if you can't get mad and throw your clubs?

Seriously. We can talk here. I'm writing this. You're reading it. It's like we're in the same AA group. Go on—look me in the eye and tell me you don't play golf because IT'S THE ONLY TIME IN YOUR ADULT LIFE THAT YOU CAN GET REALLY MAD AND OBNOXIOUS WITHOUT HAVING TO EXPLAIN OR APOLOGIZE!!!

And even if, like me, you've reached the point where you get mad only once or twice a year, *you still have the option.*

Can you hit a member of your immediate family? Of course not. Curse out your boss? I know I haven't tried it. Can you even be insubordinate with a traffic cop who's two levels up from protoplasm? Get serious. Those guys can revoke an entire life. You reach a point in life where you don't even want to alienate your insurance agent!

But golf? There it sits. Ready to be flung. The last vestige of adolescent freedom. A whole world of emotional possibilities.

Let's just say that the pros' version of the game has no therapeutic component at all.

If you're a Tour pro and you wrap your 1-iron round a live oak, give your putter some well-deserved frequent-flier mileage and tell the little old lady beside the green to take her emphysema somewhere else while you putt, the Tour Policy Board, man, like, gets all in a huff. And if you tell 'em, "Hey, dudes, don't have a cow," their eyes just glaze over. They give you the Distant-Relative-of-Mac-O'Grady Stare.

The Tour of the '90s make you nostalgic for Tom Weiskopf. Okay, okay, maybe that's too extreme. But you almost wish the *old* Curtis Strange—The Human Snap—would come back.

9. YOU'D HAVE TO PLAY IN FRONT OF OTHER HUMAN BEINGS.

From the start, this has never been a good idea.

When a Tour pro yips a tiny putt on a green like glass, and he's dying inside because he's just missed his fifth cut in a row, and he reeeaaalllyyy doesn't want to spend the rest of his life giving driving-range lessons to the wives of the Duluth Elks Lodge, that's when thousands of fans remind him just what a pathetic case he is.

"Ooooooooooooooooooooo-ooo-ooo-ooohhh!!!"

Why don't they just hold up the "Death to Choking Dogs" signs?

Then he has to walk to the next tee. He's trying to get the miss out of his mind. But the gallery *has* to console him. "Bad break, Bubba!" "Don't worry! Anybody can miss from eighteen inches!"

So he thinks, "Let's see . . . if I strengthen my grip, close my stance, transfer my weight real quick, shut the clubface and pronate my wrists real fast, maybe I can smoke a snap hook and take out a whole family of five."

But that never helps. There's always more fans, and they all know how awful it is to shoot 82, have dinner at Taco Bell, then look forward to a bed at a Red Roof Inn.

10. SOME MISCELLANEOUS REASONS.

▼ You'd have to play in the rain.

▼ Sometimes the lightning siren doesn't work.

▼ Sooner or later, you'd get paired with Hubert Green. His record is 73 waggles in a sandtrap in Rochester. "If he'd backed off and started over," J.C. Snead once said, "I'd have struck him dead right there."

▼ If you were to sign up with teaching guru David Leadbetter right now, he'd have a lesson open at 11 A.M. on Friday, March 6, 2012. Maybe then he'll figure out what's wrong with your swing.

▼ The first time you play with Jack Nicklaus, he'll be genuinely nice to you, which will make you feel

even smaller than you already do (if that's possible), and you will wonder, quite correctly, why you even bothered to spend your life playing a game in which another man has permanently retired the trophy.

▼ Sooner or later you're going to wonder, "What exactly does Rocco Mediate?"

▼ You will want to kill Ken Green but after years of plotting you will go crazy not being able to figure out how.

▼ Eventually you'll have to tell Curt and Tom Byrum that they really don't look the slightest bit alike.

11. OH, YOU DIDN'T THINK THERE *WAS* A NUMBER ELEVEN. SILLY YOU.

Number eleven is the "but-on-the-other-hand."

Get this. The 40th man on the PGA Tour's money list wins almost $400,000 a year. If he works at it at all, he can double that through endorsements, corporate outings, speeches and general, All-American grifting and grafting. Even if he doesn't win a tournament. Even if he's never home. Even if he never smiles or gets mad or cheats or wears a shirt made from natural fibers.

The 80th man on the money list, some clown who probably can't chew gum and mark his ball at the same time, wins about $250,000 a year, can make six figures easily on the side and has his pick of the blonds in the front row of the gallery at the Colonial.

Even the guy who is 100th on the money list makes close to $180,000 a year, and any able-bodied man should, in five years, learn to play a simple game like golf as well as Ed Humenik, who happens to be 100th on the list that is in front of me right now. So it's an old list.

And even *he* can scam some poor, star-struck Hardee's Classic pro-am hacker from Coal Valley, Illinois, into a full partnership in a chain of Jiffy Lubes. Heck, by the time Ed Humenik is my age he'll probably *own* a newspaper, not work for one.

Yes, the money is good. That can't be denied. But who needs money and fame when you have to live such a life?

How You, Too, Can Play the U.S. Open

This one's easy: You enter the damn thing!

Well of course the U.S. Open Championship is really only "open" to professionals and top amateurs (two handicap or 2.7 handicap index), but the fact is that even an amateur can enter the Open simply by forgetting the whole concept of a handicap and declaring himself a professional. (The same goes for women and the U.S. Women's Open; handicap of four or 4.4.)

The fourth line of the United States Golf Association's official entry form reads "Amateur, Pro or . . ." That's where you write in "Pro." All that's left is for you to attach a $75 check to your entry and nominate where you want to play your 36-hole local qualifying. The USGA provides a list of some 80–90 clubs, and if the course you choose can't accommodate the requests (current entries run more than 5,500), you may be moved.

So here's some advice: Don't pick the course closest to home; pick the course where you figure two rounds of golf is worth a lot more than $75. In 1989, for instance, you could have chosen Mission Hills, a sumptuous layout in Rancho Mirage, California, where the LPGA plays its annual Nabisco Dinah Shore event; Crooked Stick in Carmel, Indiana, site of the 1991 PGA Championship and the 1993 U.S. Women's Open; the Country Club of Rochester, where Walter Hagen played his golf; Llanerch Country Club outside Philadelphia, where Dow Finsterwald edged Billy Casper when the PGA switched from match play to medal play in 1958.

The top 600 qualifiers, according to a complicated formula known only to the USGA, proceed to sectional qualifying. (The ladies' start with sectional.) Now we're looking at two additional rounds, at no extra cost, at such private oases as the San Francisco Golf Club; Skokie Country Club, outside Chicago, where Gene Sarazen won the 1922 U.S. Open; and the Portland Golf Club in Oregon, where Ben Hogan won the 1946 PGA. Of course, if you have to turn professional purely for the opportunity of playing in an Open, then you probably don't have a chance of ending up one of the 600 survivors.

There is a catch. If you fail to score within 10 strokes of the course rating, then you'd better have a good excuse. Failing that, your name goes on a USGA blacklist. Not only will you be banned from further Opens—which some might wear in the grill room as a badge of honor—but you may be banned from all other USGA championships, and should you apply to be reinstated as an amateur, the USGA might toss your application in a pending file and let it grow lichen.

Why would the USGA be so cruel? One, they like their championships to be taken seriously. Two, those players who *are* serious don't like to wait and watch you hit your eleventh shot into the same branches of the same bush (interrupts their rhythm, I'm told). And three, this is such a good idea that the USGA has to find *some* way to deter America's golfing millions.

How You Might Not Be Able to Enter the U.S. Women's Open

If you were born a man. In 1989 the United States Golf Association changed the eligibility requirements for the U.S. Women's Open, Senior Women's Open, Women's Amateur, Women's Mid-Amateur, Women's Publinx and Girls' Junior from "women golfers" to *"golfers who were female at birth."*

Credit Charlotte Wood, a 57-year-old woman from Texas who was a 47-year-old man from Texas when he—she?—went under the knife in 1982. Wood finished third in the Senior Women's Amateur and reached the last four of the Women's Mid-Amateur in 1987. She tried to go a few places better in 1988 but withdrew after the rest of the field—all women at birth, one presumes—complained.

Although Wood could probably make a good case in court that she be allowed to enter—never mind sexual discrimination, it's perfectly legal for transsexuals to have the appropriate changes made to their birth certificates—she has so far decided it's not worth the effort.

▼ *U.S. Amateur Championship.* Open to all amateur golfers with a handicap index of 3.4 or lower, or a handicap of three or lower.

▼ *U.S. Women's Amateur.* As above, but with a handicap index of 5.4 or lower, or a handicap of five or lower.

▼ *U.S. Amateur Public Links Championship.* Open to "bona fide" public-course players who have not held privileges at courses closed to the public or which maintains its own course (i.e., not a daily fee course usually) unless the privileges come through an educational or military institution or via an entrant's employment. No handicap maximum, but 36-hole qualifying is held at the tournament site.

▼ *U.S. Women's Amateur Publinx.* Ditto, for females at birth.

▼ *U.S. Junior Championship.* Open to any male who has not reached his 18th birthday by the day of the final round and with a handicap index of 9.4 or lower, or a handicap of nine or lower.

▼ *U.S. Girls' Junior.* Same as above—but for females at birth—except the handicap index must be 12.4 or lower, or the handicap 12 or lower.

▼ *U.S. Senior Amateur.* Must be fifty-five years old by the date of sectional qualifying and have a handicap index of 8.4 or lower, or a handicap of eight or lower.

▼ *U.S. Senior Women's Amateur.* Must be fifty years old by the day of the first round and have a handicap index of 12.4 or lower, or a handicap of 12 or lower. And be female at birth.

▼ *U.S. Senior Open.* Must be fifty years old by the start of an appointed date (contact USGA) and, if an amateur, have a handicap index of 8.4 or lower or a handicap of eight or lower.

▼ *U.S. Mid-Amateur.* Must be twenty-five years old by the date of sectional qualifying and have a handicap index of 5.4 or lower, or a handicap of five or lower.

▼ *U.S. Women's Mid-Amateur.* As above, but with a handicap index of 9.4 or lower, or a handicap of nine or lower. Don't forget the female at birth thing.

How to Get U.S. Open Tickets

More important: *When* to get U.S. Open tickets. Today the Open traditionally sells out way ahead of time. In the case of the 1987 Open at the Olympic Club in San Francisco, the tickets were gone two *years* ahead of time, before the club could even print up a brochure. So apply at least two years in advance.

The U.S. Women's Open should not be as hectic, but with the graduation of Jack Nicklaus and Lee Trevino to the Senior circuit, tickets to the Senior Open could become tougher than the "junior" version. In any case, better safe than sorry. Call early.

U.S. OPEN

1993 (June 17–20): Baltusrol Golf Club, Springfield, New Jersey

Tickets:
Box 9
Shunpike Rd.
Springfield, NJ 07081
(201) 376-1900
(201) 376-7609

1994 (June 16–19): Oakmont Country Club, Oakmont, Pennsylvania (outside Pittsburgh)

Tickets:
Oakmont Country Club
Hulton Rd.
Oakmont, PA 15139
(412) 828-8000

1995 (June, dates to be announced): Shinnecock Hills Golf Club, Southampton, New York

Tickets:
Box 1436
North Highway
Southampton, NY 11968
(516) 283-3525

U.S. WOMEN'S OPEN

1993 (July 22–25): Crooked Stick Golf Club, Carmel, Indiana

Tickets:
U.S. Women's Open
1150 N. Meridien St, Suite 303
Carmel, IN 46032

1994 (July 21–24): Indianwood Golf Club, Lake Orion, Michigan

Tickets:
Call club at (313) 693-3330

1995 (July 13–16): Broadmoor Golf Club, Colorado Springs, Colorado

Tickets:
Contact USGA at (908) 234-2300

U.S. SENIOR OPEN

1993 (July 8–11): Cherry Hills Country Club, Englewood, Colorado (outside Denver)

Tickets:
4125 S. University Blvd.
Englewood, CO 80110
(303) 761-9900

1994 (June 30–July 3): Pinehurst Country Club, #2 Course, Pinehurst, North Carolina (in the middle of nowhere)

Tickets:
Box 4000
Highway 5
Carolina Vista Dr.
Pinehurst, NC 28374
(919) 295-6811

1995 (June 29–July 2): Congressional Country Club, Bethesda, Maryland

Tickets:
Contact USGA at (908) 234-2300

The Five Best Places to Watch a Major Championship

The huge grandstand behind the 17th green at St. Andrews.

1. 17TH HOLE AT ST. ANDREWS

There's a 400-foot long grandstand right behind the hole, from which 7,000 at a time can watch the litany of horrors that always occurs at the Old Course's Road Hole. Part of the stand—the center, naturally—is reserved seating, but the other 5,000 seats are up for grabs. Check the pairing sheet for a stretch of big names, get there 20 minutes early to guarantee a seat, carry a blanket if the wind is coming off the sea, and settle in to watch the pros appear around the dogleg created by the Old Course Hotel. They will stand over their balls and wonder how the hell they're going to avoid the Road Bunker in front, the road itself behind, and still hold the narrow green. This is spectating at its sadistic best.

2. 13TH AT AUGUSTA NATIONAL

The popular place for photographers and elderly fans and their folding chairs is behind the green of the par-five second, which either receives a long approach or allows a fairly easy up-and-down from sand. I prefer the grandstand behind the 13th which, although small, allows fans first to judge the tee shot on this dogleg par five on how far round the corner the player has been able to draw it and then vicariously make the decision whether or not to go for the green. I'll always remember Curtis Strange facing such a decision in The Masters in 1985, soon after taking the final-round lead. Seated next to me was Herbert Warren Wind, who took a glimpse through his binoculars and suddenly started spitting phlegm all over the place as he blurted, "My god! He's taking a metal wood!" Of course, Strange was wrong and Wind was right and Curtis will never be forgiven. But I'll tell you what: It was great theater for anyone lucky enough to witness it.

3. 8TH HOLE AT PEBBLE BEACH

I'll even name the exact spot. There's an electrical box, or something like that, about two feet high, to the left of the landing area for the drive on this magnificent par four. If you're tall enough, stand close to it; if you're my height (five-eight on my tiptoes), stand on the electrical thing. It'll accom-

From the other side of the carry on the 8th at Pebble Beach.

modate one foot. It sounds like a lot of work, but it's the best way to see what Jack Nicklaus has called "the best second shot in golf": a mid or long iron across the Pacific to a green framed by sand.

4. THE 6TH TO 10TH HOLES AT TURNBERRY

When Greg Norman won the 1986 British Open at Turnberry, I did a strange thing: I stopped following the leaders and started following the leaders. By this I mean I decided to follow them from about 100 yards back. I waited for the players, the press and the crowds to pass, and then nipped across the sixth fairway (against tournament guidelines, I must confess) to walk along the top of the cliffs above the Firth of Clyde. All of these five holes follow the water. A shirt-sleeved policeman gave me a long look, but instead of frog-marching me back behind the ropes, he issued a breezy "Wonderrrful, isn't it?" And it was. Norman and Tommy Nakajima had dragged all the fans up to the green with them and soon had the place in utter silence as they putted. All we could hear from our place in the rear were the waves lapping on the beach below and a few seagulls and oyster catchers shooting the breeze. The sun was glinting off a calm sea, silhouetting a few yachts, and towering to the sky, just offshore, was Ailsa Craig, that massive hunk of granite. Believe me, the scene is just as breathtaking from the "mainland" side of the fairways.

5. ANYWHERE AT SHINNECOCK HILLS

U.S. Opens are fairly horrible spectator events, usually because classic Open courses are lined with trees that may look good, but which block 90 percent of the decent sight lines. There are exceptions to this, such as the auditorium provided by the slope behind the final green at The Olympic Club in San Francisco, but Shinnecock Hills, out on the eastern tip of Long Island, is about the only Open course that is truly "open" to spectating (Pebble Beach is a close second). It's not a links course, in that the turf is not classic, sandy linksland. But the relative lack of trees and roll of the land suggest links, which means spectators often find themselves standing on little humps, slightly above the action with nary a bough in their way. The sea air and the area's vulnerability to sudden mood swings in the weather are other good reasons to watch an Open here.

Five Good Ways to Watch Any Golf Tournament

1 Pick a spot for the day and stay there. Par threes are always popular. The final hole never hurts.

2 Pick a group of players and follow them. Asked why he'd paired Ben Crenshaw, Lee Trevino and Tom Watson together in the U.S. Open at Shinnecock Hills in 1986, USGA boss Frank Hannigan replied that it was his day off, and he liked watching those three play.

3 Find a cluster of good groups. This is a tough one, but if you have Norman, Strange and Ballesteros in successive groups and a course whose holes turn in different directions often enough, it's not a bad idea to watch them come through, run up ahead, watch them come through, run up ahead . . .

4 Spend time at the practice range. Ballesteros is the best to watch—he'll shape shots until sundown. But the longer you spend, the more characteristics you'll notice. Trevino cackles the whole time. Peter Jacobsen always jokes with the caddies. Paul Azinger likes to talk about his swing. Strange never seems happy. Nick Faldo spends more time practicing positions within the swing, normally in the takeaway, than he does actually hitting balls. Most of the others just pound, pound, pound.

5 Watch it on television. Sad to say, it's about the only way to witness the whole story.

If You Can't Make It to a Major...

As golf's major championships make up but four weeks on a schedule of more than 50 tournaments, there are plenty of other events to choose from. Some of the nonmajors make for fairly slim pickings—no offense meant to the Quad Cities Open—but others are worthy of closer attention. Here's a sample of nine such tournaments, with appropriate details.

1. AT&T PEBBLE BEACH NATIONAL PRO-AM

Folks still refer to this event as "The Crosby," as it was informally known before Kathryn Crosby, wife of crooner Bing, removed the family name from the tournament marquee in 1986 as a protest against sponsorship by the telecommunications conglomerate. But they could call this tournament *anything*—my preference would be the "Crosby Clambake," the original moniker—and it would remain a popular tournament.

Why? Simply because it is played in part over Pebble Beach, which happens to be one of the finest pieces of golfing real estate you'll find. Even though the pros are partnered by movie stars, business moguls and dermatologists-to-the-stars, all of whose swings make German hammer-throwers look elegant, nothing can spoil the surroundings. Even if the weather turns foul—and it very often does at this time of year—there are few better places to watch a golf tournament than on the Monterey Peninsula.

Note: Until 1991, Cypress Point was one of the tournament courses, but chose to withdraw rather than alter its membership policies to admit minorities and women. It was replaced by Poppy Hills, a public layout part-owned by the Northern California Golf Association. Most of the players hate it.

When played:
Late January/early February

Where played:
Pebble Beach Golf Links, Poppy Hills Golf Course, Spyglass Hill Golf Course,

all in Pebble Beach, California (Monterey Peninsula)

Tickets:
Day: $20; Week: $60–$90 ($10 for teenagers)

Ticket information:
(800) 541-9091

Parking:
Free

Hotels:
The Lodge at Pebble Beach (408) 624-3811; The Inn at Spanish Bay (408) 647-7500

Restaurants:
The Lodge at Pebble Beach, The Inn at Spanish Bay, Hog's Breath Inn (in Carmel). A tip: The 1991 tournament program ran a complete dining guide to the Monterey Peninsula. Maybe the tournament office can find you a copy.

Other points of interest:
Big Sur, Cannery Row, 17-mile Drive, Monterey Bay Aquarium; San Francisco (two hours' drive). Or you can just park yourself out near Pt. Pinos and watch the surf crash and the seals bark.

Nearest airport:
Monterey Peninsula Airport, San Jose International, San Francisco International

2. NISSAN LOS ANGELES OPEN

It's been around since 1926 and has been won by the likes of Ben Hogan, Jimmy Demaret, Sam Snead, Arnold Palmer and Tom Watson. The Riviera course, a George Thomas design from

1926, is a classic layout that has also held the 1948 U.S. Open and the 1983 PGA Championship. What was once a great tournament, and is now just a good tournament, could return to its glory days if the tournament organizers would allow the punishing kikuyu rough to grow closer to ankle-deep and pinch a few of the fairways. Then it would be a U.S. Open-caliber course. Again.

When played:
February

Where played:
Riviera Country Club, Pacific Palisades, California; (213) 454-6591

Tickets:
Day: $15; Week: $40

Ticket information:
(213) 482-1311 or (213) 480-3232

Parking:
$5 per day, $15 per week (shuttle service operates)

Hotels:
Miramar Sheraton (800) 325-3535; Holiday Inn (800) 465-4329

Restaurants:
Plenty in Los Angeles area. Strattons (Westwood), Toppers (Huntley Hotel, Santa Monica), Gladstones (Malibu)

Other points of interest:
Universal Studios, Hollywood, Beverly Hills, Venice Beach

Nearest airport:
Los Angeles International

3. THE PLAYERS CHAMPIONSHIP

In its never-ending struggle to have major status accorded to the Tour pros' "own" championship—the one administered by the staff of the players' member organization—what was once the Tournament Players Championship has been renamed to sound similar to The Masters. They've also dropped the pro-am and even colored the gallery ropes and stakes green to emulate Augusta National.

Although the tournament lacks tradition—it's been going only since 1974—this usually is a good tournament to watch. It draws a strong field, and the TPC at Sawgrass (the original Tournament Players Club) allows some of the best views of the action anywhere in the country.

Most overrated view: The 17th hole, the par three with the island green. It's like Kesey used to say: "You're either on the bus or off the bus," and golf fans who judge a pro's skills completely on his ability to hit a green with a short iron or end up wet would probably be better served thrill-wise at the local drag strip.

When played:
March

Where played:
TPC at Sawgrass, Ponte Vedra Beach, Florida; (904) 285-3301

Tickets:
Thurs., Fri.: $20; Sat., Sun.: $30; Week: $90

Ticket information:
Galleries limited to 30,000. Renewal forms mailed to existing ticket holders. Call (904) 285-7888 for information on ticket outlets and ordering by telephone.

Parking:
$2 per day

Hotels:
Marriott at Sawgrass, (800) 251-1962; Holiday Inn Jax Beach, (800) 465-4329; Sheraton Jax Beach Resort Inn, (800) 325-3535; Ponte Vedra Inn & Club, (800) 874-3558

Restaurants:
Ragtime, Sliders, Homestead (all in Ponte Vedra), Hans' Bistro (Jax Beach; order the snails)

Other points of interest:
PGA Tour and ATP headquarters, St. Augustine, area beaches, golf courses

Nearest airport:
Jacksonville International (50 minutes)

4. MCI HERITAGE CLASSIC

Always one of the best tournaments of the year, for several reasons:
• Harbour Town is a magnificent course. Pete Dye, with the help of his wife, Alice, and of Jack Nicklaus, put together a shortish, tight layout with tiny greens (I still haven't figured out why they had to enlarge number 15, a long par five that demanded a precise wedge for the approach).
• Because the layout is so good, it draws a top field.
• The finishing stretch (three-shotter, sharp dogleg par four, wet 'n' sandy par three, magnificent par four along the water of Calibogue Sound) is one of the best in golf.

Here's another indication of how good the Heritage can be: Heritage winners include Arnold Palmer (1969), Hale Irwin ('71, '73), Johnny Miller ('72, '74), Nicklaus ('75), Tom Watson ('79, '82), Greg Norman ('88).

When played:
April, usually after The Masters

Where played:
Harbour Town Golf Links, Hilton Head Island, South Carolina; (803) 671-2231

Tickets:
Day: $25; Week: $75

Ticket information:
(803) 785-3333 or (800) 845-6131

Parking:
Free

Hotels:
Sea Pines Resort, (800) 845-6131; Marriott, (800) 228-9290; Hyatt Regency (800) 228-9000/9001

Restaurants:
Hilton Head has more than 200

Other points of interest:
Tennis, horse riding, nature preserves

Nearest airport:
Hilton Head; Savannah, Georgia (one hour)

5. THE MEMORIAL TOURNAMENT

Perhaps the most prestigious tournament without major status, the Memorial always draws a strong field. Two reasons: It is hosted by Jack Nicklaus, who has a predilection for having his tournament run smoothly down to the last detail, and it is played on Nicklaus's finest design—Muirfield Village, perhaps America's best post-war golf course. The tournament recently moved from pre-Memorial Day dates to later (too much television competition for actual Memorial Day dates), which is good news in that the course, which normally is in excellent shape, will be in better-than-excellent shape. The course has several amphitheater greens, as well as excellent clubhouse and practice facilities, including a circular range so players can practice in the wind direction of their choice.

When played:
Early June

Where played:
Muirfield Village Golf Club, Box 396, Dublin, Ohio 43017; (616) 889-6700

Ticket prices:
Daily tickets for practice rounds only. Week (grounds only): $85

Note: The Memorial is like The Masters in that tickets are distributed to the same spectators each year. Anyone wishing a place on a waiting list should contact the tournament at (614) 889-6700.

Parking:
Free

Hotels:
Stouffers Dublin, (800) 468-3571; Marriott Courtyard (800) 228-9290; Holiday Inn (800) 465-4329; Marriott

North (800) 228-9290; Sheraton North (800) 325-3535; Embassy Suites, (800) 362-2779; Hyatt Regency and Hyatt Capital Square, both (800) 228-9000/9001

Restaurants:
The Refectory, Fifty-Five at Crosswoods, The Vault (downtown Columbus), LaScala, TGI Fridays, The Bogey Inn

Other points of interest:
State Capitol, Columbus Zoo, German Village and Brewery District, COSI (Center of Science and Industry)

Nearest Airport:
Port Columbus International

6. ANHEUSER-BUSCH CLASSIC

Curtis Strange hosts this tournament at the Kingsmill Resort on the banks of the James River outside Williamsburg, Virginia. The tournament doesn't draw a very strong field, as its dates often con-

flict with those of the British Open—one good reason Strange has a mediocre Open record. All the problems incumbent with midsummer heat and humidity don't help, either. It is, however, one of the best tournaments to visit with children since Busch Gardens and a bunch of other family attractions are nearby.

When played:
July

Where played:
Kingsmill Golf Club, 100 Golf Club Rd., Williamsburg, Virginia; (804) 253-1703

Ticket prices:
Thurs., Fri.: $15; Sat., Sun.: $20; Week: $60

Ticket information:
(804) 253-3985

Parking:
Free

Hotels:
Hilton, at resort entrance, (800) 445-8667; Quality Inn, (800) 228-5151; Ft. Macgruder (800) 446-4082; Kingsmill Resort (800) 832-5665; Courtyard by Marriott (800) 321-2211; Best hotel in the area is Williamsburg Inn, (800) 447-8679

Restaurants:
Whaling Co., Mr. Liu's, Riverview Room at Kingsmill

Other points of interest:
Busch Gardens theme park, Colonial Williamsburg, Jamestown Settlement, Yorktown Battlefields

Nearest airport:
Richmond and Norfolk. There is commuter service to Newport News.

7. B.C. OPEN

You've read the comic strip, now watch the golf tournament. Johnny Hart, creator of those neolithic laughs, happens to be a golf nut who lives in the area and who is the honorary chairman of the event. B.C. never draws a star-studded field, but it's a well-run tournament and as an added attraction puts on a players–caddies softball tournament on the

eve of the tournament and an outdoor concert during the tournament (see below).

If you're wondering where the name of the golf course came from, try the industrial giant, Endicott-Johnson.

When played:
mid- to late-September

Where played:
En-Joie Golf Club, Endicott, New York (outside Binghamton); (607) 785-1661

Tickets:
Thurs., Fri.: $15; Sat., Sun.: $25; Week: $50

Ticket information:
Write to B.C. Open, Box 571, Union Station, Endicott, NY 13760

Parking:
$4 (valet) per day

Hotels:
Best Western Homestead and Best Western Johnson City, (800) 528-1234 or (800) 268-8993; King's Inn (607) 754-8020; Holiday Inn Binghamton, (800) 465-4329; Owego Treadway, (800) 631-0182; Red Roof (800) 843-7643; Hotel DeVille (607) 722-0000

Restaurants:
Plenty in Binghamton and Johnson City. In Endicott: Surf and Turf, Number 5, Vestal Steakhouse, Gance's Cafe, Orlando's, Rita's, Cortese

Other points of interest:
Tournament features a concert around the 18th green on Friday night. Past performers include Ray Charles, Chuck Mangione, the Oak Ridge Boys, the Gatlin Brothers and Air Supply.

Nearest airport:
Edwin Link Field/Broome County Airport

8. WALT DISNEY WORLD/OLDSMOBILE GOLF CLASSIC

Although the Disney comes during a part of the schedule when most players are either planning to go overseas or have actually gone, the tournament has been known to draw a moderately strong field because the Magic Kingdom, Epcot Center, and Donald, Mickey and Goofy provide a mite more entertainment for the players' families than, say, catching up on the latest pizza concoctions at the nearest Milwaukee shopping mall. If there is a PGA Tour event that could be said to be a family event, this is it.

When played:
October

Where played:
Walt Disney World's Magnolia, Palm and Lake Buena Vista courses, Lake Buena Vista, Florida (Final round on Magnolia); (403) 824-6298

Ticket prices:
Thurs., Fri.: $10; Sat., Sun.: $18

Ticket information:
(407) 824-2250

Parking:
$3 per day

Hotels:
Walt Disney World is full of them. Call (305) 824-8000 for reservations.

Restaurants:
In hotels

Other points of interest:
Walt Disney World, Epcot Center, Disney/MGM studios

Nearest airport:
Orlando International (15 miles)

9. KAPALUA INTERNATIONAL

The tournament's been around since 1983, always as an unofficial event, and is now played over the Kapalua resort's newest course, the Plantation,

designed by Ben Crenshaw—and that is the main draw here (apart from the obvious advantage of being in Hawaii). Crenshaw did something weird when he built the Plantation: He gave golfers oodles of room in the fairways and built massive greens with little protection. But he also built in numerous sirens: On a short par four on the back nine, for example, the golfer could easily hit to a 100-yard-wide landing area—three times the normal size—and have a short iron to the green. But if he flirts with the bunkers and rough on the left, he might just drive the putting surface. Of course, most players choose the latter option and end up in jail. It's a delicious design philosophy.

Kapalua draws a strong field of pros who are either on their way to or home from tournaments in Japan, which means it's quite possible to see the likes of Crenshaw, Curtis Strange, Peter Jacobsen or Lee Trevino participating.

When played:
November

Where played:
Kapalua Resort (Plantation course), Maui, Hawaii; (808) 669-5607

Ticket prices:
Free

Ticket information:
(808) 669-4844

Parking:
Free

Hotels:
On resort

Restaurants:
On resort

Other points of interest:
Tournament parties, which have included such entertainers as Huey Lewis, Charley Pride and the Gatlin Brothers.

Nearest airports:
Kapalua-West Maui, Kahului

How to Get Masters Tickets

Before the 1990 tournament, it was possible to reply to classified ads in Augusta and Atlanta newspapers and pay through the nose for hallowed tournament tickets. Or scalp them in Augusta during tournament week.

As it turned out, most tickets were not even tournament tickets. A counterfeiting ring was uncovered during the 1990 event, and several culprits were arrested. The following year's tickets had *holograms* on them! Pretty damn impossible to copy, I'd say.

The same people get Masters tickets each year, and a subscription is canceled about as frequently as the Cubs win the World Series. There is a waiting list for cancellations, but even it is so oversubscribed that it was closed down in 1978 with the last name on the list prepared to wait 50 years—and expecting to.

About the only way now to see The Masters is to know someone with tickets (the tournament does not object to ticket-holders lending them to friends) or have a member of your immediate family betrothed to one of the Nicklaus kids. Or qualify for the tournament.

But you can get tickets for the practice days at the club gates. This is not a bad deal. Watching the pros try and figure out the greens before the tournament begins is to watch grown men cry. If you do go for a practice day, try to make it Wednesday. It's on that afternoon that most of the field participates in a par-three tournament at the club's idyllic, nine-hole par-three course. This is as loose as The Masters gets, with some players bringing along their children (one year, Peter Jacobsen's son played in a sandtrap while Daddy holed out) and others hitting powder balls, playing left-handed or hitting simultaneously—anything to lighten the mood. For further information, contact the club at Augusta National Golf Club, Washington Rd., Augusta, GA 30913.

"Best of Luck, Arnold Palmer"

The first order of business in Arnold Palmer's morning, whether he's in his northern headquarters in Latrobe, Pennsylvania, or stationed at his southern command in Orlando, Florida, is to sign his name.

Palmer receives almost 15,000 autograph requests a year, and although that would mean good money for a baseball player, Palmer sends his John Hancock out for free.

The requests run the gamut. The most popular, of course, are photograph requests; Palmer supplies most of the photos, too. About 2,000 of the requests are for autographed Palmer paraphernalia to be sold at auctions run by everything from elementary schools to television stations. It was directly as a result of these requests that Palmer learned long ago never to throw away a glove after a round. Also popular are autographed books, but whatever the donation, it is always accompanied by a form to be returned to Palmer with details on what the item(s) fetched.

Palmer, of course, is not the only pro that handles such requests, although he and Jack Nicklaus are undoubtedly the most sought-after. As a matter of fact, any pro will sign a photograph and probably write in the desired message, so long as you go through the proper channels, which means if you contact their agents.

So if there is a golfer out there whose autograph you want, for whatever reason—you played with him in a pro-am, perhaps, or sat beside him on an airplane—consult the following. Allow up to a month for delivery, as many golfers spend several weeks on the road and will not be able to manage such requests until they take a week off.

Paul Azinger.

MEN

Player	Source
Paul Azinger	Leader Enterprises 390 North Orange Ave., Suite 2600, Orlando, FL 32801
Severiano Ballesteros	Fairway, S.A. Ruiz Zorilla 16-2°J Santander 39009 Spain
Andy Bean	International Management Group (IMG) One Erieview Plaza Suite 1300 Cleveland, OH 44114
Chip Beck	IMG (see Andy Bean)
Mark Calcavecchia	IMG (see Andy Bean)
Billy Casper	Pinnacle Enterprises 8133 Leesburg Pike, Suite 580 Vienna, VA 22182

MEN

Player	Source
Fred Couples	The Players Group 8251 Greensboro Drive Suite 1150 McLean, VA 22102
Ben Crenshaw	Scott Sayers 2905 San Gabriel Suite 213 Austin, TX 78705
Raymond Floyd	IMG (*see Andy Bean*)
Al Geiberger	Advantage International 1025 Thomas Jefferson, NW Washington, DC 20007
Bill Glasson	IMG (*see Andy Bean*)
Hubert Green	Pros, Inc. 100 Shockoe Slip Box 673 Richmond, VA 23206
Ken Green	Eddie Elias Enterprises 1720 Merriman Rd. Box 5118 Akron, OH 44313
Ben Hogan	Ben Hogan Company 2912 West Pafford St. Ft. Worth, TX 76110
Hale Irwin	Hale Irwin Golf Services 745 Old Frontenac Square Suite 200 St. Louis, MO 63131
Peter Jacobsen	IMG (*see Andy Bean*)
Tom Kite	Pros, Inc. (*see Hubert Green*)
Bernhard Langer	IMG (*see Andy Bean*)
Bruce Lietzke	IMG (*see Andy Bean*)
Davis Love III	Pros, Inc. (*see Hubert Green*)
Sandy Lyle	IMG (*see Andy Bean*)
Johnny Miller	Johnny Miller Enterprises Box 2260 Napa, CA 94558
Larry Mize	Cornerstone Sports Chateau Plaza Suite 940 2515 McKinney Ave. Lock Box 10 Dallas, TX 75201

Hale Irwin.

MEN

Player	Source
Jodie Mudd	Doug Baldwin 333 First Avenue West Suite 500 Seattle, WA 98104
Larry Nelson	Cornerstone Sports (*see Larry Mize*)
Jack Nicklaus	Golden Bear, Inc. 11760 U.S. Highway One North Palm Beach, FL 33408
Greg Norman	IMG (*see Andy Bean*)
Arnold Palmer	Arnold Palmer Enterprises Box 52 Youngstown, PA 15696
Gary Player	IMG (*see Andy Bean*)
Mike Reid	Brent Turley 2029 Century Park East, Suite 422 Los Angeles, CA 90067
Chi Chi Rodriguez	Eddie Elias (*see Ken Green*)
Joey Sindelar	Advantage International (*see Al Geiberger*)
Sam Snead	Uni-Managers International 10880 Wilshire Blvd., Suite 1800 Los Angeles, CA 90024

MEN

Player	Source
Craig Stadler	Brent Turley (*see Mike Reid*)
Payne Stewart	Leader Enterprises (*see Paul Azinger*)
Curtis Strange	IMG (*see Andy Bean*)
Hal Sutton	Sutton Enterprises Suite 117—Energy Square 212 Texas St. Shreveport, LA 71101
Lee Trevino	Lee Trevino Enterprises 1221 Abrams Rd. Suite 327 Richardson, TX 75081
Ken Venturi	Eddie Elias (*see Ken Green*)
Lanny Wadkins	Pros, Inc. (*see Hubert Green*)
Tom Watson	Charles Rubin, Esquire 1313 Commerce Tower 911 Main St. Kansas City, MO 64105
Fuzzy Zoeller	Eddie Elias (*see Ken Green*)

All others: Contact them through the PGA Tour, 112 TPC Blvd., Ponte Vedra Beach, FL 32082.

Where to Find . . . a Bob Jones Autograph

You'll be hard-pressed to squeeze one from him, but Mark Emerson of Columbus, Ohio, has about 50 of them. He also has the John Hancock of every U.S. Open winner back to 1913, every British Open winner back to 1892 and every PGA Championship winner since the event began in 1916. That's what happens when you set out to collect every major winner, a project Emerson began a few years ago and abandoned with "mixed success" in 1990 after spending thousands of dollars on newspaper advertising ("Autographs Wanted!") around the world. Which is not to say Emerson is not still looking—he recently paid $5,000 for an Old Tom Morris autograph. Which *is* to say that if you have a good, clean autograph Emerson has been hunting for years, you won't have much trouble getting a Bob Jones. Call (614) 771-7272.

Nancy Lopez.

WOMEN

Player	Source
Amy Alcott	Giaciolli and Co. Crocker Bank Bldg. 225 Santa Monica Blvd. 3rd Floor Santa Monica, CA 90401
Pat Bradley	Robert Nation 1924 Market St. Camp Hill, PA 17011
JoAnne Carner	Don Carner 3030 S. Ocean Blvd. Palm Beach, FL 33480
Beth Daniel	Pros, Inc. (*see Hubert Green*)
Jane Geddes	IMG (*see Andy Bean*)
Juli Inkster	IMG (*see Andy Bean*)
Betsy King	IMG (*see Andy Bean*)
Nancy Lopez	IMG (*see Andy Bean*)
Meg Mallon	David Binkley 1533 North Woodward Ave., Suite 300 Bloomfield Hills, MI 48304
Ayako Okamoto	P.G. Planning, Inc. Aoyama Sky Bldg. 5F 2-7-17, Kita-Aoyama Minato-Ku, Tokyo 107 Japan
Patty Sheehan	Rebecca Gaston Box 11675 Reno, NV 89510
Jan Stephenson	IMG (*see Andy Bean*)
Kathy Whitworth	Pros, Inc. (*see Hubert Green*)

All others: Contact the Ladies Professional Golf Association, 2570 Volusia Ave., Suite B, Daytona Beach, FL 32114.

The Major Golf Organizations— and What You Can Get from Them

PGA Tour

112 TPC Blvd.
Ponte Vedra Beach, FL 32082
(904) 285-3700

Headed up by Commissioner Deane Beman, the PGA Tour also runs the Senior PGA Tour for the over-50 set, and the Nike Tour, mostly for younger players yet to make the big tent.

What You Can Get:
A *PGA Tour Media Guide,* with player profiles, a section of Tour records and results and statistical information, costs $8.95. The Partners Program will send you videotapes of "Shell's Wonderful World of Golf" as part of your $38 membership.

AMERICAN JUNIOR GOLF ASSOCIATION

2415 Steeplechase Lane
Roswell, GA 30076
(404) 998-4653

The AJGA runs almost 30 tournaments in 18 different states for boys and girls aged up to 18. Competition is fierce.

What You Can Get:
The $35 membership includes application fees for five AJGA tournaments. Beyond that, each application costs $2. The $35 also gets you a year's subscription to *Golf Magazine, Golf Digest, Golf World* or *Golf Illustrated,* an AJGA Calendar, discount airfares to AJGA tournaments with American Airlines, the AJGA's monthly newsletter, a rule book and a bag tag.

THE PROFESSIONAL GOLFERS' ASSOCIATION OF AMERICA

100 Ave. of the Champions
Palm Beach Gardens, FL 33418
(407) 624-8400

The PGA of America is the umbrella organization for club professionals. It supervises the training and accreditation of its membership—in other words, it ensures that the game is taught properly. It also runs the PGA Championship, one of golf's four major professional championships.

What You Can Get:
The PGA doesn't sell its media guide, which is a shame, because it lists the addresses and telephone numbers for the officials in each of the 41 PGA local sections around the country—a good source if you're looking for lessons. It has published (with Macmillan) a consumer version of its *PGA Teaching Manual: The Art and Science of Golf Instruction.* You may also want to subscribe to *PGA Magazine.* Part of this monthly publication is reserved for pros only; the rest—news, features, results, new products—can be enjoyed by anyone with more than a casual interest in the game. A year's subscription costs $23.95 in the U.S., $29 in Canada. Write to: *PGA Magazine,* Box 1347, Elmhurst, IL 60126-1347.

THE LADIES PROFESSIONAL GOLF ASSOCIATION

2570 Volusia Ave., Suite B
Daytona Beach, FL 32114
(904) 254-8800

The LPGA has two divisions, one for touring pros—the ladies you occasionally see on television—and one for teaching pros.

What You Can Get:
The LPGA will sell you its media guide for $10.

THE NATIONAL GOLF FOUNDATION

1150 South U.S. Highway One
Jupiter, FL 33477
(407) 744-6006

The NGF tracks the growth of and trends in the golf market and prints its findings in various publications.

What You Can Get:
Golf Facilities in the United States, a geographic analysis of the more than 12,000 facilities across the country, costs $150 (or $75 to NGF members). Its *Golf Projections 2000,* along with a slide presentation, costs $300 ($150 to NGF members). The NGF also has an extensive catalog of books and videos (instructional and noninstructional) and will even sell you clothing. However, the most useful NGF material available—in that you can get the books and videos at several other sources—are its "Executive Summaries." These are short pamphlets devoted to such subjects as "Efficient Bag Storage," "Planning the Golf Car Path," "Establishing Green Fees" and "Ball Flight Laws." They cost $2 each, with a minimum order of $10. For a full listing of summaries, send a check or money order for $2 to the NGF at the above address.

How to Get British Open Tickets

There are a couple of ways of going about this.

1. Book a tour package with a golf tour operator. Most of the major operators, such as PerryGolf or Wide World of Golf, offer 10- and 14-day packages that combine play at some of Britain's (and sometimes Ireland's) most famous courses with a visit to the British Open. A full list of operators appears on pages 20–23.

2. Write in advance to the Royal & Ancient Golf Club of St. Andrews. Its offices are at Links Place, St. Andrews, Fife, KY16 9JD, Scotland, Great Britain (from where it administers all British Opens); (011 44) 334-72112.

3. Show up on the day of play. The R&A usually reserves a large block of tickets for daily admission.

The venues for upcoming British Opens are:

1993—Royal St. George's, on the southeastern tip of England, July 15–18.
1994—Turnberry Golf Club, in Ayrshire, on the southwest coast of Scotland, dates to be announced, but count on mid-July.
1995—Old Course, St. Andrews, Scotland, dates to be announced, as above.

THE UNITED STATES GOLF ASSOCIATION

Golf House
Far Hills, NJ 07931

The USGA governs the game in this country, is the curator of the game and vociferously maintains the game as a predominantly amateur pastime.

What You Can Get:
The USGA's catalog is discussed elsewhere in this book. Suffice to say here that it includes books, videos, prints, clothes and various knickknacks that appear to have no reason for existence whatsoever. You may want to find out more about the USGA Members Program, a membership organization designed to raise funds for the USGA. There are several categories of donation, a percentage of which is tax-deductible in each case:

$25—This is the basic package. It gets you an annual subscription (eight issues) to *Golf Journal,* a copy of the Rules of Golf, a bag tag, a bumper sticker, an ID card, various travel discounts, a copy of the USGA's gift catalog and an advance copy of the program for the following U.S. Open. Spouse rate in this category is $5.

$15—A junior rate, for 18-and-unders, that gets the same as above. Only difference is that the bag tags IDs you as a junior.

$100—Gets you all the basics, plus notice of limited edition golf books sold by the USGA, a towel and a green repair tool. Spouse rate is $25.

$250—Gets you the $100 package, plus a limited edition golf print, an annual on the U.S. Open and the opportunity to purchase advance tickets to the U.S. Open or any other USGA championship. Spouse rate is $50.

$500—The $250 package, plus a videotape of the most recent U.S. Open and a gift to be named later (it changes from time to time). Spouse rate is $100.

$1,000—The $500 package, plus a reproduction of a book from the USGA's rare book collection and two tickets to the U.S. Open or any other USGA championship. Spouse rate is $300, but you won't get two more free tickets—you'll get the chance to buy two more in advance.

some looney groups— and what you can get from them

These are ersatz affinity groups that exist primarily to purvey fun souvenirs and knickknacks. They're extremely harmless.

GOLFAHOLICS ANONYMOUS

c/o Mark Oman
Box 222357
Carmel, CA 93922
(408) 624-4386

What You Can Get:
A full range of gifts: shirts, sweatshirts, towels, headcovers, hats, visors. Books include *How to Live with a Golfaholic, The Sensuous Golfer* and *The 9 Commandments of Golf.* GA's "Driving Kit" includes a license-plate frame that reads "Keep Swinging." They'll sell wholesale or retail. Note: This is not a membership society.

GOLF NUT SOCIETY OF AMERICA

Nut House
Bush Prairie, WA 98606
(206) 687-5774

What You Can Get:
Your $25 annual membership fee gets you an entrance examination (to tell you how damaged you really are), a bag tag, a membership certificate, a subscription to the *Golf Nut News* newsletter, invitations to local golf-nut tournaments and tour packages with fellow nuts. Surprise, surprise—there's a gift catalog. It includes golf bags, shag bags, sweaters and sweatshirts, towels, headcovers, visors and umbrellas.

LAID BACK GOLFERS' ASSOCIATION

Box 12774
Oklahoma City, OK 73157
(405) 948-8555
(800) 843-5242

Golf is one division of Laid Back Enterprises, along with fishing, tennis, skiing and aerobics. It does organize local tournaments, which it terms "LBGA Mulligan Classics."

What You Can Get:
Caps, visors, towels, sweatshirts, T-shirts, goofy balls (the water ball, for example, is a real ball wearing flippers and a mask) and posters.

Inside a Televised Golf Tournament

by John Goldstein

John Goldstein is a former associate producer of NBC's golf telecasts who now works as a freelancer in the same field. He was hired in 1979 as a golf statistician (the network's first) and thereupon made the job up as he went along.

He compared himself to a baseball squad's utility infielder: playing different positions, filling various roles when needed. He produced features; wrote "voice-over" copy for the openings to the telecasts; helped write the graphics that pop up on the screen; fed the announcers statistical and personal information on the players and conducted quickie interviews—"talking heads," as they're known—with the leaders which were later meshed into the telecast. When the show was on the air, he was to be found in the tower behind the final green, feeding information to the announcers on five-by-eight-inch cards and communicating with the truck via closed-circuit telephone, talking either to the producer ("Don't forget Wadkins on 18; an eagle puts him a shot out of the lead") or the graphics coordinator ("Azinger needs an up-and-down for the win; now's a good time to show that sand-save stat").

To try to capture at least one aspect of the many tasks that go into bringing an important golf tournament into your living room or den, we asked John to keep a diary during the 1990 Players Championship, held at the Tournament Players Club at Sawgrass, about half an hour's drive south of Jacksonville, Florida.

Here's what he gave us.

MONDAY, MARCH 12

7:30 P.M.

Arrive at the Marriott next to the Tournament Players Club at Sawgrass. It's been a little more than 24 hours since we finished the telecast of the Honda Classic down in Ft. Lauderdale. In my brief respite between tournaments I played a round of golf with my father near his home in Boynton Beach, made a few telephone calls, flew to Jacksonville, rented a car and drove about 45 minutes to the hotel. Now I order up room service and flip on the tube. Calm before the storm.

TUESDAY, MARCH 13

8:00 A.M.

I talk my way through a half-dozen security checks (left my parking credential in the hotel room) and arrive at the NBC compound, a small village of trucks and trailers that for the next six days will be home to 95 technical personnel and 15 production people. NBC will also hire a temporary support staff of 55, who will work as scorers and spotters on the course, as well as six "runners," whose duties will include everything from

How NBC gets The Players Championship from course and booth to screen.

making sure the crew has coffee and doughnuts in the morning to picking up network executives at the airport.

8:10 A.M.

I speak to the technical manager, Ernie DeRosa, about lining up a camera crew to shoot a feature on Tom Kite, the defending champion. He assures me he'll have the crew within a couple of hours—as soon as the equipment is unloaded from the trucks.

8:30 A.M.

I start scouting for a suitable location for the Kite interview which, I hope, will take place later today. I discover a quiet office in the rear of the tournament headquarters building, whose inhabitant is more than happy to vacate midafternoon, when we'll move in with lights, cables, a camera, a monitor and a tape machine, as well as a cameraman, a lighting director, a tape operator and, I hope, a Tom Kite.

10:00 A.M.

In the rented trailer that serves as our production office, the first of a myriad of meetings takes place. The producer, Larry Cirillo, and the director, Andy Rosenberg, have been joined by the senior members of each engineering area—audio, video, tape and maintenance—to map out the technical game plan for the week. This doesn't happen at every tournament, but The Players Championship is NBC's biggest event, our showcase. We've brought in extra equipment and manpower to produce a total of 10 hours (we're on air two hours Saturday, four hours on Sunday and supply USA Network with four hours of coverage on Thursday and Friday), so everyone wants to make sure we're all on the same page. Still, this meeting doesn't affect me, so I head off in search of my elusive camera crew.

10:30 A.M.

Found them. I'm joined on the practice tee by a cameraman (with hand-held minicam) and a tape operator. We're stockpiling "talking heads"—video portraits—of every player on the range. The guys will take a minute to grin foolishly into the camera on Tuesday rather than on Sunday, when the tensions can be high and the patience level low. I spot Ben Crenshaw, who I want to interview for my piece on Kite. They were junior golf rivals back in Austin, Texas. As always, "Gentle Ben" is obliging. And, as always, his answers are thoughtful and articulate.

11:30 A.M.

Kite teed off for his practice round about two hours ago, so I go to the ninth green to find him. I talked to him last week to set up the interview, but I still have to nail down a time and place. He's not on the ninth when I arrive. There is, however, an elderly couple sitting on folding chairs, who look like they've been there a while, so I ask if Kite has been through yet. A bespectacled man turns around to reply. It's *Byron Nelson!* When the winner of 52 tour events, 11 in a row in 1945, and 18 in the 1945–46 calendar year, informs me that Kite is in the next group, I stammer my thanks and awkwardly introduce myself. My day is made.

11:40 A.M.

Because he's the defending champion, Kite has his dance card filled—interviews, press conferences, social functions—and he's not sure he can do the interview today. He tells me to check with him again after the shoot-out, a light-hearted competition that starts with 10 players on the first tee and eliminates one per hole until only a winner is left. I realize I'll have to follow the shoot-out, which is not the most productive use of my time, but there's no other way of knowing when Kite may be eliminated. It's to tee off at 2:30.

2:15 P.M.

I send the camera crew to the interview location and tell them to wait there until I return with Kite.

2:30 P.M.

Kite and the other nine names tee off at the 10th at the TPC. I trail along in a golf cart, rooting against him—I figure that the earlier he finishes, the better the chance he'll do the interview today.

5:30 P.M.

Wouldn't you know it. Kite *wins* the shoot-out. But he agrees to give me a few minutes. I take him to the location, where the crew has been standing for three hours. This doesn't bother them; they're now into overtime. It *will* bother NBC's budget department. Kite seems bothered, too, but he's a pro: When the camera rolls, his impatience is concealed.

6:00 P.M.

The interview completed, Kite bolts from the room. He's already late for a dinner being hosted by PGA Tour Commissioner Deane Beman. The crew begins to "tear down" the equipment, and I head back to the production trailer.

6:30 P.M.

First cold beer of the evening.

WEDNESDAY, MARCH 14

8:00 A.M.

Back on the practice tee. We tape more heads, and when Kite arrives we shoot various angles of him practicing. Any feature about Tom Kite that doesn't include a scene or two on the range has missed the story.

9:30 A.M.

As arranged, Tom's wife, Christy, meets us near the tee. This will be the final interview for the feature. She seems relaxed on camera, and her answers are good. I ask her if she's surprised that her husband, who's small, light and legally blind, has been so successful. "There's no way of predicting who will be the good ones out here unless you can see inside them, and find out what makes them tick and how hard they're willing to work," she replies. She will definitely make it into the piece.

TV
Tricks of the Trade, II:
A Storm
in a Golf Cup

I t was 1979. The networks had microphones positioned on the tees and fairways at golf tournaments. Now-retired NBC audio engineer Jerry Caruso figured, "Why not the cups?"

Caruso, with the help of one other audio engineer, came up with a two-by-three-inch, 20-milliwatt transmitter, powered by a pair of nine-volt batteries and mounted on a small board at the base of the cup. For an antenna, he fed a thin length of copper wire up the side and looped it around the cup about two inches below the surface of the green.

When a ball dropped, it activated a microphone that responded only to vibrations. The plop of the ball was then transmitted to an antenna in the camera tower behind the green—at a spot high enough to "look" into the hole.

The PGA Tour approved the use of the cups at the 1980 Bay Hill Classic and thereafter ten of them were installed at each NBC-televised event.

Alas, although the invention earned Caruso an Emmy, the miked cups ran afoul of budget cuts in 1987.

—John Goldstein

10:00 A.M.

Go to the tape truck to screen the interviews, take notes and think about what portions to use. Kite's interview is about 20 minutes long; his wife's and Crenshaw's are about five minutes each. The final piece will run approximately four minutes.

11:30 A.M.

Start to prepare statistics for the announcers, using the PGA Tour's computer printout. I type up a performance chart, listing every player in the field and how he's done this year: events entered, the amount of times in the money, earnings and position on the money list and best finishes. The Tour's printout provides all that, but it's a bulky document that's not really portable. Although typing my own chart takes an hour and a half, when I finish I'll have a compact, concise and portable source of information with the most important facts. Another reason for doing it: As I type, I subconsciously memorize things about players that I might be able to use during the telecast.

1:00 P.M.

Our first production meeting. The trailer is standing room only. In addition to the NBC production people and announcers, there are several representatives from the USA cable network, which will carry portions of the first two rounds. The most popular topic for discussion is how to coordinate the USA talent—host Bill MacAtee and on-course commentator Peter Kostis— with our own guys.

2:00 P.M.

With everyone still assembled, we review a tape of last year's Players Championship.

2:30 P.M.

With an edit session scheduled for 6:00 P.M., I duck out and head for the press room to write the Kite feature. I make a final decision on which "sound bites" to use, script the parts that Bryant Gumbel, our main announcer, will voice-over and decide what video I'll need—Kite on the practice tee, Kite winning the 1989 tournament, etc. I also send a runner out to buy a copy of a CD by Bob Seger that contains the song "Like a Rock." Why this song? I happened to hear it on my car radio a few weeks earlier and, knowing I'd be doing the Kite feature, figured it would work well and filed it away in my mind.

4:30 P.M.

I round up the tapes I'll take to edit at the PGA Tour Productions facility a few miles away on the road to Jacksonville. Usually all our editing is done in our mobile tape truck, but the guys in there are overloaded with other work and we're to go on the air tomorrow. Another advantage of using the Tour's facility: They've got every tournament from the last 15 years in their tape library.

6:30 P.M.

The slow process of editing begins. John Delvecchio, a Tour Productions editor, is talented and certainly knows golf, and my notes are in pretty good order, so the three-minute, 58-second piece takes only six hours to put together. *Only.*

12:45 A.M.

After making a back-up copy of the tape, I drive back to my hotel, crack open the minibar for a cold beer, and collapse.

THURSDAY, MARCH 15

9:00 A.M.

Before leaving my hotel, I start compiling information on five-by-eight-inch cards about the players we're most likely to see today. The data is biographical (name, age, hometown, college, amateur record) as well as statistical (career wins, earnings, position on money list), and will come in handy for the announcers when a guy takes two minutes to line up a putt.

11:00 A.M.

Now in the production trailer, I type up much of the same information I wrote on the cards and give it to the graphics coordinator. Many of these tidbits will appear on screen during the telecast.

Noon

Since I've used shots of the 1989 U.S. Open in the Kite feature—he was the third-round leader but blew a gasket in the fourth—I call the United States Golf Association to arrange a fee. The cost: $500 for anything up to one minute.

2:30 P.M.

The announcers take their position for rehearsal. They simulate a telecast for a short while, but mostly this time is used by the director and engineers. After two days of setting everything up, this is the first opportunity for the director to look at all his camera angles; for the engineers, it's a chance to set the levels on their equipment.

4:00 P.M.–6:00 P.M.

On the air. On USA Network, that is. Early-round coverage is always hit-or-miss. Many of the eventual leaders teed off in the morning and are finished for the day. Others are playing holes out of the range of cable coverage (we don't provide 18-hole coverage until the weekend). Basically you just go with the big names and whichever contenders come into camera range.

6:05 P.M.

Announcers and production staff meet for a postmortem and to discuss what changes will be made for tomorrow's broadcast. One problem: The last names of USA's Peter Kostis and NBC's Bob Costas are pronounced almost identically, which created some confusion when the producer gave instructions into their earpieces. Tomorrow they will be known as "Peter" and "Bob."

6:45 P.M.

First cold beer of the evening.

FRIDAY, MARCH 16

9:00 A.M.

Don't tell my bosses. I'm going out to play tennis for an hour. Those sumptuous spreads in the production trailer and all those late dinners (not to mention those *cold* late dinners) are not doing wonders for my waistline. I have to get some exercise.

11:00 A.M.

After putting together today's five-by-eights and graphics, I visit the tape truck to view the "tease" that will open the telecast. The tease, as the word implies, is intended to interest the viewer in the telecast ahead. You know, "Forget about the NCAA hoops on CBS—we've got a story right here you just can't miss!" The opener is a short piece featuring the golf course and the first-round leaders, Jodie Mudd and Mark Calcavecchia, and it won't take long to come up with the voice-over copy. I head for the press room.

11:30 A.M.

Back to the tape truck, where I oversee the "sweetening" of the Kite feature—the addition of music and graphics.

2:30 P.M.

I sit in with Bill MacAtee as he voices-over the tease in the booth between the ninth and 18th greens. Usually the booth above 18 is where the "host" announcers sit. For The Players Championship, however, we set up a central area where players can come in for interviews after their rounds. We call it the "Little House on the Fairway."

4:00 P.M.–6:00 P.M.

On the air (USA again). In effect, the four hours of USA coverage is treated as a dress rehearsal for the weekend coverage. No offense meant to the cable network, but our checks are signed by NBC.

6:15 P.M.

Now it's time to get serious. The NBC announcers and a few production personnel meet informally with some of the leaders, including Hale Irwin and Davis Love III, in a private area of the locker-room. It helps us get to know the players, who are often conveyed as "faceless," and to pass their personalities along to the viewers. Just as important, in my estimation, it makes the players feel more comfortable with the people who cover them at NBC.

7:00 P.M.

After the players depart, the rest of us discuss tomorrow's tease. We settle on a melange featuring the significance of the tournament, the difficulty of the golf course and the irresistibility of the leading men. The coproducer and one of the associate directors trudge back to the tape truck for another long night of editing.

7:45 P.M.

First cold beer of the evening.

SATURDAY, MARCH 17
11:30 A.M.

A moment of truth. Our executive producer, making a rare golf tour appearance, wants to screen the Kite feature. Since Gumbel's voice is not yet on the tape, I nervously read his part while the boss watches impassively. He seems to approve, but he'd like to hear more about Kite growing up in the shadow of Crenshaw. Since it's out of the question to ask Tom to sit down for a follow-up interview before his round, it's decided to ask him to join Costas—that's "Bob"— in the Little House while the feature airs and have Bob follow up with a question or two.

1:00 P.M.

Back on the practice tee to shoot talking heads of the leaders. Irwin leads by one from Mudd and Rocco Mediate. Most players don't mind answering a couple of quick questions, but some want no part of the camera before they play. We respect their wishes and don't push.

2:30 P.M.

The skies open up and a torrential downpour causes suspension of play. All the hard work and careful planning have gone for naught—we will not carry a single live golf shot today. Nevertheless we have two hours of network airtime to fill. The scramble is on.

4:00 P.M.–6:00 P.M.
On the air. A battle plan has been quickly drawn up and swiftly executed. Gumbel and Johnny Miller are in the tower on 18. Costas is in the Little House. Mark Rolfing, who usually follows the play on the course, and Fuzzy Zoeller, an occasional guest announcer, man a hastily arranged "studio" in the locker-room, where I also am stationed to collar players and dole them out to the various sites like Halloween candies. Curtis Strange and Greg Norman are sent to Costas; Gumbel and Miller get Mediate; Rolfing and Zoeller visit with Irwin and Mudd. In all the confusion, I forget about Kite, who has left for his hotel. A production person is dispatched to retrieve him, and later in the telecast Kite sits somewhat reluctantly with Costas as the feature airs and the follow-up questions follow up. Interspersed in all the talking are segments of Thursday's first-round coverage. Mercifully, the clock strikes six.

6:15 P.M.
Another meeting, this one to discuss the long day awaiting us tomorrow. We also take the opportunity to schedule our next meeting.

7:15 P.M.
First cold beer of the evening.

SUNDAY, MARCH 18
6:00 A.M.
Camera crews are sent out to tape shots of the moon in a still-darkened sky and players warming up at sunrise. We'll use this in the tease. The same weary crews start tracking the action when third-round play resumes at 7:15 A.M.

9:00 A.M.
A few of us are in the control truck watching the bank of monitors, picking out the best (and worst) shots to use for a third-round recap. We discuss the pros and cons of televising golf on a tape-delayed basis, perhaps a condensed, one-hour highlight package of each round. There are two very good arguments against the idea: (1.) There wouldn't be enough commercial minutes to make golf profitable, and (2.) It just wouldn't be as much fun as it can be live—for the viewers or for us.

11:00 A.M.
The third round is over at last. Mudd leads Calcavecchia and Ken Green by a stroke. We hustle to accomplish in two hours what we normally do in six: edit a tease, prepare graphics, shoot the talking heads we'll need.

12:45 P.M.
The announcers convene on the 18th tower to put their voices on the aerial footage of the holes that they'll cover. The footage was shot from a helicopter earlier in the week. Some do it in one take; others elicit that ancient jibe from the truck, "Don't worry—we've got plenty of tape."

1:45 P.M.
Minutes before we go on air, Gumbel voices over the tease. This is also the last chance for a run to the Port-a-John: we'll be on the air for four hours today.

On the air. Mudd never relinquishes the lead, but Calcavecchia stays close enough to keep it interesting. Nevertheless, four hours is a long time to cover a tournament, so we break the show up a bit. Talking heads are rolled in, as is footage of Calcavecchia finishing second in each of the previous two weeks, at the Honda and at Doral. Up in the 18th tower, I try to find out the last time someone finished second three weeks in a row, but I can't come up with it. No matter. It occurs to me that if Calcavecchia does finish second, he'll go to the top of the 1990 money list without a win to his name. I pass that on to Gumbel and Miller. As the rest of the field comes in, Costas conducts a couple of interviews in the Little House. Out on the course, Calcavecchia gets to within one shot of the lead with a birdie at 16, but Mudd responds with a clutch birdie at 17, the short but treacherous par three with the island green. Mudd taps in his winning putt (he wins by one) at 5:53 P.M., which leaves us just enough time for a brief interview with the winner and the presentation of the trophy. The credits roll.

6:05 P.M.

First of *many* cold beers this evening.

How to Shoot a Golf Tournament

by Steve Szurlej

There's more to capturing a golf tournament on film than pointing-and-shooting from the best seat in the house.

Consider that a golf photographer must lug several pounds of equipment over acres of often hilly terrain, sometimes in horrendous weather, normally fighting a rabid gallery, occasionally in pursuit of a solitary shot. And then a caddie or tournament official will saunter between the subject and the lens and all will be lost.

On the other hand, the rewards can be, well, rewarding. One photographer who has been rewarding us for years with his work is Steve Szurlej, staff photographer for Golf Digest *and* Golf World *(and* Tennis*). Here he tells how the golf photographer goes about an often misunderstood business—and offers a few tips for the amateur, too.*

You probably think you'd kill for my job. I get the best seat in the house at the top tournaments and all I have to do is take photographs. What a life.

Whoa, there. The job is not as glamorous as you think. Let me tell you about it.

Let's start with getting to work. While you're sitting in bumper-to-bumper, rush-hour traffic, I'm probably sitting on an airport runway, wedged into an airline seat and staring up the behinds of a dozen airplanes waiting to take off in front of me. I've already negotiated highway traffic. Now, as I ponder runway traffic, I realize that I miss the good old days before deregulation, when I could get anywhere from New York, my home airport, nonstop. Now I can't get from A to B without going through some hub, and I always worry that one or more pieces of baggage won't change planes with me. I carry about 50 pounds of cameras, lenses and film on board with me and check one suitcase and up to four cases of additional equipment—it depends on the assignment. Ever tried carrying six cases at once? Did you see John Candy in *Trains, Planes and Automobiles?*

Ever had your gear stolen? You always fear that it will happen. In New York last year, it almost did. I was standing in line at La Guardia Airport, waiting to check my bags through to Portland, Oregon, where I would shoot the Fred Meyer Challenge, a charity pro-am organized by Peter Jacobsen. I noticed this odd-looking guy staring at my gear and decided to keep an eye on him. At one point, he bent down. I thought he was just sort of stretching, but the next thing I knew he was heading full-tilt for the exit with the bag carrying all my cameras! As I screamed at the top of my lungs, a skycap intervened, but the guy got past him. Fortunately, two cops outside nabbed the thief and I spent the next hour—while the plane waited for me, I might add—filling out police reports. What a start to a shoot.

Okay, so finally we reach our destination. Assuming the rental car doesn't break down and the hotel room doesn't have an ice machine or an all-night party next door, I'm ready for my first day on the golf course.

Unless, of course, it's Wednesday. Rule number one for the golf photographer who has a desire to remain injury-free is this: *Don't work pro-am day.*

I'd rather play golf. Better that than ducking shots from amateurs that come from directions you could never imagine. About the only safe place on Wednesday is the pros' practice area. On the other hand, if you're not an accredited photographer, Wednesday is your last chance to shoot pictures of players, as PGA Tour rules prohibit spectators from carrying cameras during play. So photograph your favorite pros, but proceed with caution. When it's time for the amateurs to hit, take cover.

Come Thursday, first-round day, I'm up early. Color quality is best when the sun is low in the sky. The light filters through the atmosphere differently and is warmer and richer. In the middle of the day, when the sun is high overhead, visors and hats worn by players can cast long shadows over the players' faces. Even if a player isn't wearing a hat, the sockets of his eyes can look dark; we call this "raccoon eyes." So the first two hours after sunrise and the last two hours before sunset are prime time for photographers. In the summer that translates to long days at the golf course. But at least it means long lunches.

When the light is low again in the afternoon, I might find a tee where the players will be playing directly into the sun. If I can find one without any clutter in the background, so much the better. The 14th tee at Bay Hill in Orlando, Florida, is an excellent afternoon tee. There's a lake immediately behind the tee and a fairway on the far side of the water. The background is so far away that it becomes a soft backdrop. More important, there is no place for spectators to get in the way.

Whatever tee I find, I may have to make a deal with the marshals who, as every golf photographer knows, are put on earth to spoil backgrounds. There's nothing that ruins a picture quite like an overweight marshal in pink plus fours holding a "Quiet Please" paddle right behind a player's head.

The marshals tend to stand behind the players because if they stood in front of them, they'd distract them when they lifted their paddles. But I'll explain to them who I am and what I'm trying to do, and I'll try to give a couple of options on where to stand. Most are amenable, and some are downright helpful. There have been instances where I've wanted to move everything around—remodel the entire tee. A Gatorade bucket might be propped up too high on a bench, for example, or there may be huge sponsor banners crowding the shot. Normally a photographer will take care of this himself first thing in the morning, when nobody is around. But sometimes you'll want to move things around in the middle of the tournament. You need the marshals on your side in those instances.

Another angle I might search for is a green that will yield great putting and short-game photographs. The key is to find an *elevated* green for a dramatic, low angle and a clean background. Let a photographer choose between a classic, old layout with elevated greens and a contemporary TPC-like layout, and he'll take the classic every time.

Unless the assignment is to shoot the golf course and not tournament action. Spectator mounds at TPCs provide excellent vantage points from which to photograph individual holes.

Having found the ideal elevated green, pin placement is the next consideration. You want the players to putt toward the light source, so a pin placed on the side of the green closest to the sun is best. If you were to draw an imaginary line from the ball through the hole and extend it to the gallery rope, there is the position to shoot from. That's something you as a photographer may want to bear in mind on practice and pro-am days.

However, you can't always get what you want. Standing or kneeling in a player's direct line of vision can be a distraction, so it's often best to move slightly off-line. How far off-line depends on the player. Some, like Jack Nicklaus, concentrate so intensely that I doubt they'd notice you if you jumped up and down. Others? Let's just say some professional golfers are easily disturbed.

Bunkers provide another great opportunity for photographs. They are the "second base" of golf. Just as second base on a baseball diamond provides so much dramatic action, with players sliding head first in a cloud of dust or acrobatic shortstops turning impossible double plays, so some of golf's dramatic photographs are to be found when players explode from sand.

Positioning is as important here as it is with putting. The second green at Augusta National has two of my all-time favorite bunkers. Lots of photographers position themselves behind the green and smile approvingly when balls go in the sand. Many do, for the hole is a downhill par five that is reachable in two, and players aren't afraid of hitting into the sand for they figure they can get up and down for birdie. The background is the uphill slope of the fairway, perfectly manicured as only Augusta National is, and the bright, white sand acts as fill light, brightening the faces—and therefore the expressions—of the players. It's an ideal situation for great bunker photographs.

Accredited photographers normally are given access just inside the gallery ropes to facilitate the job at hand. Some spectators don't appreciate the need for this and occasionally will spare no words in informing you of their objections. I assure you that it is rare when a photographer blocks the view of a spectator. If it does happen, the photographer certainly draws no pleasure from it. But more often than not the gallery is good-natured enough to let a photographer get on with his or her job, and some will lend a hand by holding an umbrella over you on a rainy day. Nevertheless, those hot, sunny days when considerable quantities of beer have been consumed by the gallery require the diplomatic moves of an envoy to the Middle East.

Now if you think that this preferred position gives the photographer a wonderful view, think again. The 400 millimeter lens that most golf photographers carry, and which will be responsible for about 80 percent of their work, drastically restricts the field of view. While I can see the action and reaction of one golfer, the surroundings—including the flight of the ball and the result of the shot—remain a complete mystery. To be perfectly honest, I don't see many shots land. When a gallery cheers as a ball dances close to the hole, usually I'm still shooting the player.

In addition to the standard 400mm lens, I carry another camera body with a 300mm lens, both supported by monopods—one-legged tripods, basically. They help support the heavy telephoto lenses without immobilizing you the way a tripod would. A third camera body with either a 24mm, 50mm or 84mm, or a midrange zoom lens, complete the hardware. Fanny packs carry the additional lenses, films and accessories. Strapped to the waist, they allow the hands to be free and ready to operate the chosen camera and lens when necessary. Total weight: Between 25 and 30 pounds.

For the highest quality images, I use a slow-speed color transparency film, ASA 64 and 100 being the speed of choice among magazine photographers. The slower the speed, the finer the grain. Newspaper photographers commonly work with color negative material. They can make black and whites easily enough from color negatives, and with so many newspapers now running color shots, they cover both bases.

Film selection is critical as lighting conditions change during the day. Both the 1989 and 1990 Masters, each won by Nick Faldo, finished in near dusk at the 11th green at Augusta National. There, tall pines block what little light is left at dusk, and even with a high-speed film, quality images are tough to come by. You can go either way. You can shoot at a lower speed and gamble that the winner won't get too animated after his victory, or you can underexpose the film—which allows you a faster shutter speed—and "push process" the film in the lab. When Faldo won in 1989, sinking a long birdie putt to beat Scott Hoch, I shot ASA 200 film at one-thirtieth of a second, with my lens as wide open as it could go (F2.8), then pushed it to 500 in the lab. As it turned out, Faldo threw his arms up in the air when he won and, other than that, remained pretty steady. His arms are a blur in most of my shots, but I have a good image of him with his arms above his head.

One thing about a playoff: At least you're in the right place at the right time. The golf photographer's worst nightmare is to hear the roar of the crowd from one green when you're two groups ahead with a challenger. If you're the lone photographer on assignment, as I often am for *Golf World* or *Golf Digest,* keeping up with the tournament is imperative. You can do this only with a thorough knowledge of the golf course, being physically aggressive and enjoying the occasional moment of luck.

One particular instance when my aggressiveness and course knowledge paid off came on the Sunday of the 1983 Masters, when Seve Ballesteros was in contention (he eventually won). I ran from the sixth green around the back of the seventh tee, picked up a concrete path that cut across the fourth hole, just below the tee, then ran uphill through trees to the right of the second fairway. Finally, I cut across the second fairway, just in front of the tee, and arrived at the eighth green just in time to capture Ballesteros chipping in for eagle. I was rewarded with a sequence full of the Spaniard's wonderful expressions.

More than any other sport, golf requires that you adhere to strict rules of etiquette. So, too, does golf photography. You can't just release the shutter whenever you feel like it. Timing is everything—just as it is to the poor chap having to hit the ball. Impact often is the moment you want to capture on film, but releasing the shutter before ball contact is made is prohibited. Conditions will occasionally allow an early release, normally because extreme telephoto lenses will put the photographer out of audible range, and photographers working together sometimes will check the safety of an early release. One will stand in for the player and the other will release the shutter from the intended location. No matter the distance, however, it's always better to be downwind when using this technique. (You probably won't have to bother with this on practice days; the players don't like the noise then, but they often tolerate it.)

If our jobs are not as easy as the public might like to believe, they are made a lot easier by the support services provided by such companies as Kodak, Nikon and Canon. At the major tournaments, such as The Masters or the British Open, they'll provide both on-site repair and film processing. This is the photographer's equivalent of Gasoline Alley at the Indianapolis Motor Speedway. If a camera breaks down, you drop it off in the pits. Simple repairs can take as little as 15 minutes; the more complicated jobs might depend on whether the repair crews have the necessary parts. Some repair jobs are just impossible, though. I still remember one photographer standing in the pits at Augusta National with his 300mm lens in pieces. He's been up on a platform above a hole when a violent thunderstorm had blown the lens to the ground. It couldn't be repaired, but he was loaned a replacement for the duration of the tournament.

The companies process film overnight, which is pretty impressive in the case of Kodak at the British Open. Kodachrome shots, you see, are processed in *Paris.* Kodak did have a Kodachrome processing plant in England, but closed it down (Ektachrome, which uses a simpler processing system, can usually be handled locally). So when I handed over my rolls each afternoon at the 1990 British Open in St. Andrews, they were whisked by motorcycle to Edinburgh and put on a plane for London, where they then changed planes for Paris. They were then picked up by motorcycle again to be whisked off to the plant. Once developed, the procedure was reversed and I had my pictures the next day.

This sort of service is more valuable than you can imagine. In the first place, I can edit the shoot as I go, instead of wading through a vast amount of slides when the tournament is over and I might be on deadline. Second, knowing what I already have might tell me what I still *need*. Third, if there's something wrong with a camera that I don't know about, I'll know soon enough when my work comes back—and, of course, I can get the problem fixed immediately in the pits.

Okay, I confess. It's not all hard work. After a few years working with the players you find moments to have fun. At the Honda Classic one year, for example, my mother took a volunteer's job tracking scores at one of the holes. She'd sit by the green and as each player holed out and left the green, she'd transmit to the Tour's statistical headquarters what each player had scored.

She didn't know any of the players, but I made sure they knew her. I was working a few holes back and told a couple of the pros I knew—Craig Stadler and Andy Bean, to name two—who she was and where she was. It was pro-am day, so they didn't mind a little fun. As each player left the green, he'd walk over and greet her like an old friend. "Hi, May! How are you today! You look *great!*" "May! Long time no see! Put me down for an eagle!" This went on all afternoon, and though she was puzzled at first, she soon cottoned on.

I think it made her day.

Golf on the Radio, Shot by Shot

The only way to hear play-by-play golf on the radio in this country is to find a short-wave radio and dial into a broadcast from Britain that is being aired on the British Broadcasting Corporation's World Service.

Unfortunately, we can't supply you with the exact wavelength. The World Service has five or six different wavelengths for each of its two North American regions (Canada/USA-Central, Mountain, Pacific; Canada-Atlantic and Eastern and USA-Eastern) and frequently changes them. Plus, different wavelengths are used at different times of day. What we can tell you is that *London Calling* is a monthly magazine for World Service listeners that lists what is on and where to find it. It costs $15 per year, from *London Calling,* Box 76, Bush House, Strand, London, WC2B 4PH, England, Great Britain.

It will be worth the effort, for listening to golf live on the radio is not unlike listening to baseball: plenty of downtime when the announcers can set the scene and spark the imagination; the same anticipation between contact and result. "Is it a home run or a warning-track out?" in baseball becomes "Is it stiff or did he catch the trap?" in golf.

But enough of the explanations. Instead, sample the action. This is an edited version of the actual transcript, supplied by the BBC, of the coverage of the 1989 British Open at Royal Troon (I've cleaned up the dialogue in some parts). The main voice in the booth is that of Renton Laidlaw, an occasional voice on ESPN's television coverage in the U.S. He's joined in the booth by John Fenton. On the course are Chris Rea, former Scottish rugby internationalist and now a correspondent for both rugby and golf broadcasts, and Tommy Horton, a former British touring pro.

To set the stage, Mark Calcavecchia, Greg Norman and Wayne Grady are approaching the final hole of a four-hole stroke-play playoff. This is the first time such a format has been used to decide a major golf tournament. As Renton Laidlaw explains, the U.S. Open has an 18-hole playoff while both the PGA and The Masters play sudden death, as do regular tournaments.

Both Norman and Calcavecchia are one under par for the first three holes. Grady, the leader for much of the tournament, is one over. The best Grady can hope for is to get a birdie while the other two make bogies. But Norman and Calcavecchia are two of the most aggressive players in the game. Both will attack the final hole. As it turns out, Norman finds the final hole at Troon a stronger adversary than he'd anticipated.

Let's pick up the action:

Renton Laidlaw:
Wayne Grady, Greg Norman and Mark Calcavecchia now move to the 18th. If you have tuned in, you're listening to Sunday Sport at the Open golf championship, and we're going to stay here at Troon until we get a winner. The time now is just after two minutes past seven.

Now we're going to join Chris Rea on the 18th. Greg Norman and Mark Calcavecchia are both one under par in this four-hole stroke-play playoff, two shots clear of Wayne Grady. They're playing the last of the four holes, the 18th.

Chris Rea:
Renton, the tee is actually hidden from my view, but the players have obviously got back and on to it. We're just awaiting the drives . . .

(At this point, a high-pitched whooooosh!click! is heard—a tee shot)

Rea:
. . . and the first one is on its way safely. Calcavecchia has driven down the right side of the fairway into a little bit of light rough. That's quite safe. The rough here is not very dangerous. It has been well trodden down. Now Norman. . . .

(A whoosh! only is heard—no click)

A practice swing from Norman. This last hole is 452 yards, fraught with danger. It's the last hole of the stroke-play section. If it's even-Stevens then they go into sudden death. Norman has not been holding back from the tee. He's hit

two cracking drives at the first and second. He swings. . . .

(whooooooooooosh!click!)

Good, clean contact. The ball comes down, the crowd like it. It's a beauty!

(Crowd noise)

But, oh, it's gone into the bunker! It has rolled into the bunker right beside me. It was almost *too* good. Norman went boldly once again, and he's hit his ball a massive distance—really too far. He's pretty hard up against the face of the bunker, so it will take some shot for Norman to reach the green.

(whoosh!click!)

Now Grady swings. He gets some modest applause from behind him. I see it coming perfectly down the middle. It's coming up to the bunker, but it's not going to go into it. An excellent shot by Grady.

What drama: Calcavecchia is in the rough in the right. Grady is in perfect position in the middle of the fairway and Norman is in the bunker.

Laidlaw:
Well, Greg Norman went for a really big shot down the middle and he's in the bunker. He's going to have to hope that Calcavecchia takes four, and that he can get it out the sand and get down in two from something like 100 yards.

Tommy Horton:
It's ironic, Renton. Calcavecchia's in the rough but his lie will be nice and tight

where the crowds have been walking. Norman has just fallen off the fairway and into a fairway bunker and is in a rotten place. Sometimes life is a little unlucky.

Laidlaw:
Who knows? They might both take five, Wayne Grady might make a birdie three and suddenly they'd be all square again and going to sudden death.

Whatever happens, there is plenty of drama here at the end of the 118th Open Golf Championship. Now we're going back to Chris Rea, who's out on the fairway. It will probably be Calcavecchia to play first. Remember he has quite a long shot and there is that out of bounds just off the putting surface at the back of the green.

Rea:
And the fairway is pock-marked with bunkers in front of him, too. There are two a bit in front of the green, two on the right and one on the left. Calcavecchia picks his club. He's having a last look at the green. He swings.

(whooooosh!whack!—an iron shot)

He makes fine contact. The crowd behind are applauding it.

(Crowd noise)

Laidlaw:
A marvelous shot! What a shot!

(Now the crowd goes crazy)

That, Chris, is an absolutely *superb* second shot. He has hit from the rough to something like five feet. What a time to produce a shot like that.

We go back now to Wayne Grady. Chris Rea is watching him play his second.

(whooosh!whack!)

Rea:
He throws it up to the green, the crowd is loving this. They're egging it on.

Laidlaw:
That's a wonderful shot, too! Almost into the hole, Chris. It bounced a couple of times and has run some five feet beyond the hole. Both Grady and Calcavecchia have chances of birdie threes. Now Greg Norman.

Rea:
He's on the upslope and needs to play an extraordinary shot. Mind you, the man is capable of some extraordinary golf.

What a thrilling finish. Wait— Norman's backing off. A noise is disturbing him, I think.

(Now a very strange moment. Just as Norman is poised to hit, the voice of BBC-TV's Peter Alliss is heard over loud- speakers on the course. The commentary that television viewers can hear in their living rooms can now be heard on the 18th hole. "He can't take even a grain of sand," Alliss is heard to say, at which Norman backs out of the bunker, laughs and speaks.)

Greg Norman:
He's telling me how to play the shot!

Rea:
It may be that one of our television col- leagues, Peter Alliss, is inadvertently telling him how to play the shot!

(Laughs)

He's certainly not going to take his advice, though.

(thwaaaaack!)

Norman has made tremendous con- tact! It's coming down in front of us, and, oh, it's gone into another bunker! Surely Greg Norman's chances have gone now.

Laidlaw:
It looks like that tee shot into the bunker is going to cost him his second Open Golf Championship [Norman won in 1986]. Calcavecchia is now within five feet of his first major championship.

The crowds are rushing down the fairway and are surrounding the bunker from which Greg Norman will now be playing his third shot. Norman has to get it up and onto the green. If he hits it too cleanly it could go through the green and out of bounds—and that will be the end of him.

Let's go down to Chris Rea. He's down there with Greg Norman.

Rea:
Almost within touching distance.

(thwoooosh!)

Oh, he's made far too good contact! He has flown the green completely, Renton.

Laidlaw:
But whether it's on the path or still in bounds, I'm not too sure. It may well be that the ball has bounced back into play.

Now Norman and his caddie are walking up to the green. Greg Norman looks very disconsolate. And now Greg has conceded that the ball is out of bounds. He's not making any effort to play any more. Wayne Grady will putt for a three to finish at level par after four holes. And he holes it . . .

(The crowd groans)

No, he doesn't.

(The crowd cheers; Grady has tapped in for his par)

So Mark Calcavecchia, from America, who parred the first hole, who birdied the second and parred the 17th, the third of the extra holes, now has a putt of five feet to win the 118th Open Golf Championship and become the first American since Tom Watson in 1983 to take the most prestigious title in interna- tional golf . . . and he holes it.

(Crowd noise)

Mark Calcavecchia has ended the European and Australian dominance of the title over the last five years. He also maintains a sequence of American vic- tories here that was started by Arnold Palmer in 1962 and continued by Tom Weiskopf in 1973 and Tom Watson in 1982.

What disappointment for Greg Norman, and for Wayne Grady, who led the tournament for almost three days. Comment, John Fenton?

Fenton:
I feel desperately sorry for Greg Norman. He opened the final round with six consecutive birdies, broke the course record with a 64 and then had to finish like that.

(The show begins to wrap up)

Laidlaw:
Well, it's victory here for Mark Calacavecchia at Royal Troon. I hope you've enjoyed our coverage of this championship. It certainly provided plenty of excitement on this final day. And we'll all look forward to your joining us for our next Open golf championship special, next year at this time at the Old Course at St. Andrews.

It's goodbye for now.

(Music and fade)

Books, Magazines, Videos

A Hefty Drive Is a Slosh: An Appreciation of P.G. Wodehouse's Golf Stories

by Stephen Goodwin

To read the golf stories of P.G. Wodehouse is to travel back to a happy time and place when the Royal and Ancient game was in the sweet bloom of youth.

The fictional Manhooset Golf and Country Club, where most of the Wodehouse stories take place, is the playground of gallant young men wearing plus fours and making judicious use of their cleeks and light irons, rejoicing in shots that are hit "on the meat" and meditating on the profound mysteries of the perfect pivot.

But golf then was as golf is now: a game in which hope merely paves the road to disillusionment, and no writer has fully grasped the ardent, fickle spirit of the game better than Wodehouse. In his stories, golf's little tragedies are revealed for what they truly are: comedies, for Wodehouse understood perfectly that, in golf, glory and gloom are inseparable. Consequently, the stories are as hilarious today as they were when first published more than half a century ago.

Admittedly, they take some getting used to. The men have names like Rollo and Eustace, and they are always saying things like "Bully!" and "Rotten luck!" and "Dash it all!" But Wodehouse, although he moved to Long Island, New York, in the 1950s, was an Englishman, born in 1881, whose tastes and temperament remained firmly fixed in the Edwardian era. His first collection of golf stories, *The Clicking of Cuthbert*, probably seemed a trifle old-fashioned even when originally published in England in 1924.

Ditto his second collection, *The Heart of a Goof*, which came out two years later. By then Wodehouse, a favorite writer of the *Saturday Evening Post*, had accumulated a large following on both sides of the Atlantic and both of those volumes were published in the U.S. as, respectively, *Golf Without Tears* and *Divots*. Wodehouse even made a few minor changes to "Americanise" the stories. For example, Manhooset,

located somewhere on Long Island, replaced Marvis Bay, the seaside resort that is the setting in the British editions.

The stories in both volumes were written in a spate not long after Wodehouse, then a man of 40, took up the game. After that initial flurry he tapered off, adding only a dozen more golf stories over the years. There is no single source of all his golf stories, but a few volumes come close. *The Golf Omnibus*, published by Simon and Schuster in 1973, contains 31 stories, which is a few short of the entire collection. Another anthology, *Fore: The Best of Wodehouse on Golf*, was published by Ticknor & Fields; although it contains two stories not in *The Golf Omnibus*, it is short of ten that are. *Wodehouse on Golf*, published by Doubleday, is also short several stories. Sadly—or surprisingly, rather—not one of those anthologies remains in print, but they can be obtained from the major golf-book dealers.

These golf stories are only one small entry on the publishing scorecard that Wodehouse turned in, for he was one of the most prolific writers who ever lived (on the morning of his death, in 1975, he was still scribbling away, at the age of 93). Altogether Wodehouse managed to produce more than 70 novels and 300 short stories, not to mention hundreds of essays and articles, reams of light verse, and scripts for both movies and plays. His most famous character was, of course, that unflappable valet, Jeeves.

Yet the golf stories seem to have had a special hold on his affections; Wodehouse, an 18-handicapper who had to be careful lest he slip back to a 20, declared himself that they were "written in blood." On every page of every story it is clear that he knew exactly what it meant to be smitten by the game, to be mindlessly—and harmlessly—deranged by golf. He knew in his bones that golf is not a metaphor for life, as so often has been said. On the contrary, life is a metaphor for golf! Indeed, it was life he kept in perspective by comparing it to golf in analogies such as this: "I am not a married man myself, so have had no experience of how it feels to have one's wife whiz off into the unknown; but I should imagine that it must be something like taking a full swing with a brassie and missing the ball."

Those are actually the words of a character called the Oldest Member, or sometimes the Sage. He is the narrator of virtually all the Wodehouse golf stories, and he tells them in prose that is as clean and crisp as a well-struck mashie shot that takes just the right amount of turf. From his favorite settee on the Manhooset veranda, the Oldest Member has seen a lot of golf and a lot of life and is never too busy to share his wisdom with the impetuous young fellow who sinks down in a chair near him, usually muttering about giving up "the blanked infernal silly ass of a game!" The Oldest Member, drawing on his infinite store of memories, will always set him straight.

There is no better means of conveying the flavor of a Wodehouse story than to summarize one. "A Woman Is Only a Woman," for instance, begins with the Oldest Member lurking on the veranda and surveying that "varied, never-ending pageant, which men call Golf." His thoughts take a ruminative turn as James Todd and Peter Willard labor up the ninth hole.

James and Peter are two friends united since their childhood by their mutual inability to master the game. They "contrived, as time went on," Wodehouse writes, "to develop such equal form at the game that the most expert critics are still baffled in their efforts to decide which is the worse player."

The pair are young men of means, but the Oldest Member assures us that they are not frivolous. Before a game of golf, Peter "would go to the trouble and expense of ringing up the office to say he would not be coming in that day," and James was equally conscientious.

The two had the full joy of their miserable golf until the day that a certain Grace Forrester arrived in Manhooset, and both our heroes fell in love with her. "Love," says the Oldest Member, "is an emotion which your true golfer should always treat with suspicion. Do not misunderstand me. I am not saying love is a bad thing . . . I have known cases where marriage improved a man's game, and other cases where it seemed to put him right off his stroke."

Naturally—for how else *could* such a dilemma be solved—Peter and James decide to play a round of golf for the supreme prize, Grace (although it is not at all clear whether she cares a fig for either of them). Off they go to wage a ding-dong battle with cleek and mashie.

Their round is too long to chronicle here in detail, but perhaps their scorecards will give you an idea of the intensity of the first nine holes:

| James | 8 | 2 | 34 | 17 | 12 | 10 | 9 | 23 | 14 |
| Peter | 9 | 2 | 33 | 17 | 11 | 11 | 9 | 23 | 15 |

The Oldest Member reports the vicissitudes of the match with the high philosophical seriousness it deserves; for, as he notes, "It is the glorious uncertainty of golf that makes it the game it is."

With James one-up at the turn, matters come to a crisis. Peter announces that he intends to forfeit the match, clearing the way for James. Struck by the noble sacrifice of his friend, James goes straight to Grace to propose; but, being a golfer, he first explains to her the theory of the great teacher, Sandy MacBean, who stresses the importance of keeping a line drawn from a point at the back of the neck to the ball at right angles to the line of flight of the ball.

"Gibberish," says Grace.

End of courtship. Peter and James rejoice in their narrow escape from a woman who has no feeling for golf, and decide to stick religiously to their four rounds a day. The moral, according to the oldest member: "There are higher, nobler things than love. A woman is only a woman, but a hefty drive is a slosh."

The arrival of a woman—"like the Serpent in the Links of Eden"—precipitates the conflict in most of Wodehouse's stories, but the plots are brilliant variations on the theme. There are cases where the man takes up the game with a passion in order to woo the woman, only to find that she has no interest whatsoever in golf. Or the man tries to rein in his natural temper while playing, then discovers that Evangeline or Adeline or Jane wants not a Milquetoast but a full-blooded fellow who gives vent to his emotions. Or, again, stories in which a woman is a scratch player who secretly wishes to take up knitting and let her handicap go to pieces.

And no matter what happens in the stories, no matter how quaintly the characters speak and dress, Wodehouse always conveys the fine fanaticism of golf. Every contemporary obsession is prefigured in these stories. The horror of slow play? Wodehouse has his Wrecking Crew, a four-ball made up of the First Grave Digger, the Old Man with the Hoe, Father Time and Consul, the Almost Human. They dodder down the fairway "like one of those great race migrations of the Middle Ages," and their pride and joy is that they have never allowed anyone to play through.

Wagers? You have heard about James and Peter, but there is also the case of Otis Jukes and Rollo Bingham, who play one hole—one long hole—from the first tee at Manhooset to the doorway of the Hotel Astor, in Times Square, for the hand of Amelia Trivett ("The Long Hole").

Finicky rules-keepers? The outcome of their match hinges on a ruling about a ball that reaches its destination in the back of a car, a "moving hazard." Superstitions? Try "The Magic Plus Fours," which are of a pattern that would make even Doug Sanders blush. Collectors? One lucky soul actually acquires, in "High Stakes," the "authentic baffy used by Bobby Jones at the Infants' All-in Championship of Atlanta, open to those of both sexes not yet having finished teething."

Every type of golfing man—and woman—makes an appearance. In "A Mixed Treasure" and "Sundered Hearts," Wodehouse gives us the man who wants to buy his game: Mortimer Sturgis, the proud owner of 11 drivers, and 28 putters—94 golf clubs in all. In "Scratch Man" we meet the old stagers who memorialize their triumphs by naming their children after their favorite battlegrounds. Their sons are christened Sandwich, Hoylake and St. Andrew, their daughters, Troon and Prestwick. There is the scourge of the links, the nonstop talker. In "The Salvation of George Mackintosh," his fiancée finally tries to kill him with her niblick, and the Oldest Member says approvingly, "If the thing was to be done at all, it was unquestionably a niblick shot." And there is Mitchell Holmes who, in "Ordeal by Golf," is portrayed as so sensitive that he "missed short putts because of the uproar of the butterflies in the adjoining meadows."

If all this sounds familiar, well, so it should. Change the names of these characters, dress them in the latest outfits from Aureus, turn the baffies into 4-woods and the mashies into 5-irons, substitute the name of Arnold Palmer for that of Harry Vardon, and these stories would be completely up-to-date. The fact that modern golfers will recognize themselves in these quaint and old-fashioned stories only adds to the humor and enjoyment.

And there is always a quiet wisdom underpinning these tales. The Oldest Member may be a little dotty, but no true golfer would dispute that the game is good medicine for the soul. We could do worse than adhere to the philosophy that Wodehouse spells out thusly: "Keep the head still . . . slow back . . . don't press . . . There is no better rule for a happy and successful life."

Editor's Choice: The Best Golf Books

INSTRUCTION

In this game instructional ideas are like opinions: Everybody's got one, and not that many serve much purpose.

But this is not necessarily the authors' fault. Publishers have actually been known to turn a buck on golf instruction, and agents—International Management Group folks, mainly—seem to love nothing better than to get their more successful clients into print. Hence *Win, and Win Again* by Curtis Strange or *Shark Attack* by Greg Norman.

But at least these are "serious" instructional books and not of the junk "Be Happy, Play Better" genre. I recently received a copy of something called *Quantum Golf,* which deals with a mystical pro called Linc St. Claire teaching the true path to self and inner happiness on a golf course in Iowa.

Come to think of it, Timothy Gallwey's *Inner Game of Golf* made a lot of noise, but my Presbyterian upbringing prevents me from recommending anything that spends more than 300 pages telling you how to feel good. Heck, if golf didn't feel downright awful most of the time, I doubt if it would be worth the effort.

Instead, here are six instructional recommendations of my own, and one from an expert, i.e., someone who believes instructional books are best left alone.

1. *Golf My Way* by Jack Nicklaus.
The flying elbow and the upright plane be damned, this is fundamental stuff from the greatest player ever, with sidebars devoted to key aspects of the swing (steady head, grounding the club, etc.) and good illustrations from Jim McQueen. But if you *really* want a sensi-

bly set-out education from Nicklaus, try to get your hands on the manual given out at the Jack Nicklaus-Jim Flick instructional schools (and scheduled to be on the consumer shelves soon). It breaks down every part of the game into "What," "How" and "Why" and is as user-friendly as golf manuals come.

2. *Pure Golf* with Johnny Miller.
It was written in 1976, when Miller was in the habit of hating himself if he didn't hole *long iron* shots. In other words, sound advice from one of the best iron players ever, even if firing your right side on the downswing is tough for amateurs.

3. *Natural Golf* with Seve Ballesteros.
The guy who wrote this, John Andrisani, is a good friend, but that's not why I recommend this. It's because learning how Ballesteros does things on the golf course is a bit like finding out how magicians pull rabbits out of hats.

4. *How to Play Your Best Golf All the Time* with Tommy Armour.
I like three things about this book: (1.) its writer, the late Herb Graffis, about the best and funniest person you could ever spend an hour or two with (and don't think Armour didn't know it); (2.) the idea that you practice Armour's advice with only an 8-iron, for numerous reasons, the best being that "The shaft of the 8-iron is short enough so, with due regard for the walls, ceiling, furniture and flooring, you can physically check up on what your mentality is absorbing" (Graffis's idea, without a doubt); (3.) the book contains highlighted sentences throughout, which would make another book on their own. Examples: "Action before thought is the ruination of most of your shots" and "The majority of short putts are missed by looking for

imaginary slopes and hitting the ball softly, trying to 'baby' it into the cup." A recent hit, *Harvey Penick's Little Red Book,* did much the same sort of "nugget" job. Quite well, too.

5. *Practical Golf* with John Jacobs.
As at his schools, Jacobs teaches you to analyze shots by the flight and trajectory of the ball. To anyone who loves golf because it is an *individual* game, this is not so much instruction as *opportunity.*

6. *Golf for Women* by Kathy Whitworth.
Fundamentally sound and important to mention, I feel, because women golfers—professionals and amateurs—still don't get enough attention.

Now to the expert's choice.
Dick Donovan, a book dealer and collector from upstate New York (who recommends the ultimate golf library on page 234), has read thousands of golf books in the 15-plus years that he has specialized in the sport. But he won't read instruction.

Except for one book—*Scrambling Golf: How to Get Out of Trouble and Into the Cup,* by George Peper. The author is now editor-in-chief of *Golf Magazine,* but when he wrote *Scrambling Golf* his day job involved the composing of jacket copy for huntin' and fishin' books. Peper first took the scrambling idea to Lee Trevino, but Trevino wanted too much cash, so Peper wrote it himself. To this day Dick Donovan maintains that *Scrambling Golf* makes more sense and is more practical than most other instructional books put together. And having too often watched Peper settle his large haunches into an otherwise unplayable lie and then scramble my last nickel from me, I'm inclined to agree.

. . . AND AN INSTRUCTIONAL BOOK THAT SHOULD NEVER HAVE BEEN WRITTEN

Some books are bad, and others are plain bizarre. *Basic Golf* was written by Bob Gordon for *nudists* and includes buck-naked models in its illustrations.

But there are a few books out there that leave you dumbfounded, wondering how on earth they made it to print.

Langer on Putting with Vivien Saunders is the perfect example.

Bernhard Langer, you see, is the modern game's worst putter. The Bavarian gent is wonderful with an iron in his hand—his 71 in the stormy second round of the 1985 British Open at Sandwich was one of the most impressive iron displays in recent memory—and most other areas of his game are solid.

But putting? Good lord, Langer has suffered the yips for two decades. He's been known to four-putt from six feet, has resorted to more eccentric putting grips than Manhattan has quack psychologists and in his own autobiography, *While the Iron is Hot,* Langer devotes several pages to these self-same putting woes. I can only assume that the British publisher watched Langer putt fairly well en route to winning The Masters in 1985 and then figured that Langer's "cure" would fly off the shelves.

HISTORY

If there's one thing golf could use, it's a book that covers its entire history in the United States. H.B. Dickie Martin's *Fifty Years of American Golf* downed tools around the Depression. Herbert Warren Wind's excellent *The Story of American Golf* takes us into the mid-fifties. Will Grimsley gets into the sixties in *Golf: Its History, People and Events.* There's been nothing as thorough as these books since.

So perhaps this category should be retitled "Nostalgia" books, and we'll include books devoted to a particular aspect of golf. Top honors would go to:

1. *The Story of American Golf* by Herbert Warren Wind.
An elegantly written account of the growth of the game through the Hogan era.

2. *The U.S. Open: Golf's Ultimate Challenge* by Robert Sommers.
A complete account of the second most important golf championship in the world. Great as a reference book and as a damn good read.

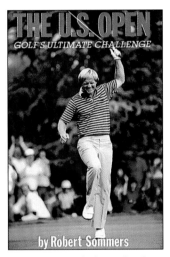
Sommers's U.S. Open classic.

3. *Golf's Golden Grind* by Al Barkow.
Deals principally with the post-war years and some of the great, colorful characters who played at that time, such as Jimmy Demaret, Lloyd Mangrum and Ky Laffoon. Good anecdotal material here; did you know, for instance, that Demaret would call low, running shots "snake rapers?" Finishes in the mid-seventies.

4. *Golf in America: The First 100 Years* by George Peper, Robin McMillan and James A. Frank.
Published in 1988 to celebrate the centennial of the game in this country, this is one of the better coffee-table publications on the shelves. But it's a production number and runs a bit thin in some areas, such as travel (resorts, etc.) and media (television, magazines, etc.).

5. *The PGA* by Herb Graffis.
A diligent and exhaustive account of golf as a business. Graffis was blind and in his nineties when he finished it.

BIOGRAPHY/AUTOBIOGRAPHY

Tough category. Anyone who says Sam Snead's *Education of a Golfer* is great has to get out more; it's terrible. Lee Trevino's *The Snake in the Sandtrap* comprises a series of thigh-slappers holding together what could have—and *should* have—been the most interesting story of them all. And Herb Graffis once told me that Bobby Jones refused to review *The Walter Hagen Story* for the *New York Times* because he knew that a legion of Hagen's stories were apocryphal at best.

So where does that leave us?

With nothing but a bunch of marginally interesting life stories, that's where. So, if you must, try *Go for Broke* by Arnold Palmer or *Down the Fairway* by Bobby Jones (a wonderful golfer, a clever lawyer and a *very* articulate writer).

N.B. Although they're not autobiographies, Dave Hill's *Teed Off* and Frank Beard's *Pro: Frank Beard on the Golf Tour* both give fairly insightful and cynical portraits of the pro game. Dishonorable mention goes to Frank Beard's book on the Senior Tour, *Making the Turn,* not because of the text itself but because the publisher saw fit to grace its cover with a photograph of *Tommy Aaron.*

GOLF COURSES/GOLF ARCHITECTURE

You'll find plenty of books filled with beautiful photographs (and some not so beautiful), but even if it's true that a picture is worth a thousand words, the best golf course/golf architecture books take time to also discuss the subject matter. To that end, our choices:

1. *The Golf Course* by Geoffrey Cornish and Ron Whitten.
This is pretty much the bible on golf-

course architecture today. It begins with the evolution of "architecture" on the links of Scotland back when bloody skirmishes with the English were still knocking golf matches off the sports pages, and moves diligently through the various "eras" of design (such as "The Pennsylvanian Influence"—Henry Fownes at Oakmont, Hugh Wilson at Merion, etc.). The duo also profile each architect and list and date their designs and redesigns (a section with a few errors, but invaluable nonetheless) and include an alphabetical listing of most courses known to man (it was here that I discovered that one J. Hamilton Stutt was responsible for the Kirkcaldy/Balwearie golf course in Scotland, my home course).

2. *The World Atlas of Golf* by Pat Ward-Thomas (and a cast of thousands, including Herbert Warren Wind, Charles Price and Peter Thomson).

It covers all the major courses in the world with two to four pages of descriptions of the building and subsequent playing of each course. Photographs and excellent course maps. Another architectural bible.

3. *The Anatomy of a Golf Course* by Tom Doak.

This is technical stuff from the young architect (and contributor to this tome). It lays out all the decisions an architect must make in the design process. So in one sense this is a *philosophy* book. Doak is very down-to-earth. Straight away he tells us that it's not the architect's job to make a course fair for example. Instead, he must get the most out of the land while testing all aspects of the game. And there really isn't much more you can ask for.

HUMOR

This is simple. Anything by P.G. Wodehouse and *Dogged Victims of Inexorable Fate* by Dan Jenkins. I also get a giggle listening to 17-handicappers wax metaphysical about *Golf in the Kingdom*. End of category.

COLLECTIONS

You just knew that Herbert Warren Wind would figure highly here. *Herbert Warren Wind's Golf Book,* from 1971, and *Following Through,* from 1985, each contain selections of Wind's elegant essays from his days with *The New Yorker*. They deal with such topics as player profiles ("Snead: Twenty Years After His First Open"), travel ("North to the Links of Dornoch") and course design ("Some Thoughts on Golf Course Architecture"). That there is some overlap should not concern you; either remains a satisfying read.
   Also:

1. *Strokes of Genius* by Tom Boswell.
Most of this first appeared in Boswell's own newspaper, *The Washington Post.* There is nothing particularly original about the subject matter of these essays—the first two offerings deal with Jack Nicklaus and Augusta National—but Boswell is easily the most convincing of today's golf writers. He'll argue a case like a courtroom lawyer, and fairly soon you're agreeing with everything he has to say. Favorite essays include "Whataya Got, Big Chief?," a profile of Fuzzy Zoeller (the title refers to Zoeller addressing a familiar face whose name has been forgotten) and "Dye, You Devil, Dye," which describes and critiques Dye's TPC at Sawgrass—"the most wonderfully ugly golf course on earth." Boswell continues that the TPC course is "a perverse paean to life's vengeful, capricious dark side" and that the program for the TPC tournament "ought to have a Dürer print for a cover—a demented, emaciated knight on a starving horse followed by a carcass-gnawing mongrel." Now *that* would be a piece of memorabilia.

2. *Golf: The Four Majors* by John Hopkins.
Here Hopkins, the golf correspondent for *The Financial Times* of London, has curated a collection of essays from such literary figures—we use the term loosely—as Alistair Cooke, Dudley Doust, Ben Wright, Dan Jenkins, Hugh McIlvanney, Peter Dobereiner, Frank Hannigan and Frank Deford to cover

every angle of the major championships. Jenkins on Tom Watson chipping in to win the 1982 U.S. Open at Pebble Beach. Hannigan on Walter Hagen's four successive PGA Championships. Marvelous stuff.

3. *A Tribute to Golf* by Thomas P. Stewart.
This book is really just a collection of stuff Stewart likes and took some 15 years' compiling: a piece on designing golf holes by Desmond Muirhead; a piece on pro-ams by Ben Wright, CBS-TV commentator; Herbert Warren Wind on The Masters; and an 1887 essay on "The Praise of Golf" by Sir. W.G. Simpson. There are a few essays by Stewart himself; several photographs by Brian Morgan, Jim Moriarty and others; and prints by Donald Moss and numerous "Unknown Artists." But really this is the appeal of Stewart's book: You never really know what's coming next. It's a wonderful work to browse.

4. *The Jim Murray Collection.*
This is sort of a trick, because there's not much golf in here; Murray covers every sport. It's the *index* that I love. Really. Only in a Jim Murray collection would you find Jack Nicklaus's entry flanked by Nick the Greek and Nijinsky (the horse, not the dancer), Tom Weiskopf surrounded by John Wayne and Johnny Weismuller, Babe Didriksen preceded by Bo Derek, Eddie Dibbs and Charles Dickens!

REFERENCE

Few golf books cover every facet of the game (although HarperCollins is to publish an updated version of *Golf Magazine*'s *Encyclopedia of Golf*), so we've divvied up reference books into particular categories.

Equipment:
For a current guide to equipment, try the Buyer's Guides in *Golf Magazine* (March issue) or *Golf Digest* (December issue). For a history of equipment, try *Golf in the Making,* originally published in 1979 by Ian Henderson and David Stirk. For equipment assembly or repair, you will find no better book than

Golf Club Design, Fitting, Alteration and Repair by Ralph Maltby, equipment guru at the GolfWorks in Newark, Ohio.

Collecting:
The original bible was *The Encyclopedia of Golf Collectibles: A Collector's Identification and Value Guide* by John M. Olman and Morton W. Olman, who ran The Old Golf Shop in Cincinnati. I say "original" because prices changed— considerably given the bull collecting market (no pun intended)—and the Olmans brought out an updated version in 1992 entitled *Olmans' Guide to Golf Antiques and Older Treasures of the Game.* Either is a good choice.

Golf Courses:
The Anatomy of a Golf Course by Tom Doak. See above.

Books:
Two of the most ardent book collectors in the country, Dick Donovan and Joe Murdoch (both of whom contributed to *The Golfer's Home Companion*), completed what can only be called a labor of love in 1987 with *The Game of Golf and the Printed Word, 1566–1985: A Bibliography of Golf Literature in the English Language.* This tome catalogs 4,800 titles, beginning with—from 1566, of course—"The Actis and Constitutions of the Realme of Scotland

The book of books: *The Game of Golf and the Printed Word, 1566–1985.*

maid in Parliamentis haldin be the rycht excellent, hie and mychtie Princeis King's James the first, Second, Third, Feird, Fyfth, and in tyme of Marie now Queen of Scottis." It also lists publishers, where published, and dates of first and subsequent editions. It doesn't list prices, principally because that depends on the quality of the book, how rare it is and how the market is doing. And how well is it doing? Consider that in the fall of 1991, Murdoch sold his collection of 3,358 titles for $650,000, immediately after which Donovan mailed Murdoch . . . a golf book. His note: "Joe, here's a start on your next collection."

Instruction:
A reference book on instruction? Kind of. The PGA of America has just issued a consumer version of its *PGA Teaching Manual: The Art and Science of Golf Instruction.* It includes such topics as "The History and Evolution of Golf and Golf Technique," "Physical Training for Golf," and several appendices that covered such topics as vision problems for golfers, "What is a good instructor?" and "Golf Swing Misconceptions."

Tournaments:
The World of Professional Golf by Mark McCormack. The gaffer of the International Management Group has been publishing this since 1966, with the corporate help of such companies as Dunhill, Ebel and now Desaru (a joint Japanese-Malaysian golf resort developer!). The annual includes detailed descriptions of the major championships, as well as shorter synopses of the major international tours (PGA, Senior, European, African, Australasian, Asia/Japan and the Women's Tours). Beyond that, the edit is skewed very much toward IMG clients; the book kicks off with 11 pages on the Sony Rankings, which IMG administers, and entire chapters are devoted to the Dunhill Cup and the World Match Play Championship, two tournaments run by IMG. Where does one find it? Contact IMG at One Erieview Plaza, Suite 1300, Cleveland, OH 44114; (216) 522-1200.

Grass:
Yup, grass. Bermuda, bent, rye and chewing fescues! St. Augustine and poa annua! James B. Beard's *Turfgrass Science and Culture* will tell you more about more types of turf than you thought existed.

. . . AND A COUPLE OF MISCELLANEOUS FAVORITES

1. *The Handbook of Golf* by Alex Hay.
A few hundred enthusiasts could probably name a few hundred golf books as good as Hay's *Handbook,* but I just happen to admire the simple and concise way that Hay covers the entire game. First you get a little history and soon you're into developing a basic swing, learning to spin the ball, playing in weird weather and so on. Hay also includes some player profiles and a glossary, and the illustrations are crystal clear. For a beginner, this is an excellent primer; for the more experienced player, it's a good "back-to-basics" book.

2. *Dogleg Madness* by Mike Bryan.
The author uses three "scenes" to describe and discuss the game: The 1986 U.S. Open at Shinnecock Hills, the 1986 British Open at Turnberry and the tiny Ozona Invitational, an amateur event in the wilds of west Texas where Bryan, a native of Austin, spent his childhood summers with his grandparents. The book isn't divided into the usual sections (history, architecture, the media). Rather, Bryan digresses when the need arises. He describes watching Kenny Knox at Shinnecock, moves on to how Knox was a Monday qualifier for the Honda Classic a few years ago but won the tournament, segues into the opposite end of the spectrum, (at the time, Curtis Strange) compares the depth of golf talent to tennis, and concludes that winning on the pro tour is nigh impossible. The finale to this little digression is great: "Some of these pros tell reporters, 'I'm out here for one reason only—to win. If it wasn't, I'd go home.' But they don't win, and they don't go home."

Hummocks, Whins and Losses

by John Garrity

• • •

The best way to meet Dr. A. MacKenzie is by surprise in some dim shop in Charing Cross Road, amid airborne dust and the perfume of old bindings and decayed pages. Taking his little volume, *Golf Architecture,* from the shelf, one can turn the pages languorously and lose oneself in the arcana of "hummocks," "whins," "rushes" and "mole drains." There is poetry in the good doctor's litany of manures: "Fish or meat guano, basic slag, malt dust, sulphate of ammonia, chalk, the refuse of leather, cloth and shoddy factories, seed crushing mills, seaweed. . . ." There is common sense, too, as in MacKenzie's correction of the notion that worm killers have manurial value: "The green-keeper will tell you that after the application the grass has come up much greener. That is due to the fact that the worms are no longer discolouring it by crawling over it with their slimy bodies."

Don't get to London much? A more practical way to meet Alister MacKenzie—who, if you don't recognize the name, also designed some of the world's great golf courses, including Augusta National and Cypress Point—is by way of a subscription to a book club called The Classics of Golf.

The idea of the club, put simply, is that noted golf historian and writer Herbert Warren Wind will nose around musty book shops while you're out smacking balls in the sun, and every couple of months he'll send you a reprint of one of his finds for $19.95 plus handling. The series opens with an incontestable classic—*Down the Fairway,* by Robert T. Jones, Jr., and O.B. Keeler—and progresses to volumes quaint (James Balfour's *Reminiscences of Golf on St. Andrews Links*) and curious (Arnold Haultain's *The Mystery of Golf*), with stops along the way for landmark instruction books by Ben Hogan, Tommy Armour and Byron Nelson.

The book club began in 1984, and the voices of some of the authors included to date are instantly recognizable:

"You will no doubt recall Keats' poem about stout Cortes staring with eagle eyes at the Pacific while all of his men gazed at each other with a wild surmise, silent upon the peak in Darien. Precisely so did Peter Willard and James Todd stare with eagle eyes at the second lake hole, and gaze at each other with wild surmise, silent upon a tee in Manhooset." (P.G. Wodehouse, *The Clicking of Cuthbert*)

"We picked up—'I.P.'d' as one said at the time, meaning the ball was 'in pocket'—and began looking for all of the other competitors in backyards along the way toward Colonial. Tiny had quit at a fishpond. Grease Repellent had struck a sundial and lost his ball. Easy Reid had met a fellow and stopped to sell him some insurance. John the Band-Aid had broken his blade putter by throwing it against a chimney. The only two still in contention were Foot and Magoo, whom we found hitting seven-irons out of Bermuda grass lawns over the rose-covered fence and onto Colonial's 1st fairway." (Dan Jenkins, *The Dogged Victims of Inexorable Fate*)

Other voices are barely tolerable, such as J.L. Low's in the extremely dense *F.G. Tait—A Record,* which joins a Scottish golf memoir to a play-by-play of the Boer War, with missed putts and missing limbs getting roughly equal sympathy.

For the most part, the collection is more Masterpiece Theater than Nevada Bob's. The facsimile editions are faithful reproductions, and each volume has a new foreword by Wind and an afterword by the likes of Ben Crenshaw, Alistair Cooke or John Updike. "We've found that reading is first and golf is second," says series publisher Robert Macdonald. "If you're not a dedicated reader, it's not going to be that appealing to you."

Having thus narrowed the market to that tiny segment of Americans who own both wing chairs and hickory-shafted putters, the founding partners have made a virtue of smallness. Macdonald, a former CBS executive, runs the operation alone from a Manhattan office a few blocks from Wind's cubby-hole office at *The New Yorker.* ("I'm more of the business person," says Macdonald. "Herb's hopeless at business.")

Orders are handled through an office in Stamford. "We know this is a very small market," says Macdonald, who pegs the Classic subscription list at about 5,000. "The so-called golf nut is not really interested in these books. It takes a much more reflective, thoughtful kind of golfer."

Although chronically behind schedule, Classics of Golf has released 26 titles to date with 36 as the final goal. If Wind and Macdonald have trouble with their remaining choices, they can always refer to the series' selection number 16 for guidance. "A good golf course," MacKenzie writes in *Golf Architecture,* "is like good music or good anything else; it is not necessarily a course which appeals the first time one plays over it, but one which grows on a player the more frequently he visits it."

So far, most of the titles in the Classics of Golf series meet MacKenzie's test. They deserve repeated visits by golfers who enjoy reading.

Where to Find . . . Jack Nicklaus's Golf Swing—in Bronze

At the Franklin Mint, which sells a series of five bronze statuettes of the Golden Bear—each about four inches high—mounted on a wooden plinth and labelled "The Full Swing." Each sequence comes with an affidavit from Nicklaus as to its authenticity, and costs $595. If that seems a tad steep, consider that a portion of the proceeds go to the PGA of America's Junior Golf Foundation. Contact the Mint at (800) 843-6468.

Who else would have his *swing* bronzed?

The Ultimate Golf Library

by Dick Donovan

● ● ●

Where to Buy Your Golf Library

If you have to go to a book dealer, contact the following experts and ask for the latest catalog available. You'll notice that several dealers are based in Britain, but that should come as no surprise as golf is first and foremost a British game.

Richard E. Donovan
   Enterprises
Publishers & Booksellers
Box 7070
305 Massachusetts Ave.
Endicott, NY 13760
(607) 785-5874

George Lewis Golfiana
Box 291
Mamaroneck, NY 10543
(914) 698-4579

Bob Grant
Victoria Square
Droitwich
Worcestershire
England

Colonel John C. Furness
Old Police House
Strathpeffer
Rosshire
Scotland

Sarah Baddiel
The Golf Gallery
Gray's Antique Market
Davies Mews
London W1
England

Dick Donovan has been buying and selling all manner of books for the past 21 years. For the past 15 he has specialized in golf. The coauthor, with Joe Murdoch, of The Game of Golf and the Printed Word, *Donovan reads and reviews every golf book published (except, he concedes, the instructional stuff). Donovan doesn't claim to have the best golf library. He confers that honor on Alistair Johnson, a Scottish-born vice-president with the International Management Group. But he knows as much as anyone about what books are out there and where you can lay your hands on them.*

Please note also that his choices for "The Ultimate Golf Library" address the reader who is at least semi-serious in assembling a golf library; the "Editor's Choice" section contained elsewhere in this book reflect only the opinions of the editor.

Golf has amassed an astounding volume of literature. Over the past 400 years more than 5,000 books and pamphlets have been published in English in 40 countries—more than enough material to whet the appetite of any earnest bibliophile.

The driving force behind my own collection is a passion for books and for the entire game of golf. But some collectors are just curious as to how the game started or are intrigued by course design or the personal and professional lives of golf legends. Statisticians and golf writers look for reference material and volumes of tournament results. And, inevitably, there are those who are inspired by financial rewards—some see a golf library as an investment.

Whatever the motivating force, many would-be collectors have sought my advice on developing a golf library. I'm happy to offer the following advice on how to proceed.

The best place to begin is your local library. Check out a few books on golf history, instruction, biographies and golf-course architecture. You'll get a rough idea of what kind of collections you could have. Then make it a *personal* collection, centered around your own area of interest.

One of the delights of collecting is the hunt for treasured books—but be aware of the scarcity of the elusive titles. Until a few years ago it was possible to scour the used-book stores, Salvation Army outlets and flea markets for an occasional find. However, the increasing number of golf-book and memorabilia collectors in recent times has made this a more difficult endeavor.

Newcomers to the field are encouraged to get to know fellow collectors through the Golf Collectors' Society and to share their successes and failures. Many GCS members can offer advice on how to proceed. You should also check out your nearest used-book store and ask them to look out for golf literature. Once the dealer feels that your are sincere about buying books, he can actively solicit titles for you. Get catalogs from booksellers to get an idea of pricing.

Be aware that this can be an expensive hobby (unless you have some strange urge to collect the *least expensive* golf books ever published!). At three auctions held in Scotland about the same time as the 1990 British Open, for example, a third-edition copy of the first book on golf, *The Goff,* from 1793, went for $36,000; James Cundell's *Rules of the Thistle Club,* from 1824, fetched $13,000, and a rare, 15-page pamphlet of golfing verse, "Golfiana, or a Day at Gullane," from 1869, went for $33,000. Obviously these are selected examples of tough-to-find materials, but I find these prices nevertheless to be an aberration of the market.

But you probably don't want to plunge into the purchase of a book that costs more than an Acura with all the bells and whistles. So I've outlined below a basic, representative—albeit classic—library. They are not all readily available, however, so I have categorized the library into sources: "Bookstores," "Bookstores or Dealers" or "Dealers Only." Don't be put off by having to go to dealers; the most prominent are listed. I have not included golf book clubs as sources.

BOOKSTORES

The Golf Course
Geoffrey S. Cornish and Ronald W. Whitten, 1981

A thoroughly researched reference work on golf courses and design. As well as giving a complete history and analysis of the subject, it identifies more than 10,000 courses, lists who designed (or remodeled) them and when, and provides important biographical data on almost every architect in history.

The Encyclopedia of Golf Collectibles
John M. Olman and Morton W. Olman, 1985 (Updated version published in 1992.)

A solid contribution. The Olmans (John is Mort's son) have assembled in one volume a collector's identification and value guide. It covers virtually every category of memorabilia.

The Mystery of Golf
Theodore Haultain, 1908

This was the first real attempt to probe the enigma of the game or, if you will, what the hell we are all doing out there.

Five Lessons: The Modern Fundamentals of Golf
Ben Hogan with Herbert Warren Wind, 1957

One of the most popular instructional books of all time. This, Vardon's *Complete Golfer* and Boomer's *On Learning Golf,* Earnest Jones's *Swing The Clubhead,* and *Bobby Jones on Golf* constitute the five most important methods of teaching, and all the others are variations on the theme.

On Learning Golf
Percy Boomer, 1942

Probably one of the simplest and easiest approaches to golf instruction. Also one of the longest-in-print instructionals.

BOOKSTORES OR DEALERS

Golf in the Making
Ian T. Henderson and David I. Stirk, 1979

A colorful and informative book that traces the history of the game through the evolution of equipment and its makers.

The Golf Courses of the British Isles
Bernard Darwin, 1910

This is a very entertaining read on the pleasures of playing golf on some of the greatest courses in the U.K. Harry Roundtree's outstanding illustrations make this a keeper. Today's architects can get a good feel for traditional design from Darwin's eloquent essays.

The Game of Golf and the Printed Word, 1566–1985: A Bibliography of Golf Books in the English Language
Richard E. Donovan and Joseph S.F. Murdoch, 1988

Excuse me if I blow my own—and Joe's—horn here. This is a more complete bibliography than Joe's *Library of Golf* mentioned later, but does not have all his annotations.

DEALERS ONLY

A History of Golf
Robert H.K. Browning, 1955

If you read only one book on the history of golf, this should be it. It is probably the most accurate reference you can find. Browning goes right back to the beginnings of the game and strives to put the history in perspective. One thing this book does better than any other is to inspire the reader to want to know more.

My Golfing Life
Harry Vardon, 1933

The reminiscences of the six-time British Open winner, whose career spanned the era of transition from the gutta percha to the rubber-cored ball, offer insights on the dynamics of match play, foursome money matches and

Vardon's travels to the United States when the game was just developing here.

Golf Architecture in America
George C. Thomas, 1927

A classic in the field of course design. Thomas, who designed the Riviera and Los Angeles Country Clubs, pulls together the concepts and philosophies of other contemporary architects and supports it all with great photographs and illustrations.

Fifty Years of Golf
Horace G. Hutchinson, 1919

The noted amateur, and the first Englishman to captain the Royal & Ancient, was a prolific golf writer. Here he presents a good read on the development of golf in England and on his feeling for golf books.

Thirty Years of Championship Golf
Gene Sarazen, 1950

Written with Herbert Warren Wind, this is a frank and entertaining look at the master golfer's life and storied career, from caddie to champion.

The Walter Hagen Story
Walter Hagen and Margaret Seaton Hech, 1956

A chronicle of the illustrious career of the man who said "I never wanted to be a millionaire—I just wanted to live like one." The Haig was a magnificent showman who changed the social standing of the golf pro forever.

Golf Is My Game
Robert Tyre Jones, Jr., 1960

Anything written by Bob Jones is worth having in a golf library. This autobiography recalls most of his major accomplishments, as well as how he developed the Augusta National Golf Club and The Masters Tournament.

The Links
Robert Hunter, 1926

Another classic contribution to the genre. Hunter was a noted sociologist but also a devotee of golf, and he provides us with one of the earliest

American treatises on the game. Excellent photographs illustrate early traditional designs.

Golf: A Royal and Ancient Game
Robert Clark, 1875

Clark collected for history all the known literature, both publicly and privately printed. A beautifully produced book.

Golf Architecture
Dr. Alister Mackenzie, 1920

Dr. Mackenzie designed Augusta National with Bob Jones, as well as several other noted courses. Here he leaves us a legacy of his design concepts in a slim, 135-page work.

Golf in America
James P. Lee, 1895

An important book, as it was one of the first golf books produced in the U.S. that was written by an American. It traces golf's beginnings and gives the reader an insight into this new social phenomenon.

The Goff
Thomas Mathison, 1743

The first book on golf was a book of verse. It's about a fictional match between the author (Pygmalion) and a local Scottish bookkeeper (Castilio).

Golf Club Trademarks, American 1898–1930
Patrick Kennedy, 1984

Kennedy has enlightened the club collectors of the world with a seminal work that assists in the identification of woodshafted clubs.

Scotland's Gift: Golf
Charles Blair Macdonald, 1928

Another key book. Macdonald was a driving force in early American golf and wrote this history of the game here. He also delves into golf's earlier history and lets us in on the genesis of the USGA.

The Story of American Golf
Herbert Warren Wind, 1948

The definitive work—and very well written—on the development of golf in the United States.

Badminton Library of Golf
1890

One of the most influential books in any golf library. Its significant writings on all aspects of the game reached a great number of enthusiasts and contributed to the deluge of golf writing that followed.

The PGA
Herb Graffis, 1975

A definitive and insightful book that chronicles in great detail the development and activities of the PGA as it grew and eventually split into the PGA of America (for club professionals, mainly) and the PGA Tour (for touring professionals).

Down the Fairway
Robert Tyre Jones, Jr., and O.B. Keeler, 1927

Recounts the extraordinary life and times of one of the greatest golfers of all time. Keeler was Jones's biographer and gives us a real appreciation of golf in the golden era.

The Golfer's Manual
Henry Farnie, 1857

Another cornerstone; the first book of prose on golf and also the first of hundreds to come on how to play it.

The Haunted Major (The Enchanted Golf Clubs)
Robert Marshall, 1920

A classic piece of golf fiction, it has the distinction of being the golf title that's been in print the longest.

The Complete Golfer
Harry Vardon, 1905

Vardon's first book probably influenced more golfers than we realize. He covers instruction, naturally, but one wonderful chapter is devoted to golf-course architecture.

Swing the Clubhead
Earnest Jones, 1952

Jones's teaching methods are still being preached today.

Bobby Jones on Golf
Robert Tyre Jones, Jr., 1966

The theories on the game by one of the game's greatest practitioners—and one of the few players who had the ability to write his own instruction.

The Library of Golf, 1743–1966
Joseph S.F. Murdoch, 1968

A must book for any golf collector, for this constitutes a delightful account of a man's love of books and the game. Murdoch's personal annotations of a few hundred selected golf titles make you want to run out and find all of them for your own library.

Hints to Lady Golfers
Maud Gordon Robertson, 1909

This was the first book written by a women golf professional.

Golfing Curios and the Like
Harry B. Wood, 1910

Mr. Wood was one of the earliest collectors and here provides us with a commentary on all sorts of collectibles, from equipment to medals to books. This is also one of the first attempts at a golf-book bibliography.

The Life of Tom Morris
W.W. Tulloch, 1908

If you want to learn the history of the game, this is required reading. Tom Morris's life spanned a considerable period and offers us good reading on the transition from the featherie era to the guttie era and on to the rubber-cored ball. He is acknowledged as the "Father of Golf Course Architecture."

The Happy Golfer
Henry Leach, 1914

This is one of my own favorites. I always learn much from Leach's essays on early golf around the world and am always stimulated to research.

The Clapcott Papers
Alastair Johnson, 1985

Clapcott was an early student on the history of the game and provided much historical research material. In this book

Where to Find . . . Golfing Christmas Cards

The United States Golf Association sells various combinations of Santa Claus and Christmas trees and snowy golf courses at $19–$22 for a box of 25 (only one set, depicting Young Tom Morris playing in the snow in St. Andrews, is nondenominational). Call (800) 632-3600.

Sportcards, of Newport, Rhode Island, has four cards, much the same theme as the USGA's, for $20–$22.50 per box of 25. Call (401) 847-5848.

St. Nick wants eight strokes: one for each reindeer.

Alastair Johnson, a noted historian in his own right, offers insightful commentary.

Golfers at Law
Geoffrey Cousins, 1958

The best history on the evolution of the rules and commentary on decisions. Fortunately, it's in layman's language.

The Game of Golf
Willie Park, Jr., 1896

Another key book and the first written by a golf professional. A quite handsomely colored cover enhances it.

The Golf Course Mystery
Chester K. Steele, 1919

The first full-length mystery with the murder scene on the golf course. Since then some 75 other works of this genre have appeared.

The Major Golf Publications

It's a jungle out there. There are golf monthlies and weeklies—no dailies yet—as well as regional magazines, newsletters and even a series of poster-style bulletins. Although we have separated them into Majors, Minors, The Others and the Brits, our intention is not to attach some sort of class system to golf publishing. While the major publications are the best-produced and have the best writing and layouts by far—they should have; only they can afford it all—the smaller publications should be judged purely on how well they do the job they purport to do.

the majors

Golf Magazine versus *Golf Digest* could be the subject of an essay question. The two have been having at each other for more than three decades, pirating each other's writers, artists and playing professionals, redesigning and redesigning again, just to get the edge.

Golf Magazine is part of the Los Angeles-based Times Mirror Company, while *Digest* belongs to the New York Times' family. Each has a circulation of more than one million, each follows a similar pattern of theme issues during the year and each is at the mercy of trigger-happy golf equipment companies who threaten lawsuits and the withdrawal of hundreds of advertising pages if a writer so much as *thinks* that one brand of golf equipment may be superior to another. One other thing: Both are well-conceived, well-executed publications that employ the top writers, photographers and illustrators in the field.

GOLF MAGAZINE

Editorial offices:
Two Park Avenue, New York, NY 10016

When launched:
1959

Frequency:
Monthly

Where circulated:
U.S. and Canada (very little overseas)

Subscriptions from:
Box 53733, Boulder, CO 80322-3733;
(800) 876-7726

Playing professionals:
Arnold Palmer, Jack Nicklaus, Greg Norman, Curtis Strange, Raymond Floyd, Peter Jacobsen, Nancy Lopez

Teaching professionals:
Ken Venturi, Dave Pelz and others

Strengths:
Golf Magazine's instruction gets two or three times the readership of its feature material, which is not so much a criticism of its features as a credit to its instruction. The magazine's "Private Lessons" section, which passes quick tips to four different types of golfer—straight hitter, long hitter, low handicapper, high handicapper—has remained immensely popular since its launch in February 1986. Jack Nicklaus

Where to Find . . . a Magazine Devoted Totally to Golfiana

In fact, it's called *Golfiana*. It's published quarterly by Bud Dufner, a member of the Golf Collectors Society, and contains half a dozen eclectic articles about golf history in each edition. A recent issue, for example, contained a history of British Opens played at St. Andrews, written by Bobby Burnet, historian at the Royal & Ancient; a profile of J.H. Taylor; an instructional article (on putting) by Jerry Travers from 1933; and a book excerpt on golf during the Reformation of the Church of Scotland in the 16th century! Single copies cost $14. Annual subs cost $40 in the U.S. or $46 in Canada. Call (618) 656-8172.

Golf seldom strays from instruction on its cover.

and his personal illustrator, Jim McQueen, were recently shanghaied from *Golf Digest*.

Weaknesses:
Sometimes has a tendency to pass off a catchy cover line as good instruction. In August of 1987, for example, the magazine told its readers that they needed *two* swings, when the fact is that most folk have trouble enough finding one. December 1992 ran "The X Factor," which had something to do with maximizing the relationship between shoulder angle and hip angle! Turned out to be a huge hit.

Writers:
Regulars include Thomas Boswell and Dave Kindred, two of the best in the business. A recent addition is Lewis Grizzard. Other contributors include Stephen Goodwin, formerly head of the literature program at the National Endowment for the Arts; Mike Bryan, who has written several good baseball and golf books, and Jim Dodson, who straddles the Mason-Dixon line by being a contributor both to *Southern* magazine and *Yankee*.

Golf Digest

Editorial offices:
5520 Park Ave., Trumbull, CT 06611

When launched:
1950

Frequency:
Monthly

Playing professionals:
Seve Ballesteros, Tom Kite, Al Geiberger, Bernhard Langer, Tom Watson, Patty Sheehan, Amy Alcott

Teaching professionals:
Bob Toski, Paul Runyan, David Leadbetter and others

Strengths:
Pages. Advertisers love the circulation and the *Digest*'s association with the *New York Times*: Special sections, such as a U.S. Open preview, often are distributed with the *Times*.

Weaknesses:
Their equipment coverage can be excessively thorough. They also can be guilty of ivory-tower journalism. To wit: Should editors who belong to golf clubs that restrict be slamming other clubs that restrict?

Writers:
The good stuff doesn't always come from such "name" writers as Dan Jenkins, formerly with *Sports Illustrated,* or Charles Price, formerly editor of, and later contributor to, *Golf Magazine*. Both Jerry Tarde, the current editor, and Peter McLeery, an associate editor, write knowledgeably and competently. Peter Dobereiner is an Englishman whose style leans toward the verbose but is seldom unentertaining. Dave Anderson, sports columnist for the *New York Times,* crops up from time to time.

the minors

Golf Illustrated

Editorial offices:
5050 North 40th St., Suite 250, Phoenix, AZ 85018

When launched:
1992 (current version)

Frequency:
10 times per year, doubling up January/February and November/December

Golf Illustrated was moved to Arizona in 1991 when its parent company, New York–based Family Media, filed for bankruptcy. Its new owners, who also publish the *Arizona Golfer,* immediately started plunging money into the magazine, principally in production costs, which is to say *Golf Illustrated* sometimes *feels* the most elegant of the golf publications. They also hired "Dick and Dave," best remembered as the old Bartles and Jaymes guys, for an advertising campaign. But without the wine coolers in hand, Dick and Dave look like any two old golfers in the land. Beyond

that, *Illustrated*'s coverage of the golf scene is workmanlike with little inspiration: A good third magazine in what is effectively a two-horse race.

Golf World

Editorial offices:
5520 Park Ave., Trumbull, CT 06611-0395

When launched:
1947

Frequency:
Weekly from mid-January through August; bi-weekly from September through November; one issue in December

Golf World was a small weekly out of North Carolina with a staunch but limited following until *Golf Digest,* under the flag of the *New York Times,* purchased the magazine. With an infusion of cash and a few more bodies, *Golf World* became a much fuller publication, comprehensively covering the pro tours while offering up the occasional instruction and equipment article. If you want your golf news by the week, this is by far the best source.

Golf Journal

Editorial offices:
Golf House, Far Hills, NJ 07931

Golf Journal.

When launched:
1948

Frequency:
Eight times per year

This is the USGA's magazine, and therefore deals heavily with USGA-related material. The game's history, lore, issues, humor and such nuts and bolts topics as rules, agronomy, handicapping and equipment. It's sometimes colorful but usually a small publication. Could use even a conservative dash of flash.

GOLFWEEK

Editorial offices:
175 Fifth St. SW, Winter Haven, FL 33880

When launched:
1975

Frequency:
Weekly

In 1975, this was a one-man operation known as *Florida Golfweek*. Two years ago, it dropped the "Florida" from its name and went national, although the meat of its readership is from the southeastern United States. It's a family organization, with the editor's sons, Tom and Bob Stine, serving as general manager and special events coordinator, respectively, and occasionally writing. Although the editorial outlook tends to be parochial at times, its actual treatment of the game—particularly in the areas of smaller tournament reports, equipment, course management and real estate fields—is very thorough. A very useful publication whose weekly arrival I have come to look forward to.

GOLF SHOP OPERATIONS

Editorial offices:
5520 Park Ave., Trumbull, CT 06611-0395

When launched:
1953

Frequency:
Nine times per year

Published by *Golf Digest, GSO* is the bible for those who operate pro shops or any other outlets that sell golf. It is a large-format, very colorful publication, heavy on the business of running the shop. It names the top 100 golf shops in America every February, breaking the list down into shops at private clubs, municipal courses, resorts, privately-owned daily fee courses and off-course discount stores.

Golf Course News.

GOLF COURSE NEWS

Editorial offices:
38 Lafayette St., Box 997, Yarmouth, ME 04096

When launched:
February 1989

Frequency:
Monthly

If you need to find pond liners or information on new developments, this is the place to look. The concept of the publication—newsprint broadsheet, normally around 42 pages—is sound, in that *someone* has to track and report on the growth in the golf-course business.

SOUTHERN LINKS

Editorial offices:
Box 7628, Hilton Head Island, SC 29938

Launched:
March 1988

Frequency:
Six times per year

Much of *Southern Links'* editorial content is nationally angled and written by such competent writers as Ben Wright, a commentator for CBS-TV, and Barry McDermott, a former *Sports Illustrated* writer. But beyond such contributions, *SL* appears to follow the well-trodden "regional" path of running articles about advertisers. It's four-color production is impressive, however.

EXECUTIVE GOLFER

Editorial offices:
2171 Campus Drive, Irvine, CA 92715

When launched:
1972

Frequency:
Six times per year

One would have thought that a publication that extols an affluent readership would be thick as, say, a *Vogue* or *Palm Beach Life* magazine. *EG* is thin in comparison. Still, it does it's job in that it contains features on new resorts, profiles, articles on architecture and equipment and a list of "luxury resorts for corporate meetings," with good hard information that will be useful to anyone charged with arranging such a get-together. This is not, however, a publication for the golfer who buys at discount. Note: The Pazdur family has produced a couple of editions in Japanese. Subscriptions include two golf resort guides and one "Private Country Club Guest Policy Directory."

GOLF FOR WOMEN

Editorial offices:
All American Plaza, 2130 Jackson Ave.
W. Oxford, MS 38655

Launched:
July 1988

Frequency:
Six times per year

One hopes this newish magazine flies. A very small percentage of the major magazines' readership is female, and while almost one out of every two new golfers is female, the ladies are also dropping out of the game at a high rate. Still, there *should* be a magazine devoted to women's golf, because they get shortchanged in almost every other area of the game. This is a good, four-color magazine with such interesting topics covered as "Playing Pregnant." There are also profiles of lady pros, fashion and travel articles and instruction by women for women.

the others

This is only a selection. In the latter half of the last decade, as golf grew increasingly popular, local and regional magazines spread like a brush fire. Some didn't make it, but now virtually every golf association has its own publication.

THE MET GOLFER

Editorial offices:
Two Park Avenue, New York, NY 10016

Launched:
1983

The official publication of the Metropolitan (New York, New Jersey and Connecticut) Golf Association, this may be the slickest of the regionals. It has improved in recent years, roughly when Times Mirror Magazines took over the parent company and was able to infuse the expertise of the support staff from *Golf Magazine*.

THE MASSACHUSETTS GOLFER

Editorial offices:
670 Centre St., Boston, MA 02130

Launched:
1990

One of the youngest regionals, *The Mass Golfer* gets high marks for its production and feature articles. It's now linked with Times Mirror Magazines, which also publishes *The Met Golfer*.

AMERICAN GOLF MAGAZINE

Editorial offices:
11661 San Vicente Blvd., Suite 402, Los Angeles, CA 90049

Launched:
1987

Much of the circulation goes to the 140 public golf courses operated by the American Golf Corporation. In fact, this publication devotes itself to the public golfer. Its instruction and rules material is universal, but the features are slanted to public tournaments, profiles, etc.

BACK NINE

Editorial offices:
Box 55427, Seattle, WA 98155

When launched:
1987

Frequency:
Six times per year

Deals with golf courses in the Pacific Northwest, while also covering instruction, local golfers and travel to other areas.

CLUB DIRECTOR

Editorial offices:
National Club Association, Washington Harbour, 3050 K St., N.W., Suite 330, Washington, DC 20001

When launched:
1983

Frequency:
10 times per year

Deals with directors of more than just golf clubs. Not a very sexy publication, on "newsletter" stock, but it is realistic. One issue I read gave good—mainly financial—reasons why the golf boom may implode by the turn of the century. It's tough to find that stuff anywhere else.

Colorado Golf.

COLORADO GOLF JOURNAL

Editorial offices:
559 2nd Ave., Castle Rock, CO 80104

Launched:
January 1987

Frequency:
Four times per year

A four-color publication that leans more toward features than tournament scores and other such data. Its spring issue contains a complete list of golf courses in Colorado.

FORE

Editorial offices:
3740 Cahuenga Blvd., North Hollywood, CA 91609

Where to Find . . . a Humorous Golf Magazine

Most golf publications like to think that they're occasionally laugh-a-minute thigh-slappers, but only one devotes itself totally to ridiculing the game. It's called *Bogeys* and is published occasionally in Glasgow, Scotland, by a golfer named Donnie Kerr. Only in *Bogeys* will you learn that Ben Crenshaw has his eyebrows handsewn in Savile Row, that Nick Faldo decided to take up golf in 1972 after an eccentric aunt gave him a hand-knitted Fair Isle sweater and that Mrs. McCormack puts a blanket over Mark's cage at night. Meanwhile, the *Bogeys* Advisory Service informs you that you can easily unsettle an opponent by setting fire to his golf bag or calling him "sweetie" for the entire round. The newsstand price is £1, but you might be able to negotiate a price and squeeze a subscription from Kerr by writing to him at WH Publications, 18 Mearns Rd., Clarkston, Glasgow G76 7EU, Scotland, Great Britain.

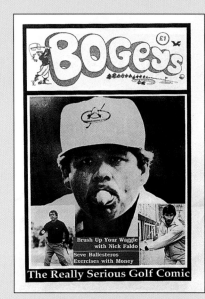

Launched:
1968

Frequency:
Six times per year

SoCalGA members are fortunate to have such an attentive publication. In addition to a small feature "well," the magazine is full up front with departments dealing with such items as "Handicap Hints," "News of the Golf Industry," "New Products," "Know the Rules" and more. It also contains news from other golf associations.

GOLF GEORGIA

Editorial offices:
2400 Herodian Way, Suite 200, Atlanta, GA 30080

When launched:
January 1988

Frequency:
Five times per year (January, February, April, July, October)

This is the Georgia State Golf Association's publication. It neither looks good or reads particularly well but, like so many of these "official" publications, it delivers good hard information on the area's golf courses.

GOLF PRO MERCHANDISER

Editorial offices:
7 East 12th St., New York, NY 10003

When launched:
January 1988

Frequency:
Six times per year

GPM is produced by the staff of *Sportstyle* and is therefore heavy into clothing fashions. Both are owned by Fairchild Publications, which also deals in *Women's Wear Daily* and *W*.

MICHIGAN GOLFER

Editorial offices:
Box 7007, Grand Rapids, MI 49510

Launched:
1982

Frequency:
Six times per year

A good regional publication that includes news and features on courses (reviews, too), tournaments, players, and more—which is to be expected from one of the most enthusiastic golfing states in the nation.

PAR EXCELLANCE

Editorial offices:
10401 W. Lincoln Ave., West Allis, WI 53227

When launched:
1984

Frequency:
Four times per year

Stocky, four-color publication covers entire midwest. Includes articles on instruction, architecture, equipment and golf courses in other parts of the country. Can't quite understand the spelling of "Excellance."

the brits

With a few exceptions, the first thing you will notice about British golf publications is that, relative to the American mags, they really could care less how well you play the game or how much you want to improve. They care more about the game itself.

In Britain, you will find columns about amateur golf or women's golf—both of which are heresies to major American publications—as well as historical pieces and profiles of players we have *yet* to hear much about. (Contrast this to American six-page instructional theses on how to hit your drives six yards longer by cleaning behind your ears every morning.)

This difference in editorial philosophies can be traced to the difference in cultures. Where American magazines go to great lengths to identify their audiences ("Our average reader has 4.3 cars, has a stock portfolio of $180,000, and his pet dog, Widdle, went to Harvard!"), then sell them what they believe they can't wait to buy, British magazines seem to believe that there are hordes of golf-damaged Britons who will read next to anything that falls in their laps. Which happens to be true.

GOLF MONTHLY

Editorial offices:
IPC Magazines, King's Reach Tower, Stamford St., London, SE1 9LS, England

Frequency:
Monthly

Until a few years ago, *GM* was an independent, rough-hewn magazine put together in Glasgow by a smallish staff. Now it is part of the vast IPC media conglomerate and has been redesigned into a more contemporary-looking book. Getting a little bit heavy on instruction, however.

GOLF WORLD

Editorial offices:
Advance House, 37 Millharbour, Isle of Dogs, London, E14 9TX, England

Frequency:
Monthly

GW is the sister publication to America's *Golf Digest*, which means you often get the same instructional articles that appeared in *GD* appearing in *GW* a few months later. But its features remain fresh.

TODAY'S GOLFER

Editorial offices:
EMAP Pursuit Publishing Ltd., Bretton Court, Bretton, Peterborough, PE3 8DZ, Cambridgeshire, England

Frequency:
Monthly

The youngest of the British golfing publications, *TG* has tried to cash in on the British golf boom by speaking to the proletariat in the game. You get your fill. A recent issue had 39 entries on its contents page, which included instruction from Ian Woosnam; features on balls, putters, wedges, match play and cheats; previews to two tournaments; and three competitions in which readers could win either a set of Ram irons and woods, a Hogan golf bag, towel, umbrella and balls, or a weekend of golf in the English Midlands.

GOLF ILLUSTRATED WEEKLY

Editorial offices:
Advance House, 37 Millharbour, London, E14 9TX, England

Frequency:
50 issues per year

This is the weekly sister publication to *Golf World* (Britain), which is the sister publication to *Golf Digest* (U.S.), which is the sister publication to *Golf World* (U.S.). Which one is Hannah is anybody's guess.

Where to Find . . .
a Print of Jack Nicklaus, Arnold Palmer and Ben Hogan in the Same Frame

Ron Ramsey is Art Director at *Golf Magazine* but moonlights as an illustrator (or is he an illustrator moonlighting as an art director?). He created the Nicklaus-Palmer-Hogan print in 1978 and has been steadily receiving orders ever since. Each print measures 16-by-20 inches and costs $20, including postage, from Ramsey Graphics, 265 Bronxville Rd., Bronxville, NY 10708. Allow three weeks for delivery.

Golf on the Silver Screen

Or Where to Find Some of the Worst Movies Imaginable.

They say that golf does not "translate well" to the cinematic medium. Which is a kind way of saying that golf movies stink.

But the fact is that sports in general don't work in movies—or at least if the film's about the sport. When the movie is really about something else but set in the *context* of a sport, it can work really well.

Breaking Away, for instance, wasn't about cycling; it was about growing up. *Bull Durham* by all accounts was about minor-league baseball. Wrong again. It was the old routine about seasoned veterans teaching young raw talent the facts of life: *Jeremiah Johnson* with sex and a seventh-inning stretch.

And so the seminal golf movie of all time actually concealed the following, somber message:

If you ever face a choice between joining a lah-di-dah country club or having your face gnawed to the bone by rats . . . take the rats.

Caddyshack was the movie. In the same way that P.G. Wodehouse portrayed and satirized so accurately the eccentric aristocracy that inhabited English golf clubs in the early part of the century, so *Caddyshack* does for those obnoxious characters who seem to have become a staple at so many well-heeled clubs today.

Rodney Dangerfield plays the nouveau-riche developer who drives a big car, steers a big boat, leaves tips that could raise the GNP of several small African nations and who has a boom box and beer taps built into his golf bag.

Ted Knight is the antithesis of Dangerfield—the old-money WASPish club captain, a local judge who actually puts stock in his blue blazer, club crest and cravat. He steams as Dangerfield precipitates the destruction of his orderly world.

The rest of the cast play supporting roles, even if their performances suggest otherwise. Chevy Chase is the slick, cocaine-sniffing entrepreneur, contemptuous of his pompous surroundings. Bill Murray plays a perpetually stoned greens superintendent—it's the role that made him as a film star (and in truth, makes the film a classic).

The place goes up in smoke at the end. Murray shapes plastic explosives into forest animals to rid the golf course of gophers, and they eventually explode to the cannons and bells of the 1812 Overture. Score one against the snobs. Who wouldn't cheer?

Beyond *Caddyshack,* however, there are slim pickings indeed among golf movies. *Follow the Sun,* in which Glenn Ford replayed the life of Ben Hogan as he returned to glory after an automobile crash, is a severely questionable piece of work. *The Caddy* stars Jerry Lewis, and that about says it all right there. You won't likely find the Ford flick, but there are some copies of the Lewis-Martin movie kicking around (most old golf movies don't move well enough for even the most ardent stocker of eclectica to hold onto them). As for *Caddyshack II,* that Jackie Mason-driven turkey

Some advice for Ben Hogan from Jerry Lewis in *The Caddy*.

probably did more to discredit the proponents of the original than it did to further the use of golf as a comedic vehicle. A real stinker.

On the other hand, some movies that are now unavailable might make marvelous viewing were they to be rereleased. Three P.G. Wodehouse stories, "Rodney Fails to Qualify," "Chester Forgets Himself" and "Ordeal by Golf," were filmed in Britain in 1924. If they were a fraction as funny as the books they'd be movie classics. And can you believe golf crossed paths with kung fu? It happened in 1981 with *Bruce Lee, We Miss You* in which a martial artist seeks to revenge the murder of his hero, kung-fu film star Bruce Lee. He encounters the murderer on a golf course, whereupon the pair duke it out at high speed with golf balls and golf clubs and the customary sound effects. Sounds like an excellent format for a PGA Tour playoff.

What follows is a list, the best we can come up with, of those movies still available and their prices, and a short list of "wannasees." Not included are movies in which golf is purely incidental. Examples: *Breaking In,* that fine Bill Forsyth movie about professional burglars, which starred Burt Reynolds (he lectures an apprentice burglar while playing golf), or *Ordinary People,* in which Donald Sutherland and Mary Tyler Moore can be seen heading from the 18th green to the 19th hole.

We've used two sources for the listings, each of which carries more than 20,000 titles, but you may want to try your local store first (especially for rentals).

▼ "VC" is Video Connection, at 4011 Secor Rd., Toledo, OH 43606; (419) 472-8863. The company takes Visa, MasterCard and Discover.
▼ "MU" is Movies Unlimited, at 6736 Castor Avenue, Philadelphia, PA 19149; (800) 523-0823. They take Visa, MasterCard, Discover and American Express.

the movies

BAT 21

Tri Star Pictures, 1988
Stars: Gene Hackman, Danny Glover

Hackman is Lt. Col. Gene Hambleton, whose plane is shot down behind enemy lines in North Vietnam in 1972. After several unsuccessful rescue missions, his rescuers come up with a plan based on Hambleton's love for golf: A pilot, played by Glover and code-named "Bird Dog," radios Hackman—code-named "Bat 21"—and tells him to "play" a familiar golf hole. He opens with the first at Tucson National, Hambleton's home course in Arizona. It runs 408 yards southeast, so Bat 21 makes his way southeast for 408 yards. Eventually they get him home, which seems to be the sort of happy ending Hollywood always churns out. But *Bat 21* actually happened. Hambleton is now in his seventies and still playing Tucson National, where he sports a 10-handicap.
VC: $19.95
MU: $19.95

THE CADDY

Paramount, 1953
Stars: Jerry Lewis, Dean Martin, Donna Reed

Lewis is a good golfer who dissolves when anyone watches him. Instead he teaches Martin to play and caddies for him. An awful film.
VC: n/a
MU: $19.95

CADDYSHACK

Warner Bros., 1980
Stars: Rodney Dangerfield, Ted Knight, Chevy Chase, Bill Murray, Michael O'Keefe, Cindy Morgan

Mayhem at a stuffy country club. See above.

VC: $19.98
MU: $19.95

CADDYSHACK II

Forget it.

DEAD OF NIGHT

Ealing Studios, 1946
Stars: Sir Michael Redgrave, Mervyn Johns, Renee Gadd, Googie Withers

Directed in part by Charles Crichton, who was behind the classic Ealing comedy *The Lavender Hill Mob* and was brought out of retirement a few years ago to pilot *A Fish Called Wanda*. Golf's involvement in this one is strange. Each guest at a country retreat recounts an incident with the supernatural. Redgrave, for example, tells of a warped ventriloquist and an equally warped dummy. The golf episode is sort of comic relief. Two golfers play a match for the right to court a girl (did someone say "Wodehouse"?). The loser immediately drowns himself, then returns to haunt his conqueror all over the golf course. One of the stars reminds me of a very puerile joke an old newspaper colleague used to torture workmates with. Q.: "Did you see Googie Withers last night?" A.: "Who's Googie Withers?" Punchline: "Everyone's, in cold weather."
VC: $19.95
MU: n/a
IMPORTANT: Be sure they don't send you the horrid *Dead of Night* fright flick starring Ed Begley, Jr.—if they send you anything at all; there's been talk of both movies being taken out of circulation.

DEAD SOLID PERFECT

HBO, 1989
Star: Randy Quaid

The cable-movie version of Dan Jenkins book was better than the reviews would have you believe. Quaid plays the frustrated pro trying to make a life of it on the pro tour. By the way, that scene where one pro makes love to another pro's wife in the undergrowth of a golf course is based on an actual incident that is said to have been captured by a television camera high up in a crane at a tournament in Texas. Jenkins, naturally, will not reveal the participants who inspired him. Jenkins himself makes a brief appearance in a motel hallway.

Note: Neither VC or MU stocked this, but it is still kicking around. My local movie store carries it, but that could be a comment about the louts who run it as much as anything else.

Sean Connery as James Bond prepares to tee off against Auric Goldfinger (Gert Fröbe) while the world's most menacing caddie, Odd Job (Harold Sakata), looks on.

GOLDFINGER

CBS/FOX, 1964
Stars: Sean Connery, Honor Blackman, Gert Fröbe

In an early sequence, Bond plays against arch enemy Auric Goldfinger (Fröbe), who is tampering with the world's gold reserves. Bond must deal not only with his opponent but also with his opponent's cheating caddie, the rotund and extremely dangerous Odd Job.
VC: $19.98
MU: $19.95

M*A*S*H

Fox, 1970
Stars: Donald Sutherland, Elliott Gould, Sally Kellerman

A Robert Altman film in which Hawkeye and Trapper like to hit balls on a makeshift layout when not wisecracking or pulling shrapnel from GIs' torsoes.
VC: $19.98
MU: $19.99

PAT AND MIKE

MGM, 1952
Stars: Katharine Hepburn, Spencer Tracy, Aldo Ray, William Ching

In this George Cukor movie, Hepburn plays Pat Pemberton, an excellent athlete who, at the urging of her fiancé (Ching), enters a golf tournament and narrowly loses to Babe Zaharias. She is signed up by corrupt fight manager Mike Conovan (Tracy), who eventually falls in love with her. When he turns down a demand from the mob that Pat throw a golf match, the mobsters attack him, whereupon Pat wades into the fray, beats up the bad guys and realizes she loves him, too. Well of course

Moe, Larry, and Curly take dead aim in *Three Little Beers.*

she wins the tournament. Betcha didn't know that Charles Bronson has a role.
VC: $19.98
MU: $29.95

THREE LITTLE BEERS

Columbia, 1935
Starring: Larry Fine, Moe Howard, Curly Howard

That's right, folks—Larry, Moe and Curly. The Three Stooges deliver beer to a golf tournament and all hell breaks loose. The Stooges' movies often come in boxed sets of different volumes, 13 in all. *Three Little Beers* can be found in Volume Four.
VC: $29.95
MU: $29.95

the wannasees

We found these in a wonderful book titled *Sports Films,* compiled by Harvey Marc Zucker and Lawrence J. Babich and published by McFarland & Co. in 1987. Several pages are devoted to golf films. These are some of the more interesting listings.

MCNAB'S VISIT TO LONDON

A 1905 film appears to tell of a Scottish golfer who visits a friend in London and proceeds to wreck the friend's house. Story of my life.

ORDEAL BY GOLF, RODNEY FAILS TO QUALIFY, CHESTER FORGETS HIMSELF

The aforementioned Wodehouse movies, originally released in 1924.

THE RAMBLIN' GALOOT

A western made in 1926, it tells of a cowboy teaching a rich banker and his beautiful daughter how to play golf. Honest.

SCROGGINS PLAYS GOLF

A British film from 1911. The *Sports Films* synopsis: "When a golfer loses his ball, he uses eggs and fruit instead." It was this movie that inspired the provisional ball rule.

GOLFING EXTRAORDINARY, FIVE GENTLEMEN

A golfer, one of five, swings and misses his ball, then falls over. End of movie. Made in Britain in 1896, it was, according to *Sports Films,* the first sports comedy ever made.

THE GOLF SPECIALIST

Nothing more than stage routines from W.C. Fields, although worth noting is that this was Fields's first talkie.

Publicity poster for *Pat and Mike.*

![A] n Orderly Guide to Golf Videos

Two popular Lee Trevino golf videos.

Golf videotapes make for a puzzling medium. There's no questioning the value of such easy access to instruction. Bad day at the course? Pop in the video when you get home.

On the other hand, very few golf videos are of a high standard in terms of production. None are composed or lit particularly well and few are scripted at all. And in the case of those that are, it is the unfortunate nature of golf instruction that the golfer reads the lines. I suppose it's impractical to have Curtis Strange go through the motions of grip, stance, address and alignment while Sir John Gielgud does the voice-over.

By and large, golf videos are issued by PGA, LPGA and Senior Tour professionals, and most of the instruction, even if unprofessionally delivered, is sound. What follows is a categorized guide to golf videos. Our source for prices is GolfSmart, the California-based consumer division of The Booklegger, which supplies most of the pro shops and discount golf stores around the country. The United States Golf Association has a fair selection of tapes on the U.S. Open and others dealing with such items as the Rules of Golf and turfgrass research, and most golf catalogs carry the best-known titles. You could also walk into a department store tomorrow and buy Nicklaus or Trevino tapes. You might also find a small selection for rent at your local video store.

One other thing to note: The PGA Tour issues a compilation of tapes from the old television show "Shell's Wonderful World of Golf." Problem is you have to join its "Partners" membership program to get a copy. Contact them at (904) 285-3700.

We have used GolfSmart as our source simply because they carry most of the good titles and they are *very* reliable. GolfSmart is at Box 1688, Cedar Ridge, CA 95924; (800) 637-3557 or (916) 272-1422.

TITLE	LENGTH	PRICE
VIDEOS BY JACK NICKLAUS		
Golf My Way, Vol. I	128 mins.	$85
Golf My Way, Vol. II	141 mins.	$85
Jack Nicklaus Plays the Greatest Holes		
in Championship Golf	65 mins.	$19.95
VIDEOS BY ARNOLD PALMER		
Arnold Palmer's Play Great Golf Series		
Mastering Fundamentals	60 mins.	$39.98
Course Strategy	60 mins.	$39.98
The Scoring Zone	60 mins.	$39.98
Practice Like a Pro	60 mins.	$39.98

Title	Length	Price
VIDEOS BY LEE TREVINO		
Lee Trevino's Priceless Golf Tips		
Chipping and Putting	25 mins.	$19.95
Getting Out of Trouble	27 mins.	$19.95
Swing, Distance and Control	25 mins.	$19.95
Putt for Dough and How to Read Greens	50 mins.	$19.95
Lee Trevino's Golf Tips for Youngsters	40 mins.	$19.95
VIDEOS BY BOBBY JONES		
How I Play Golf	180 mins.	$245.00
Bobby Jones's Instructional Series		
Vol. I	45 mins.	$69.95
Vol. II	60 mins.	$69.95
VIDEOS BY CURTIS STRANGE		
Win—and Win Again	70 mins.	$29.95
ENSEMBLE VIDEOS		
PGA Tour Golf (Hal Sutton, Craig Stadler, Lanny Wadkins, Tom Kite, Payne Stewart)		
The Full Swing	60 mins.	$29.95
The Short Game	60 mins.	$29.95
Course Strategy	60 mins.	$29.95
The Master System to Better Golf, Vol. I		
The Short Game (Craig Stadler)	20 mins.	$14.95
Driving (Davis Love III)	20 mins.	$14.95
Iron Accuracy (Tom Purtzer)	20 mins.	$14.95
Putting (Gary Koch)	20 mins.	$14.95
A compilation of the four	60 mins.	$39.95
The Master System, Vol. II		
Fairways and Greens (Paul Azinger)	20 mins.	$14.95
Tempo (Fred Couples)	20 mins.	$14.95
Trouble Shots (Bobby Wadkins)	20 mins.	$14.95
A compilation of the three	60 mins.	$39.95
The Master System, The Seniors		
The Driver and Wedge (Miller Barber)	25 mins.	$14.95
Rhythm, Tempo, Sand & Chip Shots (Dale Douglass)	25 mins.	$14.95
Long Irons, Putting (Orville Moody)	25 mins.	$14.95
A compilation of the three (with some additions, we presume)	115 mins.	$39.95
PUTTING VIDEOS		
Ben Crenshaw		
The Art of Putting	44 mins.	$19.95
Dave Stockton		
Precision Putting	30 mins.	$49.95

TITLE	LENGTH	PRICE
THE SHORT GAME		
Paul Runyan's Short Way to Lower Scoring		
Putting and Chipping	35 mins.	$29.95
Pitching and Sand Play	26 mins.	$29.95
Raymond Floyd		
Sixty Yards In	60 mins.	$59.95
John Jacobs's Short Game	60 mins.	$69.95
VIDEOS FOR WOMEN		
Nancy Lopez		
Golf Made Easy	48 mins.	$39.95
Donna White		
Beginning Golf for Women	40 mins.	$14.95
JoAnne Carner		
Keys to Great Golf	90 mins.	$39.95
Jan Stephenson		
How to Golf (*sic*)	50 mins.	$29.95
Women's Golf (with Peggy Kirk Bell, DeDe Owens, and other female teachers)		
Full Swing	40 mins.	$29.95
Approach Game	40 mins.	$29.95
VIDEOS BY THOSE WHO TAUGHT THE BEST		
Jack Grout (who taught Nicklaus)		
Keys to Consistency (Long game)	59 mins.	$39.95
The Last 100 Yards (Short game)	45 mins.	$39.95
Phil Rodgers (Nicklaus' short-game guru)		
The Short Game	72 mins.	$39.95
Jimmy Ballard (who taught Curtis Strange, Sandy Lyle, and more)		
The Fundamental Golf Swing	69 mins.	$49.95
David Leadbetter (who taught Nick Faldo)		
The Full Golf Swing	90 mins.	$59.95

Where to Find . . . Videotapes of the Great Tournaments in Golf History

If you forgot to set your VCR to catch Jack Nicklaus winning the 1986 Masters, fear not: You can buy a video of the proceedings—without a doubt, the best golf tournament in recent history—and watch it to your heart's content. Ditto every U.S. Open Championship back to 1962—which omits, unfortunately, Arnold Palmer's win at Cherry Hills in 1960.

We have used two sources for tournament videotapes. The first is GolfSmart, the Californian mail-order house (listed as "GS"). Call (800) 637-3557 or, in California, (916) 272-1422.

The second is the United States Golf Association, in New Jersey (listed as "USGA"). Call (800) 336-4446. Members of the USGA Members program pay $14.95 for all but the 1990 Open films.

In each case, ask for Beta availability.

Tournament/Winner	Length	Price
1992 Masters/Fred Couples	60 mins.	$19.95 (GS)
1991 Masters/Ian Woosnam	60 mins.	$19.95 (GS)
1990 Masters/Nick Faldo	60 mins.	$19.95 (GS)
1989 Masters/Nick Faldo	52 mins.	$19.95 (GS)
1988 Masters/Sandy Lyle	60 mins.	$19.95 (GS)
1987 Masters/Larry Mize	60 mins.	$19.95 (GS)
1986 Masters/Jack Nicklaus	60 mins.	$19.95 (GS)

Tournament/Winner	Length	Price
1992 U.S. Open/Tom Kite	60 mins.	$29.50 (USGA)
1991 U.S. Open/Payne Stewart	60 mins.	$19.95 (USGA)
1990 U.S. Open/Hale Irwin	60 mins.	$19.95 (USGA)
1989 U.S. Open/Curtis Strange	55 mins.	$19.95 (USGA)
" " "	40 mins.	$29.95 (GS)
1988 U.S. Open/Curtis Strange	50 mins.	$19.95 (USGA)
" " "	30 mins.	$19.95 (GS)
1987 U.S. Open/Scott Simpson	59 mins.	$19.95 (USGA)
" " "	60 mins.	$29.95 (GS)
1986 U.S. Open/Raymond Floyd	28 mins.	$19.95 (USGA)
1985 U.S. Open/Andy North	30 mins.	$19.95 "
1984 U.S. Open/Fuzzy Zoeller	37 mins.	$19.95 "
1983 U.S. Open/Larry Nelson	36 mins.	$19.95 "
1982 U.S. Open/Tom Watson	36 mins.	$19.95 "
1981 U.S. Open/David Graham	36 mins.	$19.95 "
1980 U.S. Open/Jack Nicklaus	40 mins.	$19.95 "
1979 U.S. Open/Hale Irwin	30 mins.	$19.95 "
1978 U.S. Open/Andy North	26 mins.	$19.95 "
1977 U.S. Open/Hubert Green	36 mins.	$19.95 "
1976 U.S. Open/Jerry Pate	27 mins.	$19.95 "
1975 U.S. Open/Lou Graham	30 mins.	$19.95 "
1974 U.S. Open/Hale Irwin	32 mins.	$19.95 "
1973 U.S. Open/Johnny Miller	31 mins.	$19.95 "
1972 U.S. Open/Jack Nicklaus	30 mins.	$19.95 "
1971 U.S. Open/Lee Trevino	34 mins.	$19.95 "
1970 U.S. Open/Tony Jacklin	33 mins.	$19.95 "

Tournament/Winner	Length	Price
1969 U.S. Open/Orville Moody	37 mins.	$19.95 (USGA)
1968 U.S. Open/Lee Trevino	39 mins.	$19.95 "
1967 U.S. Open/Jack Nicklaus	39 mins.	$19.95 "
1966 U.S. Open/Billy Casper	40 mins.	$19.95 "
1965 U.S. Open/Gary Player	36 mins.	$19.95 "
1964 U.S. Open/Ken Venturi	32 mins.	$19.95 "
1963 U.S. Open/Julius Boros	39 mins.	$19.95 "
1962 U.S. Open/Jack Nicklaus	33 mins.	$19.95 "
1956 U.S. Open/Cary Middlecoff	17 mins.	$24.95 "
1991 U.S. Women's Open/ Meg Mallon	50 mins.	$19.95 (USGA)
1990 U.S. Women's Open/ Betsy King	53 mins.	$19.95 "
1989 U.S. Women's Open/ Betsy King	38 mins.	$19.95 "
1988 U.S. Women's Open/ Liselotte Neumann	50 mins.	$19.95 "
1991 U.S. Senior Open/ Jack Nicklaus	53 mins.	$19.95 (USGA)
1990 U.S. Senior Open/ Lee Trevino	53 mins.	$19.95 "
1983 British Open/Tom Watson	52 mins.	$79.95 (GS*)
1981 British Open/Bill Rogers	52 mins.	$79.95 "
1980 British Open/Tom Watson	52 mins.	$79.95 "

Anthologies

The History of Golf (four tapes)	Six hours, 40 mins.	$119.98
(MPI Home Video, 800-323-0442)		
Great Moments of The Masters	52 mins.	$49.95 (GS)
The U.S. Open History/Jim McKay	60 mins.	$29.98 (GS)
" "	55 mins.	$29.95 (USGA)

*GolfSmart's stock of British Open videotapes is limited and changes regularly. Call to check availability.

Games

Six Popular Golf Games That Don't Hold Up Play

1. LAS VEGAS

Should be played as a four-ball.

Split a four-ball into two teams of two. After each hole, put each team's scores, after subtracting handicap strokes, "together." A team that scores a four and a five on a hole, for example would register a "45." If the other team takes a five and six, it would register 56. Subtract the low number from the high number and award the difference as "points" to the low team. Keep a running tally.

A team's low score always comes first except when the other team scores a net birdie. Then the other team's *high* score comes first, and the point difference is even greater.

2. WOLF

Can be played as a three-ball or four-ball.

Each player takes a turn at being the "wolf" on a hole. After everyone has teed off, he chooses his partner for the remainder of the hole. If a wolf's team wins the hole, the players claim a point. Each hole is played as a low-ball game and has to be won outright by the wolf.

Variations on this game involve the wolf accepting or rejecting a partner after *each* tee shot is hit, or deciding to go it on his own. In the latter case, he wins double points if he wins the hole.

3. SNAKE

Can be played as a two-ball, three-ball or four-ball.

When a player three-putts, he is said to be "holding the snake." Should another player then three-putt, the snake is passed on. Whoever is holding the snake when the round is finished pays up.

4. HIGH-BALL

Should be played as a four-ball.

In a group of vastly differing handicaps, this keeps the worse players in the match. A point is awarded for low score on the hole. If the two low scores tie, the better of the two worse scores act as a tiebreaker.

For instance, let's say Team A shoots a 3 and a 5.

Team B shoots a 3 and a 6. Team A would win the hole by virtue of the 3s offsetting each other and the 5 beating the 6.

5. SKINS

Best played as a three-ball or four-ball, but can be played as a two-ball.

A "skin" is a set amount up for grabs at each hole. If one player wins the hole outright, he collects a skin from each of the other players in the group. If the hole is tied—not necessarily by every player in the group—the next hole is carried over so that it is worth two skins. The skins accumulate until a hole is won outright.

6. YARDAGE

Can be played as a two-ball, three-ball or four-ball.

Instead of a player or team winning a hole, he or they win the yardage of the hole. Most yardage at the end of the round wins. Yes, it helps to win the par fives.

Putting It All Together— a Golf Jigsaw

The Golf Day mail-order catalog stocks a 500-piece jigsaw puzzle depicting the par-three 15th hole at Cypress Point Golf Club on the Monterey Peninsula, California. When completed, it measures 18 by 24 inches. It costs $12.95. Call (800) 669-8600.

Just one thing. Isn't it the 16th that's the post-card hole at Cypress?

Short-Distance Golf

Do not confuse pitch-and-putt with short-distance golf; the former involves short swings on short holes with regular golf balls, and the latter involves full swings on short holes with balls that fly half the distance of regular balls. It also involves a Florida-based organization known as the American Modified Golf Association.

The AMGA was formed in 1985 by Bill Amick, a golf-course architect who was known in the 1960s for helping establish the real estate development/golf course combination and as a proponent of converting sanitary landfills into golf courses, an idea that never really flew. Some said it stunk.

Amick also built many executive courses made up of par threes and short par fours—"challenge courses," he called them—but all the while he remained fascinated with an idea that his original architectural mentor, William Diddell, had pioneered in the 1940s: a ball that flew shorter distances and would lead to golf courses requiring less land.

Amick found the perfect specimen in the mid 1980s when Troy Puckett, an engineer with the MacGregor equipment company, developed the "Golden Bear Cayman" ball.

The ball is the same size as a regular ball but is half a regular ball's weight and compression (50 as opposed to 90 or 100). It is plastic-coated and foam-filled and is controlled aerodynamically not by dimples but by methodically arranged pimples. The ball's flight distance and tendency to hook or slice are proportionally less than those of a real ball.

The half-distance ball originally was developed for a course Jack Nicklaus designed at the Britannia Resort on Grand Cayman, an island in the Caribbean. Nicklaus laid out a nine-hole course for regular balls and superimposed an 18-hole plan that could be played with Caymans.

Soon Amick brought the concept to the United States. After helping MacGregor improve the ball's aerodynamic stability and putting performance, he designed the Eagle Landing Golf Club in Hanahan, South Carolina, the first course built *solely* for short-distance play.

Today, there are around 30 courses that either encourage their patrons to use the Mactec ball (the new name for the Cayman) or have actually held "Modified Golf" tournaments.

Individual membership costs $25 a year. Corporate or club membership costs $125. The money gets you general information on where you can find modified golf courses and tournaments and a quarterly newsletter. If you become really proficient, you might even win a spot on the U.S. modified golf team that each year competes against a squad of Japanese modified golfers.

Contact the AMGA at Box 1984, Daytona Beach, FL 32115; (904) 767-1449.

Where to Find . . . the Arnold Palmer Golf Game

If Joe Veltri had his druthers, you'd find it in every toy store in Palmerdom (i.e., the world). Veltri, known as "Spanky" to his friends, is a former car-wash operator from suburban Pittsburgh who, through a remarkable chain of events, landed the rights to one of the most popular golf games in recent memory.

You may recall the game. It had a little plastic model of Arnold Palmer attached to a golf shaft. You pulled a trigger on the shaft and Arnie's shoulders swung back in a perfect three-piece takeaway, then swung through and whacked a tiny polystyrene ball down your hallway and into the kitchen. Better still, you could choose from an array of little woods and irons.

Well, the game disappeared a while back. Then, one day in 1988, one of Veltri's employees brought to work a version that had been uncovered in his grandfather's attic. Veltri got into the habit of playing around with it when business was slow—on rainy days usually—and could not for the life of him work out why the game wasn't available anymore. So he called Palmer's people to find out who made it, and what he found out instead was that no one knew where the original molds for the game were nor who owned the rights. Veltri then spent a year and $70,000 of his own money chasing around the world after the molds for the game (half the molds were in Britain, it turned out, and half were in Florida) and the rights. Finally Veltri sold the car wash and went into the Arnold Palmer business.

Today's model differs from the original in that the clothes are painted—the original was plain plastic—and Arnie's hair has been tinged with streaks of grey. There's also been talk of a little competition for Arnie (pun fully intended). Watch for a Lee Trevino or a Gary Player.

The retail cost is $64.95. If you can't find it in a toy store, call (800) 927-2563. Check that number. The sharper among you will recognize the "92" as Palmer's total victories worldwide, and the "7-2563" as the P- A - L- M - E in "Palmer." Spanky just ran out of numbers.

Arnold Palmer and friend.

A basic Lomma course for a basement set-up.

So How Small Do You Want It?

Here's the how-to and where-to for getting hold of:

- ▼ A basic miniature course
- ▼ A luxury miniature course
- ▼ Components-only for a mini-practice area
- ▼ A *micro* golf course.

THE BASICS

Lomma miniature golf courses crop up in the strangest places: on the decks of ships, on rooftops and in some of the most remote corners of the globe. There are three Lomma courses in Libya, for example, a couple in Iceland (indoor, of course) and Central America is swarming with the things.

Why? Two reasons. First, American companies and government agencies who have corporate colonies abroad think nothing of setting up a minigolf course to amuse their already golf-damaged employees. Second, and this is the key to Lomma's prolific success, the Lomma courses are basically no-frills, do-it-yourself affairs that cost relatively little.

A basic Lomma nine-hole course, with obstacles, putters, scorecards and pencils will set you back $5,900. The basic payment plan is half up front and the balance is paid in 12 monthly installments. But if you pay half up front and the balance in one lump sum, in *cash,* you'll get a 10 percent discount. Pay half up front and the balance in six monthly installments and you'll get 7½ percent off.

The top-of-the-line Lomma course is a 19-hole "Pro Am" course that will set you back $29,900 (minus any discount). Lomma introduced this one in 1991, and it's a slight departure from traditional miniature courses in that it is devoid of traditional obstacles, such as windmills, clowns, loop-the-loops and wishing wells. These have been replaced by holes with hazards and different cuts of rough, i.e., different textures and thicknesses of artificial turf. (If you do want the traditional obstacle course, it comes with the same components as below, with obstacles replacing the hazards, and costs $19,900). The full Pro-Am course package includes:

- ▼ 20 greens (17 regular greens, a triangular green

and a pair of "his" and "her" greens, the idea being that "he" hits to one green on a Y-shaped hole, and "she" hits to the other.)

- ▼ A last-shot box that stores the balls
- ▼ 19 fairways, each three feet wide
- ▼ 19 tee pads
- ▼ 27 hazards, including sandtraps, water hazards, mounds, ramps, etc.
- ▼ 19 flags
- ▼ 19 scoretables
- ▼ 19 flower boxes, for decorating around the holes
- ▼ 120 putters, right- and left-handed
- ▼ 144 balls
- ▼ 4,320 pencils
- ▼ 5,000 scorecards
- ▼ 5 plastic signs
- ▼ One club rack
- ▼ An owner's manual.

Whatever the course ordered, it will normally arrive in large packing crates, along with a Lomma rep. He will go over the construction instructions with you and the four local laborers that Lomma recommends you hire, and then leave you to it. If you intend to make a business of minigolf, the Lomma rep will also give you details on the two-day public relations and promotions seminars the company throws at its Scranton headquarters, free of charge.

For full information, contact Lomma Enterprises, 1120 South Washington Ave., Scranton, PA 18505; (717) 346-5559.

A LUXURY COURSE

You've probably seen these things towering above the roadsides in America's favorite vacation spots: Myrtle Beach, the New Jersey shore, all along the east coast of Florida. You can recognize them by waterfalls, palm trees, holes that slope like ski runs and festoons of large fiberglass jungle fauna—which is why so many of them are known as Junglegolf, Jungle Caverns, Jungle Lagoons, and so on.

Most are the work of Golf Projects of America or, to be specific, of James "Poddy" Bryan. He's been in this business since the 1950s, designing and providing building specifications for the most part, but also building more than 30 miniature golf courses himself. Bryan is now spreading into related fields, such as driving range/minigolf complexes and minigolf courses that adhere to the more subtle aesthetic principles of full-scale golf-course architecture as opposed to the bombastic style of his jungle golf creations. To wit, he makes more use of ridges and contours, has designed several cuts of artificial turf to emulate different cuts of rough (definitely a trend for all operators) and cuts three different cups so that each hole can be played differently—just like the real thing.

Bryan's courses don't go for a song, and they take up to four months to build, but they do attract crowds. He has been known to take on jobs that cost as little as $100,000 to construct, but generally the total coast of building a luxury course is in the $300,000 range.

A JungleGolf miniature course from James Bryan.

▼ A five-foot high gorilla, in brown or black—$1,068
▼ An electric Ferris wheel—$904
▼ A five-foot high, six-foot long whale that can spout water—$1,042
▼ An eight-foot high, blinking lighthouse—$743
▼ An 11-foot high, 12-foot long elephant—$4,270. This is Wittek's most expensive obstacle.

For further information and a fairly goofy catalog, contact Wittek Golf Supply, 3650 N. Avondale Ave., Chicago, IL 60618; (312) 463-2636.

If Bryan handles the design and building specifications only, he charges 12½ percent of the estimated cost of the whole project, or $37,500 for a $300,000 project, plus expenses. If he builds it, too, he charges an additional 10 percent of the total cost—taking the fee to $67,500—plus salaries, expenses and housing for his construction supervisors (two, usually). If that sounds high, consider that Bryan claims many of his projects have paid for themselves in the first year. In fact, he refuses to get involved in projects that he doesn't feel will be in the black within five years.

For full information, contact Golf Projects of America, 2826 N. Kensington St., Arlington, VA 22207; (703) 533-7939.

COMPONENTS ONLY

Wittek Golf Supply does sell plans for an entire miniature golf course, but is one of the few sources that will actually sell a course component-by-component.

Wittek sells two types of putting felt, in green, blue or red, and two types of artificial turf, in two shades of green. It also sells more than 50 minigolf obstacles, such as windmills, wishing wells, various animals and cartoon characters.

The felt costs from $4.95 to $8.50 per square yard, while the turf comes in at $5.95 to $7.50 per square yard.

The obstacles cost considerably more. The low end, a wooden arch with a wooden log swinging from it, costs only $168, but once you get into the wacky world of giant fiberglass mice, you're talking high three and sometimes four figures. Here are some examples:

A MICRO COURSE

This was the brainchild of Ryan McCullough, a high school student from Fargo, North Dakota. He first built a prototype of a table-top golf game then did what Madison Avenue types call putting a product "in test." He showed it to his buddies at a local park. They liked it. Ryan and his dad, Ronald, went into production.

The game measures four feet by eight feet (it is mounted on a collapsing table) and has nine holes—each a par two—snaking up and down ramps. The game comes with 15 little mallets and 36 marbles, as well as 500 scorecards, 144 pencils, 50 "free-game" cards and a banner. The McCulloughs calculate that, as a business, you can pull in around $200 if you set up in a mall on a busy Saturday and rent the equipment out for 50 cents a round.

The entire package costs $695, plus shipping and handling.

Contact: Micro Golf, 417 Main Ave., Fargo, ND 58103; (701) 237-0986.

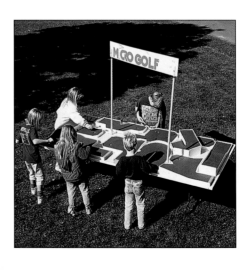

A 4′ × 8′ micro course.

Golf with a Piece of Plastic

You think it's tough hitting a golf ball accurately? Try playing 18 holes with a Frisbee.

That's what "disc golfers" do. They progress around 18 "holes," throwing various forms of flying discs into baskets fixed halfway up 18 poles—known as "pole holes." All the baskets have chains hanging in the middle to act like a basketball backboard.

If this sounds a little weird, consider first that thousands of disc golfers who fling plastic around the more than 300 disc courses in the U.S., Canada, Europe, Japan and Australia find their actions perfectly normal. Some find them lucrative, too. There are almost 200 tournaments held around the world every year, with a total entry of some 10,000 golfers, and almost $250,000 handed out in prize money. The best disc golfers can take home almost $10,000 a year.

The top players have elevated technique in the game far above the idea of letting rip with a Frisbee. Although the sport probably was first played with Frisbees only—it was invented in 1957, soon after the California-based Wham-O Manufacturing Company came out with the Frisbee—today's top players opt for discs of different sizes and shapes for different shots. Although changing discs for drives or "putts" or curves is standard, some players will actually roll a disc as much as 400 feet to avoid trees.

Trees are just one obstacle that face disc golfers. Although there are no sandtraps and holes measure roughly one-third the length of normal golf holes, the disc golfers do have to consider wind (much more so than a ball golfer), terrain and other weather conditions. If an amateur can get around an 18-hole course in 72 or fewer "shots," he can consider himself an expert.

Most of the equipment in this country is sold through Headrick's Disc Golf (Ed Headrick, former CEO of Wham-O, is credited with being disc golf's James Naismith), but formal play is governed by the Professional Disc Golf Association (which, despite its name, is open to anyone). The PDGA issues rule books, sanctions tournaments, tracks statistics, publishes a bimonthly newsletter and establishes the field, based on points won at other events, for the annual PDGA World Disc Golf Championship. That particular event is split into divisions for pros, women, masters (ages 35–44), grandmasters (45 to 54) and senior grandmasters (55 and over). A separate national championship is held for amateurs.

To obtain a book of disc golf listings or to find out more about disc golf, contact the PDGA at Box 240363, Memphis, TN 38124; (901) 323-4849.

Disc golf is not without its waits at the tee.

"Putting" out.

Goofy Golf

Miniature golf mania had to be one of the craziest crazes of the Roaring Twenties. There were private courses for sophisticated flappers and a chain of wildly successful "Tom Thumb" courses.

Today, miniature golf holds a special, if less manic, niche in pop culture. Classy and challenging courses are everywhere, less frivolous and not as nutty while retaining the charm of the game.

It's only natural that software companies would try to recreate a game in which an elephant can devour your ball and you will never need a caddy.

MINI-PUTT

Accolade
550 S. Winchester Blvd.
San Jose, CA 95128
(408) 985-1700

Formats: IBM/Tandy 1000, Apple IIGS, Amiga, Atari ST
Price: $29.99–$39.99

Mini-Putt offers everything the demanding minigolfer could possibly want. Players sign in, then select from four different courses that are of varying degrees of difficulty. The holes feature all the traditional wacky hazards, such as ramps, tunnels and windmills that we have come to know and love, as well as some surprises. A cannon shoots your ball toward the hole, for example; a fantasy castle sports a tricky drawbridge.

The minigreens are marked with arrows indicating rolls and swales, and there is a handy map thrown in so you can see where you have to go—the hole is not always in sight.

ZANY GOLF

Electronic Arts
1820 Gateway Dr.
San Mateo, CA 94404
(415) 571-7171

Formats: IBM, Tandy, and compatibles
Price: $40

Zany Golf is even stranger—and more challenging—than *Mini-Putt*. The graphics are superb and each hole is wackier than the next. Case in point: One hole has a hamburger guarding the cup. You have to get the buns jumping to reveal the hole, while a ketchup bottle squirts at the green.

In *Zany Golf*, you move a cursor to where you'd like to place the clubhead. This sets the direction and strength of your swing. Then you fire away.

Players begin with five strokes. You have these strokes, plus whatever is par for the hole, to play. Run out of strokes and you have to return to the start. Or look at it this way: You have to restart when you reach five over par.

That can be exasperating, but the ninth hole, Frankenstein's Private Club, is more than enough to keep you coming back until you can save your five strokes.

I'd recommend you have more than one player compete. That way you can stay in the game just a tad longer.

The Best Computer Golf Games

by Matthew J. Costello and Mark Danna

• • •

Golf *should* be an easy game to simulate.

It doesn't have beefy players huffing and puffing around the screen, as you'll find in computerized football or hockey. There's no computerized baseball caroming off a computerized back wall at 90-plus computerized miles per hour as a computerized center fielder scrambles to hit his computerized cut-off man.

No, golf's physical elements are more "focused." There's a person, usually a man, holding a club. A fairway and a green beckon, and on the ground in front of him is a ball. All he has to do is hit it. Given the sophistication of software today, that should translate easily.

And would, if it weren't for all golf's variables.

Terrain, for instance. How can a computer ever capture all the different landscapes golf courses can offer? Or a gusting wind that can whip a golf ball out of bounds? How can a computer simulate the scene as a darkened sky replaces a bright sun and turns everything a greenish gray? For that matter, how would a computer handle a caddie who chews gum?

Golf, as game designers quickly found out, is simple in its basic concept but beyond that a game of nuance and strategy, where one lie can be perfect and the next can be perfectly horrible.

But the best computer golf games on the market

Jack at play with his *Course Design* program.

are those that try to capture the feel, the challenge and all—or as many as possible—of the elements of real golf. Here are the best of them. As these companies are constantly updating and improving their lines, you may want to call ahead for a catalog. The numbers are listed.

the serious simulations

JACK NICKLAUS UNLIMITED GOLF & COURSE DESIGN

Accolade
550 South Winchester Blvd.
Suite 200
San Jose, CA 95128
(408) 985-1700
(800) 245-7744

Formats: IBM PC, Amiga
Price: $59.95

The product has three parts: The Bear's Track, a fictional, oceanfront, 18-hole course; a recreation of Muirfield Village, the site of The Memorial Tournament in Columbus, Ohio, and probably Nicklaus's best design; and the pièce de résistance, an architectural program that will knock your designer socks off.

As with other Accolade golf games, the graphics are superb. So, too, are the sounds of golf balls flying and landing on different surfaces. Course conditions can be set for dry, normal or wet; greens can be made slow or fast and wind direction and speed can be set to whatever you wish. And with such graphic enhancements as flying divots and spraying sand from bunker explosions, as computer games go, this may be as real as it gets.

Accolade has also improved, by about 50 percent, the speed at which screens are redrawn. There are instant and reverse-angle replays, a best-score list and even a hole-in-one club.

What sets this game apart from the field, however, is the *Course Design* program. Choosing from different types of land, you can either build your own champi-

Superb graphics along with the basic menu of *Unlimited Golf*.	A tree, one of the many choices of vegetation in *Course Design*.

onship course or recreate famous holes. From an inventory of backgrounds and objects, such as trees, shrubs, hazards and buildings, or by using a sophisticated painting program, you can design any kind of golf hole your heart desires. Creating lakes, hills and valleys, uphill and downhill lies and "climatizing" the backgrounds in desert hues, spring greens or fall colors is easily done with simple on-screen prompts, keystrokes and on-screen advice from the Golden Bear himself.

MEAN 18

Accolade
550 South Winchester Blvd.
Suite 200
San Jose, CA 95128
(408) 985-1700
(800) 245-7744

Formats: Macintosh, Apple II GS, IBM PC, Amiga
Price: $19.95–$44.95

Mean 18 is a classic. Voted "Best Simulation" by the Software Publishers Association, the main disk offers four courses: Augusta National, the Old Course at St. Andrews, Pebble Beach and the fictional "Bush Hill." All have excellent graphics and realistic sound effects.

Preround options include Stroke Play (up to four players), Match Play (two players), and Best Ball (four players); pro or regular tees, and expert or beginner levels (beginners get perfect aim and club recommendations).

Before each hole, the screen shows an overhead with par and yardage information. The next screen has three windows. A large, main window shows a view from the tee (actually from several feet behind the golfer). A smaller window allows club selection, aim (moving the main window right or left a number of increments), an instant aerial cam replay of your shots to the green (but not your putts) and access to a score sheet. Finally, a vertical window to the left of the main screen displays your Power Meter.

One strong feature of the *Mean 18* Power Meter is that its Swing Zone is divided into 10 segments— more than most games—and each one represents 10 percent of your club's maximum distance. This allows you to be extremely precise in your calibrations.

The upper section of the Power Meter is used for overswinging. Allowing the power bar to rise all the way to the top automatically gives you maximum power and lets you skip the second click, but it also exaggerates hooks and slices caused by improper clicking in the bottom section of the meter.

When putting, you get an overhead of the green, scaled in size to how close your ball is to the pin. A handy movable long black line extending from your ball to the hole helps immensely in lining up putts.

Mean 18 also has an architectural feature you can use to redesign any of the courses. The drawbacks, however, are that all saved changes are permanent and you cannot change the position of the cups. No Sunday pin placements, in other words.

The only glaring fault in *Mean 18* is the slow speed at which the screens are redrawn, up to 10 sec-

Teeing off at Augusta National in *Mean 18*.

For variety, Famous Courses add-on discs are available for the IBM PC and the Apple II GS. For the IBM and compatibles, Volume 2, priced at $12.95, features Inverness, Turnberry and Harbour Town; Volumes 5 and 6, combined on one disk for $24.95, has Butler National, Bay Hill, Concord (hotel), Medinah, Riviera and Spyglass Hill. For the Apple II GS, Volumes 3 and 4, on one disk for $34.95, offers The Olympic Club (Lakeside), Las Colinas, Muirfield (Scotland), Doral, Castle Pines and Kapalua.

PGA TOUR GOLF

Electronic Arts
1820 Gateway Dr.
San Mateo, CA 94404
(415) 571-7171

**Formats: IBM, Tandy, and compatibles, Sega Genesis
Price: $49.95**

Electronic Arts staked a claim to the booming sports game market with highly successful games for football (*John Madden Football*), baseball (*Earl Weaver Baseball*) and other sports. These computer games offered fast-paced action with a statistical depth that would make any sports fan happy.

PGA Tour will make an electronic "hacker" happy, too. You have a choice of several games, while you can also select the size of your group, the tees you want to play from and which of four Tournament Players Clubs (including the TPC at Sawgrass) you want to play. There's even a driving range should you

onds a screen, which I suppose is computerized golf's version of slow play. Some quibbles include an absence of wind as a factor, no options for backspin or high or low shots; easily read greens with generous portions of flat, straight terrain (would that we could find some of those in real life!); an instant replay which shows only a long, black line of flight, and a scorecard that records eagles and double eagles, should you be skilled enough to score any, as birdies.

But *Mean 18*'s strengths far outweigh its weaknesses. This game is highly recommended. The sights and sounds are terrific, the above mentioned Power Meter is well-designed, and the unseen-but-discriminating gallery applauds and howls enthusiastically after any truly superb approach shots and spectacular putts.

The National Championship

If you really get hooked on *Mean 18* you can parade your talents against players of similar caliber around the country in weekly tournaments. You'll need an IBM PC or compatible, a modem, and a subscription to the Computer Sports Network, which allows you to access CSN's main computer in Houston, Texas.

Four-round tournaments on 54 different courses are held throughout the year, 30 of them at the same time as the corresponding event on the PGA Tour. Players' scores and statistics are downloaded into CSN's data base at the end of each round, and weekly winners of each of four flights win trophies. Every player accumulates points which, at the end of the year, can be exchanged for discounts on actual golf clubs, balls and accessories.

The tournament golf software costs $39.95, but the cost per tournament can run as low as $3–$5 per round if you refrain from accessing CSN in prime time. Actual play is done off-line, so you are billed only for each start-up and finish. The final cost involves buying additional courses. A three-course disk costs $9.95.

For further information, contact Computer Sports Network, 2900 Wilcrest, Suite 400, Houston, TX 77042; (800) 727-4636.

The opening screen for *PGA Tour Golf*—you can practically smell the potato salad in the sun. Yecch!

wish to warm up. You will also have to select the 14 clubs you want to play with during the round.

When you're set to tee off you are treated to a dramatic overview of the course. There's a terrific fly-by view of the first hole, as though a helicopter was giving you a personal preview. The graphics of trees, grass and sand are superb.

Then a pro, such as Paul Azinger or Joey Sindelar, appears on the screen and offers a little strategic advice. Azinger's advice, for example, on the tee shot to the island green, par-three 17th at the TPC at Sawgrass: "Wind on this hole always makes club selection difficult. Go for the center of the island no matter where the pin is."

An info box tells you what hole you're on, the number of strokes you've taken, the distance to the pin and your status thus far in the round.

Actual play is easy and maintains all the options you'd get with the real thing. You aim a crosshair in the

direction you want to hit the ball and execute the swing with the usual three clicks on the keyboard, mouse or joystick. The first click starts the backswing, the second starts the downswing and the third determines the point of impact. If you want to hook the ball, you impact early. Slice it? Impact late (but bear in mind that you may put too severe a curve on the ball and end up in trouble).

You'll use the Power Bar to vary the power of the swing. The screen shows you your *potential* yardage based on the club chosen, wind and other factors. It's for you to figure out how far you want the ball to go and then start your downswing when the power bar has reached the right percentage.

Putting is handled similarly, and you can adjust the distance potential of the putter yourself from a range of five to 120 feet.

That's basically the game, but it is the extras that make this a very detailed simulation. There are nine different lies, and you can see a close-up of just what your ball is sitting in. There are also different types of strokes, such as a punch shot or a putt from the fringe.

GREG NORMAN'S SHARK ATTACK

Virgin Games, Inc.
18061 Fitch Ave.
Irvine, CA 92714
(714) 833-8710
(800) 874-4607

**Formats: IBM/Tandy 1000, Amiga, Atari ST,
Commodore 64
Price: $14.99–$19.99**

The Great White Shark's computer game is labelled as "The Ultimate Golf Simulator." That might be a bit optimistic, but *Shark Attack*—a product of eight man-

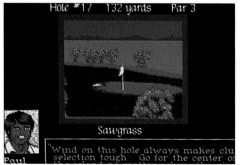

Advice from the Zinger.

Playing a chip shot.

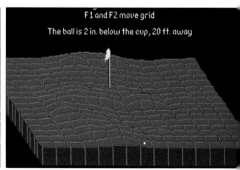

The putting green, *PGA Tour Golf*.

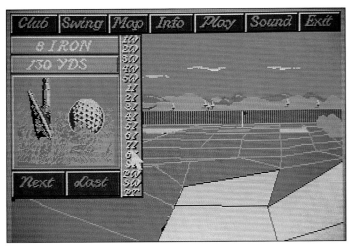

An approach from the rough in Greg Norman's *Shark Attack*.

years of design and development—is very good indeed.

The simulator has many innovations. It dares to break from the normal three-click method of computer golfing. As in most games, there is a "power bar." This one's vertical. You start the swing and let the mercurylike gauge rise as high as you want. When you have amassed enough power for the desired yardage, you hit the button to initiate the downswing, and a needle at the bottom of the gauge starts wavering. The idea is to let the mercury fall and hit the button when it's right on the needle.

Both match play and stroke play are offered and should you so wish you can eliminate some of the options, such as wind or weather or the caddy and his automatic choice of club.

If there's one real weakness in *Shark Attack*, however, it's that putting is not as challenging as it should be. Greens are presented with contour lines, lacking somewhat in realism but supplying the information you need. A directional cursor appears on the screen and you use the power bar to determine how hard you hit the ball.

Shark Attack comes with 10 players in the database and has room for 50 of your own creation. Such attributes as experience, swing, grip and fitness can be adjusted for computer players, while you can allot handicaps to your human players.

arcade golf

The Nintendo system showed that a defunct idea—video games—could be miraculously brought back to life. Nintendo is now the most popular Christmas gift; its annual sales exceed $3 billion. In fact, even though Nintendo is now challenged by newer game systems, it is almost as ubiquitous as the VCR. The Nintendo Entertainment System offers a number of entertaining golf games.

NINTENDO GAME BOY GOLF

Nintendo of America, Inc.
Box 957
Redmond, WA 98052
(206) 882-2040
(800) 633-3236

Format: Game Boy
Price: $89.95 for Game Boy, $19.95 for Golf

Portability is the prime asset of the Nintendo Game Boy, a hand-held video system incorporating an eight-bit microprocessor, a three-inch, high-resolution, black and white LCD screen, and push-button controls. Golf is just one of the many interchangeable cartridges available for the Game Boy, which comes with stereo headphones (so as not to disturb others) and a Video Link cable to link two Game Boys for a little competition.

Although the graphics, sound and music are cartoonish, it's hard not to be charmed by this tiny universe where play begins with your caddy urging you to "Fight!" as a football fight song plays and where your player jumps up and down, with full musical accompaniment, whenever he scores a birdie.

The main screen has a large window—relatively speaking—which shows the tee, the first part of the hole and a flashing cursor with which you'll aim. A smaller window below includes the hole number, par, yardage, current score, wind direction and strength, a graphic with the lie of the ball and the selected club. A small but nice touch is the way that flags wave in the direction of the wind.

On the plus side, Game Boy is very portable, its screens are redrawn instantly and you can save a game and pick up where you left off. Rain delay, perhaps.

On the down side, the accompanying yardage chart is not to be trusted—in some instances, this writer found himself having to take two to four more clubs—the horizontal swing gauge is not sectioned off, making exact power selections difficult, and some of the holes are very contrived, such as the one whose green is divided in two by rough!

NINTENDO GOLF

Nintendo of America, Inc.
Box 957
Redmond, WA 98073
(206) 882-2040
(800) 633-3236

Formats: Nintendo Entertainment System
Price: $39.95

The first Nintendo golf game remains one of the best. You select either Mario or Luigi—both of whom are taking a breather from the more strenuous demands of *Super Mario Brothers*—to play for you.

You get an overhead view of the hole as well as the perspective from the tee or Mario's or Luigi's current lie. A small arrow tells you wind direction and speed. The game uses the three-click system for ball-striking, and you use the "select" button to pick your clubs. The screen tells you what par is and keeps track of your score.

Nintendo Golf plays easily and, despite its cartoony quality, it has a nice *feel*. When your player turns, you get a changing view of what's directly ahead. And there are some mighty difficult holes on the course and some fantastic water hazards. But you

Choosing a wedge, *Arnold Palmer Golf*.

can use a hook or slice to curve your ball around trouble. Hitting a ball off the screen, however, will cost you a stroke.

Once on the green, crosshairs appear. You line them up between your putter and the cup, taking into consideration the arrows on the green that indicate hills and rolls. A satisfying "plunk" sound greets a successful putt.

JACK NICKLAUS'S GREATEST

Konami Inc.
815 Mittel Dr.
Wood Dale, IL 60191
(312) 595-1443

Formats: Nintendo Entertainment System
Price: $30–$40

This is a fast-playing version of the computer game. You can play some of Nicklaus's favorite holes, with selections from Pebble Beach, St. Andrews, Castle Pines or others. You can play solo or play against either programmed players or real-life opponents.

The game comes with a driving range option, as well as a practice green and a wind gauge that can be helpful.

ARNOLD PALMER TOURNAMENT GOLF

Sega Genesis Video Entertainment System
Sega of America
3375 Arden Rd.
Hayward, CA 94545
(415) 591-7529
(800) 872-7342

Formats: Sega Genesis
Price: $190 for system, $50–$60 for golf game

What sets this golf game apart from the others is its club selection option, which allow you not only to pick the 14 clubs in your bag, but even the material your clubs are made of. In the "Practice" mode, you can choose from Black Carbon, Glass Fiber (fiberglass) or Super Ceramic, which can drive, without any wind, 230, 245 and 265 yards respectively. In "Tournament Play," you begin with the basic Black Carbon and have to earn the longer-hitting sets by returning good scores.

Also unique are the 12 levels of expertise which

can be set to your specification in the Practice mode and which you step up with experience in Tournament Play. A higher level means more power, skill and better caddie advice, but the degree of difficulty also increases.

Format options include Tournament Play, 12 rounds against 15 computer players (you don't have to play the whole dozen at once); a practice round of stroke play, either alone or with another player who may share your controller or use his own; match play against the computer; or simple practice, with no actual competition.

Play takes place on one of three, 18-hole, par-72 courses. The U.S. course runs 6,919 yards, borders a lake and is very difficult. The Japanese course, at 6,690 yards, has many water hazards, bunkers and out of bounds. The British course, at 6,950 yards, is rustic and is dotted with bunkers and bushes just off the fairways.

Before you swing, a "Player Information Window" yields wind, lie, choice of club and stance. Power is determined by three clicks (if you miss the second power click, you can replay the shot), while you aim your shot by moving to the right or left a yellow triangle appearing above the flagstick.

In addition to the unique aspects mentioned above, the great strength of this game lies in the graphics. When you land behind a tree, it looms up in front of you. Other great visuals include the wind, which is displayed by a weather vane on which a cock's head notes direction and a revolving cap indicates speed.

Cute touches include a television-style announcer, who doles out tournament updates and standings; a

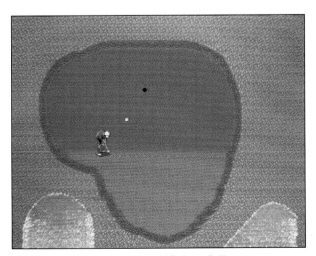

Putting in *Arnold Palmer Golf*.

female caddie; and comments that appear on the screen, such as "Oh no, that was too short!" or "What did you aim at?"

POWER GOLF

NEC Technologies Inc.
1255 Michael Dr.
Wood Dale, IL 60191
(708) 860-9500

Formats: TurboGrafx-16 video system
Price: $159 for system, $59 for golf game

TurboGrafx-16 is NEC's 16-bit game machine, which looks like a CD player and whose little game "cards" are the size and shape of credit cards but a bit thicker.

You can choose one of three modes: Stroke Play, Match Play or Competition. The last is recommended by the accompanying manual for up to three players and comes with a long-drive and closest-to-the-hole contest. Unique to *Power Golf* is the option to sit back and watch the computer play—an exercise in course management.

There are three players to choose from: A young PGA touring pro, a female golfer and a senior pro. But don't be fooled into thinking the young Tour stud is the hotshot here. He's only a standard player with good shot direction, and who can drive the ball about 211 yards. It's the senior who has pro quality swing and almost-pro drives, about 220 yards. However, since his swing is faster, timing is trickier and takes longer to master. The LPGA pro has a sound, unhurried swing and hits up to 181 yards—a good player for beginners.

Power Golf has a controller with buttons and a directional pad, and the usual three-click system for swinging. Unlike most other games, however, a fourth click, when properly executed, can vary backspin and trajectory (Nintendo Game Boy has a similar capability).

Unfortunately, *Power Golf* has several serious weaknesses. Some of the holes are just too contrived. Counting tee, green and fairways, one hole was composed of five islands. There is only one course to play, and it's fictional. The undelineated power gauge demands a lot of guesswork. You can't save a game and, most ominous of all, the accompanying manual doesn't know the difference between a slice and a hook.

Three Golf Board Games

In Pursuit of Par, TPC at Sawgrass Edition

Pursuit of Par Inc.
516 Commerce Dr.
Panama City Beach, FL 32408
(800) 421-8180

Price: $35

This is the most realistic of the board games available, and the one we recommend if you want to buy just one of its kind.

Based on Pete Dye's TPC Stadium course in Ponte Vedra, Florida, the site of The Players Championship, Pursuit of Par comprises four double-sided boards sporting colorful graphics that have been drawn up from aerial photographs of the course.

There is a choice of four tees: red, white, blue and the championship tips. Clubs are chosen from men's and women's distance charts. Two dice determine distance and direction, and a third affects recovery shots from rough, traps and trees. Two wedge-shaped distance/direction gauges help align shots. Balls are marked on the board with special pencils and are easily wiped off with a damp cloth after each hole is played.

Nice touches include small photographs and brief descriptions of each hole and handsome scorecards bearing the TPC logo.

On the downside, this board game, like many others, will not give you the thrill of competition that a computer game can provide; it's based much more on chance than on skill. On the other hand, it's portable and a heckuva lot cheaper than a computer.

Ultimate Golf

Ultimate Gifts, Inc.
Box 2023
Danvers, MA 01923

Price: $44

Rendered on two sides of the board are 18 of the greatest golf holes in the world, from Pebble Beach, St. Andrews, Cypress Point and more. One to four players select from a full set of clubs: 14 cards, each with yardage and accuracy results based on rolling two dice. Shots go straight or to either side at one of four angles and are measured by a type of slide-rule gauge. Special cards should be consulted when a ball lands in the rough, in a bunker or on a green.

As with Pursuit of Par, Ultimate Golf, when compared with computer games, has plusses and minuses. The biggest drawback in this game is the time that has to be devoted to manual labor: shuffling through cards, lining up scales and precisely placing markers.

Pro Golf

The Avalon Hill Game Company
4517 Harford Rd.
Baltimore, MD 21214
(800) 638-9292

Price: $12

The Avalon Hill Game Company excels at creating demanding simulation games. Their award-winning war games run the gamut from Waterloo to Vietnam, but they also have a line of challenging sports games. Pro Golf is a quickly understood and entertaining game that lets you use today's players to recreate the battle for all the marbles at the U.S. Open.

Although we categorize Pro Golf as a board game, there is no board. There is instead a book describing each hole at Pebble Beach, a pad of scorecards and a roster of 36 player cards. Each player card is a minichart packed with the possible results each swing might bring.

A player chooses a swing from those listed on the chart. He then rolls two dice, matching the two numbers, lowest first (so a 2 and a 6 would be a roll of "26"). This number is then matched to the column for the chosen swing. If the player has chosen a drive, a 26 may mean a long shot to the left, a short slice, or any of many more possibilities.

Putts are made by rolling a number larger than the distance to the pin, which may raise a few eyebrows among those who have faced an easy putt but have sent it screaming past the hole.

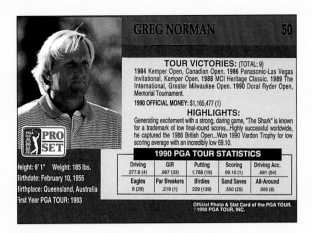

GREG NORMAN   50

TOUR VICTORIES: (TOTAL: 9)
1984 Kemper Open, Canadian Open. 1986 Panasonic-Las Vegas Invitational, Kemper Open. 1988 MCI Heritage Classic. 1989 The International, Greater Milwaukee Open. 1990 Doral Ryder Open, Memorial Tournament.
1990 OFFICIAL MONEY: $1,165,477 (1)
HIGHLIGHTS:
Generating excitement with a strong, daring game, "The Shark" is known for a trademark of low final-round scores...Highly successful worldwide, he captured the 1986 British Open...Won 1990 Vardon Trophy for low scoring average with an incredibly low 69.10.

1990 PGA TOUR STATISTICS

Driving	GIR	Putting	Scoring	Driving Acc.
277.6 (4)	.667 (33)	1.768 (19)	69.10 (1)	.681 (54)
Eagles	**Par Breakers**	**Birdies**	**Sand Saves**	**All-Around**
8 (29)	.219 (1)	229 (139)	.550 (25)	305 (6)

Official Photo & Stat Card of the PGA TOUR.
©1990 PGA TOUR, INC.

Height: 6'1" Weight: 185 lbs.
Birthdate: February 10, 1955
Birthplace: Queensland, Australia
First Year PGA TOUR: 1983

For Card Collectors

Given the world's addiction to card collecting, it was inevitable that golf cards would hit the market—even if they were issued as something of a reincarnation. The PGA Tour issued player cards more than a decade ago, but when the idea failed to catch on, the cards became giveaways at junior golf clinics.

Then baseball card mania began for real a few years back and the PGA Tour figured it simply had been ahead of its time. So, late in 1990, Pro Set, one of the major players in the card business, issued "official" PGA Tour golf cards. The inaugural set contained 75 PGA Tour players and 25 Senior players. That was followed in 1991 by a run of 285 cards, 75 Senior and the rest PGA Tour. *That* was followed in 1992 by Pro Set filing for Chapter XI bankruptcy!

Another set appeared briefly in 1990, from England, of all places. But this set never made it to the stores, partly because the cards were a bit, well, amateurish. Whoever made them obviously didn't know his subject or he would have known that "Jerry Lanston Wadkins," as one card read, is known as "Lanny" or that "Thomas Sturges Watson" has been known to answer to "Tom." Can you imagine a baseball card labelled "Albert W. Lyle"?

The most intriguing cards of all also come from England, and they, too, are reincarnations. They originally appeared in the 1930s, as cigarette cards in Imperial Tobacco brands. Now Imperial Publishing has rereleased them.

The "Famous Golfers" set includes 25 caricatures of such ancient greats as Harry Vardon and James Braid; the "Prominent Golfers" set includes 12 famous players, such as Bobby Jones and Glenna Collett Vare and the "Golf" set comprises 25 instructional tips from names that probably only those with an interest in golf history will recognize: Dai Rees (demonstrating the stymie!), George Duncan and Percy Alliss (father of Peter, now behind the mike for ABC-TV), to name three.

Contact Imperial at 011-44-81-518-7722.

OFFICIAL PGA TOUR CARD

IAN BAKER-FINCH

**Golf cards, from the
PGA Tour Pro Set.
Non-Aussies available, too.**

Our Writers and Photographers

Jim Finegan has visited just about every corner of this golfing earth with the strangest golf swing alive: left shoulder poking at the heavens, right elbow jutting out behind him, clubhead waggling back and forth like a surveyor's plumb line, all leading up to a WHACK!!! with a huge loop. You'd never guess that this wisp of a man is a three-time champion at the Philadelphia Country Club and once went 81 holes at Pine Valley—by consensus the toughest layout in the world—without scoring higher than bogey! Few golfers have such a passion for the game, and never does Jim's golfing heart beat faster than when he's chasing a ball through classic British duneland in a slight gale. Which is why we're glad he's written "A Love Affair with Links Golf."

Stephen Goodwin's qualifications to write on the works of P. G. Wodehouse? First, he once headed the literature program at the National Endowment for the Arts (and now lectures at George Mason University). Second, he's written a few books himself, among them *The Greatest Masters* (an account of Jack Nicklaus's victory in 1986). Third, he's a contributing editor of *Golf Magazine*. But most important, he has a short game that may actually be funnier than those of some of Wodehouse's bungling characters. Stephen is the only golfer I know who can screw up a simple chip by getting his pitching wedge caught in the leg of his pants.

I had the pleasure of editing **Tom Boswell**'s columns for *Golf Magazine* for several years, during which time we came to realize that we had the same view of golf: It is an impossible game which becomes unbearable if not approached with equal measures of love, commitment and ridicule. That's why he's the perfect person to tell you why you don't want to play the PGA Tour.

John Goldstein, who kept a diary for us during The Players Championship, formerly was an associate pro-

ducer with NBC-TV's golf telecasts and is on a first-name basis with about every player on all the major pro tours.

Roger Graves, who writes on running a golf discount store and how to become a PGA of America professional, among other things, wrote for us from firsthand experience, which is to say he nearly became a pro, still owns a piece of the store, covers golf for *The Salt Lake Tribune* and still manages to fit in several rounds of golf per week. I'm a little worried about Roger.

Mike Royko may be the funniest columnist in America. Although he now toils for the *Chicago Sun-Times,* we've reprinted one of his pieces from the *Chicago Tribune* from 1979. The column, which forges a link between golf equipment and bovine genitalia, was brought to my attention by Ron Riemer, the Chicago-based guru of golf-equipment advertising at *Golf Magazine.* All kidding aside, some say Riemer is funnier than Royko. . . .

I asked *Golf Digest* staff photographer **Steve Szurlej** to write on how to shoot a golf tournament because I once heard him describe how to shoot a tennis match and figured that if so much technique went into tennis, goodness knows what goes into golf.

Well, now we know.

Robert Walker contributed a host of wonderful photographs to this book. I've always felt that Robert has one of the most "artistic" pairs of eyes in the business.

For me to put together a book of this scope without the help of *Golf Magazine* staff photographer **Leonard Kamsler** would be akin to leaving your closest relative out of a family reunion. In fact, Leonard is fond of describing the staff at *Golf Magazine* as his family, and that goes for everyone whe has ever worked there. It's a big family—but, hey, Leonard's a big guy.

I don't know **Bill Hogan** beyond a few phone calls. But he spent several years putting together *Golf Gadgets,* which I suspect will soon become a golfing cult classic. He's picked the best and worst for us.

David Earl, who tells how he built his own putting green, is the only member of the staff of the United States Golf Association to have been named "Golf Nut of the Year" by Golfaholics Anonymous. He also is the only USGA staffer with a diamond embedded in one of his front teeth and to have swapped chords with Bo Diddley. Make of that what you will.

When the United States Golf Association has to whip a golf course into shape for a major championship, it calls on **Rees Jones,** who describes for us the various steps involved in building a golf course. If the name sounds familiar, it's because Rees is the son of Robert Trent.

Matthew J. Costello and **Mark Danna** both write about computer golf games. The latter is a free-lance writer, while Danna is a former staffer at *Games* magazine (remember that?) and a champion of Frisbee golf.

Joe Murdoch tells us all about golf auctions, but I wish this charming old man would tell us how he managed to sell his collection of almost 3,500 golf books for a cool $650,000! Interesting story: When the sale went through, Dick Donovan, who compiled with Joe *The Game of Golf and the Printed Word,* the definitive listing of everything written about golf, immediately sent him a copy of Herbert Warren Wind's *The Complete Golfer.* This was the first entry in the old collection, bought for Joe by his wife several decades ago. "Start again," read the accompanying note.

Tom Doak, who writes on greens, bunkers and short par fours, has barely turned 30 and already has designed and built half a dozen golf courses around the country. The Doakster—as he's known around the halls of *Golf Magazine,* where he is a contributing editor—is a partisan of the old, enjoyable style of golf. If you ever get lost in northern Michigan, ask directions to High Pointe, in Franklin. That was Tom's first major solo project.

I first met **Dick Donovan,** who suggests the perfect golf library, in 1990 in the parking lot of the Crail Golf Club in Scotland at 11:00 P.M. on a Friday night. He'd played Crail that afternoon with hickory-shafted golf clubs. I'd just birdied the final hole in total darkness. You want normal golfers, go to Florida.

Although I'd spoken to **Janet Seagle** several times on the telephone, it was not until the USGA held a media day for the 1990 Curtis Cup matches at Somerset Hills Golf Club in New Jersey that we finally crossed paths. After the customary greetings, Janet did some offbeat things with the day's pairings so we could play together. We had a marvelous time.

I first encountered **Chris Yurko** when he joined *Golf Magazine* as an assistant editor, which was not that long before he headed off to Columbia University's Journalism School. When I last encountered him, he was entering a supermarket near Columbia by the "Exit" door, whereupon he grabbed a six-pack of Red Stripe, paid for it in the wrong check-out line and disappeared into the night.

Rob Sauerhaft is *Golf Magazine*'s resident equipment expert, a former captain of the Colgate University golf team, and the proud—and we mean *proud*—owner of the world's worst golf-shirt collection.

Philip Gibson is a subeditor (that's a copy editor in these parts) with *Golf Monthly* in Britain.

Fred Vuich, who took the photograph of Muirfield Village Golf Club that adorns the cover of this book, is a staff photographer with *Golf Magazine.*

I also would be criminally remiss if I neglected to thank John Boswell, my agent, who set this project rolling, and Jeff Neuman at Simon & Schuster, who gave me free rein—probably too free—to include what I felt would be most interesting and entertaining to those interested in and entertained by the game of golf.

Index

Photo Credits

Titleist: 3 (top), 131, 132

Robert Walker: 3 (bottom), 8 (top, middle), 14, 38, 40, 41, 45, 48, 57, 64, 65 (top), 68, 106, 157, 167, 187, 194, 200, 201, 202, 236, 237, 238

Pebble Beach Co.: 7 (top, middle), 36 (right), 75 (both)

John Jacobs Practical Golf Schools/Mona Roman Advertising: 7 (bottom), 108, 109, 110 (bottom)

Accolade: 8 (bottom), 259, 260 (both), 261

PerryGolf: 9, 11, 13, 17, 19, 21, 22, 33

British Tourist Authority: 24

Desert Highlands: 36 (left)

Doug Ball/SCORE Magazine: 50

Bob Weeks/SCORE Magazine: 51

USGA: 52 (top, bottom), 53, 79, 81, 89, 235

The Bobby Jones Collection/Hickey Freeman: 54

Rees Jones, Inc.: 61 (all), 62 (both)

Leonard Kamsler: 65 (bottom), 99, 175, 227, 233, 234 (left)

Mike McAlister: 76, 77

Golf Magazine/Andrea Eisenman: 95

Stevenson's Studio: 101, 110 (top)

Dave Pelz: 104 (all)

Ben Hogan Company: 128 (both)

Matzie Golf Co.: 123, 144

The GolfWorks: 145, 151, 152

PGA of America: 159, 160

Mike Calbot: 171 (both)

Steve Burton: 195

Columbia Pictures: 219, 243 (right)

"GolfSmart": 225, 244 (both)

Franklin Mint: 229

Paramount Pictures: 241

United Artists: 242

MGM: 243 (left)

Electronic Arts: 249, 262 (all)

James Bryan: 255

MicroGolf: 256

Jeff Carlick: 257 (both)

Shark Attack: 263

Sega: 264, 265

PGA Tour, Inc.: 267 (both)